CHILDREN AND WRITING IN THE ELEMENTARY SCHOOL

CHILDREN AND WRITING IN THE ELEMENTARY SCHOOL

Theories and Techniques

RICHARD L. LARSON

Herbert H. Lehman College
of the
City University of New York

New York
Oxford University Press
London   Toronto   1975

For Zelle

Preface

Oxford University Press published *Teaching Freshman Composition* in 1967 and *Teaching High School Composition* in 1970, both edited by Edward P. J. Corbett and Gary Tate. These volumes are collections of essays by several authors on the teaching of written composition at the levels mentioned in the titles. Knowing that there is a substantial, and rapidly increasing, body of literature about the teaching of written composition in the elementary school (here defined to include roughly the first eight grades in the traditionally organized school system), I urged the preparation of a volume of essays on writing in the elementary school. When Professors Corbett and Tate agreed that they would not be able to work on such a volume, I decided to undertake the project myself.

In planning the volume, I had in mind four principal goals: The first was to bring together, and place side by side, writings by leading theorists from Great Britain and from the United States, since teachers from the two countries collaborated so productively at the Anglo-American Conference at Dartmouth in 1967 and since the approaches taken to the writing of young children in the two countries often contrast with, and complement, each other in illuminating ways. Second, I sought to present some of the seminal thinking that has been recently published about how discourse works (and about the kinds of discourse that one can identify in the speech and writing of young children) as a background against which readers can consider specific suggestions about techniques and emphases in the teaching of composition inside— or outside—of the elementary classroom. Third, I sought to assure that the concerns of those teachers who wish to emphasize the "basics" of spelling, punctuation, syntax, and organization were confronted alongside the concerns of those who want the teacher of writing to emphasize development of the child's imagination and those who look upon writing as a "rhetorical" act usually performed by a symbol-using being in order to induce some sort of response in another such being. And, fourth, I tried to offer some views that will help teachers in what is one of their most important activities—one that is, however, much neglected in the professional literature on the teaching of writing— reacting to and commenting on students' writing. In organizing the book, and in preparing headnotes and questions for discussion, I have tried to allow the different perspectives on all these subjects to illuminate each other. I hope that users of the book will continually be alert to the possibility of comparing the assumptions, implications, and attitudes toward the teaching of writing that emerge from the several essays.

I would like to thank Edward Corbett and Gary Tate, both of them personal friends, for allowing and encouraging me to take up the work of assisting teachers of written composition in the elementary school. I want also to thank John Wright and Harriet Serenkin, my editors at Oxford University Press, for their support of the project and for their patient assistance with the development of the manuscript. Finally, I thank all those who generously agreed to allow me to reprint portions of their work.

The value of what I have gathered now remains to be determined by prospective and practicing teachers of writing in our schools, who will be able to say whether the essays in this volume help them to do a more effective job with their classes and with individual students than they might otherwise have done.

White Plains, New York   Richard L. Larson
May, 1975

Contents

Introduction

My experience with elementary schools in Hawaii and New York City suggests that written composition does not appear conspicuously in the Language Arts curriculum of many elementary schools and that it receives only passing attention as a subject for teaching in many elementary classrooms. Yet, it is incalculably important for children in elementary school to receive encouragement and to be given regular opportunities for writing. Young children need the chance to experiment with language, to observe the differences between spoken and written language, to learn how writing enables a person to organize and interpret experiences, to see how writing helps them to express feelings and perceptions, and—of course—to discover how writing can communicate ideas and feelings to others. All of these uses for writing—typically taught in the classes on written composition in secondary schools—are quite as important for young children as for older children. Furthermore, the elementary classroom is a propitious place to seek them, because young children as a rule are less likely to be inhibited by pressures for them to succeed and to conform to established conventions than are older children. Young children, in the opinion of many teachers, are more willing to enjoy experiments with language than are those who have to worry about their work—about whether the language they use satisfies the demands of teachers who are helping them prepare for standardized tests or college entrance examinations or who are helping them learn to write well enough to earn a living. This anthology, then, is intended in part as an argument for increased attention to composition in elementary classrooms as well as an instrument to help teachers in their professional work on the teaching of writing.

In elementary classrooms where children practice composition, the teaching of writing may appear artless and unpremeditated. Although an atmosphere of casualness can signify a comfortable and productive writing class, it does not mean that the teacher's work has not been carefully planned. Indeed, it is essential for teachers of writing to understand well how various kinds of discourse work and to plan the structure of their writing programs as well as the strategies they will follow in responding to students' writing. The teacher of writing, at any level, has a good deal to think about before the school year begins, and during the year. The teacher makes a good many decisions, even if unconsciously, that affect what children write and the attitudes they develop toward writing— attitudes that may durably influence the children's willingness to write and the kinds of writing they produce. It is useful for teachers to think about the kinds of decisions they make as they teach writing.

These decisions include the goals of the writing program on which the teacher will ask students to embark. The goals, in turn, reflect a teacher's decision about the philosophy of composition that he or she will adopt. And the teacher has to decide what kinds of writing he or she will ask the students to attempt and what kinds of assistance he or she will give to students as they work. Other decisions include the kinds of comments—oral and written—that the teacher will make on students' work and the ways in which the teacher will make judgments about students' progress in writing— not to mention how the teacher will discuss that progress with students' parents. This book is intended to offer new and experienced teachers, alike, some help in the making of these decisions.

This collection advocates no single philosophy or set of doctrines about composition; it is not a textbook with a single point of view.

Rather, it is intended to furnish information, drawn from the works of scholars and teachers in England and America, that will acquaint teachers with various options in philosophy and teaching techniques. The choice of a philosophy, a strategy, teaching procedures, and ways of talking about writing always remains with the teacher. The intent of this volume is that teachers will be able to make better-informed choices as a result of their attention to it than they might otherwise have been.

The first group of essays lays some conceptual groundwork to aid teachers in establishing a program in composition. Essays by Britton and Moffett suggest ways of viewing and classifying pieces of discourse, including those by young children.

A piece of writing is a way of communicating facts and perceptions to another person as well as an expression of how a writer sees him or herself and his or her experiences. A teacher can better understand what is going on in students' writing if he or she has a plan for grouping or identifying what students show him or her. While the distinctions made by Britton between writing produced in the role of ''spectator'' and that produced in the role of ''participant,'' and between ''transactional'' and ''poetic'' pieces, are often not clearcut, a knowledge of them may still advance a teacher's understanding of the student's language and of the way the student is presenting himself or herself. James Moffett's thoughts about level of abstraction in writing may help teachers to understand pieces produced by students, in addition to offering suggestions about the arrangement of writing activities.

But to teach writing one needs more than an understanding of the scales along which various kinds of writing may be arranged; one also needs information about the development of children—information that may furnish clues to what various uses of language imply about the development of a given student. Essays about Piaget's work and its implications for education give information about children's psychological development that should help the teacher of composition see what the student can, and perhaps cannot, reasonably be expected to do at different ages. Golub's discussion and Hunt's research on children's syntax indicate that a teacher can learn about a student's feelings and his or her growth in powers of perceiving and thinking, as well as about the development in his or her understanding and control of language, from direct analysis of students' writing. Curriculum planning requires both the general concepts arrived at by research psychologists and the specific observations of how a teacher's own students are developing; a skilled teacher will relate the two.

Since the child's personal growth is an increasingly prominent concern among teachers of writing, each teacher may want to consider whether his or her philosophy of curriculum should reflect that concern above others. To encourage reflection on this question, we include a piece from Dixon's essay *Growth through English,* in which he discusses the philosophy of curriculum that he finds most attractive. The selection presents only Dixon's view of the curriculum, though the headnote identifies two views that Dixon does not adopt. In examining Dixon's essay along with the others in the first section, you should consider what other views of the elementary school English curriculum (particularly writing) may be advanced and how they cohere with the views of discourse and of children's development presented in this section. Do the other essays in Part I encourage you to adopt a philosophy of curriculum other than Dixon's? The essays in Part I should encourage deliberation about who you are, or would like to be, as a teacher of writing.

Part II concerns the specifics of classroom technique—or, more particularly, teaching techniques that work, inside or outside of a classroom. One goal of a teacher is to stimulate the student's imagination, thereby helping him or her to reach discoveries about his or her world. The selections in this part suggest ways for the teacher to encourage students to be inventive and imaginative in language. The teachers whose ideas appear here want students to understand the world in which they live—to understand it through their senses and their imaginations as well as through their minds and analytical faculties. These teachers recognize the value to students of having fun with language, of trying out ways of making language reveal reality or create a new reality, of shaping and organizing reality according to the students' ways of seeing it. The essays by Haggitt and Kohl speak of exercises in the investigation of the students' worlds, and selections by Robbins, Carlson, Koch, Groff, and

Whipp speak of how the world can be given shape through poetry and through stories. While the authors suggest particular forms, exercises, and activities, they also keep in mind the goals of writing for children—the liberation of their imagination and the increase in their facility to use language.

After the teacher has encouraged students to write, and after the students have written (or while they are writing), the teacher needs to respond to what they write. The selections in Part III raise the question: What does one notice and what can one say about students' writing? What the teacher notices may be quite different from what he or she says. Writing reveals the emotional life, the growth, the fears, the concerns of the writer, and though these matters may affect what the teacher does with students, sometimes they are not discussed directly. Instead, the teacher may talk about striking features of language; habits of expression; ways of capturing ideas and feelings still more forcibly; ways of arranging ideas into some more satisfactory patterns. The teacher may also help students to value what they have written, to enjoy it, to want to write more, and to want to share with others what they have written. The essays by Wallace Douglas and Leslie T. Whipp range from concerns about the qualities of feeling that students express and the perplexities they reveal to the precise details of the language patterns they employ. Teachers will find it useful to compare how these authors approach the describing of student work. They should consider whether in different circumstances, with different kinds of students, they might wish to use Douglas' and Whipp's ways of talking about, and responding to, students' writing. Teachers should also try to develop their own ways of responding to that work.

Many teachers of writing feel responsible for giving direct instruction in building sentences and paragraphs, improving spelling, and correcting syntax, just as much as for stimulating the student's imagination and encouraging play with language. The selections in Part IV speak to these pressing concerns. Frazier advises teachers about ways of enlarging the vocabulary of their students; he encourages discussion of whether direct efforts at vocabulary building are appropriate and of how such efforts can be coordinated with students' writing activities. Christensen and O'Hare deal with instruction in the forming of sentences: whether specific grammatical and rhetorical systems furnish suggestions for students to follow in putting words end to end, in bringing together subjects, predicates, and modifiers in ways that will inform and move readers. Trosky, Wood, and Watts deal with the connecting of sentences into paragraphs; and they raise the issues of whether it is useful to teach students to follow specific patterns of organization and whether the standard practices in teaching expository paragraphs are the most useful techniques for assuring order in students' thinking and coherence within what they punctuate as paragraphs. Nancy Martin and Jeremy Mulford suggest a way of viewing correct spelling and the observance of mechanical conventions in perspective—in relation to what for young children are larger ends of writing. The advice given in Part IV, particularly by O'Hare, Martin, and Mulford, is not the traditional doctrines of textbooks on composition; it focuses on writing as a creative process, a way of getting language to work, rather than as revision—the way many textbooks seem to treat it.

Though the question of how a writer relates his or her work to the audience is implicit in many of the selections in Parts I to IV, much of the advice in those selections subordinates concern for audience in the teaching of young students to concerns for the exercise of their imagination and their achievement of pleasure in writing. While these emphases may, in a given teacher's judgment, be the most appropriate ones for the elementary classroom, most student writers will eventually have to confront the needs and interests of their intended readers. Part V, therefore, contains two pieces, one by the present editor and one by Robert Fichteneau, that argue the importance of helping even young students recognize the value of addressing at least some of their writing to a distinctive audience. These authors suggest ways of giving students some experience with the ''rhetorical'' dimensions of writing: those dimensions that touch on the interaction of writer, reader, and subject—which is the traditional concern of the student of rhetoric.

Each of the selections in this anthology, each of the positions taken by the experienced teachers who are offering advice drawn from their research and experience, requires the reader's careful evaluation. Any given piece will appeal more to one reader than to another; the advice offered in each will seem immediately useful to some, controversial to others. At the very least, however, these selections should help teachers to see why writing is an essential activity of the elementary grades—an activity about which a substantial amount of knowledge and insight (often not shared in classes on "language arts" in the elementary school) has been developed.

Reading and talking are, of course, central parts of the elementary curriculum. Writing, the act of putting words together for particular purposes, can facilitate the teaching of reading by helping students to understand more fully how language works; it can encourage talking, by giving students a subject to talk about and even an incentive for talking. Writing also has its own justification in the elementary curriculum; it is the act by which a student explores his or her world and feelings, the art by which his or her dreams and discoveries, wishes, and perceptions are preserved for others to apprehend and enjoy. If the school should be a place for enjoyment and a place for discovering what before had not been seen, then writing deserves, and should have, an unchallenged place in every elementary classroom.

—Richard L. Larson

BACKGROUND READINGS: THEORIES OF WRITTEN DISCOURSE AND OF THE DEVELOPMENT OF CHILDREN

Now That You Go to School

James N. Britton

This anthology begins by introducing some distinctions that can be made among the kinds of written language children use, and by discussing how these kinds of writing contribute to the development of children's power to use language. In the following essay, James Britton suggests a distinction between writing done in the role of spectator and writing done in the role of participant and then suggests a further distinction between *expressive* and *transactional* writing. He also introduces the concept of *poetic* writing to describe some special kinds of discourse that children may produce. As he makes these distinctions, he considers the value that these different kinds of writing have for children.

James Britton, Professor of Education at the University of London, is one of the leading investigators of children's writing in England. He collaborated with colleagues at the University of London on a project to examine and classify large numbers of examples of children's writing. He was chairman of the York Conference on the Learning and Teaching of English in 1971.

From *Language and Learning* (Allen Lane The Penguin Press, 1970; Pelican Books, 1972), pp. 164–170, 173–180. Copyright © James Britton, 1970. Reprinted by permission.

I am inclined to believe that young children rely upon speech for all that they want to communicate and that when they write before going to school their writing takes the form of a "construct" or a performance. I have seen many examples of stories written, illustrated and decorated, the pages stitched or clipped together to make little books. They exist as objects in the world: miniature or even make-believe objects. I have in fact one such production made when the child could write only a word or two (she was under four years old): its six pages, each about an inch square, are filled with saw-tooth lines of mock writing in which at rare intervals there stands out a word: WWWW THE MMMM

We have already noticed a parallel between a poet's use of language and a child's speech, both exemplifying "the delight of utterance." That delight dovetails here with the joy of making an object; and puts the writing firmly in the spectator role. Teachers have built upon this foundation, and a good deal of early writing in the primary school is not aimed at telling anybody anything but at producing "written objects"—something to be mounted and displayed, or collected in a folder; something that deserves to be embellished, illustrated and to go along as part of the possessions of the group. This is spectator role writing: is it therefore a kind of poetry, a kind of literature, or are there other defining characteristics to be accounted for?

Postponing any answer to that question, let us first observe that writing begins as written down speech. It may take into its fabric words and phrases imported from written language the child has heard or read (as for example, the three-year-old boy who dictates stories for his mother to write down and recently included a use of "for" which certainly comes not from his own speech but from hearing stories read: ". . . for he had nowhere to go"). But the fabric itself of their writing remains written down speech. We would hardly expect a child to do otherwise than to draw upon his speech resources when he wants to write.

However, all forms of speech are not equally useful as starting-points for writing. Occasionally we have found stories written by children who seemed to have at their command only dialogue—

social interchange—and this proves a very unsuitable medium for telling a story. Here is the beginning of one by a girl of ten:

> Oh Mummy do you think it would be all right to go and watch daddy.
> Well I shall want some shopping. it will be closeing day tomorrow.
> All right I will go for you. But do you think you will come. this after-
> noon   daddy will not be fishing then will he   no. Oh here comes
> Robin Mummy can he do the shopping yes—dear. He can do the
> shopping if you get the things we will need we shall want the rugs,
> saddles, spaddes, buteckes, and the dogs lead. If you go and do that I
> will get some sandwiches and cake for tea on the beach. goodness me
> it twelve oclock I must get dinner daddy will be home soon . . .

I suspect that "speech for oneself" (the running commentary and the forms of narrative and planning speech that develop from it) constitutes an important stage in the process of learning to write. It is sustained speech, it becomes in due course internalized, and it does not rely upon feed-back from a listener. However that may be, it is clear that any more or less sustained narrative speech is likely to be a lead-in to writing. For this reason it has been suggested that children should be encouraged to amplify their contributions to a conversation with their teachers: "Yes, and then what happened?" "Was there anything else you saw?"—and so on. Or, as James Moffett puts it:

> . . . the first step towards writing is made when a speaker takes over
> a conversation and sustains some subject alone. He has started to
> create a solo discourse that while intended to communicate to others is
> less collaborative, less prompted, and less corrected by feedback than
> dialogue. He bears more of the responsibility for effective com-
> munication. . . . The cues for his next line are not what his interlocu-
> tor said, but what he himself just said. (Moffett, *Teaching the Uni-
> verse of Discourse* 1968, p. 85)

From this point on, we can envisage two parallel main lines of development. As the child becomes more familiar with diverse forms of the written language—forms adapted to different audiences and different purposes—he will draw more and more upon those forms in his own writing. We shall have more to say about this in a moment. At the same time, every new field of interest for him is likely to be investigated, explored, organized first in talk. The talk, as it were, prepares the environment into which what is taken from reading may be accommodated: and from that amalgam the writing proceeds.

"Ordinary speech," according to Edward Sapir, "is directly *expressive*" (Sapir, *Culture, Language, and Personality* 1961, p. 10), and since I want to apply the term, in some degree at least, to most of the writing that goes on in the Primary School, it is important to inquire more exactly what it means. Sapir opposes it to *referential:*

> . . . in all language behaviour there are intertwined, in enormously complex patterns, isolable patterns of two distinct orders. These may be roughly defined as patterns of reference and patterns of expression. (Sapir, *Culture, Language, and Personality* 1961, p. 11)

He goes on to say that language is

> rarely a purely referential organisation. It tends to be so only in scientific discourse, and even there it may be seriously doubted whether the ideal of pure reference is ever attained by language.

Though the two patterns are "intertwined in enormously complex patterns," it seems reasonable, and consistent with Sapir's views, to suppose that an utterance which was predominantly expressive might be distinguished from one which was predominantly referential; and this we propose to do, calling the one "expressive" and the other "transactional."

The word "expression" is used to name a variety of ideas and some of these, the most general, we can rule out as not contributing to the meaning of "expressive" as we want to use it. "Expression" may be used as equivalent to "formulation" or "externalization": in this sense the policy of a political party may find its *expression* in a manifesto. Again, "expression" is used as a way of referring to a piece of language as such—as when we refer to a word as "an ugly expression" or a phrase as a "trite expression," "a loose expression" and so on. On the other hand, when we say that a man "reads with expression," this—in so far as it means anything at all—comes nearer to the meaning we require. If I read with expression a part of me, my voice, is giving indications of what I think the writer means by his words. In a similar fashion the expression on my face is likely to be giving such indications. But the expression on my face is likely, every moment of my waking life, to be giving indications *about me*—about my state of mind and the mood and so on. And there is a sense in which, in the case of me reading, whatever indications my "expression" gives are indications, at least in part, of the way I think and feel about the story or about the people, events, and everything else in the story.

If I exclaim when I am surprised or delighted or angry or hurt—either in words or by making "purely expressive" noises—moaning or cooing or whatever else might be my counterpart of a cat's purring, a dog's growling, an infant's yelling—then that represents the extreme of what we mean by "expressive." With a full knowledge of the situation in which I am making such a noise, a listener is able to discover from it something about me. But in addition, as we have seen earlier, I continually declare the sort of person I am by the way I construe the world—by what I make of my encounters with people, events, ideas, works of art, fictions and all the rest. Whatever I talk about, therefore, I am likely to be at the same time signalling to a listener—intentionally or unintentionally—things about myself. The occasions when we deliberately try to avoid doing this are rare enough to be remarked upon: we say "expressionless" either about a voice or a face (and I think the term is much more frequently translatable as "not giving away his own attitude to what he is saying" than it is into "failing to bring out the meaning of the words he is speaking").

As we have suggested, a mere grunt can tell us something if we know the person who is making it and can see why he is doing so; it follows that in different situations the grunt will tell us different things. Similarly, the more expressive my utterances about the world are, the more liable they are to mean different things in different situations; and in this case it is likely that the differences will be heightened by the way the words are spoken—the tone of voice, gesture, facial expression. "So, you're home then!" could be an affectionate and excited welcome to a returned exile or the sarcastic opening of a family brawl.

Talk that is predominantly expressive, then, tells us a good deal about the speaker and relies heavily for its interpretation on the situation in which it occurs—that is to say, it draws heavily upon a common response to a shared situation, or it relies heavily upon the listener's knowledge of the speaker's situation.

Let us suppose someone is relating what happened to him on a past occasion. In a police court he is likely to do so in a neutral, even expressionless tone: as though to allow the bare facts to speak for themselves. But to an intimate friend he may reveal at each point his attitude towards what he is relating: and this is to bring to life the events as he experienced them—which is the only way they can be made to "seem real," since the speaker is his listener's only link with those events.

When we chat with our friends in a relaxed way, our talk is likely to be mainly expressive: we verbalize what runs through our minds and with people we know well we do not need to fill in the background—we can speak as though we spoke to ourselves or even meditated silently and did *not* speak. If in the course of this chatter one of us says something that the other wants to question or dispute or explore further, then this sets up a demand for speech that pays more attention to "things our there"—to facts or logical, causal or chronological relations; and at the same time we demand that the speaker take into account his listener's point of view. In both cases this constitutes a need to be more *explicit,* that is, a need to switch from predominantly expressive to predominantly transactional speech.

A young child's speech will be expressive for the very reason that in his egocentrism he finds it difficult or impossible to escape from his own point of view, to take into account his listener's—or indeed to suppose that "things as they are" could differ from "things as he sees them." A child will take time therefore to learn how to respond to the demands of a situation requiring transactional speech.

But there are other situations that demand a change of another kind: a change from expressive not to transactional speech but to "formal" or "poetic" speech. And here we depart from Sapir's frame of reference and must justify ourselves for including what he omitted.

Let us begin by noting that the change from expressive to transactional speech comes when *participant* demands are made—that is, when language is called upon to achieve some transaction, to *get something done* in the world. The other change arises when demands are made from the opposite end—for a more powerful exercise of language in the spectator role.

We may gossip idly about our neighbours, or swap yarns about war service, or the place we work in, or about holidays: all this will be expressive speech, and, with a few possible digressions, in the spectator role. If I grow interested in your chatter because I vaguely begin to wonder whether the place you went to might suit me for a holiday, I may move the talk from the spectator role into the participant—but at this idle level it would remain expressive speech. But if the possibilities really begin to be of practical interest to me—say for next year—then I may initiate a move from expressive to communicative speech. ("You say it's near Whitby. How far is it from the station?")

Suppose, on the other hand, I grow interested in the account of your holiday experiences *as a story*—become involved in the same way as I would become involved in a novel or a play: then I shall not want to shift your talk in the direction of things I want to find out—in fact, apart from making encouraging noises, I shall not want to interrupt at all. And you, as you warm to my interest, may begin to concentrate on giving your story a *more satisfying shape:* your talk becomes more and more of a performance, more of a construction, a verbal object. All this indicates a move away from the expressive and in the direction of the *formal* or *poetic*. . . .

It is perhaps easier to describe and to apply the categories when we turn from speech to writing: it was for the purpose of differentiating among writings that they were devised.[1]

The earliest forms of written down speech are likely for every reason to be expressive: among them we may distinguish writings

---

[1] In the course of a Schools Council project on the development of writing abilities in children of eleven to eighteen being carried out at the University of London Institute of Education.

in the spectator role and others in the participant role, but the distinction will not be a sharp one. It is when the demand is made for participant language that *any reader* can follow, or to spectator role language to satisfy an *unknown reader* that the pressure is on for a move from expressive writing to transactional and poetic writing respectively.

Children will not be able to comply fully with these demands at once. In fact, as we have suggested, it is by attempting to meet them that they gradually acquire the differentiated forms. In order to trace development therefore, we need to include two transitional categories along with the three we already have. Thus:

$$\text{Transactional}/\longleftarrow/\text{Expressive}/\longrightarrow/\text{Poetic}/$$
$$\quad 1 \qquad\quad 2 \qquad\quad 3 \qquad\quad 4 \qquad\quad 5$$

Most of the writing produced in the Primary School is likely to lie within the three central categories. I propose to explain the diagram in two ways: first by attempting to differentiate the two poles more clearly; and secondly by giving illustrations of Primary School work in the transitional categories.

By what contrasts, then, can transactional be differentiated from poetic writing? That an informative, scientific report is an example of the one, and a story or a poem an example of the other—this is something that may usefully be in our minds as we follow the contrasts in detail.

1. First, this by way of recapitulation: transactional writing is writing in the role of participant fully differentiated to meet the requirements of that role: and poetic writing is fully differentiated to meet the requirements of the role of spectator. Thus, what is said [earlier in the book] to distinguish the two roles is the background against which to consider the more particular points that follow.

2. Transactional writing is intended to fit into, to articulate with, the ongoing activities of participants: poetic writing is a way of interrupting them—interrupting them by presenting an object to be contemplated in itself and for itself. Thus a piece of transactional writing—this present page for example—may elicit the statement of other views, of counter-arguments or corroborations or modifica-

tions, and is thus part of a chain of inter-actions between people. A response in kind—another piece of such writing—is always a potential of transactional writing. Poetic writing, on the other hand, demands a "sharer," an audience that does not interrupt. A reader is asked to respond to a particular verbal construct which remains quite distinct from any other verbal construct anybody else might offer. A response in kind is not therefore inherent in the situation.

This very broad distinction has an interesting corollary: what is contributed to the ongoing activity by a piece of transactional writing may well survive when the writing itself is forgotten. Thus, for example, Lindley Murray's English Grammar could be shown to have contributed ideas that are found in many succeeding grammars. It is in fact common practice for informative books to be brought up to date: over a period of years Kirk's *Handbook of Physiology* became Haliburton's, which in turn became Mc-Dowell's—and no doubt somebody else will substitute his name in due course. Can one imagine, on the other hand, Charles Dickens producing his version of Fielding's *Tom Jones*—to replace the original—and that in turn being rewritten by C. P. Snow? Poetic writing, if it survives, survives as itself, in and for itself. (*Rosencrantz and Guildenstern are Dead* may so survive—and so will *Hamlet!*)

3. A reader "contextualizes" transactional writing in the course of reading it—by segments, so to speak. Poetic writing is contextualized, not by segments but as a whole.

John Lyons has pointed out that the initial context for any utterance

> must be held to include . . . the knowledge shared by hearer and speaker of all that has gone before. More "abstractly" it must be held to comprehend all the conventions and presuppositions accepted in the society in which the participants live in so far as these are relevant to the understanding of the utterance.

As a conversation develops, he sees this initial context as consistently building up, "taking into itself all that is relevant . . . from what is said and what is happening." (Lyons, *Structural Semantics*, 1963, pp. 83–5)

As we read a piece of transactional writing, we build in to our initial context whatever fits—piece by piece. We reject what does not fit, the things in fact that do not appear to interest or concern us. What we finally take—from, for example, an informative report—is the sum total of these pieces that we have "built in" with the addition of anything we may have made of them by creating further connexions ourselves. We may have found much or little that "fitted in"—as you may have found in reading this chapter.

But the writer who embarks on a piece of poetic writing, I believe, deliberately works *against* this process of contextualization by segments. It is internal relations, relations *within the construct,* that he tries to set up, and in doing so he has to resist the processes by which a reader might relate to parts of the shared context that lie outside his area of concern. It is a "hard shell" he needs for his object. As readers, we must first recreate the object, in all its inner relatedness, and only then try to relate it as a whole to our own concerns, our own lives. If after reading a poem we think to ourselves, "So they practise witchcraft in Peru," or "I didn't know Yeats was a spiritualist"—we are framing responses that are inappropriate to poetic writing. Of course we make such responses, and can profit from them: but if they are not secondary to a response of the kind we have described above—the recreation of a verbal object and its contextualization as a whole—then we have missed the point of the poetic enterprise.

The distinction here, then, is between contextualizing piecemeal, in transactional writing, and contextualizing as a unique whole, in poetic writing.

4. Expressive writing becomes more public as it moves in either direction; but the means by which it seeks to reach a wider audience differ as between the two poles. As expressive writing more fully meets the demands of a transaction, it becomes *more explicit.* That is to say, some features that might be omitted from the expressive version because they are *implied* when we write for someone of similar interests and experiences to our own, have now to be brought into the writing. Again, some features that would interest a reader who was interested in *us*—and so enliven the writing—will be omitted in deference to the unknown reader who may be ex-

pected to want to know what it is we have to say but not what sort of a person it is that says it. Both these changes could be described as attempts "to say X more explicitly"—whatever X may stand for.

As expressive writing moves towards poetic, however, it reaches a wider audience by quite another means; by heightening or intensifying the *implicit*. By the deliberate organization of sounds, words, images, ideas, events, feelings—by *formal arrangement* in other words—poetic writing is able to give resonance to items which in a less carefully organized utterance would be so *in*explicit—so minimally supported or explained in the text—as to be merely puzzling to a reader who was not intimate with the writer and his situation. For example: "The grey girl who had not been singing stopped" (*a*) might not be baffling as an initial or isolated piece of expressive language—say a comment you make to someone who knows you well and is sitting beside you looking at the same things as you are; but (*b*) as the opening of a piece of public communication is utterly baffling: much prior identification and explanation is needed before it makes sense to a stranger seeking information as to "what is going on." And yet (*c*) it is the first line of a poem—a piece of poetic writing addressed to the world at large. ("New Year's Eve" by John Berryman, in Alvarez (ed), *The New Poetry* 1962, p. 34) And as it finds its place in the precise and complex organization of forms that constitutes the poem, it no longer baffles a reader.

It cannot be ignored that there lies behind these attempts to distinguish the pole of transactional writing from that of poetic a suggestion that the one "has meaning" in a way the other does not—and *vice versa*. If we ask "What does it mean?" of a piece of transactional writing, we shall not expect the same sort of answer as we expect when we ask it of a poem or a novel. For this reason philosophers have spoken of the "meaning" of a transactional text and the "import" of a poetic one. And of the import of a work of literature, Paul Valéry, the French poet, has this to say:

> In sum, the more a poem conforms to Poetry, the less it can be thought in prose without perishing. To summarize a poem, to put it

into prose, is quite simply to misunderstand the essence of an art. Poetic necessity is inseparable from sensory form, and the thoughts set forth or suggested by a poetic text are in no way the unique and primary concern of discourse, but are rather the *means* which move together *equally* with the sounds, the cadences, the metre, the embellishments, to provoke, to sustain a particular tension or exaltation, to produce in us a *world*—or a *mode of existence*—altogether harmonious. (Valéry, "Concerning *Le* Cimetière Marin," in H. M. Block and H. Salinger, eds., *The Creative Vision*, 1960, p. 35)

To turn now to illustrations of writing in the transitional categories. Here is a piece by a ten-year-old boy:

HOW I FILTERED MY WATER SPECIMENS
When we were down at Mr Haris's farm I brought some water from the brook back with me. I took some from a shallow place by the oak tree, and some from a deep place by the walnut tree. I got the specimens by placing a jar in the brook and let the water run into it. Then I brought them back to school to filter. . . .

He tells us exactly what he did, and then finishes:

The experiment that I did shows that where the water was deeper and was not running as fast there was a lot more silt suspended as little particles in the water. You could see this by looking at the filter paper, where the water was shallow and fast there was less dirt suspended in it.

This, I suggest, has moved a good way out of the expressive in the direction of the transactional. But it is still transitional: there are expressive features—things that tell us about the writer rather than form part of what he is intending to communicate. Thus, it was Mr Haris's farm—he had been there before and all his class-mates had been too: to refer to it meant something to the members of that group. And the shallow place in the stream *was* by the oak tree—he had been there and he knew: and the deep place *was* by the walnut tree. These bring the experience to life for him and enliven it for those who are interested *in him*. But they are not a part of the message he sets out to communicate.

I must hasten to add that far from censuring these as imperfections I welcome them at this stage for this writer. They indicate development upon what I believe to be the right lines. Expressive language provides an essential starting point because it is language close to the self of the writer: and progress towards the transactional should be gradual enough to ensure that "the self" is not lost on the way: that on arrival "the self," though hidden, is still there. It is the self that provides the unseen point from which all is viewed: there can be no other way of writing quite impersonally and yet with coherence and vitality.

My second example is a piece by a seven-year-old girl:

> Class I had Monday off and Tuesday off and all the other classes had Monday and Tuesday off and we played hide-and-seek and my big sister hid her eyes and canted up to ten and me and my brother had to hide and I went behind the Dust-bin and I was thinking about the summer and the buttercups and Daisies all those things and fresh grass and violets and roses and lavender and the twinkling sea and the star in the night and the black sky and the moon.

This clearly is pretty close to expressive speech—and is familiar in another way—in the way it slips into one of those catalogues that small children love to write. I want to suggest here that in so far as the writer moves away from the expressive at all she moves in the other direction from the last piece—that is to say towards the poetic. I can prove nothing: it is in the reading aloud that I suspect his move. It seems to me that as the child wrote, the *sound* of what was written began to have some effect upon what she wrote next: she falls, so to speak, into a rhythm.

Such a submission to sounds is no extraordinary matter: most children who chant nursery rhymes or later reel off galloping verses show considerable skill at improvising in metre—sometimes "off the cuff" at length. But it is not a galloping rhythm that takes hold in this piece, and its effect seems to me to be on more than simply the rhythm: what is said, I suggest, is chosen under the influence of a sharpened attention to the form.

Most of the writing in the Primary School is likely, as I suggested earlier, to be expressive or transitional between expressive and the poles of transactional and poetic. It is desirable that it should be so. What the children write in the spectator role will not therefore be "literature": it will be moving out in that direction and the point at which we make the cut—the degree of formal organization required to merit the name "literature"—this is a matter upon which we can speculate, and, mercifully, upon which we do not have to agree.

QUESTIONS FOR DISCUSSIONS

1. Are the distinctions Britton makes in this essay useful to the classroom teacher? Should the teacher be influenced, in any of his activities, by the distinctions Britton offers? Under what circumstances might the distinctions be important?

2. How may the following uses of language be classified in Britton's scheme?
   a. discussion in the classroom (i.e., about a piece of writing)
   b. a boy's note to a girl friend
   c. the conversation of a family after dinner
   d. entries in a diary
   e. a recipe
   f. talk among friends on a playground
   g. an invitation to a PTA meeting
   h. a paper written for a test in school
Do you learn anything about these uses of language by classifying them?

3. Britton implies in this essay that there is value in distinguishing the audiences for which different pieces are written. Elsewhere he differentiates the audiences that children address: the writer himself; a "trusted adult"; a teacher (general); a teacher (specialist); an examiner; a layman (with the child writing as "expert"); a peer group; a group with whom the writer is working; and an unknown (presumably distant) audience. In what way is it of interest to the teacher to determine for what audience(s) the child is writing? How

should a teacher's activities differ in dealing with writing addressed to different audiences?

4. Would "transactional" writing ever benefit from having the characteristics Britton associates with "expressive" or "poetic" writing? *Could* transactional writing ever have these characteristics?

I, You, and It
James Moffett

James Moffett has greatly influenced the work of many teachers and developers of curriculum in American schools. His contributions to curriculum and teaching techniques include *A Student-Centered Language Arts Curriculum, K-13* and a companion volume of essays on the teaching of English entitled *Teaching the Universe of Discourse*.

The following essay, written in 1965, is a concise distillation of many of Moffett's major and recurring ideas about written discourse. Though written primarily for college teachers, it advances a way of looking at discourse that could be, and has been, influential in the shaping of elementary school curricula in composition as well. In reading the essay, concentrate mainly on how Moffett classifies various kinds of discourse and on his suggestions about the structure for a curriculum that will offer students practice in each kind of discourse.

James Moffett taught at Phillips Exeter Academy and did research at the Harvard Graduate School of Education. He is now a writer and consultant on school programs.

From *College Composition and Communication* Vol. 16, No. 5 (December 1965), 243–48. Copyright © 1965 by the National Council of Teachers of English. Reprinted by permission of the publisher and the author.

Consider, if you will, those primary moments of experience that are necessarily the raw stuff of all discourse. Let us suppose, for example, that I am sitting in a public cafeteria eating lunch. People are arriving and departing, passing through the line, choosing tables, socializing. I am bombarded with smells of food, the sounds of chatter and clatter, the sights of the counter, the tables, the clothing, the faces, the gesticulations and bending of elbows. But I am not just an observer; I am eating and perhaps socializing as well. A lot is going on within me—the tasting and ingesting of the food, reactions to what I observe, emotions about other people. I am registering all these inner and outer stimuli. My perceptual apparatus is recording these moments of raw experience, not in words but in some code of its own that leads to words. This apparatus is somewhat unique to me in the way it selects and ignores stimuli and in the way it immediately connects them with old stimuli and previously formed conceptions. It is difficult to separate this sensory recording from the constant stream of thoughts that is going on simultaneously and parallel to the sensory record but may often depart from it. This verbal stream is the first level of discourse to be considered. The subject is *what is happening now,* and the audience is oneself.

Suppose next that I tell the cafeteria experience to a friend sometime later in conversation. For what reason am I telling him? Would I tell it differently to someone else? Would I tell it differently to the same person at another time and in different circumstances? These are not rhetorical questions but questions about rhetoric. The fact that my account is an unrehearsed, face-to-face vocalization, uttered to *this* person for *this* reason at *this* time and place and in *these* circumstances determines to an enormous degree not only the overall way in which I abstract certain features of the ongoing panorama of the cafeteria scene but also much of the way I choose words, construct sentences, and organize parts. Compare this discourse with the third stage, when my audience is no longer face to face with me, but is farther removed in time and space so that I have to write a letter or memo to him. Informal writing is usually still rather spontaneous, directed at an audience known to the writer, and reflects the transient mood and circumstances in which the writing occurs. Feedback and audience influence, however, are delayed and weakened. Written discourse must replace or compensate for the loss of vocal characteristics and all physical expressiveness of gesture, tone, and manner. Compare in turn now the changes that must occur all down the line when I write about this cafeteria experience in a discourse destined for publication and distribution to a mass, anonymous audience of present and perhaps unborn people. I cannot allude to things and ideas that only my friends know about. I must use a vocabulary, style, logic, and rhetoric that anybody in that mass audience can understand and respond to. I must name and organize what happened during those moments in the cafeteria that day in such a way that this mythical average reader can relate what I say to some primary moments of experience of his own. In other words, whether this published discourse based on the cafeteria luncheon comes out as a fragment of autobiography, a short story, a humorous descriptive essay, or a serious theoretical essay about people's behavior in public places, certain necessities frame the discourse and determine a lot of its qualities before the writer begins to exercise his personal options.

These four stages of discourse—inner verbalization, outer vocalization, correspondence, and formal writing—are of course only the major markers of a continuum that could be much more finely calibrated. This continuum is formed simply by increasing the distance, in all senses, between speaker and audience. The audience is, first, the speaker himself, then another person standing before him, then someone in another time and place but having some personal relation to the speaker, then, lastly, an unknown mass extended over time and space. The activity necessarily changes from thinking to speaking to writing to publishing. (Thinking as inner speech is at least as old as Bergson and William James and as new as Piaget and Vygotsky.) For me no discussion of language, rhetoric, and composition is meaningful except in this context, for there is no speech without a speaker in some relation to a spoken-to and a spoken-about.

Starting with our cafeteria scene again, I would like to trace it as a subject that may be abstracted to any level I would wish. Please understand that by ''subject'' I mean some primary moments of experience regardless of how dimly they may appear in the discourse. There are four stages in the processing of raw phenomena by the human symbolic apparatus, although, again, one may recognize many gradations in between. This continuum can best be represented by verb tenses, which indicate when events occurred in relation to when the speaker is speaking of them. Suppose I represent the cafeteria scene first as *what is happening,* which would be the lowest level of verbal abstraction of reality: the order and organization of events would correspond most closely to phenomenal reality, and my verbalization of them would be the most immediate and unpondered that is possible. That is, my symbolic representation in this case would entail the least processing of matter by mind. If next I treat the events at the cafeteria as *what happened,* the subject will necessarily partake a little more of my mind and a little less of the original matter. Although the order of events will still be chronological, it is now my memory and not my perceptual apparatus that is doing the selecting. Some things will stick in my mind and some will not, and some things I will choose to retain or reject, depending on which features of this scene and action I wish to bring out. Of the details selected, some I will dwell upon and some I will subordinate considerably. Ideas are mixed with material from the very beginning, but the recollection of a drama—a narrative, that is—inevitably entails more introduction of ideas because this is inherent in the very process of selecting, summarizing, and emphasizing, even if the speaker refrains from commenting directly on the events.

Suppose next that I speak of my cafeteria experience as *what happens.* Obviously, if we consider it for a moment, the difference between *what happened* and *what happens* is not truly a time difference, or at least we must realize that what we are calling a time difference is actually a difference in the level to which I choose to abstract some primary moments of experience. I am now treating my once-upon-a-time interlude at the cafeteria as something that recurs. I have jumped suddenly, it seems, from narrative to generalization. Actually, as we have said, ideas creep in long before this but are hidden in the processing. Now they must be more explicit, for only by renaming the experience and comparing it with other experiences can I present it as what happens. No primary moments of experience recur. What we mean is that we as observers see similarities in different experiences. Only the human mind, capable of sorting and classifying reality, can do this. What I do, for example, is make an analogy between something in the cafeteria experience and something I singled out of a number of other experiences. I summarize a lot of little formless dramas into pointed narratives and then I put these narratives into some classes, which I and others before me have created. In this third stage of processing, then, the cafeteria scene will become a mere example, among several others, of some general statement such as "The food you get in restaurants is not as good as what you get at home," or "People don't like me," or "Americans do not socialize as readily with strangers in public places as Italians do," or "The arrivals and departures within a continuous group create changes in excitation level comparable to the raising and lowering of electric potential in variously stimulated sensory receptors." It is apparent that these sample generalizations could all have contained the cafeteria experience as an example but vary a great deal in their abstractness, their range of applicability, their objectivity or universal truth value, and their originality.

The transition from a chronological to an analogical discourse is of enormous importance in teaching. The student must forsake the given order of time and replace it with an order of ideas. To do this he must summarize drastically the original primary moments of experience, find classes of inclusion and exclusion, and rename the moments so that it becomes clear how they are alike or different. Most students fail to create original and interesting classes because they are unwittingly encouraged to borrow their generalizations from old slogans, wise saws, reference books, and teachers' essay questions, instead of having to forge them from their own experience. Many students leave out the illustrations completely and offer only their apparently sourceless opinions. Others, reluctant to leave the haven of narrative, tell several anecdotes and never show how they are related. But these are failures of teachers, not of students. Proper writing assignments can lead the students to good generalizations.

In what I will call the last stage of symbolizing a subject, you may wonder why I still refer to the cafeteria, since none of that experience appears any longer in the discourse, which is now a highly theoretical essay. That is deceptive; it is behind the discourse, buried in the processing and so combined with other experiences, and so renamed, that we do not recognize it any more. The "subject" seems to be a theory, some combining and developing of generalizations. This stage is telling *what will, may,* or *could happen.* Some general assertions previously arrived at by analogical thinking are now plugged into each other in various ways according to the rules of formal logic. Suppose we take some generalizations about the behavior of Americans and the behavior of Italians and the behavior of South Sea islanders and we transform and combine these statements in such a way as to come out with an anthropological conclusion that was not evident in any of the original moments of experience nor even in the generalizations about them. It took manipulations of logic to show the implication of the earlier statements. To go beyond this stage is to enter the realm of mathematical equations. What will, may, or could happen is a high-level inference entailing tautology, verbal equations. My own essay is an example of stage-four abstraction. I am setting up a series of equations among "levels of abstraction," "distance between speaker, listener, and subject," verb tenses, human faculties, and kinds of logic. I will then conclude a theory about composition curriculum by combining generalizations about what happens in discourse with what happens in the learning process of people. What enables me to do this is that something fundamental to the operation of our nervous system underlies all these man-made conceptions.

I have traced separately, and grossly, two abstractive progressions—one in which the speaker's audience becomes more remote and diffused over time and space, and another in which the speaker's subject becomes less and less matter and more and more idea. Each relation—and of course the two must be taken together—entails certain necessities, and shifts in these relations entail changes all down the line, from the organization of the whole discourse to individual word choice. As we move through the progressions, perception gives way to memory and memory to ratiocination; chronology gives way to analogy and analogy to tautology. But each faculty and kind of logic depends on the one before. In view of what we know now about abstractive processes and the cognitive and verbal growth of children, this order seems pedagogically sound to me. In other words, the necessities inherent in devising a rhetoric for an increasingly remote audience and in abstracting moments of experience to higher and higher symbolic levels are precisely the limitations which should shape our writing assignments.

According to Piaget, and Vygotsky agrees with him, the early egocentric speech of children becomes gradually "socialized" and adapts itself to other people. At the same time his mental outlook decenters; that is, he gradually yields up his initial, emotionally preferred vantage point, and expands his perspective so as to include many other points of view. Of course, both these kinds of growth never really stop. The movement is from self to world, from a point to an area, from a private world of egocentric chatter to a public universe of discourse. Cognitively, the young person passes through, according to Jerome Brunner, three phases—the enactive, the iconic, and the symbolic. First he knows things by manipulating them with his hands, then he begins to classify and interpret the world by means of image summaries, and finally he can carry out logical operations in his head modeled on his earlier physical manipulations. Most teachers have always known that in some way the child should move from the concrete to the abstract, but the whole notion of an abstraction ladder has never been clear and still requires more study. I have found the communication engineers' definition of coding to be very helpful in all this: Coding is the substitution of one set of events for another. What I call the processing of matter by mind is in fact the substitution of inner events for outer events. These inner events are neural, and we don't yet know very much about them. We can be sure, however, that as the child's nervous system develops, these neural operations become more complicated. A series of writing assignments is a series of thinking assignments and therefore a sequence of internal operations. All stages of a developmental sequence are crucial and none can be left out. Teachers have got to become more sophisticated about this sequence and more aware of the effects in the student of his trying to do what we ask.

As a model for a composition course, imagine the trinity of discourse—first, second, and third persons—to be a single circle that separates into three overlapping circles which move out until they merely touch. The discourse unity of somebody talking to somebody else about something is what we must never lose, but we can create phases, not by decomposing composition into analytical elements but by gradually pushing the persons apart. Language and rhetoric are variable factors of each other and of shifting relations among persons. We abstract not only from something but for someone. Rhetoric, on the other hand, is to some extent dictated by the abstraction level we have chosen; in drama and narrative one appeals mainly by concrete recognitions, and in exposition and argumentation mainly by one's classes and logical justice. So the rationale of our composition course lies in some crossing of the two progressions I have sketched. This is not only possible but will spiral the curriculum. For example, we ask the student to tell what happened in four different rhetorics—to himself as the spontaneously recalls a memory, to a friend face to face, to someone he knows in a letter, and to the world at large in formal writing. Generalizations and theories can be dealt with first in interior monologues, then in dialogues, in letters and diaries, and only at the end in essays. The student is never assigned a subject, only a form and the forms are ordered according to the preceding ideas. Thus, the assignments are structural and sequential.

Specifically, I would have the student write in this order: all kinds of real and invented interior monologues, dramatic monologues, dialogues, plays, letters, diaries, fragments of autobiography, eye-witness accounts, reporters-at-large (modeled on those in the *New Yorker*), case studies, first and third person fiction, essays of generalization and essays of logical argumentation. Many teachers may feel that such a program slights exposition in favor of so-called personal or creative writing. In the first place, one doesn't learn exposition just by writing it all the time. An enormous amount of other learning must take place before one can write worthwhile essays of ideas; that is in the nature of the whole abstraction process. All writing teaches exposition. Furthermore, I cannot conceive a kind of discourse which does not contain ideas; even in concrete description, contrasts, similarities, and notions of causality and progression are strongly implicit. Monologues, dialogues, letters, diaries, and narratives may either contain explicit ideas or be shaped by ideas, What do we mean by a *pointed* narrative? What are Socratic dialogues about? And why do we have students digging for meaning in literary works of imagination if they are not full of ideas? The issue is not idea writing versus other kinds of writing but rather which *form* the ideas are presented in. All modes must be taught. The panic to teach exposition is partly responsible for its being taught so badly. Teachers do not feel they can take the time to let a student abstract from the ground up. But if they do not, he will never learn to write exposition.

There are several corollaries of the program I am proposing. Since it attempts to exercise the student in all possible relations that might obtain between him and an audience and a subject, one corollary is that he not be allowed to get stuck with one audience or at one range of the abstractive spectrum. It is essential that he address someone besides the English teacher and get some kind of feedback other than red marks. As one solution, I suggest that he be accustomed to write to the whole class as being the nearest thing to a contemporary world at large. Compositions should be read in class, and out of class, reacted to and discussed. One must know the effects of one's rhetoric on someone who does not give grades and does not stand as an authority figure. I suggest also the performance and publication of student works as frequently as possible. Monologues, dialogues, letters, and diaries give the student the opportunity both to address a real or invented person outside the classroom and to adopt a voice not his own.

What most frequently freezes the student at one end of the abstractive spectrum is too much writing about reading. Perhaps because of the great influence of college essay exams and of literary exegesis, composition courses often boil down to "how to write about books." This is a narrow notion of exposition. Abstracting about someone else's already high abstraction, whether it be a book or a teacher's essay question, means that certain essential issues of choice about selecting and treating material and creating classes are never permitted to come up for the student. When I assign a topic such as "loyalty" or "Irony in A. E. Housman," all I am asking the student to do is to find illustrations for my classifications. By doing half of his work for him, I am impoverishing his education. Rather than assign literary exegesis, I would have him write in the forms he reads. As practitioner he will naturally be a better literary critic than a student who only analyzes. Rather than assign book reports and essays on books, I would encourage the student to incorporate into his essays of generalization illustrations and ideas drawn from his reading and to mix these with his own experiences and observations; in other words, get *him* to create the classes into which he can fit people and actions drawn from both books and life. There is a real place for reading in a composition course, not as subject matter to write about but as a source of experience and as a repertory of discourse. After all, reading provides some excellent primary moments of experience.

From the perceptual level on up the student should be forced in effect to confront all the right issues of choice. Only in this way will he develop the faculties necessary to produce the ideas of exposition. On the same grounds, I am leery of asking the student to read about writing. I have spent a lot of time unteaching the dicta of composition texts and manuals of advice. Trial and error best develops judgment and taste, if this trial and error process is keyed in with the student's learning schedule. Explanations and definitions of good style, technique, and rhetoric create more problems than they solve. The issue here is not only one of cognitive development but of psychological independence. We must give students an emotional mandate to play the symbolic scale, to find subjects and shape them, to invent ways to act upon others, and to discover their own voice.

QUESTIONS FOR DISCUSSION

1. In what ways does Moffett's method of categorizing discourse resemble, and in what ways does it differ from, Britton's? Both writers talk of a "continuum." How is each writer's continuum organized?

2. For the teacher interested in improving his ability to understand and interpret children's writing, whose classifications are more

helpful: Britton's or Moffett's? Or are they equally beneficial? Why?

3. How might Moffett's classifications of discourse be translated into an elementary school curriculum in composition? Which of his classes of discourse, if any, might be directly taught to children of various ages?

4. According to Moffett's way of viewing discourse, what connection is there between talking and writing? Would talk anticipate or reinforce any of the kinds of writing Moffett discusses? Which ones and why?

5. Moffett says that "proper writing assignments can lead students to good generalizations." In Moffett's view, what do you infer to be the qualities of a "proper writing assignment"? What sorts of assignments might be "improper"?

7. Look back at Moffett's essay after reading the next two essays about Piaget's discoveries and hypotheses. How well do you think Moffett has taken into account the work of Piaget in his comments on kinds of discourse and on curriculum?

Genetic Epistemology and the Implications of Piaget's Findings for Education
Herbert Ginsburg and Sylvia Opper

Over the last decade the work of Jean Piaget has attracted increasing attention from educators and theorists of curriculum, especially in English and
Language Arts. Piaget may best be described as a ''genetic epis-
temologist''—one who studies the growth of ways of knowing and of
power to learn. His numerous writings mostly describe how children of different ages see the world and learn. He himself has not written extensively
about education. Therefore it becomes necessary, in introducing Piaget's
work to a teacher of writing, to present interpretive commentary on his
work that identifies those findings likely to be most directly helpful to
teachers.

One of the most thorough and informative introductions to Piaget published recently is a book by Herbert Ginsburg and Sylvia Opper entitled
Piaget's Theory of Intellectual Development: An Introduction. The selection that follows is taken from the concluding chapter, in which the authors
look at some of what Piaget has to say to a teacher. The discussion is quite
general and is not aimed only, or even primarily, at the teacher of Language Arts. It will therefore be necessary for teachers of English and of
writing to apply Piaget's ideas to their particular field.

From *Piaget's Theory of Intellectual Development: An Introduction*, pp.
219–32. © 1969 by Prentice-Hall. Reprinted by permission of the publisher.

IMPLICATIONS FOR EDUCATION

In the present section, we will consider some general implications of Piaget's views for education. While Piaget himself has hardly dealt with the problems of education or with other practical applications of his work, it is clear nevertheless that his theories are particularly relevant for educational practice. Piaget's investigations into the development of a number of logical, physical, and mathematical notions, as well as other aspects of the child's thought, implicitly contain a number of ideas which, if suitably exploited and developed, could prove valuable to educators and educational planners. The potential of his findings for education has so far scarcely been acknowledged, and it is only fairly recently, during the past ten years or so, that psychologists and educators have begun to appreciate the importance of Piaget's theories. Attempts are currently being made in various countries, especially in Great Britain, to modify existing school programs in line with the discoveries of the Geneva group, and these attempts could profitably be extended to other parts of the world. We will therefore attempt to extract from his theories a number of general principles which may be of value to the educator. It should be emphasized at the outset, however, that our intention is not to propose particular curricula or materials on the basis of Piaget's work. We will not describe, for example, a teaching sequence on number or on logical implication; rather, our concern is with general guiding principles which emerge from Piaget's psychological research. The implementation of these principles requires the special skills of the educator, not the psychologist.

Differences Between Adults and Children

Piaget's theory as a whole suggests a proposition, which, although quite general, should have important consequences for education. The proposition is that the young child is quite different from the adult in several ways: in methods of approaching reality, in the ensuing views of the world, and in the uses of language. His investigations concerning such matters as the concepts of number, or verbal communication, have enabled Piaget to contribute to a change, indeed one might almost say to a metamorphosis, in our ways of looking at children. As a result of his work we have become increasingly aware that the child is not just a miniature, although less wise adult, but a being with a distinctive mental structure which is qualitatively different from the adult's. He views the world from a unique perspective. For example, the child below the age of 7 years truly believes that water, when poured from one container to another, gains or loses in quantity, depending on the shape of the second container. For him there is no inconsistency in stating that a given amount of water gains or loses in quantity merely by being poured from one container to another. Or in the case of number, the young child, although able to count to 20 or more, has no conception of certain fundamental mathematical ideas. He may think, for example, that a set of five elements contains more than a set of eight elements, if the physical arrangement of the sets takes on certain forms.

These and many other unexpected discoveries concerning the child's notions of reality lead us to the surprising recognition that the child's world is in many respects qualitatively different from that of the adult. One reason for the child's distinctive view of reality is a distinctive mental structure. The young child (below about 7 or 8 years of age) centers his attention on limited amounts of information; he attends to states rather than transformations; he is egocentric, and fails to take into account other points of view; and he is incapable of forms of thought, like reversibility,[1] which allows symbolic manipulation of the data of experience. Even the older child (between 7 and 11 years), although capable of fairly subtle mental operations, is strongly tied to concrete situations. He reasons best only about immediately present objects, and fails to take into account the possibilities inherent in a situation.

One result of the child's cognitive structure is a view of reality which seems chaotic and unnatural to the adult. Another conse-

[1] When a child can mentally retrace the steps that brought about the events or objects he is looking at or can see the connection between performing an operation (e. g., pouring water from one vessel to another) and reversing the operation (i. e., pouring the water back into the first vessel), he is said to understand "reversibility." (Ed.)

quence is that the young child's use of language is different from the adult's. That is, the words that the child uses do not have the same meaning for him as for the adult. This point has sometimes been overlooked in the past. It was usually assumed that if a child used a particular word, this word naturally would convey the same meaning as when an adult used the same word. Adults believed that once a child has learned the linguistic label for an object, he has available the underlying concept. But Piaget has shown that this is often not the case. The child does learn his words from the adult, but assimilates them into his own mental structure, which is quite different from the adult's. The words "same amount to drink," for example, are interpreted in one way by the 4-year-old, and in another way by the adult.[2] Only after a period of cognitive development does the child use these words and understand them in the same way as the more mature person.

The implication of this very general proposition—that the young child's thought and language are qualitatively different from the adult's—is also very general. It must follow that the educator must make a special effort to understand the unique properties of the child's experience and ways of thinking. The educator cannot assume that what is valid for him is necessarily valid for the child. For example, while the educator himself may learn a great deal by reading a book or listening to a lecture, similar experiences may be far less useful for the young child. While the educator may profit from an orderly arranged sequence of material, perhaps the child does not. While the educator may feel that a given idea is simple and indeed self-evident, perhaps the child finds it difficult. In short, it is not safe to generalize from the adult's experience to the child's. The educator's assumptions, based as they often are on his own learning experience, may not apply to children. What the educator needs to do is to try to improve his own capacity to watch and listen, and to place himself in the distinctive perspective of the child. Since the meaning expressed by the child's language is often idiosyncratic, the adult must try to understand the child's world by

[2] The child may interpret the phrase in a much more concrete, specific, and limited way than an adult, because the child's capacity to deal with abstractions and relationships of quantity is not yet well developed. (Ed.)

observing his actions closely. There are no easy rules or procedures for the educator to use in order to understand the child. What is needed chiefly is considerable sensitivity—a willingness to learn from the child, to look closely at his actions, and to avoid the assumption that what is true or customary for the adult is also true for the child. The educator needs to interact with the child in a flexible way in order to gain insight into the latter's current level of functioning. With this attitude—a willingness to observe the child, to learn from him—the educator can begin to understand the child, and tailor the educational experience to the child's needs.

Activity

Perhaps the most important single proposition that the educator can derive from Piaget's work, and thus use in the classroom, is that children, especially young ones, learn best from concrete activities. . . . Piaget places major emphasis on the role of activity in intellectual development, especially in the early years of life. In Piaget's view, one of the major sources of learning, if not the most essential one, is the intrinsic activity of the child. The child must act on things to understand them. Almost from birth, he touches objects, manipulates them, turns them around, looks at them, and in these ways he develops an increasing understanding of their properties. It is through manipulation that he develops schemes relating to objects. When new objects are presented, the child may at first try to apply to them already established schemes. If not successful, he attempts, again through manipulation, to develop new schemes; that is, new ways of acting on and thereby comprehending the world. This understanding may not be on a verbal level. In fact, verbal understanding is not usually accomplished at the outset; it takes a long time. The child must begin by acting on objects, that is, by manipulating them. Over a period of time, these overt, sensorimotor schemes can become internalized in the form of thought. Still later the child may be able to express on a verbal level the notions he has developed on the basis of interaction with the world.

For these reasons a good school should encourage the child's activity, and his manipulation and exploration of objects. When the teacher tries to bypass this process by imparting knowledge in a verbal manner, the result is often superficial learning. But by promoting activity in the classroom, the teacher can exploit the child's potential for learning, and permit him to evolve an understanding of the world around him. This principle (that learning occurs through the child's activity) suggests that the teacher's major task is to provide for the child a wide variety of potentially interesting materials on which he may act. The teacher should not teach, but should encourage the child to learn by manipulating things.

Acceptance of the principle of active learning requires a considerable reorientation of beliefs concerning education. Teachers (and the public at large) usually consider that the aim of education is to impart knowledge of certain types. According to Piaget's theory, this conception is in error for several reasons. First, teachers can in fact impart or teach very little. It is true that they can get the child to *say* certain things, but these verbalizations often indicate little in the way of real understanding. Second, it is seldom legitimate to conceive of knowledge as a *thing* which can be transmitted. Certainly the child needs to learn some facts, and these may be considered *things*. But often the child does not learn facts if the teacher transmits them; the child must discover them himself. Also, facts are but a small portion of real knowledge. True understanding involves action, on both the motoric and intellectual levels. Consider for example the understanding of class properties. A traditional view might propose that the child learns some facts about classification; for instance, that a square is a geometric form. Piaget's view, on the other hand, argues that understanding of classification consists of a sequence of activities. First the child physically sorts or otherwise manipulates objects. He feels various forms and in this way, among others, perceives the differences among them. He may put different forms in different places. Later, he can sort the objects solely on a mental level. He does not need to separate things physically, but he can do it mentally. Later still, he can perform inclusion operations on the (imagined) classes of objects. He can consider that a hypothetical class includes and is "larger than" its constituent sub-class. Thus, knowledge of classification does not merely involve facts, but actions as well: physical sorting, mental sorting, mental inclusion operations. Furthermore, most of these actions are non-verbal.

The teacher's job then is not so much to transmit facts or concepts to the child, but to get him to act on both physical and mental levels. These actions—far more than imposed facts or concepts—constitute real knowledge. In this connection it may be useful to conceive of the child's understanding in terms of three levels.

The first of these levels is motoric understanding. Knowledge at this level implies that the child can act directly on objects and manipulate them correctly. He can adjust his movements to fit the properties of the objects, and thus indicate that he has understood them at the level of motor responses. For instance he can move objects, or lift them up, or turn them around. Another level of understanding is that of internal activity on an intuitive basis. The child performs actions on the objects in a very abbreviated and internal manner. Because the activity can be performed so much faster on a mental level than on an overt level, the child is able to do more in a given period of time. He is also no longer limited by spatial and temporal restrictions. Finally, there is the level of verbal understanding. The child is able to deal with concepts on an abstract verbal level, and he can often express his mental operations in words.

Several important comments can be made concerning these levels of understanding. First, the higher levels—intuitive and verbal—depend upon the lowest; that is, the motor. Manipulation of things is a prerequisite for higher, verbal understanding. The young child cannot jump to the higher levels before establishing a basis in concrete manipulation. Therefore, concrete experience should precede learning from verbal explanations or written materials. Second, these different levels need not necessarily be restricted to given ages. It is unlikely, for example, that the preoperational [3] child is completely intuitive in his approach, or that the adolescent is completely verbal. Rather it seems probable that at a given period of development one mode of understanding will predominate over, but not exclude the rest. For both these reasons, that is, the priority of concrete manipulation and the presence of all modes of understanding at all age levels (at least beyond infancy), children

---

[3] The "preoperational" period in a child's development is characterized by the child's focusing on a small amount of information or on one aspect only of a problem (e. g., the height to which a liquid rises in a container into which it has been poured) to the neglect of other data or characteristics of a problem. (Ed.)

must have a chance to be active in the classroom, to touch and feel things, to find out what they do, to explore, and so forth. This is what real knowledge is about.

Cognitive Structure, New Experience, and Self-Regulation

Piaget's theory stresses the interaction of current cognitive structure and new experiences for the arousal of interest and the subsequent development of understanding. One way of putting the matter is to say that interest and learning are facilitated if the experience presented to the child bears some relevance to what he already knows but at the same time is sufficiently novel to present incongruities and conflicts. If you will, recall the moderate novelty principle as an example which was discussed in the case of infancy (but applying to older children as well). Piaget's proposition is that the child's interest is aroused when an experience is moderately novel; the experience is not so radically novel as to be unassimilable into current cognitive structure; and it is not so familiar as to surfeit the child. This principle is relativistic: the experience does not contain in itself any intrinsic properties of interest. Rather, interest derives from the interaction between the state of the child's mind and the thing to be known.

Equilibration [4] theory emphasizes that self-regulatory processes are the basis for genuine learning. The child is more apt to modify his cognitive structure in a constructive way when he controls his own learning than when methods of social transmission (in this case, teaching) are employed. Do recall Smedslund's experiments on the acquisition of conservation.[5] If one tries to teach this concept to a child who does not yet have available the mental structure necessary for its assimilation, then the resulting learning is superficial. On the other hand, when children are allowed to progress at

[4] "Equilibration" is a concept designating a person's ability to interact with his environment and experience, adjust his understanding of the world to accommodate his new experiences, and at the same time maintain a coherent and stable view of the world. Equilibration is essential to learning and growth. (Ed.)

[5] "Conservation" is a concept designating a person's ability to recognize that two entities (e. g., two bodies of water in different shape containers) are of the same weight or density or number or length (or the same in other characteristics) even though their physical appearance (e.g., shape) has been changed. (Ed.)

their own pace through the normal sequence of development, they regulate their own learning so as to construct the cognitive structures necessary for the genuine understanding of conservation.

These principles, if taken seriously, should lead to extensive changes in classroom practice. They imply, first, that teachers should be aware of the child's current level of functioning. Unless such an assessment is made, the teacher will find it difficult to judge what is apt to arouse the interest of his students. Second, the principles imply that the classroom must be oriented more toward the individual than the group. Since there are profound individual differences in almost all areas of cognitive development, it is unlikely that any one task or lesson will arouse the interest of or promote learning in all members of the class. For some children the task may be too easily assimilated into current mental structures, whereas for other students the problem may require a greater degree of accommodation than the student is at present capable of mastering. The result is boredom for the first group and confusion for the second. Third, children must be given considerable control over their own learning. Some may need more time than others to deal with the same material; similarly, children may approach the same problem in different ways.

To promote interest and learning, then, the teacher should tailor the curriculum to the individual. This means that the group should effectively be disbanded as the only classroom unit, that children should often work on individual projects and that they should be allowed considerable freedom in their own learning. Several objections are usually raised to this sort of proposal. First, if this were done, how could the teacher assure that all the children learn some common, required material? The answer is that he could not, unless the children's interests overlapped. But why is it essential for all children always to learn the same things? Second, under an individual learning arrangement, would not the children just waste their time or engage in mere play? This attitude, shared by many teachers, reveals a derogatory opinion concerning children's intellectual life, and a lack of faith in them. The attitude is clearly wrong too. Piaget has shown that the child is quite active in acquiring knowledge, and that he learns about important aspects of reality quite apart from instruction in the schools. In the first two years of life, for example, the infant acquires a primitive understanding of causality, of the nature of objects, of relations, of language, and of many other things, largely without the benefit of formal instruction or adult "teaching." One need only watch an infant for a short period of time to know that he is curious, interested in the world around him, and eager to learn. It is quite evident, too, that these are characteristics of older children as well. If left to himself the normal child does not remain immobile; he is eager to learn. Consequently, it is quite safe to permit the child to structure his own learning. The danger arises precisely when the schools attempt to perform the task for him. To understand this point consider the absurd situation that would result if traditional schools were entrusted with teaching the infant what he spontaneously learns during the first few years. The schools would develop organized curricula in secondary circular reactions; they would develop lesson plans for object permanence; they would construct audio-visual aids on causality; they would reinforce "correct" speech; and they would set "goals" for the child to reach each week. One can speculate as to the outcome of such a program for early training! What the student needs then is not formal teaching, but an opportunity to learn. He needs to be given a rich environment, containing many things potentially of interest. He needs a teacher who is sensitive to his needs, who can judge what materials will challenge him at a given point in time, who can help when he needs help, and who has faith in his capacity to learn.

Limitations and Opportunities

There are certain limitations on what the child can learn. His thought develops through a series of stages, each showing both strengths and weaknesses. Any one stage is characterized by the ability to perform certain actions typical of the particular stage, and, on the other hand, by the propensity to commit certain typical errors. Intellectual development is a progressive process. New mental structures evolve from the old ones by means of the dual processes of assimilation and accommodation. Faced with novel experiences, the child seeks to assimilate them into his existing mental framework. To do this, he may have to adjust and modify the framework, or accommodate to the requirements of novel experience. New knowledge is never acquired in a discontinuous fashion, but is always absorbed into preexisting structures in such a way that prior experience is used to explain novelty, and novelty is adapted to fit previous experience. Mental development is more than a mere accumulation of isolated and unrelated experiences; it is hierarchical process with the later acquisitions being built upon, and at the same time expanding upon the earlier ones.

One implication of the stage theory is in a way "pessimistic." Since intellectual development seems to follow an ordered sequence—a sequence which, until proof of the contrary, appears to be universal—the young child is incapable of learning certain kinds of concepts. It would serve no purpose, for instance, to try to teach a child of the preoperational period the principle of inertia, or any other abstract notion which requires the existence of reasoning at a formal operational level. A current trend prevails in the United States which believes that it is possible to teach anything to a child of any level of development, providing the appropriate method is used. Piaget's findings tend to stress the contrary. Certain things cannot be taught at any level, regardless of the method adopted. It is of course possible to accelerate some types of learning to a certain extent by use of suitable environmental stimuli. For instance, if a child of the preoperational period is fairly close to achieving the structure of concrete operations, suitable physical experience may expedite the process, with the result that the structure may be acquired somewhat earlier than if no such experience had been presented. But presentation of the same experience to an infant would not have the same effect. The infant lacks much of the experience and mental development necessary to achieve concrete operations and would consequently not have available an appropriate mental structure into which he could fruitfully assimilate the planned experience. In all likelihood, the infant would assimilate the experience to fit his own level of understanding. He might learn something from it, but not what the teacher had had in mind. The experience, therefore, although being suitable to accelerate the achievement of concrete operations for the preoperational child, would have quite a different effect on the infant. The effects of experience are limited, then, by the intrinsic ability of the child at a particular stage of development.

Thus, one aspect of Piaget's stage theory is "pessimistic"; that is, it assumes that there are some things children cannot learn. But there is an "optimistic" side to his theory too. At each stage of development the child is capable of certain forms of thought, and he has spontaneously developed certain notions of reality. For example, Piaget has found that concepts of topological geometry (distinctions between closed vs. open figures, etc.) develop in the child before those of Euclidean geometry (measurement of angles, distances, etc.) and projective geometry (measurement of perspective, coordinates, etc.). Understanding of topological notions appears fairly early in life, whereas the child only begins to understand the notion of Euclidean and projective geometry at around 7 years of age. Thus, while the 5-year-old may be incapable of learning projective concepts, he has already developed an intuitive understanding of topological notions. Each stage of development is characterized by both strengths and weaknesses.

There are several implications stemming from Piaget's proposition concerning the strengths and weaknesses of each stage of development. First, as we have already stressed, the teacher must try to be aware of the child's current level of cognitive functioning. To some extent the teacher can rely on Piaget's discoveries for this information. But Piaget's work is not sufficient, since it covers only a limited number of the subjects which are usually studied in schools. Therefore, the teacher himself must make an assessment of his students' capabilities. Even if revelant research were available, the teacher must still perform such an assessment since it is extremely likely that there are wide individual differences with respect to the understanding of any concept at almost any age level. The teacher's job is not easy. He should not place great reliance on standardized tests of achievement. Piaget's clinical method has shown that the child's initial verbal response (the type of response that is given to a standard test) is often superficial and does not provide a reliable index of the real quality of his understanding. Tests often tap only the surface, and they also often test the wrong things. Again the teacher must observe the children carefully and attempt to discover both their intuitive competence and weakness in any area.

Second, once the teacher has some awareness of the child's current level of functioning, he can make available to the child experiences which facilitate development. For example, in the case of geometry, the teacher might first present his students with opportunities to learn about topological concepts (these opportunities would not, of course, involve teaching, but perhaps acquiring materials which emphasize topological distinctions and at which the child, under the teacher's general guidance, can work independently). If such an arrangement were followed, the young student would feel comfortable with topological notions. His available mental structures would assure understanding of some topological concepts and others could be elaborated without great difficulty. Thus, his first school experiences with geometry should build upon and exploit what he already knows in an intuitive way.

Social Interaction

In Piaget's view, physical experience and concrete manipulation are not the only ways in which the child learns. Another type of experience leading to understanding of the environment is social experience, or interaction with other persons, be they peers or adults. The effects of this type of experience, although almost negligible during the first few months of life, become increasingly important as the child grows older. We have pointed out earlier that one of the prime deterrents to an objective understanding of reality is the child's egocentric thought. He cannot view things objectively at first because he can only see them as related to himself. The very young child assimilates external events directly into his own action schemes. Things are only relevant to the extent that they concern his own private preoccupations. He cannot view objects or events from any other perspective besides his own. This egocentrism naturally prevents the child from gaining an objective view of objects or of persons. Gradually, as the child becomes capable of decentering his attention, as he begins to focus on various aspects of reality simultaneously, as he comes to understand another person's point of view, then he gains a more objective knowledge of reality.

One method which promotes the relinquishing of egocentrism is social interaction. When one child talks to another he comes to realize that his is not the only way of viewing things. He sees that other people do not necessarily share his opinions. Interaction inevitably leads to conflict and argument. The child's views are questioned. He must defend his ideas, and he must justify his opinions. In doing this he is forced to clarify his thoughts. If he wants to convince others of the validity of his own views, his ideas must be expressed clearly and logically. Other people are not as tolerant of his inconsistencies as he is himself. So we see that, apart from the more commonly stressed affective side of social interaction, or the need to get along with other people, there is an important cognitive component. Social experience not only helps people to adjust to others at an emotional level, it also serves to clarify a person's thinking and helps him to become in some ways more coherent and logical.

In both types of experience, physical and social, the teacher can help the child to develop his potential for activity. By providing a variety of objects which the child can manipulate, the teacher provides a setting for the empirical discovery of physical properties of things or the opportunity for understanding at the motoric or intuitive level. By providing the opportunity for social interaction, the teacher promotes an exchange of opinions which ultimately leads to understanding or learning at the verbal level.

It should be made clear that social experience is not independent from physical experience. Verbal exchange of opinions is not feasible on certain subjects until the prior physical experience which gave rise to the opinion has occurred. In fact during the early stages of development, it seems that physical experience, or motor activity, plays a relatively more important role than language in the discovery of reality. Once the child has acted on an object or a situation, language can then serve as a major tool to internalize the experience into a compact category of experience. But the child's activity or experience is of paramount importance especially during the early stages of development.

The implication of Piaget's view is that social interaction should play a significant part in the classroom. Children should talk with one another. They should converse, share experience, and argue. It is hard to see why schools force the child to be quiet, when the results seem to be only an authoritarian situation and extreme boredom. Let us restrict the vow of silence to selected orders of monks and nuns.

Traditional Methods of Instruction

Piaget's theory implies that there are grave deficiencies in "traditional" methods of instruction, especially in the early years of school. By "traditional" methods, we mean cases in which the teacher uses a lesson plan to direct the students through a given sequence of material; attempts to transmit the material to the students by means of lectures and other verbal explanations; forces all students to cover essentially the same lessons; and employs a textbook as the basic medium for instruction. Under such an arrangement, the students take fixed positions in a classroom; talk to one another only at the risk of punishment; are required to listen to the teacher; must study the material which the teacher feels is necessary to study; and must try to learn from books. It is, of course, the case that teachers differ in the degree to which they employ traditional methods. No two classrooms are identical, and it would be difficult to find one which is traditional in all respects and at all times. Nevertheless, traditional methods are still highly influential in education today, as even casual observations of the schools reveal.

Traditional procedures of instruction are based on several assumptions concerning the nature of children and their learning. One assumption is that students of a given age level should learn essentially the same material. There is some truth to this assumption. Children of a given age level in a particular cultural context are usually of a similar level of cognitive development and, therefore, generally cannot learn certain concepts but are capable of dealing with others. But traditional schools often implement this principle in a ludicrous manner. By forcing all students to cover the identical material each day, the traditional method ignores the fact that there are individual differences in the pace of learning. Also such a procedure fails to take account of the factors producing interest and genuine learning: these occur when a new experience is character-ized by a moderate degree of novelty in relation to the individual's current cognitive structure. In a classroom if different children who possess different cognitive structures are presented with an identical experience, then some will either find the experience boring or so new as to be unassimilable.

A second assumption is that children learn through verbal expla-nation on the part of the teacher, or through written exposition in books. Of course, this is sometimes true. But as we have seen, children require concrete activity for genuine learning. Verbal ex-planation or written exposition can be effective only after a basis in concrete activity has been established.

A third assumption of traditional education is perhaps implicit in the first two. It is that if students were given a greater degree of control over their own learning, that is, if they were allowed to select what is to be learned and the ways in which it is to be learned, then they would waste their time and learn little. There is some truth to this assumption; if the students did not have some adult guidance they might indeed waste some time. But this does not imply that students should have almost no control over their own learning. As Piaget has shown, a major part of learning de-pends on self-regulatory processes. Also, outside of school, chil-dren manage to acquire an understanding of certain aspects of real-ity. Therefore, students can be trusted to take a major share of the responsiblity for directing the learning process. Adults can certainly help, but an attempt to take complete control of the child's learning is self-defeating.

A fourth assumption is that uncontrolled talking in class is disruptive to the educational process. Certainly, a great deal of noise may prevent students from learning (although our observation is that they are bothered by noise much less than teachers). But Piaget points out that conversation, and the resulting clash of opin-ions, is often beneficial for mental growth. To exclude intelligent and spontaneous conversation in schools is therefore unneces-sary. . . .

We will close this section on education, and this book, with a quote from Piaget. It states Piaget's educational goals and at the same time describes his own accomplishment.

The principal goal of education is to create men who are capable of doing new things, not simply of repeating what other generations have done—men who are creative, inventive, and discoverers. The second goal of education is to form minds which can be critical, can verify, and not accept everything they are offered. The great danger today is of slogans, collective opinions, ready-made trends of thoughts. We have to be able to resist individually, to criticize, to distinguish between what is proven and what is not. So we need pupils who are active, who learn early to find out by themselves, partly by their own spontaneous activity and partly through material we set up for them; who learn early to tell what is verifiable and what is simply the first idea to come to them. [6]

QUESTIONS FOR DISCUSSION

1. A good school, according to Ginsburg and Opper, "should encourage the child's activity and his manipulation and exploration of objects." Assuming that this is a wise judgment based on Piaget's work, what kinds of writing, and what kinds of activities related to writing, might best support, or contribute to, these kinds of encouragement?

2. How can writing activities help a child to gain knowledge of the world? Can they assist the child in developing equilibration? Or is the development of a child's knowledge and his ability to adapt his world view to new experiences largely independent of the writing he does in school?

3. What sorts of instruction, or guidance, in writing—what sorts of "interference" by the teacher—might best help the child toward

[6] R. E. Ripple and V. N. Rockcastle, eds., *Piaget Rediscovered* (Ithaca, New York: Cornell University Press, 1964).

the kinds of gains Piaget thinks characteristic of a child's epistemological development? Or should the teacher even be trying to advance what appears to be a normal process of development in each child?

4. What clues, if any, can a child's writing give about the kinds of progress he is making in developing his views of the world and his power to learn and know about the world?

Piaget and Grades K-6
Arthur Bessell

The following essay by Arthur Bessell shows the relationship of Piaget's
theories to some specific events in the Language Arts curriculum. Bessell is
reporting on his observations of oral work and dramatics in the British
primary schools. But since talk and drama are assuming increasingly prominent roles in elementary school teaching, and since they are directly connected to writing activities in the first six years of school, this report may
help teachers understand and interpret the written as well as the oral language of their students.

Arthur Bessell is Advisor for Primary Education, Cheshire Education
Authority, Chester, England.

In a lesson of dramatic movement, during a discussion of the children's movements, a third grade boy puts his hand up to say he
knows the difference between twisting and turning. He begins to
explain but hesitates, struggles for words and cannot produce a sentence. Suddenly he smiles and finds a solution, "I can't tell you but

From *Elementary English* Vol. 49, No. 2 (February 1972), 167–70. Copyright © 1972 by the National Council of Teachers of English. Reprinted by
permission of the publisher and the author.

I can show you." He proceeds to demonstrate very clearly the difference.

In preparation for some dramatic work on "a journey," a question was asked as to whether the journey to Africa would be by a plane or a boat. A third grade girl with a high I.Q. said, "It couldn't be a plane; there would be nowhere to land." When she was asked why not, she replied, "It's all jungle." For her, Africa was an undifferentiated whole, that is jungle. Any pictures of African desert, mountains, grassland, presented with a caption or some specific "African" attribute such as a lion or giraffe would have been classed as not Africa. She had no hesitations, no queries, she knew.

Again in dramatic improvisation, a situation which provides many revealing moments for the observant teacher, a boy in a position of authority tells another to put his shoe back on. The second boy pushes it on and goes through all the motions of fastening the shoe laces. The shoe he put on was a slip-on shoe with no laces. Yet to demonstrate the concept of shoe, to act out putting a shoe on, laces were an essential part of the process. All this took place in spite of the fact that the shoe he was working with required no laces. . . .

In a close study of 70 fifth graders, creative writing in an English elementary school, over 80% of the characters in them were flat, single attribute figures. They were like the T.V. Western character: all good, wearing a white hat, riding a white horse, and clean shaven, or they were on a black horse, wore a black hat, and had a moustache. There were a few children, 12 out of 70, who produced characters with more than one characteristic; i.e., the boy who stole to buy food for a hungry blind lady. Many children in the elementary grades see people, other than their family, as having a single all pervading characteristic.

A small group of fifth graders were acting out improvisations. Two of them were lost and thirsty in the desert. They realistically gasped and staggered. Two other children were on the edge of an oasis, raising water from a well and tending a small plot of ground. The hoes, buckets, plants were imagined. The well was three desks pushed together. The acting was realistic. As a boy returned to the well he saw the desperate travelers. "Dad," he shouts, "there's some drunks here." They find they are not drunk and authentically bathe their brows, bind their sores and ease their thirst. Reality was too strong for imagination. Verbally learned information about deserts was overridden by first hand experience of the wavering footsteps and staggering of a drunken man. For the boy it was a sensible comment, not a foolish piece of behavior. He commented from within his strong concrete experiences and immediately returned to very realistic acting.

Each of these examples can be multiplied many times. They appear in situations where the children are allowed to volunteer information and are encouraged to make their own contribution rather than choose from alternatives presented by the teacher.

There are two points I wish to make. First of all, children's errors and slips, their incomplete and partially right answers are often more illuminating and informative of a child's stages of language development and his thought processes and are of greater value for future action by the teacher than are the number of correct answers in a formal right, wrong testing situation. An examination by the teacher of what went wrong and a good humoured follow up with the child will often reveal more possibilities and needs than a concentration on competitive grades or scores. Secondly, the teacher must have a background of children's language and thought development, particularly the stages passed through in attaining the ability to think logically and hypothetically. Statements about the "stupidity" of children, their "inability" to learn, or as a student teacher said, "I told them how to do it and they got it wrong. I showed them again and they got it wrong again. What else can you do?" are little help. The work of Piaget and his followers, examining the growth of children's understanding in many fields, including morals, mathematics, science, and language can be of particular help for a teacher trying to understand the children he teaches. Apparent errors can often be seen not as "wrong" answers but as "right" answers from a child at a particular point along a continuum of development, moving towards the ability to think hypothetically and logically.

The stages in Piaget's continuum most relevant to the K-6 age range are the stages of preoperational and concrete thinking. In both stages there is a good deal of egocentric thought. The children think in a way which allows events and experiences to be seen only from the child's point of view and with that point of view bounded by his five senses. Knowledge will only be true if it agrees with his personal experience. For example, in many children's paintings, the sky is nearly always separated from the roofs of buildings. The sky is up above. When he looks up there is apparently nothing immediately above him. A long way above, to his senses, is blue or grey sky. The teacher telling him he is wrong may lower the teacher's standing rather than improve the child's understanding. A teacher taking a group of children outside to look at a distant sky-line and then stimulating a discussion may have begun a move away from egocentric understanding.

Another characteristic of this stage is the way a child will centre his attention on a single striking feature. He will consider one attribute and ignore many others. A fifth grader in improvised drama was acting a Viking raid on England. He shouted, "Come on chaps." When asked later if this was appropriate language he said, "Yes, that's the way English people speak." One feature out of many this boy had seen in connection with England had been seized upon and was considered the one characteristic which denoted all Englishmen.

A third characteristic closely connected with the second is the way a child will seize on a single characteristic and spread this one section of meaning to whole sentences completely distorting the intended meaning. A child who was told there was still three quarters of an hour to work in seizes upon the word quarter which to him meant a small amount and interpreted the sentence to mean there was only a little time left. After about 30 minutes he began to get very frustrated, expecting the lesson to be well over. Piaget highlights this aspect in describing how children reasoned when asked to match proverbs with explanatory sentences in "The Language and Thought of the Child."

A fourth characteristic is the child's certainty that there is a causal link for everything. Events which occur closely together provide reasons for one another. The day Tom sat by me I got all my work wrong is explained as Tom made me do badly at my work. Even though it may have been harder work or a dozen other things. Connections appear clear to a child. He has no doubts. He does not ask for an explanation. When his work turns out incorrect the teacher's "Why didn't you say you didn't understand," doesn't make any sense when he did understand and was fully able to carry out the task as he understood it. A class of second grade children was introduced to letter writing. They were taught that the text of the letter began four letter spaces in from the edge of the page. While writing letters in the third grade, a group of about ten of them held this one fact to be the essential to writing letters. It would make them interesting. It was the reason for a "good" letter and could not be a "poor" letter if this criteria was fulfilled.

A fifth characteristic is closely related to the others. A child may make little attempt to adapt his speech to the needs of the listener and will not adapt his listening to the needs of a speaker. He is locked within his own viewpoint. An interested class, apparently listening to a story will produce apparently irrelevant questions, much to the annoyance of a teacher. Yet the question about last night's television may have started five minutes ago with a single word in the story. An eighth grader driving through Iowa in a car suddenly said, "Have you ever seen a micro-wave cooker?" This statement came with no apparent beginning or reason. The sunset had reminded him of cafeteria lamps over heated food, this had led to food heating, he had visited St. Paul Science Museum where there was a food automat with micro-wave heating. This process of thinking which ends up with an answer or question apparently unconnected with the present experience, be it story or discussion, also stems from a concentration upon successive states rather than upon the transformations by which these states take place. A second grader would probably have been unable to retrace the steps in the way the eighth grader did.

A sixth characteristic is one of disequilibrium where the child is drawn into clear contradictions. The elementary child illustrates this in his willingness to give a cheerful "goodnight" after a terrible hour of bad behavior and punishment. The present moment is all. More infuriating, he will also, seeing a specific temptation, an elastic band to shoot or a pencil to drum, follow good work and reward with a complete about face making little sense to the teacher.

Finally there is the very important characteristic of irreversibility. This is the inability to return to a starting point in logic and is implied in many of the above characteristics. This is usually described in mathematical terms but I think shows itself in children's writing when you see a story title, "The Haunted Castle" and as you read you find that the story is about something else altogether. Each individual step led one step further. The story was not seen as a whole from beginning to end and in reverse but was rather a series of added steps never to be retraced.

The stages overlap and run together and are perhaps best summed up by the term ego-centricity. A child may be more egocentric in some areas than others. In an area with which he is familiar he may be much farther along the continuum towards abstract logical thought than in an area where he has little experience. The city child may have a rich understanding of the concept of public transport. He may be aware of its many features and great variety of vehicles, yet his concept of trees may have all the problematic characteristics of egocentric thought. Yet the child will believe he "knows" both concepts and will speak of them with equal certainty.

In considering the teachers' role, it is important that the teacher responds with equal sympathy and attention to answers given in both areas. His concept of trees may be inadequate, near the beginning of the continuum, have little detailed differentiation of detail but it is not "wrong," or "stupid" or "dull." Given the right experiences a sympathetic adult, and peers to share those experiences, with, he will move towards the facility and complex understanding he has of public transport.

The relevance of this for teachers of language arts, dealing as they are with the whole of a child's language and meaning and not just with the narrow, though necessary skills of punctuation and spelling seems to be that the child's answers, particularly his apparently wrong, or careless ones should be explored. More positively, that open ended tasks stemming from first hand experience; e.g., creative writing, improvised drama, a discussion/exploration approach to science and social studies be presented to him rather than single word answers, convergent questions and filling in blanks in workbooks. The latter will reinforce his egocentricity, emphasize a right/wrong approach so inhibiting to language development.

Two quotations from J. H. Flavell will both summarize my position and emphasize the techniques to be used by the elementary school teacher.

> It is clear that the mechanism which Piaget holds responsible for the development of a rational morality is exactly the same as that which he thinks engenders rationality in general, . . . both morality and logic are fired in the crucible of the spontaneous give and take, the interplay of thought and action, which takes place in peer-peer interaction . . . It is only through a sharing of perspectives with equals—at first other children and later as the child grows up, with adults, that a genuine logic and morality can replace an egocentric, logical, and moral realism.[1]

The second quotation reinforces the first.

> . . . thought becomes aware of itself, able to justify itself, and in general able to adhere to logical-social norms of noncontradiction, coherence, etc., and that all these things and more can emerge only from repeated interpersonal interactions (and especially those involving arguments and disagreements) in which the child is actually forced again and again to take cognizance of the role of the other. It is social interaction which gives the coup de grace to childish egocentrism. [Flavell, pp. 156, 157.]

QUESTIONS FOR DISCUSSION

1. Bessell appears to encourage teachers to explain or interpret features of a child's talk and writing by having them refer to Piaget's theories of the child's intellectual development. Do you think that, as a general rule, this sort of interpretation by the teacher is a wise

[1] J. H. Flavell, *The Developmental Psychology of J. Piaget* (1963), p. 296.

procedure? What are the dangers of explaining a child's use of language by referring to particular notions he is capable of understanding or to operations he is capable of performing at a given age?

2. Does Bessell's argument point to the desirability of encouraging some kinds of writing and the inadvisability of encouraging others in the first six or seven years of school?

3. What sorts of responses to children's writing does Bessell appear to encourage? (By ''responses,'' we refer here to statements or questions the teacher might offer to the child or the class that is discussing a piece of writing.)

Recent Measures in Syntactic Development
Kellogg Hunt

The focus of the two previous articles has been on the characteristics of children's thinking and their ways of seeing the world at successive ages. In the following article, Kellogg Hunt discusses how observable characteristics of children's written language change as children grow older. Hunt points to observable features of syntax and discusses what changes appear in these features as one examines samples drawn from successively higher grades.

Kellogg Hunt, who teaches at Florida State University, has pioneered the application of techniques employed by transformational-generative grammarians to the study of writing in the schools. His monograph *Grammatical Structures Written at Three Grade Levels* (1965) won an award for distinguished research from the National Council of Teachers of English.

Any teacher of English can tell a fourth-grade theme from a twelfth-grade theme. Probably anyone in this room could make still finer distinctions: he could tell the average fourth-grade theme from

From *Elementary English* Vol. 43, No. 7 (November 1966), 732–39. Copyright © 1966 by the National Council of Teachers of English. Reprinted by permission of the publisher and the author.

the average eighth-grade theme. Just how would he detect the difference? For one thing he would rely on word choice. The vocabulary of the average eighth grader is measurably different from that of the average fourth grader. But also the teacher would feel that some of the sentence structures used by the eighth grader were too mature to be used by a fourth grader. Sentence structure, not vocabulary, is my subject for this paper.

The educational researcher respects the teacher's intuitive sense of maturity, but he wishes he knew how to measure it quantitatively, by counting something—if only he knew what to count. He knows of course that it takes centuries to build up a science. All during the Middle Ages the alchemists were poking away at the information which eventually led to modern scientific chemistry. It took centuries to establish the science. The science of measuring syntactic maturity is barely emerging from the stages of alchemy. It scarcely deserves to be called a science at all. But we do know a few things.

For the last thirty years we have known at least three things about the development of language structure. First, as children mature they tend to produce more words on any given subject. They have more to say. Second, as children mature, the sentences they use tend to be longer. Third, as children mature a larger proportion of their clauses are subordinate clauses.[1]

In the last two years it has been possible to add a few more measures, and I will come to them later. But first let me turn back to the statement about subordinate clauses and try to make clear its significance for the teaching program. It would be worse than useless for a fourth-grade teacher to say to her students, ''Now if you will go back to your last paper and add more subordinate clauses to the main clauses, you will be writing like Miss Hill's wonderful sixth graders or Miss Summit's wonderful eighth graders instead of my own miserable fourth graders.'' Such an approach would be worse than useless. But the facts behind so useless a statement are not useless; they are useful if we know how to use

[1] Dorothea McCarthy, ''Language Development in Children.'' *Manual of Child Psychology,* ed. Leonard Carmichael. New York: John Wiley & Sons, Inc., 1954.

them. Let us look at some fourth-grade writings. We find pairs of main clauses like this:

> There was a lady next door and the lady was a singer.

Now an older student would not be likely to repeat the noun *lady*. He might rewrite the two clauses in any of several ways: one way would be to reduce the second main clause to a relative adjective clause.

> There was a lady next door who was a singer.

Now instead of two main clauses and no subordinate clauses, we have one main clause and one subordinate clause.

Let me give you a few more examples of pairs of fourth-grade main clauses. In every instance one of the main clauses could have been reduced to a relative adjective clause.

> Moby Dick was a very big whale. He lived in the sea. (who lived in the sea.)

> His owner was a milkman. The milkman was very strict to the mother and babies. (who was very strict . . .)

> Once upon a time I had a cat. This cat was a beautiful cat. It was also mean. (who was a beautiful cat.)

> One day Nancy got a letter from her Uncle Joe. It was her great uncle. (who was her great uncle.)

> I have a new bicycle. I like to ride it. (which I like to ride.)

> We have a lot on Lake Talquin. This lot has a dock on it. (On Lake Talquin we have a lot which has a dock on it.)

> Today we went to see a film. The film was about a white-headed whale. (which was about a white-headed whale.)

> The jewel was in the drawer. It was red. (The jewel which was red . . .)

> Beautiful Joe was a dog, he was born on a farm. (that was born on a farm.)

One colt was trembling. It was lying down on the hay. (One colt which was lying down . . .)

A convenient way to measure the frequency of subordinate clauses is to divide the total number of clauses, both subordinate and main, by the number of main clauses. I will call this the "subordinate clause index." [2] It is expressed as a decimal fraction. The index will always be 1 (for the main clause) plus whatever number of subordinate clauses are attached to it.

I find that average fourth-grade writers have a subordinate clause index of about 1.3; that is, they write a subordinate clause three-tenths as often as they write a main clause. Average eighth graders have an index of 1.4; they write a subordinate clause four-tenths as often as a main clause. Average twelfth graders have an index of 1.68. They write a subordinate clause about six-tenths as often as a main clause. If you jump now to the superior adult writers who produce articles for *Harper's* and *Atlantic* you find that they have an index of 1.78: they write about seven-tenths as many subordinate clauses as main clauses. However, some mature article writers have much higher indexes. One had a score of 2.36, indicating that his average main clause had one and a third subordinate clauses related to it.

The general trend of development is fairly clear: for fourth grade the score was 1.3, for eighth 1.4, for twelfth 1.6, and for superior adults 1.7.

It would be interesting to go back to the grades earlier than the fourth to see if the number of subordinate clauses is smaller back there. Fortunately Professors O'Donnell, Griffin, and Norris at Peabody have provided us with data within the last year. [3] Reporting on their results for speech alone, they find a general increase in number of subordinate clauses from kindergarten to the seventh grade where the study ended. These kindergarten students have an

[2] The "subordination ratio" which has been used for thirty years has usually been figured in another way.

[3] Published as an NCTE research monograph entitled *A Transformational Analysis of the Language of Kindergarten and Elementary School Children,* NCTE Research Report #8. Champaign, Illinois, 1967.

index of 1.16. Putting their figures and mine together, we see that the trend is clear. From the first public school grade to the last the number of subordinate clauses increases steadily for every grade.

This tendency has implications for teaching language. Without ever using the words "main clause" and "subordinate clause," the language arts teacher who sees pairs of main clauses like those I have mentioned can show her students another way of saying the same thing.

One further refining statement can be made about subordinate clauses and the index of their frequency. There are three common kinds of such clauses: noun, movable adverb, and adjective. The other kinds, such as clauses of comparison, are uncommon. Though the total of all three increases with maturity, not all three increase equally. Noun clauses in general are no index of maturity: the number of them is determined instead by the mode of discourse, the subject matter, all the way from the early grades to maturity. Movable adverb clauses do seem to increase with maturity in the very early grades, but the ceiling is reached early, and after the middle grades the frequency of them tells more about mode of discourse and subject matter than about maturity. But adjective clauses are different. From the earliest grades to the latest the number of them increases steadily, and among skilled adults the adjective clause is still more frequent than it is with students finishing high school. We see, then, that the subordinate clause index is a team which moves ahead, but it moves ahead because one member does almost all the work. The other two sometimes pull ahead but sometimes pull back too, depending on factors other than mental maturity.

But of course subordinating clauses is not all there is to syntactic development. In every pair of examples I have given so far, it would have been possible to reduce one of the clauses still further so that it is no longer a clause at all, but merely a word or phrase consolidated inside the other clause. In this fashion two clauses will become one clause. The one clause will now be one word or one phrase longer than it was before, but it will be shorter than the two clauses were together. By throwing away some of one clause we will gain in succinctness. The final expression will be tighter, less diffuse, more mature.

Let me illustrate now with the same examples, and then back up the examples with figures to indicate that older students do indeed more often make one longer clause out of two shorter ones.

A clause with a predicate adjective can all be thrown away except for the adjective.

Once upon a time I had a *beautiful, mean* cat.
The *red* jewel was in the drawer.

Eighth graders write more than 150 percent as many single-word adjectives before nouns as fourth graders do.

If a clause contains a prepositional phrase after a form of *be* you can throw away all but that prepositional phrase.

The jewel *in the drawer* was red.
Today we saw a film *about Moby Dick*.

Eighth graders use such prepositional phrases to modify nouns 170 percent as often, and twelfth graders 240 percent as often, as fourth graders do.

If the clause contains a *have* you can often put what follows the *have* into a genitive form and throw away the rest.

I like to ride *my* new bicycle.
Our lot on Lake Talquin has a dock on it.

Twelfth graders used 130 percent as many genitives as fourth graders do.

If a clause contains a predicate nominal, it can become an appositive, and the rest can be thrown away.

There was a lady next door, *a singer*.
His owner, *a milkman*, was very strict to the mother and babies.
One day Nancy got a letter from her *great uncle* Joe.

Eighth graders wrote a third more appositives than fourth graders.

Often clauses with non-finite verbs can all be thrown away except for the verbs, which now become modifiers of nouns.

Beautiful Joe was a dog *born on a farm.*
One *trembling* colt was lying down on the hay.
One colt, *lying down on the hay,* was trembling.

Eighth graders wrote 160 percent and twelfth graders wrote 190 percent as many non-finite verb modifiers of nouns as fourth graders did.

I have used this set of examples twice now, to show two different things: first, how it is that older students reduce more of their clauses to subordinate clause status, attaching them to other main clauses; and secondly, how it is that the clauses they do write, whether subordinate or main, happen to have more words in them.[4] Those extra added words are not padding. They are all that is left out of useless whole clauses when the padding has been thrown away. From a six-word clause five words may be thrown away, with only one word salvaged. So adding that one more word to some other clause indicates a substantial gain. Though an increase of one word in clause length may not sound very impressive, a gain of five words or so in succinctness is indeed impressive. What was said in two clauses totalling twelve words is now said in one clause of seven words.

It is not as if some fourth-grade teacher had said "Add one word to each clause you have written." Instead it is as if she had said, "In this sentence you can throw away all but one word or one phrase. You can consolidate that word or phrase with this other expression into a larger, more comprehensively organized, unit of thought."

Substantial evidence is accumulating that as school children mature they do indeed learn to put their thoughts into longer and longer clauses. My own first research dealt with children of strictly average IQ, that is, with children having scores between 90 and 110. I worked first with three grades, fairly widely spaced: fourth

---

[4] A clause is here defined as one subject or one set of coordinate subjects with one finite verb or one finite set of coordinated verbs. Thus *I went home* is one clause, and so is *Jim and I went home and rode our bikes.*

The average clause length for any body of writing, however long or short, is simply the total number of words divided by the total number of clauses. For a sentence such as *She said he ought to try harder,* there are 7 words and 2 clauses, so the average clause length is 3.5 words for that body of writing.

grade, when students are just beginning to write with some degree of comfortableness; twelfth grade when the student of average IQ writes about as well as he ever will, perhaps; eighth grade, half way between the beginning and end of that public school period. The clauses written by these fourth graders were 6.6 words long. Clauses by eighth graders were 20 percent longer and clauses by twelfth graders were 30 percent longer. But development does not stop there. The writers of articles for *Harper's* and *Atlantic* write clauses about 175 percent as long as those written by fourth graders of average IQ. In fact, in clause length, the superior adult is farther ahead of the average twelfth grader than the average twelfth grader is ahead of his little brother back in the fourth grade.

If the evidence is as sound as it seems to be, then one ought to be able to predict on the basis of it. If this tendency to lengthen clauses is a general characteristic of linguistic development, then one might predict in several directions. He might predict that if growth is fairly steady after the fourth grade, then it probably is perceptible before the fourth grade too. And if growth occurs in writing, then it probably occurs in speech too. If one is going to measure the development which occurs earlier than the fourth grade, of course, it is speech, not writing, he must study.

Fortunately the Peabody study has provided us with some confirming evidence within the last few months. Notice the slight but steady increase as I read these figures. The clauses spoken by the kindergarten children are 6.1 words long. For first graders, 6.7 words. For second graders 7.1 words. Third graders 7.2. Fifth graders 7.5. Seventh graders 7.8. At every grade level there is an increase in the clause length of their speech. Clause length plots as a smooth rising curve, all the way to the maturity of *Harper's* and *Atlantic* articles.

One might predict in yet another direction. He might predict that children with superior IQ's will have matured more in language structure at even an early age. Since my results are not conclusive at this time, I am not sure whether, as early as the fourth grade, children with IQ scores above 130 write, on the average, slightly longer clauses and write a larger proportion of subordinate clauses than fourth graders with average IQ. By the time children of superior IQ reach the twelfth grade, however, their superiority in clause-length is unmistakable. They are almost as far ahead of average twelfth graders as average twelfth graders are ahead of fourth graders. In fact, in clause length, twelfth graders with IQ above 130 are closer to writers of *Harper's* and *Atlantic* articles than they are to twelfth graders of average IQ.

These longer clauses written by older students are not produced by combining just two clauses, but by combining four or six or eight. Superior adults can combine a dozen clauses into one, by the process already briefly suggested.

So, for a third time, I suggest that teachers who understand the findings of language development research may be able to apply those findings in the classroom. For years teachers have occasionally combined pairs of clauses as we were doing here a few minutes ago. But so far as I know it has never occurred to anyone to show that six or eight or a dozen are often consolidated into one mature clause. It is by this process that little sentences grow into big ones.[5]

Here is a clause written by an average eighth grader. "He was a rare white whale with a crooked jaw." That consolidates five clauses. (1) He was a whale. (2) The whale was white. (3) The whale was rare. (4) The whale had a jaw. (5) The jaw was crooked. Average fourth graders do not ordinarily write like that. In fact, in five thousand clauses written by fourth graders we found a single nominal that resulted from as many as five of these consolidations only three times. Five is simply too many for a fourth grader, but he often consolidates three.

Despite this eighth grader's relative maturity, even he failed to consolidate clauses where he might have. He missed opportunities. He wrote:

Moby Dick was a dangerous whale. People had never been able to catch him. He was a rare white whale with a crooked jaw. He was a killer too. He was long and strong.

[5] See "How Little Sentences Grow into Big Ones," a paper by Kellogg W. Hunt read at the NCTE's Spring Institute on New Directions in Elementary English, Chicago, March 7, 1966, to be published with the proceedings of that institute.

There are many ways to consolidate this further and I won't rewrite the whole passage. The first two clauses could well be consolidated and so could the last two:

> Moby Dick was a dangerous whale that people had never been able to catch. He was a killer too, long and strong.

I am recommending, then, that throughout the elementary and secondary grades the process of clause-consolidation is one of the things which the language arts program should study. Transformational grammarians speak of this process as the result of embedding and deletion transformations.

Finally I want to describe to you a new unit of measurement which is very convenient for syntactic development research. It is certainly more significant than sentence length which is still reported to be the most widely used measure of language maturity.[6] To introduce this unit let me read a theme as written by one of our fourth graders. The theme is one sentence long.

> I like the movie we saw about Moby Dick the white whale the captain said if you can kill the white whale Moby Dick I will give this gold to the one that can do it and it is worth sixteen dollars they tried and tried but while they were trying they killed a whale and used the oil for the lamps they almost caught the white whale.

In sentence length this fourth grader is superior to the average writer in *Harper's* and *Atlantic*. Now let me cut that sentence up into the new units. Each unit will consist of exactly one main clause plus whatever subordinate clauses happen to be attached to or embedded within it.

1. I like the movie we saw about Moby Dick, the white whale.
2. The captain said if you can kill the white whale, Moby Dick, I will give this gold to the one that can do it.
3. And it is worth sixteen dollars.
4. They tried and tried.

[6] For instance, see the article on "Language Development" in the 1960 edition of the *Encyclopaedia of Educational Research*.

5. But while they were trying they killed a whale and used the oil for
   the lamps.
6. They almost caught the white whale.

For lack of a better name I call these units "minimal terminable
units." They are "terminable" in the sense that it is grammatically
acceptable to terminate each one with a capital letter at the beginning and a period or question mark at the end. They are "minimal"
in the sense that they are the shortest units into which a piece of
discourse can be cut without leaving any sentence fragments as res-
idue. They are thus "minimal terminable units." I wish I could call
these units "the shortest allowable sentences" but instead I call
them "T-units," for short. To repeat, each is exactly one main
clause plus whatever subordinate clauses are attached to that main
clause.

In ordinary prose about half the sentences consist of just one
such T-unit. The other half of the sentences consist of two or more
T-units, often joined with *and's*. Such sentences are "compound,"
or "compound-complex." Cutting a passage into T-units cuts each
compound sentence or compound-complex sentence into two or
more T-units. Now if it were true that as writers mature they put
more and more T-units into their sentences, then sentence length
would be a better measure of maturity than T-unit length. But such
is not the case. Occasionally a very young student will string one
T-unit after another after another, with *and's* between or nothing
between. The passage I read a moment ago combined six T-units
into one sentence. The result of this tendency is that my fourth
graders average more T-units per sentence than superior adults do.
That fact upsets sentence length as an index of maturity. That same
fact explains why T-unit length is a better index of maturity than
sentence length.

A useful name for the average number of T-units per sentence
might be "main clause coordination index." It probably should not
be called "sentence coordination index."

Now let us pull all these various indexes together into a
single piece of arithmetic. "Average clause length" is the number
of words per clause. "Subordinate clause index" is the number of

clauses per T-unit. "Average T-unit length" is the number of words per T-unit. "Main clause coordination index" is the number of T-units per sentence. "Average sentence length" is the number of words per sentence.

These five measures are very useful analytically and are all related arithmetically. The number of words per clause times the number of clauses per T-unit equals the number of words per T-unit. That times the number of T-units per sentence gives the number of words per sentence. The first index times the second equals the third. The third times the fourth equals the fifth. Clause length times subordinate clause index equals T-unit length. That figure times main clause coordination index equals sentence length.[7]

Finally, as a review, let me mention again the tendencies that have been known for thirty years concerning the development of language structure. First, as students mature they tend to have more to say about any subject. Second, as students mature their sentences tend to get longer. Third, as students mature they tend to write more subordinate clauses per main clause.

In the last few years a few more statements about syntactic development have been added. First, as students mature they tend to produce longer clauses. From kindergarten to at least the seventh grade, and probably beyond that time, this appears to be true of speech. And from the beginning to at least the twelfth grade this appears to be true of writing. Clause length is a better index of language maturity than sentence length. You will recall that clauses can be lengthened by a process that is here described as reduction and consolidation. That same process is described by generative-transformational grammarians as embedding transformations. Second, a convenient unit, intervening in size between the clause and the compound sentence is the "minimal terminable unit," defined as one main clause plus whatever subordinate clauses are attached to it or embedded within. This too is a better index of language maturity than sentence length. You will recall that "T-units" can be

[7] Kellogg W. Hunt, "A Synopsis of Clause-to-Sentence Factors," *English Journal,* 54 (April 1965), 300–309. Also Kellogg W. Hunt, *Grammatical Structures Written at Three Grade Levels,* Research Report #3, NCTE, Champaign, Ill., 1965.

lengthened either by lengthening clauses or by increasing the number of subordinate clauses per T-unit. In the writing of average students throughout the public school grades, the one factor is about as influential as the other in effecting longer T-units. But the equality of influence stops there. The average twelfth grader has approached the ceiling in number of subordinate clauses. To advance beyond the level of the average twelfth grader, the writer must learn to reduce and consolidate clauses much more often. Superior twelfth graders do not write more subordinate clauses than average twelfth graders. Instead they write much longer clauses, just as superior adults do.

But making one clause out of two is child's play. Long before the average child gets to the fourth grade he can consolidate two, though he does not do so very often. Some average fourth graders consolidate three into one. Some average eighth graders consolidate four into one. Some average twelfth graders consolidate five into one. Superior twelfth graders consolidate six and seven. Superior adults consolidate more than that.[8] For a teacher to stretch a youngster, to push against the limits of his present accomplishment, two is nowhere near enough.

So far I have talked only about building up little sentences into bigger ones. Before I close I want to mention the other side of the coin, breaking big sentences down into little ones, as the mature reader or listener does with such lightning speed.

In recent months we have compared the syntactic traits that make a sentence hard to write and the syntactic traits that make it hard to read. We have compared the sentences written by children with those read by them but written by adults. For our reading samples we have used the *McCall-Crabbs Reading Lessons,* since the readability of each passage therein is supposedly already established. The passages cover roughly grades four to nine.

We find that sentences more difficult to read do not have more T-units per sentence. The number is about the same whether the

[8] Kellogg W. Hunt, *Sentence Structures Used by Superior Students in Grades Four and Twelve, and by Superior Adults.* USOE Research Project No. 5-0313. Available from ERIC Document Reproducing Service, Bell and Howell, 1700 Shaw Boulevard, Cleveland, Ohio 44112.

sentences are easy or difficult. Listen to this sameness for grades 4 to 9: 1.13, 1.12, 1.13, 1.10, 1.13, 1.10.

You will remember that as children mature they tend to write subordinate clauses more often. But as sentences written by adults get easier or harder to read there seems to be no change. Listen to this sameness for passages that are 80 percent comprehensible to children in grades 4 through 9: 1.4, 1.4, 1.4, 1.4, 1.4, 1.4. (It sounds as if the record player were stuck in the same groove.)

But the clause length of passages, for 80 percent comprehension, increases steadily for grades 4 through 9 just as it increases as children write. Here are our figures so far: 8.45, 9.13, 9.59, 10.19, 11.01, 10.83.

In other words, the difficulty in reading sentences usually lies down inside the clause. Longer clauses tend to be more difficult. On the basis of previous research on what constitutes these clauses, it seems clear what it is that makes longer clauses harder to read and harder to write. On the whole, longer clauses have a larger number of sentences or clauses reduced and consolidated into one. It is by that process that little clauses grow into big ones.

Little by little the evidence piles up that the reduction and consolidation of many clauses into one is intimately related to syntactic growth both in writing and reading. If writers must build up clauses, then readers must break them down. A whole new range of applications is opened up for approaching reading difficulty.

For many years we have known that longer sentences tend to be harder to read. But in the last few months we have learned more about why that is true. It is not because longer sentences have more T-units coordinated into them, for they do not. It is not because they have more subordinate clauses attached to main clauses, for they do not. Instead it is because the clauses are longer. And the clauses are longer, it can be inferred, only because more have been consolidated into a single one.

All this has implications for the teaching of reading in the early grades. Teachers need to be trained in clause-consolidation so that children can be taught what otherwise they must discover unaided. They will discover it. That we know. But at present they must do so unaided.

Here is another place where the results of research should crawl out of the learned journals and into the classroom.

QUESTIONS FOR DISCUSSION

1. In what ways might the empirical, quantitative research of the sort represented by Professor Hunt's work be useful to the classroom teacher?

2. Hunt implies that "maturity" in syntax—a major element in writing—can be identified by the amount and kinds of consolidation (consolidation of clauses into other clauses, or separate sentences into main and subordinate clauses) found in an example of a student's writing. Are you satisfied with this index of "maturity" in writing? If one defines "maturity" of style partly in the way Professor Hunt does, is anything left out of one's idea of "maturity"? What? Is the omission serious?

3. Do you think that it might be wise to teach, directly, the kinds of consolidations talked about by Hunt, so as to accelerate a student's syntactic development? Would such teaching produce "better writing"?

4. Do you see any connection between the kinds of development discussed by Hunt and the cognitive and psychological developments in children described by Piaget? What connections might there be?

Stimulating and Receiving Children's Writing: Implications for an Elementary Writing Curriculum
Lester Golub

This article presents examples of children's writing (in their own handwriting) from each of the first six grades and looks at the imagination, feeling, and values revealed by the authors of these pieces. In the essay, Lester Golub illustrates important differences between the kinds of interests and concerns expressed by children of various ages in their writing. This view of writing connects it to the overall process of personal growth in the child—a process which, as the next essay by John Dixon will show, is of increasing concern to teachers of writing and to curriculum planners today.

Lester Golub taught at the University of Illinois, Chicago Circle. He has conducted extensive studies of children's writing, noting particularly syntactic characteristics and the ways children respond to various stimuli. The results of his work have been published in *Elementary English* and the journal *Research in the Teaching of English*.

From *Elementary English* Vol. 48, No. 1 (January 1971), 33–46. Copyright © 1971 by the National Council of Teachers of English. Reprinted by permission of the publisher and the author.

"Above everything else I would like to see our schools staffed by men and women who have poetry in their souls." (Sybil Marshal, *Adventure in Creative Education*)

Why not poets in the classroom as well as firemen, astronauts, physicists, candy makers, and lion trainers? But, the poet is different. He makes his living by writing, by stirring the reader's imagination by using his own imagination, by manipulating language. He is expendable in our pragmatic society, but without him there would be no song, no discovery of the inner voice of man that is in all of us. And that is what writing is all about, discovering our inner voice and expressing it in such a way, with language, that it stimulates some sort of sensitive, creative response in the listener or the reader. This explanation of writing must be kept in mind as we teach children to write, since it is the stimulating of this inner voice and the response it creates in others which becomes our teaching goal. In a way this goal will be too simple for those who teach from traditional language arts textbooks, where grammar, mechanics, and usage predominate. For the sake of this discussion, let us discard these texts and look squarely at the problem of stimulating and "receiving" children's writing which is their thinking in their most intimate voice.

In discarding the mechanical and grammatical dictates of language arts texts we are left face to face with the child of nine through twelve who has learned to read some simple and not so simple prose, who has learned to manipulate the pencil at an excruciatingly slow rate and who has thoughts on his mind which he *wants* to express. Not only do the children in grades three through six with whom we have worked *want* to express their ideas in writing, they also *like* to express their thoughts in writing. Once the writing is done, they want to express themselves aloud with members of the class. Why, then, do children grow to detest writing in the upper grades? Can it be that their linguistic imagination and their inner voice which permit our students to know themselves have been extinguished?

Writing as a growth process. Although most children, by the time they begin school, know how to structure the English language using the rules of an introductory text in transformational grammar, rules pertaining to declaratives and interrogatives, affirmatives and negatives, active and passive voice, simple sentences, conjoined sentences, and embedded sentences, they have no explicit grammatical or rhetorical knowledge. This preschool linguistic genius still communicates like a child.

Giving a very simple stimuli of asking a child to describe a picture so that another child can identify it will offer the following difficulties for the child: (1) He will have difficulty relying exclusively on language. He wants to use his whole body for expression. (2) He will show egocentrism by using terms and experiences not shared by the listeners. (3) He will fail to use contrasts so that the listener can associate similarities and differences, assuming that the listener knows much more about the subject than he actually does.

This simple discourse situation presented to a preschool child illustrates to the teacher of children's writing just how deeply embedded are the writing difficulties which we attempt to alleviate in the process in teaching writing. In asking a nine year old child to tell a story he has heard, the teacher must be aware of the child's ability to order information so that the reader has consecutive information at each point of the narration, the teacher must be aware of the child's ability to embed sentences to convey likely figure-ground relationships in his linguistic and psychological subordination, the teacher must be aware of the child's logical conjoining of words and sentences by the use of coordination, the teacher must be aware of the child's production of a sequence of thoughts that describe a line of thought, the teacher must be aware of the child's ability to shift styles depending upon his intended reader, and the teacher must be aware of the child's ability to use metaphor to capture similarities and differences in a situation. None of these writing abilities are dependent upon grammatical knowledge, none are well developed in early childhood or in early and late adolescence. There are no definitive limits to any of these skills, and even professional writers struggle to maintain or reach these mentalistic behaviors. The struggle which professional writers encounter in surmounting these problems is at the rhetorical level rather than the grammatical level. A case in point is illustrated in Jack London's semi-autobiographical novel, *Martin Eden.*

In spite of all that we know about the structure of English, there is very little which we can do to make a child write or talk like an adult, a first grader like a fourth grader, a seventh grader like a twelfth grader, and a twelfth grader like a professional contributor to *Atlantic* or *Harper's.* Yet children who are learning to read can and must simultaneously be learning to write. It does not take the child long to realize that the style of a note to Grandmother explaining that he will take off from school the day before Thanksgiving in order to have a longer visit with her is different from a note containing the same information but directed to the school principal. Even a supermarket list can be ordered in a logical order so that merchandise can be picked off the shelves in the most expedient way. In the classroom, stimuli for eliciting children's writing should in some way permit the child and the teacher to become aware of the rhetorical problems in writing. The quasi-linguistic problems such as spelling, capitalization, and punctuation, so apparent when an adult looks at children's writing, must be deemphasized by the teacher. Rather, the teacher should attend to the child's linguistic and rhetorical development which is as inevitable as the child's physical development.

The following samples of children's writing will illustrate growth patterns in linguistic and rhetorical thought problems encountered by children at different grade levels. At each level, the stimulus for eliciting the written response was different and can be inferred from the response.

These children are retelling an experience from their reading. How might the teacher "receive" these two samples. Children 1A and 1B have done well. Linguistic errors are negligible. In reading child 1A's sample, the teacher senses an omission in the logical development in the sequence of events. This problem was not unique to child 1A. However, child 1A is able to place a time sequence in his passage with the word *then.* Child 1B allows the reader to make this logical connection by placing his sentences in a logical order. Needless to say, both children have good kernel sentence sense. The teacher need not state all of these facts to the children, but he

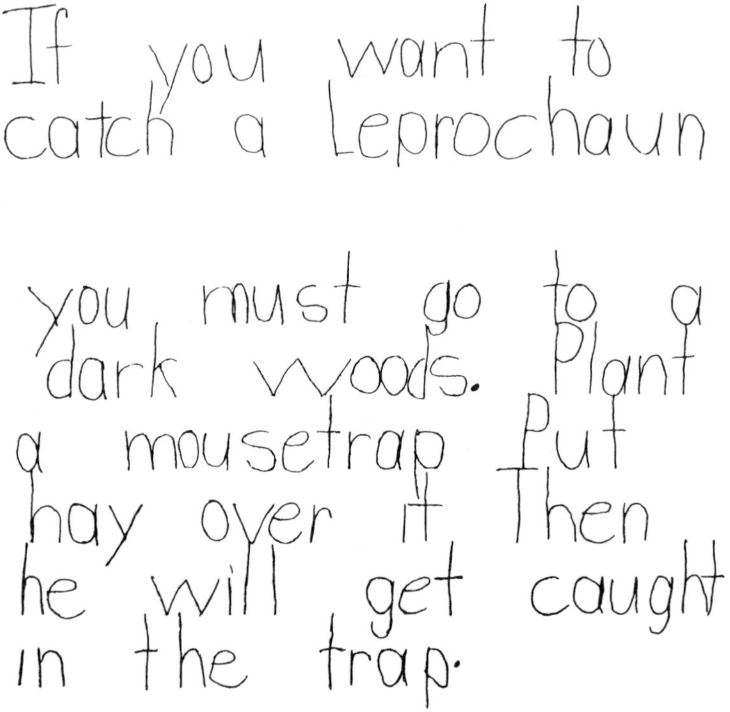

If you want to
catch a Leprochaun

you must go to a
dark woods. Plant
a mousetrap put
hay over it Then
he will get caught
in the trap.

Figure 1A

now has a beginning for further language exercises with the children. The teacher is beginning to "receive" the children's writing. The special meaning of "receive" as used here implies that the teacher listens to or reads the child's message, he accepts the message in the mode in which it is delivered without criticizing the language of the message, and then responds to the message in such a way that his response suggests a stimulus to which the child can once again respond in either the oral or written language mode. With this communications process, the dialogue between the child, his peers, and the adults in his environment remains open and continuing.

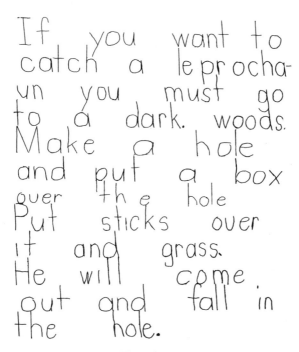

If you want to catch a leprocha-un you must go to a dark. woods. Make a hole and put a box over the hole Put sticks over it and grass. He will come. out and fall in the hole.

Figure 1B

The first impression in comparing grade one with grade two is that grade two has more information packed into each writing sample. However, syntactically they are not very different. The information is apparent in the vocabulary, the coordination, and the metaphor. Student 2A is having difficulty in ordering events and in placing referents and their modifiers. Student 2B demonstrates the problem of egocentrism. The babies and the rabbit family exhibit human emotions such as love and pride and finally the student forgets the rabbits completely and is preoccupied with her friends, especially Patty. The child is no longer able to identify with the animals. As children start to write about themselves, "receiving" their writing becomes more difficult for the teacher.

The difference between thought and language in grades two and

Peter Rabbit

Once, upon a time there lived a rabbit his name was Peter. He lived with his mother and father under the big tree. He has whiskers as big as my little finger. Then his mother died and his father did to. He has blue eyes. He has long pointed ears and he is Pink.

The End

Rusty

Figure 3A

Mr. and Mrs. Rabbit had 5 babys
Mrs. Rabbit is a Rabbit
She had 5 babys Mr Rabbit like the
little babys. + my Pord of Mrs. Rabbit.
+hink they are Pretty. Mr. and Mrs
Rabbit sould be Pord too. one baby
has blue eyes. two has pink eyes.
two has black eyes the are very Pretty
I Love Mr. and Mrs. Rabbit and the
5 babys they like my very best friend
She is Patty I have a lots of friend
But Patty is my very best friend.
The End

Figure 2B

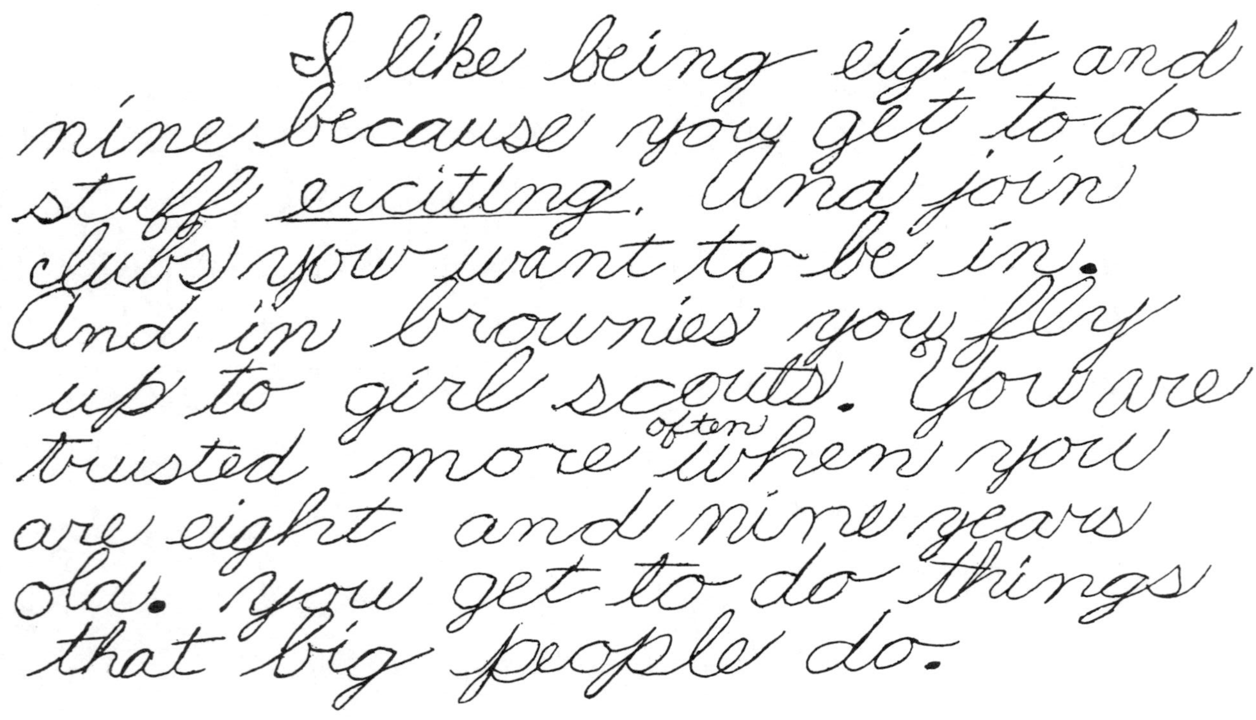

I like being eight and nine because you get to do stuff exciting. And join clubs you want to be in. And in brownies you fly up to girl scouts. You are often trusted more when you are eight and nine years old. You get to do things that big people do.

Figure 3A

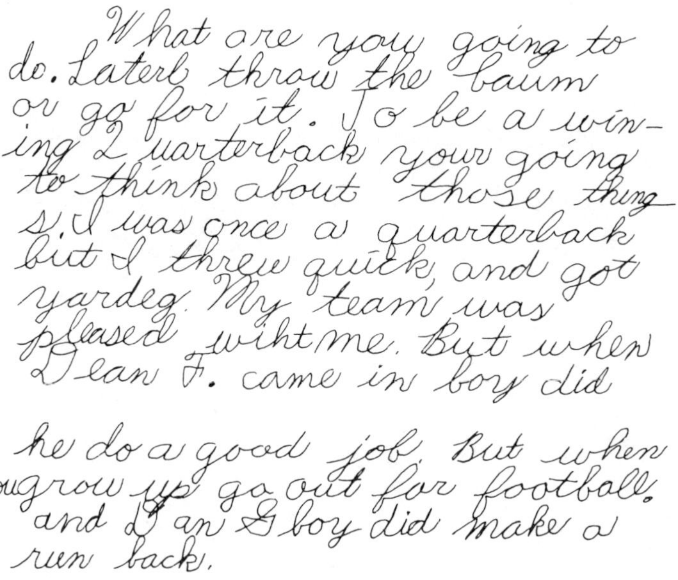

What are you going to do. Laterl throw the baum or go for it. To be a wining 2 uarterback your going to think about those things. I was once a quarterback but I threw quick, and got yardeg. My team was pleased wiht me. But when Dean F. came in boy did

he do a good job. But when you grow up go out for football, and I an I boy did make a run back.

Figure 3B

three is astounding. By grade three the child is writing cursive, he is using coordination and subordination to express relationships. His ego-centrism appears appropriate to the writing stimuli offered the child. Here the teacher's knowledge of literary analysis will help him see that a value system is being displayed by both student 3A and 3B. Other people's value systems are not always easy to accept. Student 3A expresses a value in being trusted, permitted to show responsibility and to grow up so that she can do the exciting things big people do. Will the teacher's value system and the child's clash at this point if the teacher cannot understand the child's world view? How will the teacher receive these values? Student 3B expresses another set of values. First, he is impressed by the importance of decisions in his life ambition, to be a winning quarterback. He also shows appreciation for other boys who are good football players. There is a complete lack of the competitive spirit in the paper. The competitive spirit is a highly praised Ameri-

Paul Bunyan And His Ox

Most of you know Paul Bunyan. He was the man in the world. He liked to work on roads. Did you know he built a brige across the Pacific Ocean. It only took him one mouth. He started in March and ended in April. Babe his blue ox cut the trees. Then he hald them down to the river Paul Bunyan lifted them up. Then he nailed them togetter He got into the muttle of the Ocean and lifted it up

The End

Figure 4A

In The Woods

One day when I was walking in the woods I saw a great big thing. I didn't know what it was. So I started to walk toward it. I saw that it was Paul Bunyan's pipe. I knew it was his because it was so big. Then I walked a little bit more in the woods and do you know what I saw then? It was Paul Bunyan's axe. So I walk ahead a little bit. and then I saw Paul Bunyan in person.

The End

Figure 4B

can value. How will a teacher receive these values? Grade three appears to be the place to start teaching writing as encoding.

In these two fourth grade samples, the reader can grasp the writer's sense of audience and his ability to express his own voice. Time sequences become better defined as the children learn to control grammatical past and present tense. A real effort is made to control and order the sequence of events. These papers will not be difficult for the teacher to receive. The problems in receiving these papers is to receive them in such a way as to create a new stimulus which will elicit a more personal response to the next writing activity.

Something important happens between the fourth and the fifth grade in the development of the child's thought and language process. There is a complexity of events in the child's expression which is also obvious in his complex sentence structure. However, the complex of ideas seems to lack a psychological depth of field which can be obtained through a skillful use of coordination and

The First Elephant

It was July 9, 423 B.C. when a little elf was swimming in Bula Bula creek. Then all of the sudden a Bula Bula monster sprang out of the water. A Bula Bula monster looks like a tuna can on its side with a car running over it. The little elf swam as fast as he could to shore but he wasn't fast enough. The monster threw a rock at the elf and hit him in the head. The elf got so mad that he tryed to put a spell on the monster but rock took all his powers away. So he climbed up a tree. After the Bula Bula monster left he climbed down. But without his powers he couldn't get home. So he spent 180 years eating ants. After 180 years he got so big and fat you couldn't see around him. Later scientists found out what happend so they colled it a elfant because it ate so many ants. Later his name was changed to an elephant.

By Craig

Figure 5A

Flower Power!

One dull day I sat down in our racky rocker and started to read the News Paper. One page 4 it said join the cools at the Super Sonic Sack. So at 4 minutes after 1 minute I went to the sack and I was able to join. One Tuesday I went to the Super Sonic Sack and we just sat around and told jokes and riddles and this cool kid said "Experience is a teacher, But here's what makes me burn, He's always teaching me things I do not care to learn. On Wild Wednesday we went camping to visit Flower Powered Boys!

Figure 5B

subordination. Student 5A is involved in a cause and effect type of relationship which is somewhat successful. Student 5B might have wanted to indicate some causal relationships, but these sequences are not successfully conveyed since there are big gaps in the student's perceptions of a world of experience probably known only through vicarious experience. The teacher has to receive the values expressed by student 5B with different psychological and sociological judgments from those used for receiving similar values expressed by a mature writer.

Clarence the Crossized Principal

One day there was a man looking for a job. He went to school to make a teleaphone call and he heard a hello in the backround and it was a music teacher a crosseyed one. He was terifyed so he ran down the hall and the other prin Mr. Peabody went out of saw him and he had to sit in the corner with a dence cap on. Then the music teacher started to sing and Mr. Peabody went out of his mind.

So then Clarence became principal He made new rules for the school, some were Do not walk in the halls, but run. The girls couldn't ware long dresses and the boys had to ware long hair. One day there was a fire alarm and he put on a raincoat. So the town's people named the school Crosseyed school of Clarenceville.

Figure 6A

The Secret Cave

One night when Kevin was sleeping he heard the strangest sound. It souned like it was coming from the Secret Cave. So Kevin got up and dressed and went to the Secret Cave. When he got to the cave there was a bat in the doorway. He was screaming. We scared him away. Then we went in and looked around. Down in the water hole was a young boy. He was dead. Someone had trough him in the hole. and held him there for a while. But who? Keven thought. Kevin went home and told his dad. And he asked Kevin if he had touched it. I said no. In the morning we called the police.

Figure 6B

The thought and language growth between the fifth and sixth grades is not so striking as that between the fourth and fifth grades. If one criteria of the word "creative" is imaginative or different, this sign of creativity is present in these two writing samples. Perhaps a better sign of creativity in children is the ability to order their thoughts. This is also evident in these two writing samples. Creativity should not be confused with the bizarre and teachers should not resort to all kinds of gimmickry as stimuli for eliciting bizarre responses from their student writers. For the purposes of stimulating responses and receiving written responses from children, the most effective criteria of creativity should be the child's expression of his sincere individuality, his ability to order his perceptions and his language, his ability to obtain a psychological depth of field to obtain meaningful relationships, and to test hypotheses and to reach generalizations which lead to further hypothesis testing.

In sample 6A, there is a degree of the rebel and the social critic coming through. The student is testing social values, especially the superficial ones. In sample 6B, there are signs of fear and anxiety, emotions which seem different from the secure emotions of love, friendship, pride, respect, and cooperation which were apparent in the lower grades. These less welcome but important emotions are difficult for teachers to receive and deal with in class.

This discussion of the development of elementary children's thought and language has deliberately not been a statistical one. Computer programs are available for obtaining word and structure counts to measure children's language growth. These language responses must be correlated against thought responses before we can completely "receive" and understand children's writing. . . .

QUESTIONS FOR DISCUSSION

1. Do the examples included in Golub's article illustrate any of the generalizations about children's growth as given by Piaget? Do they illustrate the generalizations about children's syntax given by Hunt?

2. Golub develops a special meaning for "receive" in the phrase "receive students' writing." Do you think that his suggested way of "receiving" students' writing is the best one, or would you prefer to "receive" the samples in a different way? How might a

teacher "respond to the message in such a way that his response suggests a stimulus to which the child can once again respond"?

3. In the beginning of the essay Golub discusses children's development of a sense of audience. Do you see such a sense developing in the examples from children of successive ages? Where does the sense of audience show itself? Do you agree with Golub's implied suggestion that in the teaching of writing in grades 1–6, attention should be given to "rhetorical problems in writing" (problems that in part require the defining of an audience for each piece of writing)?

4. How do Golub's implied views on the teaching of writing resemble those of James Moffett, and how do they differ?

Language and Personal Growth

John Dixon

A main theme of the Anglo-American conference on the Teaching of English held at Dartmouth College in 1966 was that students' uses of language are essential to the development of their understanding of their world, themselves, and their place in that world. John Dixon, in his book, discusses the two models of the English curriculum that have controlled a good deal of teaching in English classrooms. The first holds that English is intended for the development of skills in the use of language; the second, that the study of English is a way of perpetuating and disseminating a cultural heritage—of offering a "criticism of life" for students to consider. Because neither model gives adequate attention to the child's experiences, as interpreted in his spoken and written language, Dixon finds these models inadequate. He thus proposes his own model.

LANGUAGE AND PERSONAL GROWTH

It is rather easy to be wise after the event; if we are to learn from our past mistakes we need to build English teaching on a second

From *Growth Through English* (Reading, England: National Association for the Teaching of English, 1967), pp. 4–13. © 1967 by Oxford University Press. Reprinted by permission of The Clarendon Press, Oxford.

axis, based on our observation of language in operation from day to day.

When we do observe children as they learn to use language for their own purposes, surprising new areas of the map emerge that modify considerably our understanding of the earlier features. Take for instance the following entry in the diary of a ten-year-old boy:

> 1st April. Rainy with sunny periods. After breakfast I went out to get some newts. I got a large jar, washed it and put a stone in it, then went to poplar pond with a stone and a tin.
>
> It was cold and very windy. After about an hour I had caught one femail newt. I was frozzen. I could hardly feel my hands they were so cold. I half filled the jar with water and a few water weeds and put the newt in. In the afternoon I tride to get another. I saw one just out of my reach. I waded out abit and foregot that I had a hole in one of my wellington boots. The water just flowd in. I didn't catch any more newts, and went home with a boot full of water. I'm going to try and get some more tomorrow and I hope I have better luck.
>
> 2nd. Very rainy dull and wet. To-day I made a fishing net, not to catch fish but newts. I caught six. I picked out the ones I thought best. I kept three and let the others go. There were lots of newts in the pond t-day I daresay they like this kind of weather.
>
> The three newts I caught, two were a bright orange on the belly with big black round spots all over, the other one was smaller and was a muddy colour and its belly was a bright orange with very small spots on it. I mean, the spots on this one were only on the belly not all over. The one I got yesterday was a dark yellow ochre.
>
> All afternoon I sat watching them, I think they are very interesting things.

It is difficult to remain indifferent to what the boy is saying: the language invites a listener and speaks directly to him. (As he writes, it is as if the boy has that sympathetic listener built imaginatively into his mind.) In sharing the experience with the imaginary listener, he brings it to life again, realizes it for himself. There are places where he has worked to make something exact: ''I mean the spots on this one were only on the belly'' . . . ''a dark yellow ochre.'' It is as if he is listening and scanning what he has just said. At other places he has wanted a different kind of communion with the listener—has stood in a different relationship to his experience. "All afternoon I sat watching them, I think they are very interesting things." It is an open invitation to join him in feeling that life is good. (Complex-sentence hunters might agree that these two plain sentences are the sign not of a failure in expression but of a rather fine type of control.) As an English teacher one can see here a path that connects this writer's intentions with Hemingway's stories of Nick. But earlier there was a different growing point, when the boy chose to say, almost aside: "There were lots of newts in the pond t-day I daresay they like this kind of weather." There he was using language to draw observations together and make a tentative hypothesis.

What, as English teachers, can we learn from such an extract? This boy starts writing with a sense of having something worth sharing. We can guess that he is used to having a sympathetic and interested listener. He wants to make his experience real again, and as he does so he makes discoveries. Using language in his case means selecting some things for scrutiny and bringing things into order. So the flux of experiences he encountered that day begin to take on a meaning—a meaning which he treasures. We can be almost sure that the language and the meaning are both *his,* not a product handed over by the teacher. This is language in operation, not a dummy run, and we have to make our classrooms places where pupils want to talk and write from impulses such as these.

This sample reminds us that language serves, and enables us to carry out, certain fundamentally human purposes. Even the private act of writing bears traces of the primary purpose in language, to share experience. The skills model is only indirectly aware of such a purpose: its ideal pupils might well be copy-typists. And that is ironical, since the insistence on correct spelling, etc., is avowedly in the interests of better communication, of unimpeded sharing! A heritage model, with its stress on adult literature, turns language into a one-way process: pupils are readers, receivers of the master's voice. How, we may ask, do these private activities of writing and reading relate to the stream of public interaction through language in which we are all involved every day, teachers as much as pupils? The heritage model offers no help in answering, because it neglects the most fundamental aim of language—to promote interaction between people. As a result drama, the literary form that directly embodies this interaction, has been interpreted as the study of texts, not acting them out. Current accounts of language as "communication" share the same weakness. They deal only in preformulated messages and ignore the discoveries we make in the process of talking and writing from experience, or in re-enacting an experience dramatically.

The fact is that in sharing experience with others man is using language to make that experience real to himself. The selection and shaping that language involves, the choices between alternative expressions so that the language shall fit the experience and bring it to life "as it really was"—these activities imply imaginative work. If we could observe all the occasions when a child uses language in this way, and put them together, we should have caught a glimpse of a representational world that the child has built up to fit reality as he knows it.

There is, then, a central paradox about language. It belongs to the public world, and an English classroom is a place where pupils meet to share experience of some importance, to talk about people and situations in the world as they know it, gathering experience into new wholes and enjoying the satisfaction and power that this gives. But in so doing each individual takes what he can from the shared store of experience and builds it into a world of his own.

When sceptical teachers ask, "Isn't that diary an example of the work of the rare few: aren't drills the only thing for the rest?" they must look again at our human purposes in using language. Recalling experience, getting it clear, giving it shape and making connections, speculating and building theories, celebrating (or exorcizing) particular moments of our lives—these are some of the broad purposes that language serves and enables. For days we may not work much beyond the level of gossip in fulfilling these purposes, but inevitably the time comes when we need to invest a good deal of ourselves and our energy in them. It is the English teacher's responsibility to prepare for and work towards such times. If instead of being *more* alert and sensitive to average pupils—more concerned with what they have to say, if only they can realize it—he neglects their day-to-day encounters with people and situations, then they will indeed be unlikely to turn to him when they are struggling to say something of importance.

It was for this reason that members of the Seminar moved from an attempt to define *"What* English is"—a question that throws the emphasis on nouns like *skills,* and *proficiencies,* set *books,* and the *heritage*—to a definition by process, a description of the activities we engage in through language.

How important these activities may be to us personally, how deeply they may affect our attitude to experience, is suggested by much of the best writing, drama and talk that goes on in English lessons. Here we see not only the intellectual organizing of experience that goes on in many other subjects, but also a parallel ordering of the feelings and attitudes with which pupils encounter life around them. For example, after an excited visit to a fine park, a class of eight-year-olds talked over their experiences. The wind in the trees, the lake, the swans, the boy who got mud up to his knees—these and many other things found their way into one or other of the pieces that the class wrote later. Janice wrote this short poem:

The wind wiseled passed the trees.
Pushing and puling the trees.
The water triying to rech it.
But still the trees remain.
The wind stops but still the trees remain.
Pepol diey but still the trees grow biger and biger.
Flower diey but still the trees remain.

Here simple elements are drawn together into a vision of transience and permanence: of things like the trees that persist, and of things like man that wither; of the forces whose stress and strain we want to withstand. Writing like this is an important moment of personal growth.

The poem sharply reminds us of the power, always available in language, to give meaning and order to the flux and fragments of reality. Thus we make use of the system and order of language to express the order we partly recognize in things. Until, like Janice, we have written (or spoken), our recognitions and perceptions are less articulate, less explicit. Once we have written, they become not merely personal but shared, related to the socially made systems of thought and feeling that our language expresses.

Of course, much of what pupils say and write and enact will be less convincing in its insight than, say, Janice's work here. So will much of our own work, for that matter. How can a teacher help pupils engaged in so personal a task to weigh up what has been achieved? All of us test the validity of what we have said by sensing how far others that we trust have shared our response. An English teacher tries to be a person to whom pupils turn with that sense of trust. The sensitivity, honesty and tact of his response to what pupils say will confirm their half-formed certainties and doubts in what they have said. A blanket acceptance of "self-expression" is no help to pupils and may well prove a worse hindrance to their growing self-knowledge than a blunt and limited response from the teacher. The more experienced the teacher is in these matters, the more he is able to draw from the pupil the certainties (first) and later the doubts.

In every lesson where written work is read aloud to the class, or where some pupils sit back while a group presents a piece of drama, there is an opportunity for the teacher to draw from the audience an appreciation of what was enjoyed, of what went home, and thus to confirm in the individual writer or group a sense of shared enjoyment and understanding. With a new class we begin by opening their eyes to all they can achieve. And, as both the individuals and the class become confident in their achievement, there will be moments when with the teacher's help a sense of partial failure can be faced too.

For certainty about language is in a sense certainty about experience. Yet finding that others share our confidence in what we have said is only the foundation for work in language. As we mature we become increasingly aware that success in language is a partial business: as Eliot testifies:

>   . . . having had twenty years. . . .
> Trying to learn to use words, and every attempt

Is a wholly new start, and a different kind of failure
Because one has only learnt to get the better of words
For the thing one no longer has to say, or the way in which
One is no longer disposed to say it. And so each venture
Is a new beginning, a raid on the inarticulate. . . .

East Coker *

We can look on two levels at the source of our partial success. First, that of everyday experience: changes in oneself, changes in the surrounding world, and changes in one's relationship to others, all interpenetrate in the growing child or student to produce their own kind of serial curriculum. "World is crazier and more of it than we think, Incorrigibly plural." And at the level of language we can say this: we make for ourselves a representational world, sense out to the full its ability to stand for experience as we meet it, come up against its limitations, and then shoulder—if we dare—the task of making it afresh, extending, reshaping it, and bringing into new relationships all the old elements. Learning to use language continues so long as we are open to new experience and ready to adapt and modify the linguistic representation (the world) we have made for experience.

KNOWLEDGE AND MASTERY OF LANGUAGE

It is in the nature of language to impose system and order, to offer us sets of choices from which we must choose one way or another of building our inner world. Without that order we should never be able to start building, but there is always the danger of over-acceptance. How many teachers, even today, welcome and enjoy the power of young people to coin new words to set alongside the old order? How often do social pressures prevent us exercising our power to modify the meaning of words by improvising a new context, as in metaphor? Sometimes, it seems, our pupils are more aware than we are of the fact that language is living and changing; we could help them more often to explore and test out its new possibilities. Inevitably, though, the weight of our experience lies in a

* From *Four Quartets* by T. S. Eliot. Reprinted by permission of Harcourt Brace Jovanovich, Inc.

mature awareness of the possibilities and limitations raised by the more permanent forms of order in language. There has already been an explicit case (at our own level) in this chapter. The question "What is English?" invites a different form of answer from, say, "What at our best are we doing in English classes?" If we wish to describe a process, *composition* for example, the first question will tend to suggest the finished product (the marks on the page even) rather than the activity of bringing together and composing the disorder of our experience. "What . . . doing" will suggest nominal forms of verbs (bringing, composing) and thus help to keep activities in mind.

At a much simpler level members of the Seminar noted that some of us referred to "talk" in class, others to "speech." In order to see why, one might consider some of the contexts in which the words are used. "Talk" tends to be used of less formal occasions—"give a speech/give a talk." In some contexts "speech" implies accent or pronunciation—"good speech, classroom speech"; "classroom talk" may then be used as the generic term, even though in normal contexts we use "spoken and written, speech and writing" and not "talk." "Speech" seems to be rarely used today for verbal interaction, whereas we do say "we talked about it, talked it over, had a heart to heart talk." Tentatively, one might assume that those who preferred "talk" wanted to encourage informal interaction in class; those who preferred "speech" were perhaps hoping for sustained and organized utterance (rather than "chat"). Until differences like this are made explicit one may be trapped in a general uneasiness about what the other man means. Equally, in making the difference explicit we may begin to look more acutely at what goes on in class.

There is, then, a kind of knowledge or awareness about language that affects our power to think clearly and "to some purpose," in Susan Stebbing's words. Whatever the subject in the curriculum, the places where such knowledge can affect language in operation need to be more fully understood than they are at present. But the teacher of English will be particularly concerned with helping pupils, in the terms of one report, to "conceptualize their awareness of language." This seemingly cumbersome phrase was chosen with some care. "Conceptualizing," a verbal form, suggests *activity* on the part of the individual pupil, whereas "concepts" unfortunately can be thought of as *things,* reified objects to be handed over by the teacher. "Their awareness" points to a recognition already there in the pupil's thinking, not yet explicit or fully conscious perhaps, but something the alert teacher will notice and draw on.

The notion of gaining a new control over what we think by increasing our conceptual awareness of language in general has an obvious appeal to a gathering of intellectuals, not least when many of them are linguists! However, the final reports were cautious in their claims for such knowledge at the school stage. The first question at issue is when and how the knowledge becomes explicit. There was some agreement that the answer should apply to an individual rather than an age group. For if we teachers encourage a pupil to conceptualize, we should ideally be doing this at the point where the demands at the operational level of language have already given our pupil the sense that conceptualizing is needed. As experienced teachers we should see this demand emerging and be ready to help it on the way. In other words, our knowledge of the route ahead is not something to impose on the student—thus robbing him of the delight of discovery and maybe dissociating such discoveries as he does make from the systematic framework he "received" from us.

The second question was what knowledge if any *does* increase our mastery of language. As there seems to be little evidence, and some disagreement, one answer was to suggest further experimentation, with a determined effort to increase the teacher's awareness of the times when the demand for language concepts arises from the pupil but goes unrecognized at present. But the response of the majority of the Seminar was to reject the terms of the question and to ask instead for language knowledge that helps the pupil perceive himself, and for that matter Man, as in some sense the organizer of his experience. It was tentatively proposed that insights of this kind would come from a joint literary-linguistic discipline, the one investigating with more detachment the intuitions of the other. In terms of our map this was a healthy reminder that even over the next decade we may well see new territories being defined.

DANGERS INHERENT IN THE THIRD MODEL

Whatever the current model for English, we shall have to recognize
and face its weaknesses. Certainly the swing to process has its own
dangers. The first is over-rejection. If the conventions and systems
of written English do not come in the centre of the map, where do
they come at all? The answer is obviously complicated, so there is
a temptation to ignore the question. Let the pupils spell or not spell
in the orthodox style, punctuate or not, struggle with ambiguities or
not, make choices of structure or not . . . it is up to them! But
though we can fight to modify conventions and systems, we cannot
ignore them. Language remains a social instrument by which we
share, fully or imperfectly, our preoccupations and interests. When
deviance from the system becomes too great, interference may
swamp and blot out the message. This very fact suggests a broad
criterion to answer our complicated question. Where the pupil himself gives signs of being puzzled, disturbed or defeated by the
forms of the written message which he is receiving or sending, the
teacher should judge whether this is not the right moment to call his
attention to the problem. We might note that the children's writing
in this chapter includes several examples of deviance, but probably
not enough to daunt readers experienced enough to take on this
book. In class it might be a different matter: only experience can
tell, for we put up with more interference when the message seems
vital to us than when it is not.

The second danger, as U.S. members pointed out at the Seminar,
is the tendency to over-simplification; of faith blundering from dull
skills into the simple formula of "self-expression". Then the
teacher can relax. Why trouble about people and things when the
self is all-important? And, anyway, what criteria can—or dare—we
use to assess what the self expresses? But this is to save the tree by
cutting its roots. As people we exist and assert ourselves in response to our world (our family, neighbourhood, teachers . . .).
The sense of our own reality is bound up with our sense of theirs,
and both intimately depend on an awareness built up through language. For, of all the representational systems, language is the best
fitted to make a running commentary on experience, to "look at life

with all the vulnerability, honesty and preparation [we] can command.'' In an English classroom as we envisage it, pupils and teacher combine to keep alert to all that is challenging, new, uncertain and even painful in experience. Refusing to accept the comfortable stereotypes, stock responses and perfunctory arguments that deaden our sensitivity to people and situations, they work together to keep language alive and in so doing to enrich and diversify personal growth.

To sum up: language is learnt in operation, not by dummy runs. In English, pupils meet to share their encounters with life, and to do this effectively they move freely between dialogue and monologue—between talk, drama and writing; and literature, by bringing new voices into the classroom, adds to the store of shared experience. Each pupil takes from the store what he can and what he needs. In so doing he learns to use language to build his own representational world and works to make this fit reality as he experiences it. Problems with the written medium for language raise the need for a different kind of learning. But writing implies a message: the means must be associated with the end, as part of the same lesson. A pupil turns to the teacher he trusts for confirmation of his own doubts and certainties in the validity of what he has said and written; he will also turn to the class, of course, but an adult's experience counts for something. In ordering and composing situations that in some way symbolize life as we know it, we bring order and composure to our inner selves. When a pupil is steeped in language in operation we expect, as he matures, a conceptualizing of his earlier awareness of language, and with this perhaps new insight into himself (as creator of his own world).

QUESTIONS FOR DISCUSSION

1. What are the implications for the writing curriculum of Dixon's view that sharing experiences and ordering and interpreting those experiences are important uses for language in the life of a young person? What responsibilities does this view entail for teachers?

2. When looking at samples of children's writing, how does one make the differentiation between language that is being used to order and share experiences and language that is recording preformulated messages?

3. How does one judge the honesty and sensitivity of students' responses to their experiences? How can one distinguish between the fresh and honest response and the stereotyped, unobserving response?

4. If "a blanket acceptance of 'self-expression' " is no help to students, what can a teacher do to encourage honest evaluation of experiences without giving the impression that, in writing about experiences, anything goes? What questions and responses to students' work will help them? Is encouraging other students to applaud what they liked going to help the writer?

5. If the primary role of "composing" is to give shape and order and value to experiences, what is the value of being concerned with skills? Does Dixon dismiss this question too lightly?

6. What ways can the teacher use to encourage students to keep alert to what is "challenging, new, uncertain, and even painful" in their experience? How can classroom procedures and practices communicate this encouragement? How might a teacher confronting students who are indifferent to their experiences and skeptical about writing try to change these attitudes?

CLASSROOM MANAGEMENT AND TEACHING TECHNIQUES

Written Composition in English Primary Schools
Howard Blake

Since the Anglo-American Conference on the Teaching of English (1966), increasing attention has been given by American teachers and school administrators to the new philosophies and new procedures for teaching composition in the British schools, particularly the British primary schools. Several American teachers and administrators have visited Britain since 1966; they have observed classes in British schools and have brought back reports comparing American methods and procedures with those they saw in Britain. Howard Blake's essay is one of these reports.

What is noteworthy in Blake's discussion is the British views of children and of learning and the goals they assume for education. As Blake discloses, the techniques used in British schools follow from a distinctive philosophy of education.

While on a Study Leave from Temple University during the second semester 1968–1969, I had the unique, stimulating experience of visiting over 400 classrooms in about fifty primary schools in En-

From *Elementary English* Vol. XLVIII (October 1971), 605–16. Copyright 1971 by the National Council of Teachers of English. Reprinted by permission of the publisher and the author.

gland to observe their procedures for teaching written composition. Having learned through various journal articles and from first-hand reports from other educator-visitors that the British have rather drastically changed their approach to primary education in recent years, I felt that personal observation in a number of the schools over an extended period of time would furnish me with new ideas about the teaching of written composition or perhaps, hopefully, reinforce some of the ideas I already had.

It was not my purpose to evaluate any of the schools I saw nor to compare their methods with those practiced in American schools. To do so adequately would have required a much greater period of time and the efforts, as well, of more than one person. My only purpose was to look for practices and patterns that have been developed by another English speaking society to teach their children how to write. I do feel that the depth of my study qualifies me to state a few impressions of their teaching practices. Hopefully, these impressions might be helpful to American teachers who are trying to extend their understandings and perhaps to develop new or different ways of dealing with children's writing.

No two English schools are alike any more than are any two American schools. While my observations resulted in the development of a number of impressions that describe the general patterns I saw, there is, of course, no single school which embodies them all. These impressions then indicate the emerging practices going on in the more forward-looking schools, as I interpreted them. It is these schools which are furnishing the contemporary models that other schools are attempting to emulate.

PRIMARY SCHOOLS TODAY

One cannot write about written composition or any other subject in any school without some understanding of the philosophy guiding that school. This point became very clear as I went about my visits.

The English primary schools have one over-riding common objective: to make children literate. Each school has full responsibility and total freedom to achieve this goal. Consequently, it is not surprising that a wide range of teaching practices are present in the

English schools. Many of the more progressive schools organize their programs according to the plan of the Integrated Day [1]; others follow rather formal plans. Most schools operate somewhere between these two extremes, but the trend is decidedly toward the Integrated Day. It is in the evolvement of this program that the excitement in British education is found today.

There is no great concern as to whether studying a given subject overlaps with others the child has studied. Neither is there any concern about the occurrence of gaps of learning. The only criteria for deciding whether a child should study a given topic are

Will it make him more literate?

Will it help him learn to learn?

Will it help him learn to think?

Will it help him become a freer, more creative and self-reliant person?

This almost total focus upon the development of the child rather than upon subject matter alone has not always been the practice in the British schools. For years the primary schools' chief function was to prepare children to take the 11-plus examination (an exam given between the ages of eleven and twelve, the last year of primary school). Those who passed this examination continued on into a grammar school which prepared them for admission into a college or university; those who failed continued into a secondary modern school that prepared them to enter into a field of vocational work not requiring a college or university degree.

Since only about 20% of the pupils satisfactorily passed the 11-plus examination, there was strong criticism that the existing curriculum was achieving very poor results. Besides, many educational leaders strongly questioned the 11-plus approach in view of known facts about child development and learning theory. Finally, in 1958, the Leicestershire County Council authorized its school of-

---

[1] In the Integrated Day few lessons as such are taught to the entire class by the teacher. Instead each child selects his own individual project and proceeds to learn about it by engaging in whatever activities he feels will lead him to understand it properly. Thus, the child's reason for learning the basic skills is that he needs them in order to be able to do his work well. The program is totally individualized. For a full explanation, see Brown and Precious, *The Integrated Day in the Primary School,* Cambridge, Ward Lock Educational, 1968.

ficials to come up with an educational program to replace the 11-plus examination. The Integrated Day was the result and Leicestershire discontinued the 11-plus examination.

Other school districts throughout the country quickly followed the lead of Leicestershire until today there is a nucleus of school systems throughout the country which have discontinued the exam in favor of the Integrated Day, or a modification of it. Notable among these school districts, in addition to Leicestershire, are West Riding, Bristol, Hertfordshire, Middlesex, Berkshire, Oxfordshire, and some of the districts in London. The Plowden Report (1967) greatly aided the move toward the Integrated Day by strongly questioning the educational philosophy that had prevailed in English schools for years and by advocating a de-emphasis upon subject matter and a greater emphasis upon the growth of the individual.

Many schools throughout the country still offer the 11-plus exam, but its use appears to be gradually growing out of practice. Non-educators, however, are beginning to question whether the "new" education is the best for Britain. Indeed, as this paper is being written local newspapers are reporting debates in Parliament in which certain members are calling for a return to an elitist system with chief attention being given to the brightest children and a return to rigid discipline. There is also in circulation throughout the country a widely read "Black Paper" that heatedly condemns the new system. Many educators fear the new system is in danger of an educational backlash as the result of the growing attack on liberal ideas. It appears that British educators are in for some difficult years until they can convince their public of the superiorities of the new system.

Besides these changes in the curriculum, it is also necessary to be aware of some other realistic circumstances. While there are many new, pleasant classrooms, there is a preponderance of old buildings with classrooms that were not designed for project work nor modes of teaching other than the lecture method. The typical class size is forty. Classes under thirty pupils are a rarity. Consequently, with the combination of newer methods of teaching and large classes, the classrooms are terribly over-crowded.

The salaries of teachers are quite low. Beginning teachers' salaries are only about one-third of that of their counterparts in north-eastern United States; experienced classroom teachers cannot expect ever to earn the salary paid to our beginning teachers.

Schools receive an annual budget of less than five dollars per pupil for the purchase of instructional supplies, books, consumable materials, and, in some cases, custodial supplies. Few funded projects are available to provide additional materials, supplies, or resources.

All these influences, both positive and negative, surely affect the educational program. Despite them or because of them there is an excitement in the English Schools today that is extremely apparent and is most refreshing to the visitor. There is a whole new breed of teachers in the schools and in the colleges of education who are developing highly creative, informal, relaxed, individualized, imaginative ways of teaching. There is a strong fervor of determination, experimentation, and esprit de corps among the teachers that gives character to their whole approach. It is this fervor which is causing the British schools to attract world-wide attention today. It is in this setting that I observed children's writing and from which I was able to develop these impressions.

METHODS AND PRACTICES IN TEACHING WRITING

Writing is integrated with all the work children do. The actual observation of writing as an isolated subject is quite impossible in most British schools. It is not something which children do on schedule in a certain part of their day; rather, it is a natural outgrowth and an expected outcome of whatever children study or experience throughout the day. In fact writing is not treated as a subject but as an expression of the very lives children lead. It might grow as readily from a study of how television works as from observing the sheep owned by the school. Clegg says that "teachers are children conscious and language conscious" (Clegg, 1967, p. 135). The teacher seizes every possible opportunity to give children a reason for writing. Writing might occur at any time; the teacher and the children together seek reasons for doing it.

Writing is not taught from a syllabus or course of study. The choice of what is to be taught and the approach to be used resides chiefly in the headmaster or headmistress (head) of each school and his staff of teachers. Ultimately, it is each teacher who makes the actual decision. The teacher is free and is expected to develop a program that will lead children to literacy. They take the point of view that children will as readily become literate through writing about *fire* as about *frogs*. They do not feel it is necessary to have children write about a structured series of topics or experiences. They believe that getting children to think is more important than scope and sequence and that it is the teacher and the child who can best make this determination. It is their belief that this approach best enables the teacher to ''encourage each child to draw sensitively on his own store of words and delight in setting down his own ideas in a way which is personal to him and stimulating to those who read what he has written.'' (Clegg, 1967, p. 4).

This freedom and latitude results in a considerable variation in the quality of writing programs between buildings and between classrooms in the same building. Despite these differences and the fact that there is no national curriculum, similar writing programs of a very high quality are found in nearly every school. A number of discernible factors account for this surprising similarity:

1. Teacher enthusiasm for good writing is very high. Teachers work tirelessly to find successful approaches.
2. The head, through his work with individual teachers and through in-service meetings, assists in bringing in new ideas and in encouraging teachers to analyze and share their progress.
3. Much in-service education in a great number of the schools takes place on a very informal level in the teachers' staff room during the three times-a-day tea or coffee breaks. The give and take among teachers and among heads and teachers during these sessions was very stimulating to me and convinced me that it is here that most of the ideas for teaching originate. The teachers work well together; they seek and use ideas from each other. ''I like it, I think I'll use it,'' is a frequent expression heard in the staff room.
4. Many school districts have instituted what they call ''Teacher

Centers,'' with a director in charge, which contain a thorough professional library and laboratories and equipment with which teachers can prepare materials for their classrooms. At the Centers a well-prepared series of in-service programs which teachers attend on a voluntary basis are offered. It also serves as a conference center for the district's educational program and as a social center for the district's teachers.

5. A great number of professional books containing suggestions for and descriptions of writing programs, along with analyses of samples of children's writing, have emerged during the past few years. Largely sharing a common philosophy, these books are widely read and discussed by most teachers and in the end make a great contribution both to the quality and commonality of writing programs throughout the country. The books listed in the bibliography for this paper are representative of those that explain the current English approach to writing and are receiving serious study by heads and teachers.

6. Inter-visitations among teachers in the same district and between districts are quite common. Frequently, for example, a district will for a three-day period entertain the heads from a number of other districts. Upon completion of their observations and discussions, the heads return to their own schools to disseminate the new ideas and help their teachers refine what they are doing. Meetings of this nature take place throughout the country, involving teachers as well as heads.

7. A number of other agencies and individuals throughout the country have great influence upon the direction of the writing program. By identifying models of good teaching, organizing institutes and conferences, and publicizing research and experience they bring about a continuous dialogue concerning effective approaches to writing. Among these are Colleges of Education, primary advisors, chief education officers, inspectors at the local and national levels, numerous educational journals, the National Association of Teachers of English, and local associations of English teachers.

The absence of a course of study has not prevented the English schools from developing a writing program of high quality with characteristics of a national viewpoint about writing. It is not surprising to find a stage in nearly every classroom, to see similar collections of children's books in nearly every classroom, and to observe teachers in nearly every classroom using a similar philosophical approach in developing writing experiences for children.

Children learn to write by writing. This was one of the most impressive aspects of my observations. Children spend much of their time writing and in the process enjoy doing so. They understand that one stage in learning about something, whether it be *Vikings* or *colors* is writing about it just as they also read, look at visual materials, discuss, or paint to also learn about it. One of the teacher's objectives is to have every child write something every day. This extensive practice of writing on nearly every subject imaginable eventually helps most children to become capable writers and to take pride in the preciseness of their written products. There is a strong carry-over between personal and practical writing. Good writing comes more automatically where extensive opportunities for writing are available.

Most children do their writing in a notebook which furnishes a record of writing experiences as well as of progress. Some schools have their older pupils keep a diary in which they write at least weekly. Some schools start the day by having pupils write for the first twenty minutes or so on whatever topic they wish. Typically, they may write on something about which they are studying or about an experience or point of view. I saw this practiced with children as young as six.

This emphasis upon writing starts with children as early as age five and continues on through the primary school. The five-year old draws pictures to illustrate a story, dictates to the teacher a story about a picture he has drawn, or a story he has to tell. He copies words and later sentences from these stories until finally he writes independently. It is from this base that mature writing is possible later on.

There is good balance between practical and personal writing experiences for children of all ages. While each child usually chooses his own topic, he is expected over a period of time to practice both kinds of writing. For both kinds there is great variety in forms. For practical writing children not only write reports about topics they are studying but also letters, interview reports, book reviews, instructions, directions, and such. For personal writing they not only write stories but also poetry, plays, small books, and such that show creative imagination as well as impressions of sensory stimuli.

The teacher uses many approaches to motivate children to write. It is not that British children just by showing up in a classroom are able to write well. The teacher is the key who sets the stage. English teachers spend much time creating an environment in which children have many things of a worthwhile nature to write about.

1. The classrooms are places in which a lot of talk goes on. They take the point of view that better writing is achieved when children first have an opportunity to talk about the subject. Oral expression is thus achieved through group discussion led by the teacher, a child, or groups of children. In many cases the notes from those discussions are recorded on charts or on the blackboard. The classrooms are far from quiet, children having the freedom to move about as they select their materials or others with whom to work, yet they are well-managed and orderly. In one classroom for ten-year olds the children, whenever discovering something new, were encouraged to share their findings by telling it to the entire class. Although every child was working on a different project at the time, the noise level never prevented the speaker from being heard. The teacher used this opportunity to help children extend their understandings by raising questions that helped them grapple with their thoughts, to organize their thinking, and to furnish supplemental information or other suggestions that would help children gain a clearer understanding. I saw many examples of this type that illustrated the importance of oral language. It is also notable that oral language more than writing or reading dominated the day for the younger children and for those of every age who did not have a good language background.

2. Independent reading is also practiced widely. Children read extensively from the wealth of colorful books available to

them. Reading, like oral expression, builds language background for better writing.

3. The teacher generally reads something to the children every day. This might consist of a book that is continued from day to day, a selection from a book or story, a poem, a part of a play, or such. They feel that reading to children not only stimulates thought and brings forms of literature to children they might not ordinarily read on their own, but that it also helps improve writing style through hearing the vocabulary, sentence construction, grammatical and syntactal arrangements, organization, and approach used by other writers. Reading to children also improves their oral language as they listen to the teacher's inflections, intonations, and other expressive features that bring meaning to language.

4. Children's writing is preceded by an extensive amount of first-hand experience. Much of this experience comes from children's reactions to materials in the classroom. When appropriate the teacher takes the class on trips into the community, invites guests, or introduces other materials or equipment into the room. The teacher makes extensive use of the entire school building and playground. Children freely use all these facilities as they learn; their classroom is not bounded by its own four walls.

   Whether doing a group writing project on the appearance of bottles or an individual project on the making of guitars, the teacher either leads the child through a period of observation and discussion or makes it possible, through making materials available, for the child to do this for himself.

5. Teachers arouse children's awareness of colors, shapes, comparisons, etc. in their environment through appeal to the senses. They learn to use their imaginations for practical as well as for personal writing. The teacher's awareness and imagination are of equal importance with that of the children in recognizing possible writing situations. As a result children become keen observers of the ordinary, subtle happenings

and phenomena in their daily lives and write about a wide variety of topics that would easily escape the unimaginative or unaware person.

For example, in one classroom for eleven year olds, after making rubbings of objects in the room such as a floor tile, rock, window pane, top of the piano, and back of a book, the children wrote about what the designs looked like. They had also written on many other similar topics, such as "A Lamb Is Born," "Triplets," and "A Lamb's First Step" (after bringing one of the school's new lambs into the room where it was observed and discussed); "Captivity" (about fish in the aquarium); "Thoughts on a New World" (after looking out the frosted windows in the classroom); and "Insomnia," "My Sixth Sense," and "Fears in the Dark" (after discussing their fears).

In another class for ten-year olds, the children had written poems and stories on a variety of topics about the chickens, then eight weeks old, which had been hatched and reared in the room. Some of the topics were "The Escape," "Hatching of the Chicks," "A Struggle for Life," "The Incubation of Hen Eggs," "The Chicks and the Eggs." They had also made detailed graphs, diagrams, drawings, etc. having to do with their growth, expenses, food consumption, and such.

6. In all writing the teacher gets children emotionally concerned so that they want to write. In creative writing, emotions are frequently aroused either by recalling an emotional moment in a child's life (such as "My Brother's First Step," "My House and Family," or "A Swimming Lesson") or by creating an emotional moment in the classroom (such as being led blindfolded, racing around the building, or discussing sounds heard in an abandoned lighthouse). Writing easily follows for most children when this objective is accomplished.

The classrooms themselves are exciting, challenging places in which children can learn and write. The rooms appear to be more like laboratories or workshops than the traditional classroom. Most children have no permanent seat, but sit in whatever place they need to work. The rooms are divided into several work areas or bays, such as:

(a) A quiet "home" area, incorporating a well-stocked library of books and magazines where children can curl up to read. The area is carpeted and equipped with armchairs, cushions, and heavily decorated with children's work.

(b) The maths area, complete with apparatus such as geoboards, equalizers, click wheels, etc. and also containing a number of assignments on cards, both of an informal and formal nature, that each child completes independently. The whole area is illustrated by children's mathematical investigations.

(c) The research/English area complete with reference and informational books, visual and oral aids, and individualized assignments on cards. Again the area is heavily illustrated with the results of children's work.

(d) The arts and crafts area equipped with a sink, various boxes containing many types of materials such as different kinds of paper, cloth, wood, and plastic. The area has storage facilities for paints, brushes, palettes, craft tools, plus large surface work areas and facilities to keep them and the bay clean.[2]

Other schools add other bays, such as one for technology in which children can study programmed materials using teaching machines, slides, and film loops. Infants' rooms usually have an area for dramatics, sewing, or music.

Each area is well-equipped and everything has a specific place in which it is kept. Each child is expected to put away the material he uses and to finish each job he starts.

Each room is typically a library in itself, having a large collection of recreational and informational books that are very colorful

[2] These four bays are used at the Michael Faraday Junior School, London. The description was graciously furnished by Headmaster D. J. Skinner who is now a Lecturer at Goldsmiths College, London.

in appearance and are arranged for easy access. The importance of a central library for each school has been de-emphasized. Where it does exist, usually in a hallway, its chief function is to house reference books.

Classrooms contain many manipulative materials, collections and specimens of all sorts such as rocks, feathers, pictures, microscopes, exhibitions of children's work, animals that are kept for a short time such as chickens, dogs, or sheep, etc. The teacher and children continually and with curiosity look at, feel, smell, discuss, and peruse these materials as the base for oral and written language.

With such an organization it is often quite difficult to spot the teacher when entering a classroom. He might be in any one of the work areas helping a single child or a small group, such as giving a word of advice about what brush and color to use to get just the right effect or suggesting another book to read that will tell something further about a topic. He might be helping a group prepare a chart to show their growth rates, listening to a child read, or reading a report or story a child has written, commenting on it privately with the child. Although apparently inconspicuous, the teacher knows fully what each child is doing and is readily available to help any one with a question.

The teaching of writing, including the mechanics, is almost totally individualized. Learning how to write is considered an independent affair for each child. The teacher deals with each individually, expecting different levels of writing from each child depending upon his ability.

For this reason there are very few group lessons. Occasionally, the teacher offers a lesson to the entire class to motivate children to write on a new subject or to learn how to observe something using a new approach, but even where these lessons are taught, typically, each child chooses his own topic. Most writing emerges not from these group motivations but from whatever he is studying about at the time. Seldom do two children write on the same topic and seldom does the teacher assign a specific topic to the entire class.

The mechanics of writing are also taught in this manner. In all the classes I observed I saw no group lessons on such matters as grammar, punctuation, paragraphing, topic sentences, capitalization, spelling, and, with the exception of not more than ten classrooms, handwriting. I saw no workbooks nor teacher-made dittos for any of these skills.

Mechanics are not considered as important to successful writing as are the ideas which the child has to communicate. Yet the mechanics are far from neglected for they feel that mere self-expression on all occasions is not adequate. When a child finishes a piece of writing he goes over it with the teacher who helps him see how he might have said something better, how he might organize it more clearly, where punctuation could improve it, etc. Depending upon the child, the teacher might tell him to write another draft or might let it stop at that point. For some children, after reading the first few sentences and realizing that the child is not writing up to his ability, he might ask him to re-write it before they look at the paper together. Most children keep a spelling notebook in which they record their misspellings and through cognizance of their errors work to eliminate them.

All these mechanical skills are thus taught incidentally and privately but the standards are high, varying greatly for each child. In this approach the teacher has the time to deal with each child individually because he is not using his time preparing or teaching a great number of group lessons. The child through this process sees the mechanics not as something separate from writing but as an essential part of it. In this manner the child spends more of his time doing actual writing than correcting each piece he writes.

Evaluation of writing is accomplished through conferences or through comments written by the teacher. Each piece of writing is evaluated thoroughly but not by grades or marks. As indicated in the previous section, the child comes to understand the strengths and weaknesses of his writing as the teacher goes over it with him or by the comments which the teacher writes on his paper. It is felt that this method of evaluation promotes rather than inhibits the flow of expression. Each piece of writing is seen as a stage in learning how to write rather than an end in itself. Praise is given freely but honestly. Frequent writing, the freedom for trial and error without being assigned a grade, and the spirit of helpfulness brings about a great self-respect and pride in writing. Folders of each child's writing, frequently examined by the teacher and child, furnish a record of writing progress.

Writing is closely related to other means of self-expression. As already indicated writing is considered an extension of the oral language and reading program and is integrated with them. But the teacher also uses other media of expression to motivate creative writing. Children use paints, clay, fabric, and other art materials extensively as they go about their studies. Much of their work is illustrated with pictures, drawings and diagrams. Informal dramatic activities also play a strong role in the writing program.

One of the most widely used forms of self-expression is that of movement. More and more schools are incorporating it into their work with children. The teacher uses movement to extend vocabulary, increase understandings, and develop increased awareness about the topic on which they are to write. For example, Guy Fawkes Day is a happy, Halloween-like celebration occurring each November 5 with the building of large community bonfires. The occasion is used by teachers not only to study British history and traditions but also as an experience for writing. One of the frequently used topics is "Fire." Movement was used wisely to help write on this topic in a class for nine-year olds. Besides discussing and reading about fire, making a fire mural, and listening to "The Ritual Fire Dance", children during movement class were asked questions such as "What motions does fire make?" Such words as *bolting, darting, dashing, frightening,* and *vibrating* were suggested. They then acted out each of these words with some children demonstrating their interpretation to the rest of the class. These words, plus other synonyms, not only showed up markedly in the writing about fire which they did later on but the children were able to write about fire with a greater depth of understanding and feeling. Success in one medium of self-expression supports success in another. English children's writing shows marked evidence of this principle.

Few schools use a textbook for every child. I saw no classroom in which each child had a language, spelling, or any other kind of "English" textbook. The same is true for all the other subjects.

Neither did I see any classes in which children were studying from workbooks.

A few schools use a textbook for beginning reading; some use none. I saw no classroom in which reading was taught from a basal reader beyond the seven-year old classes. The whole aim in reading, if a text is used at all, is to get the child away from it as early as possible. They feel the child will find he needs to read to be able to complete successfully the work which he has to do and that the pursuit of this work furnishes all and more reading practice than any reading text could possibly provide. The reason for reading is self-imposed rather than adult-imposed.

There are single copies of most current basal texts in every classroom but they are used chiefly as reference materials by the teacher and children. Teachers frequently use texts to help individual children who need additional practice or information. But the schools put most of their "book" money into library collections, and, as already explained, these collections are bountiful, with splendid books on all subjects. Clegg believes that accuracy in writing comes chiefly from plentiful reading and writing rather than from textbooks. (Clegg, 1967.)

The writing program requires many instructional materials and many of these are prepared by the teacher. Few gimmicks are seen in the English classrooms although there are a great many commercial manipulative materials for mathematics, reading skills, science, and such. A few teaching machines are seen and their use is increasing. Books abound.

But the rooms are filled with materials and equipment most of which has been made or collected by the teachers with the help of children and parents. A cursory first impression of most classrooms is that they appear to be "junk shops," but careful examination reveals this to be far from true, for each item in the room has been thoughtfully selected for a specific purpose and the room is well-organized.

It would be impossible to make a list of the materials and equipment found in one classroom. Besides those mentioned throughout this paper, the materials I saw being used at one time in a class for ten-year olds might furnish some insights to their kinds and enormity: a rock collection, teeth from a cow, a peacock feather, a piece of marble, a chunk of melted glass, a medal on a pendant, a small toy lamp, a rabbit's tail, a clump of moss, a vase of dandelions, some crab legs, a collection of coins, a chicken feather, a candle, some sea shells, a piece of jagged glass, some grains of corn, a piece of thistle, a wheat stalk, some strips of paper, and a brick. These items comprised probably no more than one percent of all those in the room. All of them are relatively costless and are very ordinary in nature. At the time I visited this class the children were having a splendid creative experience as they observed (sometimes using a magnifying glass or microscope), discussed, and finally wrote about each item.

Most all the ideas for writing of this type originate from the teacher's imagination and understanding of writing. There are, however, a few commercial materials being used to furnish supplemental work in a few schools. Among these are *Learning to See* (Rowland, 1969), *Exploring Language* (Sealey, 1968), and *Let's Imagine* (Eyre, 1968).

In this kind of teaching it takes more imagination than money. As I observed it the more imaginative the teacher the greater the "junk," the fewer the textbooks, and the higher the quality of thinking and writing.

Examples of children's writing are widely displayed. Children's writing of all kinds is profusely displayed in the classrooms and hallways. The teacher frequently outlines poetry or a story with a green or red border when placing it on the bulletin board or wall. Displays are not intended to "show off" the writing of the good writers; they exist simply for children to see what each other has written.

Children's writing notebooks are shared with each other. Booklets are made from their collective stories, reports, or poems. Many schools have a school newspaper or a literary magazine. As children read each other's writing and see their own writing read by others they learn to see quality in their work, to care about what they produce, and to feel their work is important. Children appreciate this form of recognition and encouragement.

The teachers' and heads' attitudes and enthusiasm have a strong positive influence upon the quality of writing. One of the most over-whelming forces affecting the British schools is the dedication, en-thusiasm, resourcefulness, and attitudes of their teachers and heads. It is their spirit which makes the English system tick; without this ingredient the whole thing would be less than the success which it is. They want the schools to be good ones and they are. They know what they want from children and they get it. They are well-trained and they continue to search for ways of improvement.

They have established classroom climates that are extremely in-formal and non-threatening. Children see their teachers more as resource persons than as instructors. This spirit of mutual help-fulness brings the relationships between teachers and pupils to a very high level. In all the classrooms I visited I saw no pupils who did not appear to be profitably occupied nor did I see indication of unusual disciplinary problems despite children's liveliness. I did not see one teacher raise his voice in a threatening manner to any child. The teacher's steady encouragement leads the children to reach a higher level of writing than they might otherwise attain because they know their writing will be accepted for what it is rather than criticized for what it is not.

SUMMARY

The reader will recognize that the methods and practices for the teaching of writing in the English schools differ little from those in most American schools. What differences there are lie mainly in the subtleties of their emerging educational system in which they are finding new and successful approaches for working with chil-dren and for helping them learn. Their schools are ". . . happy, active well-kept places from which zest and eagerness in staff and pupils seem to have dispelled problems of control and discipline." (Clegg, 1967, p. 133). Their methods show there is little difference between play and learning. Their attractive, stimulating classrooms give children the idea that learning and fun go together. They are finding that through informal, open education children learn much from each other as well as from the teacher.

It might appear from my description that all English children learn to write well. Far from it. Writing is a difficult art. It is as hard for English children to learn it as for any other children. The impressive thing to me was that, in my judgment, through their approach to writing and to education, a higher proportion of English children consistently produce writing of higher quality than American children. I hope that this paper reveals at least some of the reasons for this difference.

Just as the English could learn from visits to our schools, American teachers can improve their writing programs through incorporating some of the English approaches described in this paper into their teaching. Their system cannot nor should not be copied, because our two cultures differ, if no more than in minor respects. Our population, for éxample, is more mobile, creating many minority and diverse groups. Perhaps we need a more divergent educational system than the British. Regardless, we should continuously study their achievements to determine whether enough teachers can be educated to bring consistent success through the English approach and whether their unstructured curriculum will produce children who are better educated.

I have tremendous respect for the English system and for the many kind and dedicated people who graciously opened their schools to me. It is they who are creating the excitement in the English system and make it worthy of emulation.

Throughout this paper, in order to conserve space, I have purposely avoided using examples of children's writing, despite the fact that I was fortunate enough while there to collect numerous samples that illustrate the practices mentioned. One example might show the quality of the writing I saw. It is neither the best nor the worst. It does represent the typical writing teachers get in terms of the child's feeling, word choice, and organization. It was written by a nine-year old boy with an average I.Q. who lived in a middle income neighborhood in south London.

BALLOONS
People are like balloons.
When they are young
They are full of air

They are smooth and round
And tough and bouncy,
They float with care
And rise up and up.
But when the air escapes from its prison,
They wrinkle and soften
And flop near the ground.
They grow gentle and weary
And creased and old,
Their colour fades
And go.
And they perish

BIBLIOGRAPHY

Brown, Mary, and Precious, Norman, *The Integrated Day in the Primary School,* Cambridge, Ward Lock Educational Publishers, 1968.

Clegg, Sir Alexander, *The Excitement of Writing,* London, Chatto and Windus, 1967.

Dean, Joan, *Reading, Writing, and Talking,* London, A. C. Black, 1969.

Eyre, Wallace, *Let's Imagine,* Oxford, Basil Blackwell Publishers, 1968. Books 1–4.

Holbrook, David, *The Secret Places,* London, Methuen and Co., 1964.

Jordan, Diana, *Childhood and Movement,* Oxford, Basil Blackwell Publishers, 1966.

Lane, S. M. and Kemp, M., *An Approach to Creative Writing in the Primary School,* London, Blackie and Son, 1967.

Langdon, Margaret, *Let the Children Write,* London, Longmans, Green and Co., 1961.

Marshal, Sybil, *An Experiment in Education,* Cambridge, Cambridge University Press, 1962.

Maybury, Barry, *Creative Writing for Juniors,* London, Batsford, 1967.

Peel, Marie, *Seeing to the Heart: English and the Imagination in the Junior School,* London, Chatto & Windus, 1968.

The Plowden Report: Children and Their Primary Schools, London, Her Majesty's Stationary Office, 1967.

Rowland, Kurt, *Learning to See,* London, Ginn and Co., 1969. A course in visual education consisting of five textbooks, each with a workbook and a teacher's guide.

Sealey, Leonard, *Exploring Language,* London, Thomas Nelson, 1968. Books 1 and 2 plus teacher's guide.

QUESTIONS FOR DISCUSSION

1. Summarize the British philosophy of primary education and the place of English in that philosophy as revealed in Blake's essay.

2. Does this philosophy operate widely in American primary education as far as you know? Is it challenged, where it is found? What are the rival philosophies that contend with it?

3. In what sense is it possible to say that in British schools, as described here, a teacher "teaches" writing? What specifically does the teacher do?

4. In order to carry out the philosophy of education in English described here, what kinds of responses might the teacher best make to students' writing? From Blake's account, does it seem that teachers in Britain make the kinds of responses you think appropriate? If not, are they being inconsistent with the philosophy of their schools?

Children Writing: Direct Experience
T. W. Haggitt

In elementary schools, teachers of writing often encourage children to see, observe, and record. The following essay, by T. W. Haggitt, an experienced teacher in an English junior school (students range from age seven to ten or eleven), carries on the suggestion that children can learn much about composing from working on the details of their immediate experiences. Haggitt raises the question of how children's impressions can be developed into unified statements or representations of what they have observed, and also of how the sensory impressions can be turned into writing that shows distinctive explorations with language—in short, into what is commonly called "creative" writing.

It is a remarkable Junior class that does not erupt into a frenzy of excitement when it sees the first snow fall. Discipline may keep the children in their seats but it is against nature. Will it settle? How big are the flakes? "Please, sir—can I go to the toilet?" Children are immensely interested in what is going on outside and this interest has strong creative possibilities. Let them go to the window or

From *Working with Language* (Oxford: Basil Blackwell, 1967), pp. 68–89. Reprinted by permission of the publisher.

even outside—you might as well give in, anyway! Let the children enthuse and gasp with anticipation at the excitement to come. At the same time we may do a little language teaching—even if it is Arithmetic on the timetable!

So far we have looked at children's writing inspired by second hand experience. It is important for the child's imagination to be so nurtured, but now let us examine how his observation can be developed. Every teacher is familiar with children who paint lollipop trees and neatly gathered curtains in houses where all the rooms appear to be seven feet above ground level. Unless a child has really looked at a tree, felt the roughness of its bark and examined its leaf and twig structure, he will paint a lollipop. Every child lives in a house of some sort, but he will still paint his house symbol until his eye has been directed to the shape of a house. Children starting to paint pictures are encouraged to look closely at their subject. Similarly, children about to write can enrich their descriptions by close observation.

Martin, aged 10, wrote:

THE FIRST SNOWFALL

The first speckles of white, pure white powder fought a loosing battle against the wet pavement. Then as more fell it started to win the battle. The powder wandered hevily about the sharply frozen air and settled comfortably in more powder on the ground. Every object in sight had a silvery white lining. The trees had white, silvery coats fitting perfectly. Although trying to dodge the flashes whitch fell on them the birds kept their breath and stayed in the air.

This was the first snowfall of the year and the children were at the window looking out on it. They looked at the general scene and talked. Will the snow settle? See how wet the pavement is. Watch the snow coming down—how is it coming down? Falling!—a better word?—floating—drifting. What does it look like?—powder!—bits of salt!—petals!—leaves!—does it twist like a leaf falling? Is there a word for that . . . spiral! By careful leading, the children's eyes were directed to the movement of the snow and a suitable vocabulary was discussed. The children looked at the effect of the snow on other things—trees, houses, the ground, birds, etc. Two things were achieved: a vocabulary had grown from an active situation, and the children had enjoyed their snow. They were then in a fit frame of mind to write about it!

Most children find writing about direct experience difficult at first. They have to take in what is around them, and from a welter of visual experience present a coherent description. Unlike a second hand experience where the progress of a plot is clearly defined, with vividly painted characters, a child has to sort out what he is to describe from real life. The teacher might draw a child's attention to a particular aspect of a situation, but there is still a lot to take in.

Here is Steven's very first attempt at direct experience writing. He is seven years old, and much of his work had to be deciphered, but he used the words printed. There had been a light snowfall and it was very cold. Steven, with the rest of the class, had gone outside with the teacher and had looked at the scene. On returning to the classroom the children first talked about it and then were asked to write down their impressions.

A COLD DAY

The ground is hard to-day. Leaves, pieces of paper and sticks stick to the ground. the grass crackles when you tred on it. Your fingers go red. We wrap up warm. flowers are stiff and pieces of paper stick to fences. Birds dig through the ice to get worms to eat. Theres little pieces of snow on the ground leaves fall of the trees and birds shiver. Windows go all dull and car windows go all dull. tree trunks are stiff and birds go to warmer places. pieces of paper go all stiff and they roll over on the grass. The sky is grey and snow is lined up by the grass. In the cracks of slabs some of the leaves curl up and stay like it.

Steven had presented a shopping list for a description, but in his list there is clear proof that he had *looked* closely. An older child would have been encouraged to put the sentences about the leaves together and to deal with the birds in one go. He would be encouraged to start in the sky and gradually lower his sights, taking in the full picture around him, but with a younger child it is sufficient to get him to record what he sees. The skill of coherent presentation will come later.

Karen sits next to Steven and about four weeks after the snow she wrote:

A WINDY DAY

   The wind blows grit and dust into my face. It tears the golden hair of the trees. Leaves have a race. The wistle is the wind when it howls. The leaves stop going along when the wind stops howling. When the wind gets the grass the grass looks as though it is moving. The winds sends kites up in the air. It is like the wind being a man who is in a furious mood and then tosses the trees to either side and who pulls the birds the wrong way. We can't see the wind but the wind is still there. The cyclists have to peddle hard. The wind pushes cars along the road.

Again the children had observed the action of the wind and talked about it. There had been a discussion on "shopping lists" and the children agreed that it was not proper to carry potatoes and cream cakes in the same carrier bag. Just as these would be carried separately, so could they carry events in a description separately. The wind gave an ideal opportunity—they could follow the movement of a leaf until it reached a fence or a building.

   Yvonne, who is also seven, saw the leaves in a race:

A WIND DAY

   Today the wind is in a boisterous mude as it ters down the street bending the trees as it challenges the trees to a fight for there lives the leaves have a race first thay are under startes orders and at one blow of the wind the leaves are off they run as fast as they can go the grass bens as if it was bowing to the King the wind swepes us off our feet and hurls us along much faster than we usually do.

Boisterous was a word introduced by the teacher to describe the mood of the wind. The children also talked about the sounds of the wind and Sharon wrote of: The telegraph wires sing a song. . . . Trees creak and groan . . . birds go fluttering in a struggle. . . . The wind is howling everywhere.

   The children wrote these words but in nearly every case the spellings had to be deciphered. The teacher was not, however, concerned with spelling—he was concerned with children using words, and their eyes.

In another class Susan, aged 10, wrote about the wind:

A WINDY DAY

The wind was howling and whistling through the twisted trees. Hats were flying everywhere and washing was dancing on the clothes line. Womens skirts were fluttering and flapping about. Hair was standing on end and bits of dirt and sand stinged our eyes and made them water. The wind seemed to swallow the smoke from the chimneys. Bushes seemed to be shivering with the bitter cold wind sweeping past. This big hand was banging the doors down and shattering the window panes. Paper was flying round getting caught on lamposts or fences and birds were hiding behind chimney pots to get away from the cruel, bitter, tormenting beast.

Technically Susan's piece is orderly yet there is still the essence of a shopping list. The piece is more descriptive than Steven's and the words used are stronger and show a greater fluency and colour. She was obviously seeking the right words to give life to her description, but its focal point is weak.

When Sharon, aged 10, wrote about the rain she confined her writing to a narrower vision:

THE RAIN

Rain falls gently on the leaves then tries to trickle off and falls through to the grass. It comes to a stop and stays a tiny drop of dew. It dribbles down the car windows then is wiped away with a grey hand. It falls on faces touching like needels and paints the pavement brown. The grey clouds drift carlessly along as rain slips delicutly through fingers of grass and slowly slithers through the flowers to settel on the middle of petals.

The car window is out of place. Sharon realized this when her work was discussed by the class. We have many class discussion times when children read out their own work to be commented on by both the children and myself. We look appreciatively on the "happy" phrase, as well as remarking on those parts of the description that do not seem to fit. In this way the children develop a critical ear for what is read to them and in so doing develop a critical eye for what they write themselves.

I ask the children to seek a focal point for their word pictures as an artist seeks a focal point for his paintings. What goes on in the background of a picture contributes to the "subject"; similarly in painting with words, the focal point of the description can be made to stand out (enhanced) by the contribution of a background.

In the summer term of his fourth year at our school Graham, aged 10, went out into the school grounds to sit in the sun and to write how it felt. He had written about five other first hand descriptions prior to this, mainly concerning the weather. He wrote:

> Golden streaks of sun beat down on my body. The grass leaned forwards with their exploring points. The pages of my book lifted their curtain pages trying to shut my eyes. A tree tryed to decieve the sun as its wooden back cast its shadow on a floor of green fingers. The clouds moved silently across an oceon of sky with a golden island in it. The sun cast its fingers of gold onto a window. A high pitched whistle of a bird seemed to grab the breeze. A tulips red shimering petals stood in a golden ray of sun, its stalk trying to be as proud as the sun.

I had asked the class to lie face downwards on the grass and to write in their rough books what they felt and what they saw. The children were told to look for "poetic" moments. How does the sun affect your body? Watch its effects on other things. Listen for sounds. What does the sound seem to do? Does it blend with the scene or disturb the scene? Tell me more about the flowers and the grass. What are things *like*? A first-year class were also asked to do the same on a hot day in spring. Gary, aged 7, wrote:

A SUNY DAY

> I like the cold breeze in the hot sun everywhere you look you see something cheerfull the birds sing cheerfull. The sky lark fluters about in the sky the trees are full with blosome I feel like putting my shorts

on. Branches are dying of thirst ants crawl on peoples books the sky is as blue as the sea the wasps fly about in the air the strings of grass are stuck together. the sun glitters on the windows and it look like jewels. The sun melts the play ground and if you touch it you will get all muky and filthy like dirty dirty arabs. The sun shines like a diamond in the sky when I roll my sleaves up I get sun burnt the cars shoot past like bombs. The earoplanes look like flies in the air the cars look like big chunks of glittering armour the grass is like plastic the wasps buze around you the Flowers are like rubber and are desprat For water. When I lie down on the grass it ticles me and makes me itche. When I pick the grass it glitteres in the sun like a peace of string.

Like a diamond—like a bomb—like flies—like plastic. I encouraged the children to use similes (I didn't introduce the word), because I wanted them to add more colour to their writing.

I expected greater fluency and colour when I took a third-year class to observe a disused canal near to the school. I told the children to look at the movement created by the breeze. Describe the movement—is it gentle or rough? Say what it looks like to you. Describe the picture on the canal and then take in the background. Michael, who later went to a secondary modern school, wrote:

VIEW FROM THE BRIDGE

    The slimy grey black water slides into the reeds and trees. A barge is bobbing up and down in the water, with men lazily getting off board her. Suddenly wind comes and makes the water lap onto the side of the bank. A piece of paper which someone had lost, was floating down the canal. Trees are drawn to the water, the trees blossom falls as though they are ashamed of the Grimy black water and try to cover the black and paint white over with there blossom, a dog nosed the grass on the bank and leaves it aside and goes on to the next piece. A large stick and a bottle bobbed up and down together as though they were walking arm in arm down a road. The long row of factories dirty and blacky grey are cramped up together, the church contrasts with new modern buildings. Big chimney-stacks looking like great Kings of the world and having black bands going around it to keep it together, and as I leave I see a dead bird floating in the water without a care.

Standing on an old bridge Susan, aged nine, wrote:

> I see the dirty buildings looking like grandfathers . . . the path by the side dirty like the water. . . . The church spire looks beautiful. It's reaching to the sky like the bottle floating on top of the water.

Not only church spires and bottles point to the sky. Blocks of flats do too and many of our children live high up in flats. We all went to the top floor of an eight-storey block of flats and looked down as a bird would. What does the street look like? What sounds can we hear? Is the scene always like this? What is it like late at night?

Donald, a very bright boy, aged 10, who lives in a flat, wrote:

HOUSING ESTATE
In this land where dirty, grey, ugly flats,
Point to other worlds,
Brown scars of civilisation,
Line the black littered rivers of land.
Miniture figures, mere toys, trample the white string,
Broken, dying, dark four wheeled machines,
Form an endless belt.
Unearthly screams, fierce barking,
Bells ringing in a single monotonous note,
Lids clanging, children crying,
Where wet flags point out the brown earth.
Later the moon shines on black shapes,
Resembling the dwelling places of daytime.
No sounds fill the night air.

Houses are brown scars, roads are littered rivers of land, and pavements become white string. I had encouraged the children to drop the words "like" in their descriptions. If it is like something else why not use another word? We were touching on metaphors without the term ever being introduced.

Each piece of direct observation writing is looked upon as a progression by which we improve a child's use of language. First

we try to narrow his vision of a situation so that he can see the poetry in it. Then we encourage him to add colour to his writing by
minute description. Tell me more about the subject. Give it texture
and describe the quality of its movement. We are keenly aware that
a mastery of the mechanics of language is an essential part of a
child's language experience. Adverbs, adjectives, metaphors and
similes enhance a descriptive account, so we encourage their use.
We need not, however, give them their names. We seek instead situations where the child is led naturally to their use.

Children can bring to each new piece of writing their past experience, whether first or second hand, and their already assimilated
vocabulary, thereby enriching it.

After a broadcast reading of *The Singing Hill* by Meindert de
Jong, in which a young boy meets a horse, other horses were discussed. The class were told of Pegasus the flying horse and words
were sought to capture the grace in the movement of Pegasus. Afterwards the children walked to a field not far away from school
where a horse is stabled. He is by no means a "Black Beauty", but
Susan, aged 10, wrote:

HORSES
　　The gigantic beauty of a stallion is fresh, his limbs glossy and
supple. As his tail dusts the ground his well-built limbs tremble as he
races round the field. The sparkling wickedness in his eyes glitters.
His mane tears out behind him as he gallops like the wind. His coat is
a burnished black and his nose only smells cunning ideas.

The horse would be pleased—he is cunning, but he can barely
raise a canter! A mixture of imagination and observation created a
canvas of words.

When the imagination of children has been aroused by exciting
incident, their writing will be exciting. A fourth-year class had
taken as a literature topic Alan Garner's *The Weirdstone of Bris-
ingamen*. They wrote, acted and painted the highlights of the story.
At the end of the summer term we visited Alderley Edge, the scene
of the book, and went over the ground Colin and Susan trod. We
had tea at the Wizard Inn and searched for Highmost Redmanhey

and looked for Clulow. We also sat on the "Edge" and Graham wrote:

ALDERLEY EDGE
   Tall thick bracken surged proudly up like one of the twisted trunks of the trees. This was the beauty of a remote place called Alderley Edge. It was a strange place undergrowth grew thick and like a great oceon of green with tall twisted giant tree's almost clutching the sky and sucking in the warmth of the sun threw its leaves. But this large rubie called the sun could not brake threw the proud trees and undergrowth and the crunch of the leaves which had droped of the trees into a jungle of foliage. Rock gouged the land Jagged teeth like rocks surged up like great heros. Caves smelt as if a hord of rats had lived there. This spinaching place had always had a large horde of jet black foul birds which had the name of crows.

   "Spinaching" place? Thick green growth like spinach I suppose, but I don't think I could have invented the word. Graham thought it fitted!
   Most of the work so far quoted in this chapter originated in the teacher's suggestion. How will a child write when there is no teacher direction? One November 6th a class of children were asked simply to "Write about Bonfire Night." Christine, aged 9, wrote:

   This was the great moment. It was time to light the bonfire. At last the caretaker of the flat came and lit it. The first shimmers of light began to glow. People began to gather round laughing merrily. The flames fought their way through the branches.
   It was now time to light the fireworks. The children came dancing and singing. Crashes and bangs came from everywhere. Lights were glowing. Children were yelling and screaming with joy. It was marvellous to see younger childrens faces light up.
   By now the fire was burning beautifully. The flames were leaping, swirling and twisting in and out of each other making lovely shapes. The fire silhouetted twigs against the sky. There were shadows leaping to and fro. The smoke came up in spirals, as it went up it seem'ed as though it tickled the moons chin. Soon it was all over, the children started to go home tired but thrilled. At last their was no noise at all except for the occasional bang in the distance.

Christine had written a great deal of direct observation and imaginative work in class. Her free work shows clearly that once a child has found joy in writing with colour and close observation, that joy will permeate all other work. Once, as an experiment, I wrote on the blackboard "The Postman." I then said three words—"Write about him," and the children wrote of a jaunty figure in black with a brown satchel cutting into his shoulders and creasing his coat. These children were practised in minute observation and so their work displayed it.

Let us get close to a subject now and look through the lens of a magnifying glass. Susan, aged 10, looked at a grasshopper and wrote:

> Here is a colossal monster. It's eyes glare at you, they look as though they are on fire. It could cull houses and villages and put them in its mouth and still lurk about for more prey. It is like a cyclone gathering all in its path. But when you take away the magnifying glass there is a little creature which is only a microscopic particle to what I have imagined.

By close observation, Susan's imagination had awakened and she saw what no one else might see. Other children looked at the same grasshopper and wrote totally different accounts, yet each account displayed vivid imagination and a sensitive use of language.

Cynthia, also aged 10, looked into her marble and saw:

A MARBLE
Mountains of fire
Lifting through moisty mist,
Slimy creatures hasten,
On microscopic planets.
Their huge claws squelch
Through the boiling embers
Of a different world.
Through my marble
I see these fantastic things.

The class had been making a study and collection of small things—things they treasured and kept in their purses and pockets.

They had discussed words describing small and minute things. Microscopes, magnifying bottles and magnifying glasses had been used. The children had also looked through the wrong end of a telescope. In fact the topic had been scientific, but as our nine-year-old boy said "English is in everything. You can't step out of its way."

Let us look again through the wrong end of a telescope and then into a magnifying glass. Stephen, aged 10, wrote:

> The snow piles on the road side could look remarkably like the Alps, or some snow-caped mountains. If you were to place a piece of glass at the foot of the Snow there would be a lake. A small clump of grass would make a fine forest. You could make your own world on a miniature scale but you could be in the Austrian Alps. A small ant or other insect climbing the snow could be a mountaineer. Small minute things can become enormous objects in imagination.

This is a far cry from the first snowfall quoted at the beginning of this chapter. The first account was pure observation writing. It was sensitive yet it "risked" nothing for the event was real. Stephen gave not only his observation but his imagination, and in so doing took a further step on the ladder of language experience.

A change is as good as a rest, and although children rarely seem to tire of experiencing their own environment, teachers often long for fresh pastures. Year after year of wind, rain and snow can become a little depressing, and it is necessary for a teacher to be fresh so that he can also be stimulating. I became a little jaded in outlook. While the experiences were new for the children, I had met them before so I decided to go a little farther afield.

In the early summer of 1965 one third-year and one fourth-year class, with three teachers (one the head teacher), undertook a field survey. We chose as our centre of research the small village of Tardebigge, about twelve miles away from school. Each Monday for six weeks the children travelled by coach to Tardebigge and stayed there the whole day, regardless of weather conditions. We had the willing co-operation of the village school headmaster for emergencies such as toilets and first aid, and the vicar of the church let us have the freedom of the church and its grounds. A friendly farmer gave us the use of his pasture land and another arranged a conducted tour of his dairy farm and herd. The British Waterways allowed us to visit the canal workshops at Tardebigge and the children met a Mr. Bate, a true craftsman in the old tradition, who used an adze and shell auger to make lock gates. We were surrounded by beauty, interest, and the excitement of a new situation.

It was my intention to explore the mathematical, historical and natural history possibilities of the area. Two weeks before we embarked on our study we made detailed preparations. We collected string to make into measuring chains and we made clinometers and angle-measuring devices we called angle guns. Yardsticks were made from laths and a perambulator became a tricycle for the sake of a trundle wheel. Parents were cajoled into giving pegs, trowels, nails, plastic collecting bowls and spirit levels. A war department surplus shop delivered two walking compasses for thirty bob and a dial sight for two pounds. Two tripods were found at 7s. 6d. each, and on these we built plane tables. We called a meeting of parents to explain our aims and then asked them for six shillings to help towards the cost of the coach fares. It was difficult to stop the parents coming with us!

The children practised on the equipment in the school environment. We drew rivers on the playground and measured their width by triangulation and work cards were issued directing children to:

1. Measure the height of the flats.
2. Take rubbings of interesting textures within the school environment.
3. Make a quadrat (a pegged out strip of ground $3' + 2'$ measured into $1'$ squares) and show on a squared piece of paper the position and type of plants.
4. Establish North by using a compass.
5. Make a sketch of the school or part of it.
6. Measure the hall or classroom or any part of the school and draw a scale plan.

We called these work cards opportunity cards and they were many and varied. Equipment was freely available and most of the smaller items were contained in eight apple boxes, clearly labelled.

For our first day in the field we divided the children into groups of 6 (there were 15 groups), third- and fourth-year children in each group. They were given a basic opportunity card to:

1. Choose a tree, name it, take bark, twig and leaf samples, measure its height, and record bird visitors, etc. Take a bark rubbing.
2. Choose a part of the hedgerow and examine it over the six weeks for development.
3. Make a quadrat (vertical or horizontal) and record what you find.
4. Examine the field and make a collection of interesting discoveries.
5. Make rubbings in the church and churchyard.

I wanted the children to use their eyes in this active situation. They were to be presented with many problems requiring detailed observation. Apart from the basic opportunity card many other opportunity cards had been devised which would tax the imagination of the children. I wanted them to talk, argue, discuss and reason. Even the teachers were surprised by some of the results.

The vertical quadrat proved a disaster. Have you ever tried to piece together string in one foot squares? It took one group of children three hours! The examination of the field proved dramatically successful. Unknown to us the field was being cut up for turf and we found beneath the turf a variety of eighteenth-century pottery and clay pipes, for the field had been used as a "dump" in the nineteenth century. One boy became so interested in clay pipes that he made a collection of pipes and wrote about them.

We wanted the children to record their work and to do this they had to write. Together with factual statements of what they did, the children also wrote daily diaries. The first accounts of Day One were rather disappointing. Children wrote of getting on the bus and having their milk. One traitor of a child wrote: "When we got there Mr. Haggitt got the chairs out of his boot and the teachers sat down."

Back at school on the following day I said I was disappointed. I told the children I had expected more colourful work, but I had not reckoned with the children's need to settle to their new and exciting situation. There was so much to see and such excitement on the first day that the children had been overwhelmed by the wealth of the new experiences and were unable to write coherently. For the rest of the week we settled down to record and explore our first day's findings. The children gradually came to grips with the situation and following Day Two, Gail, aged 10, wrote in her diary:

DAY TWO

When we arrived at school we were all very excited at the prospect of going to natures green fields. Even the slow drizzle dident dampen our spirits. The coach stood waiting. The sky was a threatning black We all climbed into the coach and we set off. The coaches engine roared and lurched in to life. Then in what seemed no time at all there we were at Tardebigge Everything sparkled with dew Mr. Haggitt then gave us some work to do including sketching a tree our tree seemed to reach up and try to grab the sky. Tall proud and erect every inch a Cupressus tree. A hase lay over the fields. Trees drooped down nearly touching the swamp-like ground. We had dinner at 12 o'clock. We were then told to carray on with our 5 things. Then we were given a card to do. ALL to soon the rain started pouring down. We had to seek shelter in the vicars garage. There we stood listening to the rain as it pounded on the roof A roar was heard and the coach was there. All to soon, we were back after a very exciting day.

In order to get the children to sit down after their picnic lunches (the food seemed to be gone in five minutes), we asked them on each of the six days to write a "creative" description of the scene before them. Sharon, aged 10, wrote:

TARDEBIGGE

In the dreamy haze of sun the breeze sweeps by. Birds in the sky delay their flight. Grass sleep gently not awakening. Traffic is a distant rumble. Birds twitter in the high tree tops lulling their young ones to sleep. Everything is a dream a carefree dream. The traffic and cars are not known in the gentle field and meadows. Everything is quiet and lonely but beautiful and calm. The grass is a bed of cushions. Sheep lie quietly gazing around. Flies flutter around gentley in this sleepy place.

During the lunch break I sat with my class and we chatted about Tardebigge. "It's not like Birmingham," said one boy. "It's so quiet." "Look at the cars on the road. You can hardly hear them," said another. Sharon herself drew attention to the bird hovering in the sky and other children remarked on the trees, the church (it had a striking clock) and the grass on which they were sitting. The children then wrote directly into their note books describing the scene. Some children ambled about seeking inspiration, but they all wrote of the calm beauty of Tardebigge.

Diane, aged 9, added a piece of information too!

The long green grass is swaying from side to side and the big yew tree is standing high so that you can hardly see the tops of the branches. In a dark corner on the left hand side of Tardebigge Church Yard the Gipsy Queen's tomb lies half broken so that you can see through. A bird flutters about on the yew tree and whistles a song. Men used to sharpen arrows on the poisonous yew trees. Long ago the large yew tree would see stretching for miles. It would have been Charle the Seacond ride on horse back across the field. The sight of a tree sudenly catches my eye.

I find out about it from the vicar and he said It's a blossom tree which blossoms on Christmas day and near.

The weather was not always sunny and on another day Susan, aged 9, wrote:

TARDEBIGGE
Tardebigge is green pastures and lovely tall trees that you could see far off in the mist, the rain dripping off the leaves on to stalks of the grass and little lambs trotting around.

And Margaret, also aged 9, wrote:

IN THE RAIN
A hundred shades
Of green grass, trees,
hedges all green. Flowers
deck the hedges that
border it. Shining dew-
drops trickle off leaves.

The Arum lily shuts up
and Jack goes to sleep.
The rain ran off our
coats as we sat under
the old yew. The grass
and the flowers bent their
heads as if the rain was
a king. Birds sing as
they scurry around look-
ing for food.

These children were practised in the art of direct observation writing, but whilst Margaret's I.Q. is about 120, Susan's is fractionally under 90. The children, however, both *enjoyed* the same experience, and wrote at their own level of competence.

Previous experience can leave an indelible mark on the minds of children. Susan had been in my class when we took Steinbeck's *Mice and Men* as a literature topic. She wrote:

A hundred yards from Tardebigge Church lies a lazy canal deep and green and beside it drops a bank. By the canal there is a path that is hard beaten by men that have used it. Green hills stand up against the blue sky. Pond skaters go skittering along the canal.

Martin was also in the same class and he wrote:

A few yards from Tardebigge the canal runs green. There is a path which runs down from the church beaten hard by sheep and horses. On the canal there is a dark tunnel it is dank and musty. Over it is a towering hill green and brown. Overhanging plants catch the debris of winter. Water seeps through old wooden locks. The towpath, shaded by the prickly hawthorn bushes, has small puddles spaced out along its hard and unmarked surface. There is no movement on the canal but the flickering of water beetles and the bubbles blown by invisible fish. The old lifeless barges lie on the edge of the forgotten canal, useless and unwanted.

Some of Martin's work, and nearly all of that selected from Susan's work, is pure Steinbeck. What went through the children's minds as they wrote these pieces cannot be analysed. No mention was made of Steinbeck, but perhaps the atmosphere at the canal struck a chord in their memories.

The general excellence of the creative writing during this field study was staggering because there was very little guidance by the teacher. We only suggested topics on which to write. The inspiration was all around and the children painted their pictures with words. All of the creative work was written on the spot in the rough note books carried by them. The work was rewitten back at school, but rarely did the children alter their original work.

Paul, aged 9, I.Q. is just over 90, as he walked through a meadow on the way to the milking shed, wrote this:

> As the cows graze in the feld the milk makes them heavy and clumsy. They lash themselves with their long tails to clear the flies from their backs. The grass is long and the sun is hot. The tractor roors as it goes past the quiet cows.

David's written work generally was dull and lacking in colour, but the farm moved him to write:

THE FARM
> Cows mooed as we entered the farm yard it smelt vile but the cows didnt seem to mind. Trees waved in the slight breeze and you could hear the cows eating the green sweet grass. you could hear the grunting pigs and the smell of the food they eat. on the way out I heard the snorting of a monster it was a bull. It malicious black body shone in the dull sun light of the day. The path dropped into a green field where cows spent the day eating and sleeping.

Exciting incident creates exciting language. It seemed that the children never stopped talking, yet all the talk was purposeful. Our children were engaged in an activity that kept their hands, their minds, and their brains occupied. The formative worth of this venture was obvious at the end of the survey. About one-tenth of the work originating from it was displayed and it filled three long corridors and two classrooms. There were models and collections galore, and at the two open evenings when the work was on view the *children* conducted parents, teachers and inspectors around the exhibition. The completed notebooks contained work on mathematics, history and nature study. Sketches abounded and the children had painted many pictures and created collages in cloth and paper. The notebooks contained on an average eighty "sides" and some exceeded one hundred.

As a climax to the study we had a lazy afternoon and travelled by canal barge from the outskirts of Birmingham to Tardebigge. We didn't ask the children to write, but they did! Janice, aged 9 (I.Q. 98), described part of her trip in this way:

> Brown is the water when the propela lifts up the mud from the bottom of the smooth crystal water. Fishes that were once swimming around and are now floating ded. The smooth current knocks the reeds down and slowly they work their way back again.

Vivienne, one year older and with an I.Q. of 120, wrote:

ON THE CANAL

The soft purring of the engine was almost drowned out by the excited buzz of noise that crept around. A small vole paddled quietly and swiftly downstream. The wash from the stern of the boat played havoc with the weeds making them play tag. Disturbed mud swirled and gushed sucking at the sides of the barge. Fern hung in the dank shadows. Water reflected water and shimmered on the roof and hung there glinting in the sunlight. Light rays glimmered on the skin of the water throwing light deep, deep down. The sun cast hard shadows everywhere and smoke belched forward from the engine.

There is no need to explain Vivienne's description, for she has drawn her word picture with clarity and sensitivity. It needed no correction. Vivienne had reached the end of her years in the Junior School and this was the last piece of work she ever wrote for me. Some of Vivienne's classmates had not her style or competence, but they all enjoyed similar language experiences and they all enjoyed writing about them.

I consider direct experience writing the most colourful and formative part of language experience. Literature topic writing and writing evoked by second hand experience have great value in encouraging children to handle characters and incidents with colour and imagination. In direct writing, however, children's eyes are opened to the poetry of a situation, and they write freely of what they see. When children at last begin to write freely, requiring no outside motivation, then they are truly exercising their natural creative talents.

QUESTIONS FOR DISCUSSION

1. What techniques can a teacher use to help children become more acute and sensitive observers of their experiences—to help them use their eyes, ears, and other sensory organs?

2. If the description written by a child seems a list rather than a unified representation, what steps can the teacher take to teach the notion of coherence and to help the child gain coherence in his or her descriptions?

3. What stimuli can be used to help children exercise their imaginations in the writing of description?

from
Teaching the "Unteachable"
Herbert Kohl

Many elementary schools, particularly those in densely populated urban areas, today enroll large numbers of students from ethnic minority groups, students from low-income families, and others who are often described as "disadvantaged." Many of these students see little purpose in attending school and have little motivation to succeed. Some of the students read well below the level expected of students in their grades.

Teachers are often poorly prepared to teach these kinds of students, and the efforts of these teachers often encounter resistance from the students. The work of Herbert Kohl is of special importance to prospective teachers, therefore, because it addresses the problems that they encounter in dealing with these disadvantaged, skeptical, sometimes alienated children. Kohl calls for a new philosophy—a new set of attitudes—in working with these students.

Kohl's ideas may be of value to teachers working with all kinds of students, not just with the disadvantaged. He urges ways of teaching writing and of using students' writing in the classroom that might help any student become more confident about what he or she writes and thus more effective in his or her writing.

SHOP WITH MOM
I love to shop with mom
And talk to the friendly grocer
And help her make the list
Seems to make us closer.

Nellie, age 11

THE JUNKIES
When they are
in the street
they pass it
along to each
other but when
they see the
police they would
run some would
just stand still
and be beat
so pity ful
that they want
to cry

Mary, age 11

Nellie's poem received high praise. Her teacher liked the rhyme "closer" and "grocer," and thought she said a great deal in four lines. Most of all the teacher was pleased that Nellie expressed such a pleasant and healthy thought. Nellie was pleased too, her poem was published in the school paper. I was moved and excited by Mary's poem and made the mistake of showing it to the teacher who edited the school newspaper. She was horrified. First of all, she informed me, Mary couldn't possibly know what junkies were, and, moreover, the other children wouldn't be interested in such a poem. There weren't any rhymes or clearly discernible meter. The word "pityful" was split up incorrectly, "be beat" wasn't proper English and, finally, it wasn't really poetry but just the ramblings of a disturbed girl.

My initial reaction was outrage—what did she know about poetry, or about Mary? But it is too easy to be cruel about the ignorance that is so characteristic of the schools today. That teacher did believe that she knew what poetry was, and that there was a Correct Language in which it was expressed. Her attitude towards the correctness of language and the form of poetry was in a way identical to her attitude towards what sentiments good children's poems ought to express. Yet language is not static, nor is it possible *a priori* to establish rules governing what can or cannot be written any more than it is possible to establish rules governing what can or cannot be felt.

Not long ago when I was teaching a class of remote, resistant children in a Harlem school, as an experiment I asked these children to write. I had no great expectations. I had been told that the children were from one to three years behind in reading, that they came from "deprived" and "disadvantaged" homes and were ignorant of the language of the schools. I had also been told that their vocabulary was limited, that they couldn't make abstractions, were not introspective, oriented to physical rather than mental activity. Other teachers in the school called the children "them" and spoke of teaching as a thankless military task. I couldn't accept this mythology: I wanted my pupils to tell me about themselves. For reasons that were hardly literary I set out to explore the possibilities of teaching language, literature, and writing in ways that would enable children to speak about what they felt they were not allowed to acknowledge publicly. Much to my surprise the children wrote a great deal; and they invented their own language to do so. Only a very small number of the children had what can be called "talent," and many of them had only a single story to write and rewrite; yet almost all of them responded, and seemed to become more alive through their writing. The results of some of this exploration are given here.

I have subsequently discovered other teachers who have explored language and literature with their pupils in this way, with results no less dramatic. The children we have taught ranged from the preschool years to high school, from lower-class ghetto children to upper-class suburban ones. There are few teaching techniques that we share in common, and no philosophy of education that binds us. Some of these teachers have tight, carefully controlled classrooms; others care less for order and more for invention. There are Deweyites, traditionalists, classicists—a large range of educational philosophies and teaching styles. If there is anything common to our work it is the concern to listen to what the children have to say and the ability to respond to it as honestly as possible, no matter how painful it may be to our teacherly prides and preconceptions. We have allowed ourselves to learn from our pupils and to expect the unexpected.

Children will not write if they are afraid to talk. Initially they suspect teachers and are reluctant to be honest with them. They have had too many school experiences where the loyalty of the staff and the institutional obligations of teachers have taken precedence over honesty. They have seen too much effort to maintain face, and too little respect for justifiable defiance in their school lives. I think children believe that there is a conscious collusion between all of the adults in a school to maintain the impression that the authority is *always* right, and that life is *always* pleasant and orderly. Unfortunately, the collusion is unconscious or at least unspoken. This is dramatically true in slum schools where the pressures of teaching are increased by understaffing and a vague uneasiness about race which is always in the air.

I was assigned to a school in East Harlem in September 1962 and was not sufficiently prepared for the faculty's polite lies about their success in the classroom or the resistance and defiance of the children. My sixth-grade class had thirty-six pupils, all Negro. For two months I taught in virtual isolation from my pupils. Every attempt I made to develop rapport was coldly rejected. The theme of work scheduled by the school's lesson plan for that semester was "How We Became Modern America," and my first lesson was characteristic of the dull response everything received.

It seemed natural to start by comparing a pioneer home with the modern life the children knew—or, more accurately, I thought they knew. I asked the class to think of America in the 1850's and received blank stares, although that presumably was what they had studied the previous year. I pursued the matter.

—Can anyone tell me what was happening around 1850, just before the Civil War? I mean, what do you think you'd see if you walked down Madison Avenue then?

—Cars.

—Do you think there were cars in 1850? That was over a

hundred years ago. Think of what you learned last year and try again, do you think there were cars then?

—Yes . . . no . . . I don't know.

Someone else tried.

—Grass and trees?

The class broke out laughing. I tried to contain my anger and frustration.

—I don't know what you're laughing about, it's the right answer. In those days Harlem was farmland with fields and trees and a few farmhouses. There weren't any roads or houses like the ones outside, or street lights or electricity.

The class was outraged and refused to think. Bright faces took on the dull glaze that is characteristic of the Negro child who finds it less painful to be thought stupid than to be defiant. There was an uneasy drumming on desk tops. The possibility of there being a time when Harlem didn't exist had never, could never have occurred to the children. Nor did it occur to me that their experience of modern America was not what I had come to teach about. After two months, in despair, I asked the kids to write about their block.

WHAT A BLOCK!

My block is the most terrible block I've ever seen. There are at lease 25 or 30 narcartic people in my block. The cops come around there and tries to act bad but I bet inside of them they are as scared as can be. They even had in the papers that this block is the worst block, not in Manhattan but in New York City. In the summer they don't do nothing except shooting, shabing, and fighting. They hang all over the stoops and when you say excuse me to them they hear you but they just don't feel like moving. Some times they make me so mad that I feel like slaping them and stuffing and bag of garbage down their throats. Theres only one policeman who can handle these people and we all call him "Sunny." When he come around in his cop car the people run around the corners, and he wont let anyone sit on the stoops. If you don't believe this story come around some time and you'll find out.

Grace, age 11

My block is the worse block you ever saw people getting killed or stabbed men and women in buildin's taking dope . . .

Mary, age 11

MY NEIGHBORHOOD
I live on 117 street, between Madison and 5th avenue. All the bums live around here. But the truth is they don't live here they just hang around the street. All the kids call it "Junky's Paradise."

James, age 12

My block is a dirty crumby block!

Clarence, age 12

The next day I threw out my notes and my lesson plans and talked to the children. What I had been assigned to teach seemed, in any case, an unreal myth about a country that never has existed. I didn't believe the tale of "progress" the curriculum had prescribed, yet had been afraid to discard it and had been willing to lie to the children. After all I didn't want to burden them or cause them pain, and I had to teach something. I couldn't "waste their time." How scared I must have been when I started teaching in Harlem to accept those hollow rationalizations and use the "curriculum" to protect me from the children. I accepted the myth that the teacher and the book know all; that complex human questions had "right" and "wrong" answers. It was much easier than facing the world the children perceived and attempting to cope with it. I could lean on the teachers' manuals and feel justified in presenting an unambiguously "good" historical event or short story. It protected my authority as a teacher which I didn't quite believe in. It was difficult for me; pontificating during the day and knowing that I was doing so at night. Yet could I cause the class much more pain or impose greater burdens with my lies than they already had? How much time could I have "wasted" even if I let the children dance and play all day while I sought for a new approach. They had already wasted five years in school by the time they arrived in my class.

So we spoke. At first the children were suspicious and ashamed of what they'd written. But as I listened and allowed them to talk they became bolder and angrier, then finally quieter and relieved. I asked them to write down what they would do to change things, and they responded immediately.

If I could change my block I would stand on Madison Ave and throw nothing but Teargas in it. I would have all the people I liked to get out of the block and then I would become very tall and have big hands and with my big hands I would take all of the narcartic people and pick them up with my hand and throw them in the nearest river and oceans. I would go to some of those old smart alic cops and throw them in the Ocians and Rivers too. I would let the people I like move into the projects so they could tell their friends that they live in a decent block. If I could do this you would never see 117 st again.

Grace, age 11

If I could change my block I would put all the bums on an Island where they can work there. I would give them lots of food. But I wouldn't let no whiskey be brought to them. After a year I would ship them to new York and make them clean up junk in these back yard and make them maybe make a baseball diamond and put swings basketball courts etc.

Clarence, age 12

For several weeks after that the children wrote and wrote—what their homes were like, whom they liked, where they came from. I discovered that everything I'd been told about the children's language was irrelevant. Yes, they were hip when they spoke, inarticulate and concrete. But their writing was something else, when they felt that no white man was judging their words, threatening their confidence and pride. They faced a blank page and wrote directly and honestly. Recently I have mentioned this to teachers who have accepted the current analyses of "the language" of the "disadvantaged.'' They asked their children to write and have been as surprised as I was, and shocked by the obvious fact that "disadvantaged" children will not speak in class because they cannot trust their audience.

Nothing the school offered was relevant, so I read the class novels, stories, poems, brought my library to class and let them know that many people have suffered throughout history and that some were articulate enough to create literature from their lives. They didn't believe me, but they were hungry to know what had been written about and what could be written about.

It was easier for the class to forget their essays than it was for me. They were eager to go beyond their block, to move out into the broader world and into themselves. We talked of families, of brothers and sisters, of uncles, and of Kenny's favorite subject, the Tyranny of Teachers and Moms.

We spoke and read about love and madness, families, war, the birth and death of individuals and societies; and then they asked me permission to write themselves. Permission!

In the midst of one of our discussions of fathers Shiela asked me a question that has become symbolic of my pupils' hunger for concepts. "Mr. Kohl," she said, "if you wanted to write something about your father that was true is there a word for it?" What she meant was that if there was a word for it she would do it, but if there wasn't she would be scared. One names what is permissible, and denies names to what one fears. Shiela led us to talk about biography and autobiography, and she did get to write of her father.

A BIOGRAPHY OF MY FATHER

My father was born in California.

He wasn't a hero or anything like that to anyone but to me he was. He was a hard working man he wasn't rich but he had enough money to take care of us. He was mean in a way of his own. But I loved him and he loved me. He said to my mother when he die whe would feel it. My father was a man who loved his work besides if I was a man who worked as a grocery store I would love it to. He wanted his kids to grow up to be someone and be big at name. He wanted a real life. But when he died we started a real life.

The children spoke of themselves as well. They knew what they felt and sometimes could say it. Sharon came into class angry one day and wrote about a fight.

ONE DAY THERE WAS A BIG FIGHT

   One day in school a girl started getting smart with a boy. So the boy said to the girl why don't you come outside? The girl said alright I'll be there. The girl said you just wait. And he said don't wait me back. And so the fight was on. One had a swollen nose the other a black eye. And a teacher stoped the fight. His name was Mr. Mollow. I was saying to myself I wish they would mind their own business. It made me bad. I had wanted to see a fight that day. So I call Mr. Mollow up. I called him all kinds of names. I said you ugly skinney bony man. I was red hot. And when I saw him I rolled my eyes as if I wanted to hit him. All that afternoon I was bad at Mr. Mollow.

I tried to talk to her about her paper, tell her that "it make me bad" didn't make any sense. And she explained to me that "being bad" was a way of acting and that down South a "bad nigger" was one who was defiant of the white man's demands. She concluded by saying that being bad was good in a way and bad in a way. I asked the class and they agreed. In the midst of the discussion Louis asked one of his characteristically exasperating questions: "But where do words come from anyway?"

I stumbled over an answer as the uproar became general.

—What use are words anyway?

—Why do people have to talk?

—Why are there good words and bad words?

—Why aren't you supposed to use some words in class?

—Why can't you change words as you like?

I felt that I was being "put on," and was tempted to pass over the questions glibly; there were no simple answers to the children's questions, and the simplest thing to do when children ask difficult questions is to pretend that they're not serious or they're stupid. But the children were serious.

More and more they asked about language and would not be put off by evasive references to the past, linguistic convention and tradition. Children look away from adults as soon as adults say that things are the way they are because they have always been that way. When a child accepts such an answer it is a good indication that he has given up and decided to be what adults would make him rather than himself.

I decided to explore language with the children, and we talked about mythology together.

I thought of Shiela's question and Louis's question, of Shiela's desire to tell a story and her fear of doing it. The children rescued me. Ronald told me one day that Louis was "psyching" him and asked me to do something. I asked him what he was talking about, what he meant by "psyching." He didn't know, and when I asked the class they couldn't quite say either, except that they all knew that Louis was "psyche," as they put it. I said that Louis couldn't be Psyche since Psyche was female. The kids laughed and asked me what I meant, I countered with the story of Cupid and Psyche and the next day followed with readings from Apuleius and C. S. Lewis. Then I talked about words that came from Psyche, psychology, psychic, psychosomatic. We even puzzled out the meaning of psyching, and one of the children asked me if there were any words from Cupid. I had never thought of cupidity in that context before, but it made sense.

From Cupid and Psyche we moved to Tantalus, the Sirens, and the Odyssey. We talked of Venus and Adonis and spent a week on first Pan and panic, pan-American, then pandaemonium, and finally on daemonic and demons and devils.

Some of the children wrote myths themselves and created characters named Skyview, Missile, and Morass. George used one of the words in his first novel:

One day, in Ancient Germany, a boy was growing up. His name was Pathos. He was named after this Latin word because he had sensitive feelings.

The class began a romance with words and language that lasted all year. Slowly the children turned to writing, dissatisfied with mere passive learning. They explored their thoughts and played with the many different forms of written expression. I freed the children of the burden of spelling and grammar while they were writing. If a child asked me to comment on the substance of his work I did not talk of the sentence structure. There is no more deadly thing a teacher can do than ignore what a child is trying to express in his writing and comment merely upon the form, neatness, and heading.[1] Yet there is nothing safer if the teacher is afraid to become involved. It is not that I never taught grammar or spelling; it is rather that the teaching of grammar and spelling is not the same as the teaching of writing. Once children care about writing and see it as important to themselves they want to write well. At that moment, I found, they easily accept the discipline of learning to write correctly. Vocabulary, spelling, and grammar become the means to achieving more precise and sophisticated forms of expression and not merely empty ends in themselves.

In my class a child had permission to write whenever he felt he had to. Barbara, a taciturn girl who had never written a word, put her reader down one day and wrote for fifteen minutes. Then she handed me this:

ONE COLD AND RAINY NIGHT

It was one cold and rainy night when I was walking through the park and all was in the bed. I saw a owl up in the tree. And all you could see was his eyes. He had big white and black eyes. And it was rainy and it was very very cold that night. And I only had on one thin coat. I was cold that rainy night. I was colder than that owl. I don't know how he could sit up in that tree. It was dark in the park. And only the one who had the light was the owl. He had all the light I needed. It was rainy that stormy night. And I was all by myself. Just walking through the park on my way home. And when I got home I went to bed. And I was thinking about it all that night. And I was saying it was a cold and rainy night and all was in bed.

---

[1] The habit of grading a written exercise according to form, neatness, spelling, punctuation, and heading is not surprising considering that the written part of the examination for the New York City substitute elementary school teaching license is graded that way. Content is irrelevant.

She explained that she had not slept and wanted to write. She only wrote occasionally after producing this paragraph. I could have encouraged her to continue writing, to build her paragraph into a story. But she didn't want to write. She wanted to exorcise an image that particular day. A teacher does not have to make everything educational, to "follow up" on all experiences and turn a meaningful moment into a "learning situation." There is no need to draw conclusions or summarize what the child said. Often teachers insult their pupils and deceive themselves by commenting and judging where no comment or judgment is called for.

Larry had been writing voluminous comic book fantasies starring Batman, Robin, and the League of Justice. One day he got bored with these heroes and asked me if he could write about himself. I said of course, and so he produced a fragment of an autobiography, after which he returned to his fantasies. He said that the autobiography helped him to invent his own League and his adventurous novels became more personal. I asked him how it helped him, and he said he couldn't say, but he knew that it did.

THE STORY OF MY LIFE

Foreword

This story is about a boy named Larry and his life as it is and how it will be. Larry is in the six grade now but this story will tell about his past, present, and future. It will tell you how he lived and how he liked it or disliked it. It will tell you how important he was and happy or sad he was in this world it will tell you all this thoughts. It may be pleasant and it may be horrible in place but what ever it is it will be good and exciting but! their will be horrible parts. This story will be made simple and easy but in places hard to understand. This is a non-fiction book.

Where I was Born

In all story they beat around the bush before they tell you the story well I am not this story takes place in the Metropolitan Hospitle.

When I was born I couldn't see at first. but like all families my father was waiting outside after a hour or so I could see shadows. The hospital was very large and their were millions of beds and plenty of people. And their were people in chairs rolling around, people in beds, and people walking around with trays with food or medicine on it. Their was people rolling people in bed and there were people bleeding crying yelling or praying I was put at a window with other babies so my father could see me their was a big glass and lots of people around me so I could see a lot of black shapes. And since I was a baby I tried to go through the glass but I didn't succeed. All the people kept looking I got scared and cryed soon the nurse came and took all the babies back to their mothers. . . .

George was shy and quiet and invented his own characters from the beginning. He was the class artist and drew pictures for everybody. He wrote for himself.

A JOURNEY THROUGH TIME AND SPACE

Chapter III—Just a Tramp

George had been in jail for so long, that he lost everything he had. He didn't even have a cent. "Well," he thought, "I guess I'll have to get a job." He went by a restaurant and got a job as a waiter. One day, a drunky came into the restaurant and ordered some wine. George brought him his wine then after he got through drinking it out of the bottle, the drunky said, "How's 'bout yous an' me goin' to a bar t'night?" George was afraid he would lose his job if he had been caught drinking. So he said, "Get out of this restaurant, or I'll call the manager!" With that, the drunken man hit George in the jaw with his fist and knocked him down. George couldn't take being pushed around any longer, so he got up and knocked the drunky down. The drunky got up and pulled out a knife. George grabbed at the knife and tried to make him drop it. They both fought for the knife knocking chairs and taking the worst beatings.

The manager was so afraid that he ran to get the police. Two policemen came in, and the minute George saw them, he knew he would have to spend another month in jail. So he jumped out the restaurant door and ran down the street. The policemen pursued George around the corner where George hid in a hallway and the police passed him. "Whew," he panted quietly, "I'm glad they're gone! But now, I guess, I'm just a tramp. If I leave town, it won't do no good." So he decided to hide in his basement ex-laboratory. He had been in jail for so long he had forgotten where it was. He strolled along the streets day and night. His clothes were getting raggety and people laughed at him. His mother taught him not to beg, even if he didn't have a penny. And George never did beg. And kids made up a song for him:

We know a bum who walks down the street,
In rain, or snow, or slush or sleet
He can't afford to do anything right;
'cause if you see him you'll pop like dynamite!

They made lots more of him like this:

We know a tramp who walks in the damp,
Like a dirty, stinkin' phoney ol 'scamp. —
He can't afford no money at all,
Or have a great big party or ball
'cause he's just a big fat slob,
And never has he gotten a job.

The kids sounded on him every day, and he never did get a decent job. But he still had his mind on being a scientist. To invent things and modernize his country.

There is no limit to the forms of writing that children will experiment with. They will readily become involved in provocative open assignments if they are convinced that the teacher does not want a correct answer to an unambiguous question, but rather to hear what they have to say. Themes such as "On Playing Around" and "Walls" do not prejudge how a child must respond. "On How Nice the Summer Is" does. The same is true for open forms of writing such as the fable or the parable. The teacher can provide the framework for many written exercises, but the substance of the children's responses must be drawn from their life and imagination.

This is only part of the story, however, the part which can be attempted with a whole class. It is much more difficult to encourage each child to seek his own voice, and to accept the fact that not everyone will have a literary one. It is a mistake to assume that all children have the energy and devotion necessary to write novels or poems. Children select the forms they are most comfortable with, and therefore it is not easy to teach writing. One cannot teach a sixth-grade class to write novels. The best that can be done is to reveal novels to them and be ready to teach those who want to do more than read. I never made "creative writing" compulsory. Writing must be taught qualitatively—how can one best express oneself, in what way? I found that the children understood these most complex questions, and took great pleasure in listening to the various voices of their classmates.

For example, after I read Aesop's fables to my class and we talked about them, they wrote fables of their own.

> Once upon a time there was a pig and a cat. The cat kept saying old dirty pig who want to eat you. And the pig replied when I die I'll be made use of, but when you die you'll just rot. The cat always thought he was better than the pig. When the pig died he was used as food for the people to eat. When the cat died he was bured in old dirt.
> Moral: Live dirty die clean.

> *Barbara, age 11*

> Once a boy was standing on a huge metal flattening machine. The flattener was coming down slowly. Now this boy was a boy who love insects and bugs. The boy could have stopped the machine from coming down but there were two ladiebugs on the button and in order to push the button he would kill the two ladie bugs. The flattener was about a half inch over his head now he made a decision he would have to kill the ladie bugs he quickly pressed the button. The machine stoped he was saved and the ladie bugs were dead.
> Moral: smash or be smashed.

> *Kenneth, age 11*

In writings of this sort we can sense the exhilaration felt by children in saying things that might have been out of bounds in the atmosphere of the conventional classroom. In fact the conventional classroom itself sometimes becomes the subject of their essays.

WHY DO RUSSIANS PLANT TREES?
> Children sit in classroom waiting for teacher to come. Teachcer walks in. Writes on the board. Question is, Why do Russians plant trees?

Some answer are, They plant trees to hide their artillery; To hide their cruelty to the people; So we can't see their secret weapons.

Teacher writes wrong on all. Real answer is Russians plant trees because trees are pretty.

William Barbour

WE CAN TEACH EACH OTHER

Inside I feel like I am a nice person; but I have to act like one too. I have to know what kind of person I am. Sometimes, I forget that other people have feelings. Teachers for example; sometimes I hurt them without knowing it. I can say or do something that is so hurtful that they can't say anything but, "Get up and get out." They say this so they can go on and teach the rest of us a lesson. But Teachers can hurt you too and they do it just to teach you a lesson.

You are a child of learning in some ways, but in other ways children teach teachers. I don't know what a teacher is like or how she feels, just like a teacher doesn't really know what I'm like or how I feel. So I can teach her what and how I think and feel. Teachers have been children before, but they seem to forget what it's like because the time changes in the way that the weather changes. So they can't say, well it's like when I was a child.

No, it's not like that, because people are changing and our minds are changing too. So children teach teachers a new lesson, about children today.

Patricia Williams

QUESTIONS FOR DISCUSSION

1. How might you sum up Kohl's philosophy for working with the children he describes? What particularly distinguishes his attitudes toward and ways of working with those children?

2. What sort of "curriculum" in language arts is Kohl advocating for students such as those he describes? Would the same sort of "curriculum" work with students in different economic and social circumstances?

3. What did Kohl do to "teach" the writing of stories? Might he have done more "teaching" of that form? Might Kohl's procedures work as well in other schools?

4. How is "personal" (autobiographic) writing related to the writing of fiction in Kohl's teaching? Is the connection useful only in the teaching of disadvantaged students?

5. Kohl's comments on "creative writing" sound as if they contradict the views of many teachers whose essays appear in this part. Do they? If so, whose view do *you* agree with?

Creative Writing through Creative Dramatics

Beatrice Furner

The following article by Beatrice Furner not only offers a general introduction to procedures useful for many kinds of creative writing, but also incorporates suggestions for the use of dramatics—an increasingly important activity for children in many elementary classrooms—as a way of moving children to understand experiences and situations and to write about them. Furner presents a complete series of activities by which stimulation of the senses and imagination, and discussion—accompanied perhaps by exercises in dramatics—can result in creative writing.

Beatrice Furner is a member of the faculty at the University of Iowa's College of Education.

In recent years teachers have heard much of the importance of creativity in the English program for the purpose of helping the child to develop the ability to use language to organize his experiences in order to understand self and world.

From *Elementary English* Vol. 50, No. 3 (March 1973), 405–8, 416.

Creative writing has received renewed attention as an avenue for response in a language program designed to help children make reality from experience since it can provide the child with an opportunity to explore a topic of significance to him and to realize his feelings, sensory responses, and experiences through language symbolism.

Many teachers have used creative writing as a satisfying, pleasurable experience or as a means to teach skills of written expression or control of various literary techniques such as characterization or description. They may wonder how approaches to creative writing can be structured to lead to outcomes of self-exploration and self-realization. The value of a topical motivation for writing, including a base of oral interchange through talk and drama will be considered.

While the value of non-directed writing experiences in which individuals write diaries, journals, or on any topic of importance to them is recognized; it also is important for purposes of self-discovery to initiate topics of pertinence for exploration. In this way, through preplanned experiences, perceptions can be heightened, sensory input provided, and the need to explore and express feelings created. Broad topics of significance to the experiences of the particular group of children should be selected. While reseach on topics of significance is lacking literature interest studies can be utilized, since children seem to feel a need for exploration and self-expression about the same problems or topics in various modes. Knowledge of a particular group of children and recognition of their expressed concerns can provide an adequate basis for topic selection. When planning for exploration, a topic should be broadened so that many avenues and levels of exploration are opened. This will provide input and opportunity for exploration on several levels to suit the individual needs of children. Thus, while a general topical motivation is undertaken, each child's choice of topic and form of expression remains individual.

For instructional purposes, it is helpful to consider the methodological steps which define the instructional tasks to be accomplished in a creative writing experience. A five-step sequence is useful for this purpose.[1]

METHODOLOGICAL STEPS IN A CREATIVE WRITING EXPERIENCE

1. Motivation period in which children's attention is focused on a broad topic in order to generate interest, develop a mood, and create a need to write.
2. Exchange of ideas to crystallize each child's thinking.
3. Writing period.
4. Sharing of ideas.
5. Follow-up activities, if appropriate.

The motivation step should be designed to focus children's attention on a broad topic with which they have had some experience. A need for self-expression is generated through use of stimulators involving discussion, use of literature, pictures, objects, films, records or tapes, reference to real and vicarious experiences of the children, and dramatic activity. The motivational devices should be used to heighten awareness, build perceptions, and to elicit response from each child. The motivators should be used as a springboard to encourage individual reaction and elaboration; not as a model or framework to be filled in.

As indicated by the double arrow, the second stage, exchanging ideas, overlaps the first. In fact, the sooner and the more frequently children can be encouraged to react personally; the more successful will be the motivational sequence in developing a need for personal exploration and expression. The use of creative dramatics as a means of exploring solutions to the problem can well provide this needed exchange. There should be a pulling together of ideas which encourages children to talk about their emerging ideas in order to crystallize them enough so that they are not lost in the transition to

---

[1] Beatrice A. Furner, "Developing a Program of Instruction in Creative Writing in the Elementary School," *Current Perspectives in Elementary Education* (Des Moines: Iowa Elementary Principals, Iowa State Education Association, 1967), pp. 51–54.

writing. Recognition of the fleeting nature of spontaneous, creative ideas underlines the importance of this exchange. Care must be taken, however, that the child does not express all of his ideas or, in group dictation, that consensus as to outcome does not occur. If this happens, children may have no further need to express and writing or dictation may become merely a mechanical process of filling in an outline. Each child should be actively generating ideas throughout the writing process.

In the writing period young children dictate their ideas to the catalytic-scribe or, after mechanics are well enough under control, write individually. In group dictation the teacher serves as a catalytic agent, drawing out ideas and extending them by reflecting them back to the individual or the group. All responses are positively reinforced and those which seem to receive group approval and which fit the emerging story line are recorded in the child's own words. Teachers must exercise care that they do not edit as they record. If our purpose is self-discovery through language symbolism, it is essential to use the child's language—not one foreign to him. Periodic rereading serves to stimulate children and to promote a sequentially developed story line. As the story nears conclusion, the teacher should help children to find a satisfactory ending. The story should be reread for proofreading purposes so that children can be sure it is just as they wish it and that no errors in recording have been made. Titling can then take place.

In individual writing the teacher should, during the writing period, serve as a catalyst, an audience, and an aid for mechanics as requested by the children. Since talk is so basic, the child may need to interact with his idea to the teacher or another child rather than to be alone with it. Provision should be made for this need. Again proofreading should be encouraged, not for mechanical perfection, but to be sure it says "what I want it to say."

As creative expression began with the interaction of talk, it should now return to it in the sharing period. Children should voluntarily be given the opportunity to share their solutions to the problem. A set for creative listening in which the listener enters in imaginatively should be developed. By becoming involved in others' solutions, the creative process can be heightened for each individual. Interaction should focus on ideas and effective ways of expressing them through language, not on elements of form.

Reading of a group-dictated story after a lapse of time during which a set for creative listening is developed permits the children to experience their solution, thus extending self-exploration.

If a sense of involvement in the problem is still high, children may welcome additional avenues of expression for extension of their ideas. Illustration or dramatization of the story or other solutions may provide the child with a means of extended exploration. For some children one of these modes may be more suitable than the original writing or dictation. The sharing of literature or music related to the topic may also add to the child's awareness of himself and his world in relation to the problem.

Follow-up activities of this sort should be based on the children's involvement with the topic. If a sense of completion has been achieved by them at this point in time, such activities should not be imposed.

Let us now more fully consider the contribution which creative dramatics can make as part of the motivational stages in a creative writing experience. In doing this it is helpful to consider the methodological steps in a creative dramatics experience [2] and their similarity to the stages in a creative writing experience.

METHODOLOGICAL STEPS IN A CREATIVE DRAMATICS EXPERIENCE

1. Warm-up exercises. (Preparatory physical and vocal exercises related to the topic.)
2. Individual or pair expressive activities.
3. Large group or class dramatization.
4. Reflection, discussion, and relaxation.

The first stage involves warm-up activities of an imitative and expressive form related to the topic to permit children to become

[2] Refer to descriptions in Barnes, *Drama in the English Classroom,* pp. 55, 59–62; Brian Way, *Development through Drama* (London: Longman, 1967), pp. 193–208; and Chris Curran, *An Approach to Using Drama in the High Schools* (unpublished Master's thesis, University of Connecticut, 1970), p. 54.

involved totally, to unwind, to begin to sense the problem, and to be open to sensory input. This then evolves into pair or small group expressive activities in exploration of the topic or theme. Interaction is important here as children encounter each other and reflect off actions and reactions of others, as would be the case in a real life situation. This may then emerge into a total class activity by bringing the groups together and relating activities of one group to another. After the improvisation or dramatization of the theme, a period for unwinding, reflecting, and considering the significance of what occurred is important. The obvious similarity to the steps in a creative writing experience can be seen.

Now how can we approach creative writing through creative dramatics? In the motivational and exchange of ideas stages children can be given opportunities to respond dramatically to various sorts of sensory input. Since these stages require divergent thinking to create a sense of problem, openness, and non-completion with opportunity for exchange of emerging ideas, dramatic activity is highly appropriate since it relies on creative thought in experiencing vicariously or re-experiencing an event to determine its meaning. Initial dramatic responses can be of the warm-up type involving imitative tasks in response to some other form of stimulus. Responses can gradually develop to be more expressive involving either individuals or small groups. As problems are explored and are generated through improvisation, the need for completion through creative expression will be developed. This need could be met through continued dramatic activity or through writing—the latter permitting individual response in a way not offered by group dramatization. Following writing in either the individual or group dictation style, dramatization of the stories, poems, or plays may naturally follow as a way of sharing or as a follow-up experience. Much of the needed warm-up for this dramatic activity will have come from the writing experience.

Such approaches have been used in the creative writing program at University Elementary School, the laboratory school at the University of Iowa.

In one instance, with second graders, a picture of a cougar looking into a car was used. Since no people were in the picture, consideration of the reasons for this and of their reactions was undertaken. Dramatization of the way the cat moved and sounded, the reactions of the people (feelings, facial expressions, sounds, and movements), and consideration of what happened provided input and created a need to explore more fully. An opening paragraph was dictated by the children, after which they wrote their ideas individually, in pairs, or small groups. They were so eager to share stories and to begin dramatization of various stories that the schedule for the remainder of the day was altered.

At the fourth grade level we have used a paragraph starter to explore the feelings of aloneness, reaction to a strange sight, and fright. The paragraph is as follows:

> Lee walked to the window to let in a little air. While raising the window, something caught Lee's eye. Lee's mouth flew open. There below the window was the strangest thing Lee had ever seen—

The paragraph is constructed to be very open-ended. Lee can be doing many things at the time, can be in many locations, can be male or female, and can see whatever each child desires below the window. Discussion of these possibilities will create a sense of problem and a need for self-expression, but actual dramatization involving the whole self does so more effectively, as children enact the opening of the window and the response to that strange sight below.

At the sixth grade level emotions have been explored through use of caricatures of frustration, smugness, joy, and boredom. After children react to what they think the drawings could be one rhyme is read, for example:

SMUGNESS
Smugness
Sits upon a wall
Way up high above it all
Looking down his nose at us—
Just before he starts to fall.

The intent of the author and illustrator to give their feelings about emotions is considered as the four poems are shared. Children's reactions are sought and they are guided to identify other emotions which they have experienced, to describe the feeling, how it sounds, looks, moves. This exchange of ideas can be intensified to create a need for self-expression by individual and/or pair dramatic activity using mime or improvisation to create the emotion. After writing children can share, illustrate, and dramatize ideas such as these written by sixth graders.

CONFUSION
Confusion is a mass of thought
Like the wind blowing some leaves,
They blow around and mix you up.

Julie

HATRED
Hatred is mostly madness,
Which often leads to sadness.
Please don't let anger turn to hate,
For oh, it is an awful fate.

Betsy

MISERY
Misery has very long arms
That do nothing but harm.
Your only escape
Is a batman cape.

Mike

The use of dramatic activity in the motivational stages of a creative writing experience is a useful addition to the exchange of ideas through talk since it involves the child physically, verbally, and emotionally in exploration of the problem. Through regular experiences of this type children can become more open to experience and sensory awareness.

QUESTIONS FOR DISCUSSION

1. Do you share Furner's conviction that dramatic activities can be a valuable part of the stimulus to creative writing? Can such activities be used even by teachers not experienced in handling creative drama in the classroom, or do Professor Furner's techniques require a teacher to be well-trained in the use of dramatics?

2. Furner speaks of the need for "exploration" of topics on many levels to suit the needs of individual children. In her discussion, what might "exploration" mean, and how does one encourage a young child in school to "explore" a topic?

3. Furner connects "exploration" with "self-discovery." What connections do you see between these two activities? How can the classroom teacher help assure that the first helps toward the second?

4. Furner implies that unordered exchange is healthy in the classroom—that multiple views and ways of looking at a subject are desirable—but that ideas need to be "pulled together" so that students can experience the desire to write yet not feel that writing is an anticlimactic record of points everyone agrees on. To achieve this atmosphere in the classroom may require a teacher skilled in leading discussions and other activities. Are there techniques that a teacher can use in order to achieve these goals? What does the teacher need to do, and not to do, if the atmosphere sought by Furner is to be achieved?

5. Furner speaks of the need for "divergent thinking to create a sense of problem," and later she speaks of exploring problems. In what sense does creative writing (or dramatic activity) depend upon the existence of a "problem"? What sorts of situations constitute "problems" that are useful in creative writing?

The Writing of Poetry— One Way In

Sidney Robbins

Many discussions about writing poetry concentrate on ways to stimulate students' imaginations. Such discussions also emphasize the necessity of accepting, without criticism, students' efforts at poetry in the hope that as the students come to enjoy writing and become more sensitive to their own experiences, their poetry will develop. These discussions, however, lack advice about how to evoke poetry from students, particularly from those students who have never before written poetry.

In the following essay, Sidney Robbins, recognizing the roots of poetry in feelings and in perception and understanding of vivid experiences, describes materials and presents questions which, in his experience, have prompted students to write poetry. He also presents his response to a poem that emerged from his exercise.

Sidney Robbins was a lecturer in English at St. Luke's College in Exeter, England.

Poetry should not conform to a theory, unbending conventional;
Although it will certainly have a form, subconscious, unintentional.

From *English in Education* Vol. 41 (Spring 1970), 50–58. Reprinted by permission of *English in Education* and Mrs. Sidney Robbins.

Poetry, like pictures, can be the outcome of any material placed stra-
   tegically,
It must flow consistently, jump connectively, perhaps not logically,
But with the essence of sensibility and sensitivity contained within,
Being an individual literary form, beyond protection,
   therefore
   escaping correction.

Pamela Southcott
(Poems from Bristol Schools, Age Group 16–19).

INTRODUCTION

The teacher of English has one underlying concern, the way in
which the children or adults he works with grow in language. All
my own experience as a teacher leads me to believe that this growth
takes place most effectively when language flows out of an absorption in feeling, out of a sense of being caught up in understanding
and perception. When children are completely given to dramatic
movement or held in the spell of a good story or deeply involved in
the writing of a poem or a story, they appear to make unexpected
leaps forward in comprehension and in their confidence and delight
in using words and rhythms and images. I have never noticed such
linguistic leaps when children have been engaged in the more mental, cold-blooded activities of word and sentence drills and comprehension and punctuation exercises. I realise that it would probably
be difficult to prove this conviction about growth in language in any
way that would be statistically respectable, but it is one that is supported by the experience of other teachers and writers.

   The key factor is this absorption which has behind it the child's
feelings and a new openness to understanding and insight. This is
why poetry is of such central importance to us as English teachers.
In a good poem the language is alive with the pressure and excitement of the poet's feeling and perception.

   In my work on poetry I place the main emphasis upon the writing
of poems. In my own teaching in secondary modern and primary
schools I encouraged the children to write poems regularly and
gave them an exercise book that was exclusively for their own
poems. This emphasis stems from a belief that each one of us,

provided we are allowed to acquire the confidence, can be expressive for our own ends in language. This writing of poems requires a background of other work in poetry; this would include a great deal of reading poetry aloud purely for enjoyment, the use of records and radio programmes, individual and group work collecting poems around themes and making them into sequences for performance, the making of individual anthologies ("Poems I like") and the occasional close study of an especially seminal and relevant poem. Essential equipment would include a large and varied range of poetry anthologies with some that contain poems by children and selections from the work of appropriate individual poets.

The quotation from Pamela Southcott's thoughtful and deeply felt poem "Wherein Lies the Art?" at the beginning of this article includes the line

> Poetry, like pictures, can be the outcome of any material placed strategically.

Part of our strategy as teachers will be to help the children focus their senses and imagination upon the feeling or experience they are trying to catch in words; our aim will be to encourage them to be as honest, accurate, sensitive and yet, vivid as possible.

LEVEL AND MATERIALS

I want to outline here a way of beginning with a class that has no, or very little, experience of writing poems before. It would also be useful with a class that was not focusing closely and attentively enough in its writing. It has worked well with primary and secondary children from the age of nine upwards, and with students and groups of teachers in "workshop" sessions at various teachers' centres. . . . Issue No. 5 of the Bulletin of the Exeter Teachers' Centre includes a 12-page anthology of poems by teachers that were written as a result of this procedure. It is a closely structured exercise and has obvious limitations—I would never use it more than once with any one group—but it does seem to be a helpful starting point for those who are unused to or inhibited about writing. Once they have discovered that they can write, many other more genuine sources of stimulus can be drawn upon.

I take into the class a collection of at least 50 vivid pictures, some cut out of coloured supplements, others in black and white. They need to be dramatic and evocative; clever pictures of single objects tend to be limiting, and advertisements are almost always lacking in integrity as pictures. The pictures must, in fact, be collected with the individuals of your class in mind. I aim at providing a real choice for each child and, since the stress is upon individual work, I insist that each child works from a separate picture. When younger children have chosen their pictures I give them a good five minutes to talk about them to their immediate neighbours; this will help them to respond more fully to the picture.

PROCEDURE

At this point I explain to the class that I am going to ask them some questions about the pictures; they won't have much time to answer them, so their responses must take the form of words, phrases, images, fragments of language. They must not answer in sentences. I am looking for rapid, fluent responses so they are not to worry at this stage about neatness, spelling or handwriting. If scrap paper and pencil would help them to write more freely, I would encourage them to use them. I tell them that after the last question I am going to ask them to write a poem, and I remind them that a poem does not need to rhyme and the lines do not need to be the same length. I also advise them not to use rhyme unless the impulse to do so is so strong that it hurts to resist it. It is important to indicate the kind of writing you are hoping for before they start; once they have begun writing nothing must interrupt the flow of their absorption.

I then put the following questions to the children, giving them two or three minutes to respond to each of them. (This pressure from time is important; Ted Hughes suggests in *Poetry in the Making,*

"These artificial limits create a crisis, which rouses the brain's resources: the compulsion towards haste overthrows the ordinary precautions, flings everything into top gear, and many things that are usually hidden find themselves rushed into the open. Barriers break down, prisoners come out of their cells.")

1. Write some words about why you chose your picture.
2. What is the main centre of attention in it?
3. Does it remind you of anything else? Is it like something?
4. Is there a second focus of interest?
5. Your picture is a frozen moment of time; a second before or after and it would have been slightly different. Write about the kind of movements you would see if it were part of a film or part of life.
6. When you get movement you usually get noise. Write about the noises or silences in your picture.
7. We have concentrated upon two senses, sight and sound. The other three may not apply to all of the pictures but take each one in turn, smell, touch (the feel, surfaces of things) and taste, and if it is relevant write about it.
8. Does the picture remind you of anything that has happened to you, some memory, experience or dream? If it does write about it.
9. Now, using your notes if you want to, write a poem.

The object of these questions is to take the child into the sensuous detail of his picture. Questions 1, 3, 8 have an additional, important significance because they are attempting to link the picture with some genuine source of memory or feeling inside the child; when such a link is established the possibilities of a worthwhile poem being written are greatly increased. I insist upon a period of complete silence after these questions so that the poems have a chance to germinate and be written; the length of this concentration in silence will depend upon the age of the children. I have experienced with groups of adults a most moving period of nearly an hour in which the silence and the concentration grew perceptibly thicker every minute.

RESPONSES

A boy in an A-Stream class of 3rd Year Juniors chose a black and white picture of a procession of demonstrators walking against the wind along Blackpool front. His response to the questions was:—

1. because of the sea in the night
2. the main things in this picture is people walking in the streets
3. it reminds of demonstrating
4. dark and white clouds moving
5. clouds moving, people walking, cars moving
6. car engine, feet on the pavement, flags swaying
7. the fishy smell of the sea
8. (no answer).

The first draft of his poem was:—

The silver sea in the distance,
and clattering footwear hitting the ground,
but the pier is as still as a tree,
the clouds moving over the water,
The road looks cold and frozen.

As the flags and banners sway
but still the shimmering waters are silver
and the smell of seaweed,
And the clouds are still the same.

When he showed his poem to me I asked him whether all the "ands" and "buts" at the beginnings of lines were necessary and pointed out that it would need a title if it were to stand on its own apart from the picture. His final version of the poem was as follows:

DEMONSTRATION BY THE SEA
The silver sea in the distance,
Clattering footwear hitting the ground,
But the pier is as still as a tree,
The clouds move over the water,
The road looks cold and frozen.

The flags and banners sway,
But still the shimmering waters are silver,
and the smell of seaweed
And the clouds are still the same.

Kevin Brown

This is only one out of innumerable ways of making a start. Its value to me lies in that it focuses upon detail and it endeavours to draw upon resources of feeling—the two essential elements that provide the material out of which a poem may emerge. The all important thing is that children should have their eye sensitively upon the object. I have come to feel that any deliberate teaching of rhyme patterns, stanza structures and formal rhythms is an inhibiting distraction for most children and tends to deflect their attention from the source of stimulus. The most fruitful, creative discipline of language comes in the attempt to be faithful in word, rhythm and image to the experience.

QUESTIONS FOR DISCUSSION

1. Do you think that Robbins's exercise might best be given after the student has had considerable exposure to various forms and styles of poetry? Or can it be used with students relatively inexperienced at reading poetry?

2. What are the principal assumptions about poetry that are built into the questions Robbins asks of students? Do you share these assumptions? Where does Robbins seem to think that poetry ''comes from''?

3. Do you agree with Robbins's view of the kind of directions that should be given to the student before the exercise is assigned? If not, what directions would *you* give?

4. Would you have responded as Robbins did to the first draft of the boy's poem that he prints here? If not, how would you have responded?

The Creative Thrust of Poetry Writing
Ruth Kearney Carlson

One essential in the teaching of poetry is to familiarize students with a wide range of poetry—poetry on varied subjects and in many forms. A teacher, therefore, needs information on where to find poems. Moreover, in order for teachers of English to acquaint students with the richness of other cultures, they need to know sources for the literature of these cultures.

In the following article, Ruth Kearney Carlson offers extensive information about the sources for such poems. She also articulates a set of values for teaching poetry and suggests some emphases for classroom work on poetry writing. The reader might consider whether her goals in the teaching of poetry, and her ways of working toward these goals, differ appreciably from those of the other writers represented in this section.

Ruth Kearney Carlson is at California State University at Hayward.

Several years ago the poet John Ciardi published an illuminating article entitled "The Shock of Recognition" which appeared in the October, 1953 volume of the *Journal of the American Association*

From *Elementary English* Vol. 49, No. 8 (December 1972), 1177–86. Copyright © 1972 by the National Council of Teachers of English. Reprinted by permission of the publisher and the author.

of University Women.[1] In this article Ciardi stated that the two things which must distinguish all successful art are Humanity and Technique. Neither is enough without the other.[2] These crystal-clear words by Ciardi help to illuminate most of the aspects of poetry creation. At present thousands of children in various schools of the United States are expressing themselves with emotion or feeling, but rarely does their poetry reflect poetic techniques which interrelate Art and Humanity. Too often these poets express an emotional intensity in a way that sound and sense are not communicated to the listener or reader. Ciardi feels that some significant effort adds a dimension to "ourselves and of the world." When one is reading through a poem and discovers a new and meaningful organization of experience, he recognizes a new part of himself. In other words he discovers something about himself that he has not known previously. This has been called "the shock of recognition" by Ciardi.[3]

One aspect of this "shock of recognition" comes from experiences which teach us to enlarge our imaginations and expectations. Our artistic experiences should cause us to utilize our senses and perceptions to the fullest extent.

In discussing poetry, the Japanese have used a term *ushin* which incorporates subjectivity, a sincerity of feeling with an objectivity of transcendental beauty. Shin Kei who lived from 1399–1471 states in his *Sasamegoto:* [4]

A certain man asked a master poet, "As for the Way of Poetry, what sort of training is necessary?" He answered, "The Crescent moon over the tall grasses of a withered moor." This was pointing to something unsaid, something bleak and lonely, that is to be intuitively grasped.

[1] Ciardi, John. "The Shock of Recognition" in *Journal of the American Association of University Women,* October, 1953, Volume 47, pages 10–14.
[2] *Ibid.,* page 10.
[3] *Ibid.,* page 11.
[4] Blyth, R. H. *A History of Haiku.* In two volumes. Volume Two, From Issa up to the Present. Japan: The Hokuseido Press. Imported and distributed by Japan Publications Trading Co., Rutland, Vermont, 1964, xi.

This style of poetic expression so beautifully grasped by the Japanese poet is depicted in various patterns of Oriental poetry including *haiku, tanka* and some *renga* verse. In most poetry of this type one has an *encounter* with something in the environment of the creator. In order to *encounter* something such as the "crescent moon," "the tall grasses" and the "withered moor" one must have a living awareness of those things in his milieu. Such awareness does not place man apart from the object viewed or sensed; a poet is so intensely aware that he becomes a part of that object. The few phrases by Shin Kei such as "crescent moon," "over the tall grasses," and "a withered moor" also give a sense of loneliness and bleakness—a feeling which must be intuitively grasped by the poet.

A Japanese *haiku* poem is a prose poem which frequently appears in 17 syllables arranged in a 5,7,5 syllabic pattern when it is translated into English. However, *haiku* of the highest quality is more than a syllabic pattern or a word game. These words are a breath of experience, phrases which are unfinished gaps of information which are completed by the reader or listener. Good *haiku* is seasonal in nature or shows a relationship of the poet to something in nature. Nothing is too insignificant to be noticed whether the poet is describing blades of grass, a thudding temple bell with its peak of snow, or a hopping cricket resting on the back of a frog. *Haiku* expresses an image as clearly sketched as a Japanese *Haiga* painting with its open spaces. Some of the criteria of a good *haiku* verse are: immediacy of experience, a nature theme, a symbol for a season, a simplicity of statement, a clear-cut image, and a sensitivity toward the importance of all things in life. A chapter by the author entitled "Dragonflies and Frogs" appearing in *Literature for Children: Enrichment Ideas* offers characteristics of Oriental patterns of verse as well as several activities for pupils and teachers.[5]

The greatest intensity of experience with nature consists of direct experiences such as study trips to a bay or the ocean; observations of flowers, trees, and insects; or multi-sensory experiences with frogs, toads, and butterflies. However, rigid organization patterns

[5] Carlson, Ruth Kearney. *Literature for Children: Enrichment Ideas.* Dubuque, Iowa: William C. Brown Company Publishers, 1970.

of classrooms sometimes prevent direct experiences. Two movies are now available which help to bring objects of nature to the classroom. These are "The Day Is Two Feet Long" (Weston Woods Company) [6] and *"Haiku, An Introduction to Poetry"* (Coronet Films). [7]

A modern sophisticated expression of experience consists of telegraphic terse, pictorial statements by Reps entitled *Gold and Fish Signatures.* [8] These poems express two basic ideas which are an identification and feeling for all things around us—a mosquito, the fish, wild birds, a grass blade, experiencing rain, a butterfly world and a "root drinking in the dark." Most of the ideas are rather sophisticated and are perhaps designed for mature pupils. These picture poems or bits of calligraphy also offer an economy of statement, a feeling that an imaginative image can be communicated through incorporating a few words into a rough statement with a paint brush.

The *tanka* verse is a five-line pattern of Oriental verse arranged in a 5,7,5,7,7 poetic pattern of 31 syllables in all. It has many of the same qualities as *haiku* but the form is not quite so delicate as two additional lines of seven syllables each are added. Some children create tanka verses in pairs. One child writes the *haiku* or *hokku* which consists of the first three lines of the poem, and a partner caps the verse with two lines of seven syllables each known as the *ageku.* More information on the tanka verse form appears in such books as *Sparkling Words: Two Hundred Practical and Creative Writing Ideas* [9] and *Writing Aids Through the Grades* by Ruth Kearney Carlson. [10]

Another interesting form similar to the *haiku* and *tanka* ones is known as the *lanterne.* This is a syllabic pattern of 1,2,3,4,1 sylla-

[6] Rubin, Peter, Conceived and Directed by. "The Day Is Two Feet Long," a cinematic Haiku. Weston, Connecticut: Weston Woods Company.

[7] *Haiku, An Introduction to Poetry.* Chicago: Coronet Films.

[8] Reps. *Gold and Fish Signatures.* Rutland, Vermont, U.S.A. and Tokyo, Japan: Charles E. Tuttle Company, 1969.

[9] Carlson, Ruth Kearney. *Sparkling Words: Two Hundred Practical and Creative Writing Ideas.* Berkeley: Wagner Printing, 2603 San Pablo Avenue, 1968 printing, Dist. by NCTE.

[10] Carlson, Ruth Kearney. *Writing Aids Through the Grades.* New York: Teachers College, Columbia Press, 1970.

bles arranged in the shape of a Japanese lantern. It is possible to join several verses together in the form of a linked or chained lantern also. This creates a more complete story. Two examples of the chained lantern appear in *Language Sparklers for the Intermediate Grades*. [11] These are "Trees" and "One Small Egg." The first three verses of "One Small Egg" follow:

ONE SMALL EGG
One
Small egg
Freckled gray.
Warmed by mother
Crack!

◆ ◆ ◆
Crack
Crack, Crunch
a small hole
Crack, its larger
Eyes

◆ ◆ ◆
Crack!
A mouth
A small head
A small gray wing
Peep!

Then the child continues to give the cycle of life until another egg is laid and another baby bird is born.

Another form of verse which was created originally by an American poet, Adelaide Crapsey, is the cinquain form. This has a syllabic pattern of 2,4,6,8 and 2 syllables. This has the iambic pattern but the iambs come naturally as syllables. Adelaide Crapsey was an invalid most of her life and lived in Saranac. Her poems sometimes included allusions to mythological or biblical figures, but young children have difficulty in incorporating this quality. Most artistic cinquains have a poignant quality, a sense of the transient quality of life.

[11] Carlson, Ruth Kearney. *Language Sparklers for the Intermediate Grades.* Berkeley: Wagner Printing Company, 2603 San Pablo Avenue, 1968.

David McCord has described the cinquain (sin-cane) in his volume *For Me to Say* [12] which also includes such forms as the tercet, villanelle, ballads, clerihew, as well as haiku. This same technique was followed in his earlier book entitled *Take Sky: More Rhymes of the Never Was and Always Is.* [13] In *Take Sky* a section entitled "Write Me A Verse" introduces Professor Swigley Brown who teaches such poetic forms as the couplet, quatrain, limerick, and triolet.

Lee Bennett Hopkins has used the cinquain form as a means of motivating urban children to write verses about their experiences in Harlem schools. Later, he experimented with this form in various schools throughout the country. The best of these poems appear in *City Talk.* [14]

Poetic styles which have been quite neglected in many anthologies for children are ones created by American Indian poets living in clans and tribes in various geographical portions of the United States. In recent years, scholars are becoming more conscious of cultural contributions offered by various Indian artists. There is no one American Indian poetic style, but individual variations amongst various Indian people.

The Indian poet considered his poetry a vital part of his existence and sang his "words of power" to help him to live a life of whole beauty. Although the Indian medicine man or shaman used herbs and fetishes to heal the ill, he also incorporated his chants and rituals in a poetic manner and the words offered him a sense of power. The Indian sang his songs or ritual poems to bring rain to the parched crops, to thank the sun for its light and warmth, and to help the corn to grow from rocky soil. Most Indian poetry has two basic qualities. Some poems are abbreviated terse statements of pictorial power similar to the *haiku* picture poem. The other poetic style consists of a lengthy poem with many refrains or repetitive phrases. An Indian poet also felt close to nature and had a direct

[12] McCord, David. *For Me to Say: Rhymes of the Never Was and Always Is.* Drawings by Henry B. Kane. Boston: Little, Brown and Company, 1970.
[13] McCord, David. *Take Sky: More Rhymes of the Never Was and Always Is.* Drawings by Henry B. Kane. Boston: Little, Brown and Company, 1962.
[14] Hopkins, Lee Bennett, Compiled by. *City Talk.* Photographs by Roy Arenella. New York: Alfred A. Knopf, 1970, page 26.

encounter with his experience. Quite often an Indian poet personified an object or used colorful images or symbols which were understood by listeners enjoying his words. An example of this is "A Song of Gotal," a part of the Gotal Ceremony of the Mescalero Apache which was formerly sung at dawn on the last day of a ritual used for the initiation of adolescent girls. This song appears in *The Sky Clears: Poetry of the American Indians* by A. Grove Day.[15]

A SONG OF GOTAL

The black turkey-gobbler, under the East, the middle of his tail; toward us it is about to dawn.

The black turkey-gobbler, the tips of his beautiful tail; above us the dawn whitens.

The black turkey-gobbler, the tips of his beautiful tail; above us the dawn becomes yellow.

The sunbeams stream forward, dawn boys, with shimmering shoes of yellow;

On top of the sunbeams that stream toward us they are dancing.

At the East the rainbow moves forward, dawn maidens, with shimmering shoes and skirts of yellow dance over us.

Beautifully over us it is dawning.

Above us among the mountains the herbs are becoming green;

Above us on the tops of the mountains the herbs are becoming yellow.

Above us among the mountains, the shoes of yellow I go around the fruits and herbs that shimmer.

Above us among the mountains, the shimmering fruits with shoes and skirts of yellow are bent toward him.

On the beautiful mountains above it is daylight.

Much poetry of various Indian tribes expresses the beautiful in life such as a symbol of the turkey gobbler which spreads its tail feathers to greet the dawn.

Another poem of beauty is a Tewa poem, "Song of the Sky Loom" which appears in *American Indian Prose and Poetry,* an anthology edited by Margot Astrov.[16]

[15] Day, A. Grove. *The Sky Clears: Poetry of the American Indians.* New York: The Macmillan Company, 1951, p. 83. This volume also appears in paperback published by the University of Nebraska Press, Lincoln, Nebraska.

[16] Astrov, Margot, Edited by. *American Indian Prose and Poetry.* New York: Capricorn Books, 1962. Originally published as *The Winged Serpent.*

The sky loom symbolizes a small desert rain. The Tewa song goes on to say:

> Then weave for us a garment of brightness.
> May the warp be the white light of morning.
> May the weft be the red light of evening.
> May the fringes be the falling rain.
> May the border be the standing rainbow.
> Thus weave for us a garment of brightness.
> That we may walk fittingly where birds sing.
> That we may walk fittingly where grass is green.
> O our Mother the Earth, O our Father the Sky.[17]

Another volume for adults is *American Indian Poetry: An Anthology of Songs and Chants* edited by George W. Cronym.[18] The Indian poet feels that poetry is song and music which come together, and the Navaho poet in "Song of the Earth" states:

> All is beautiful,
> All is beautiful,
> All is beautiful, indeed.[19]

Four books which have Indian poetry and have been published for children during the past year are *In the Trail of the Wind: American Indian Poems and Ritual Orations,* edited by John Bierhorst;[20] *The Trees Stand Shining, Poetry of the North American Indians* selected by Hettie Jones;[21] *I Breathe a New Song: Poems of the Eskimo,* edited by Richard Lewis,[22] and *2-Rabbit, 7 Wind:*

[17] *Ibid.,* p. 221.

[18] Cronym, George W., Edited by. *American Indian Poetry: An Anthology of Songs and Chants.* With an introduction by Mary Austin. Illustrated by J. B. Platt. New York: Liveright, 1962.

[19] *Ibid.,* p. 139.

[20] Bierhorst, John, Edited by. *In the Trail of the Wind: American Indian Poems and Ritual Orations.* New York: Farrar, Staus and Giroux: 1971, Illustrated with period engravings selected by Jane Byers Bierhorst.

[21] Jones, Hettie, Selected by. *The Trees Stand Shining.* Paintings by Robert Andrew Parker. New York: The Dial Press, 1971.

[22] Lewis, Richard, Edited by. *I Breathe a New Song: Poems of the Eskimo.* Introduction by Edmund Carpenter. Illustrations by Oonark. New York: Simon and Schuster, 1971.

Poems from Ancient Mexico Retold from Nahuatl Texts by Toni de Gerez.[23] Each of these volumes gives young writers models of poetry chanted or created by tribes or clans of American Indians. The book by Toni de Gerez depicts little known facts about the cultural life of Indians at the time when Spanish conquistadors conquered Mexico. Ancient Nahuatl texts told the songs and thoughts of the "coyote hungry-for-wisdom" people. Here is a sample of a Nahuatl poem translated into English:

Listen!
I am the singer . . .
look how my song
bends down over the earth
in the house of butterflies my song is born.[24]

Some other examples of Eskimo songs and poetry appear in the Winter 1970 issue of *The University Review,* a publication of the University of Missouri, entitled "Writers in the World Tradition of English Literature," which has been edited by Priscilla Tyler.[25] This includes "The Song of the Seal" by Jimmy Killigvuk, "The Whaler's Moon" by Howard Weyahok and "Not a Lately Song" by Lorraine D. Koranda.

Pupils who wish to create poetry in the style of an American Indian group might do the following. First, they should study the customs and rituals of an American tribe. They should learn some of the geographical characteristics of the land where the Indians lived. In some cases they might study the myths or legends of a particular clan or tribe as much Indian poetry is interlinked with myths and tales. A fourth step might be the poetic style which could include a poetic image or an extended image such as the turkey gobbler for night and dawn or the sky loom for the trickling rain. Almost all Indians of the southwest used a repetitive refrain or a repetition of

[23] De Gerez, Toni. *2-Rabbit, 7-Wind: Poems from Ancient Mexico Retold from Nahuatl Texts.* Designs in second color from ancient motifs. New York: Viking, 1971.
[24] Viking Books Brochure, Viking Junior Books, Spring, 1971, page 13.
[25] Tyler, Priscilla. "Writers in the World Traditions of English Literature" *The University Review,* a Publication of the University of Missouri. Vol. 37, Number 2, December, 1970.

phrases in poetic songs and rites. A fifth step could be the selection of a theme related to life or nature such as ''Chant for the Growing Beans,'' or ''A Song of the Polar Bear.'' Then the child poet could attempt to create a poem modeled after a sample poem published in some of the sources previously mentioned.

In recent years modern pupils have enjoyed experimenting with many of the poetic styles utilized by modern poets. One of the patterns which is quite popular is a form of visual poetry described by various names but commonly known as concrete poetry. One of the most thorough descriptions of this type of verse appears in a volume edited by Mary Ellen Solt entitled *Concrete Poetry: A World View.*[26] An introduction to the volume states that an International Exhibition of Concrete and Kinetic Poetry was held in 1964 which distinguished three types of concrete poetry: visual or optic, phonetic or (sound) and kinetic (moving in a visual succession). Some poets speak of either visual or sound poetry but in most cases concrete poetry uses reduced language words, syllables, or letters. The concrete poet is concerned with the arrangement of words on a page and feels that his object is to be perceived rather than to be read. In the words of Solt: ''The visual poem is intended to be seen like a painting; the sound poem is composed to be listened to like music.'' [27]

John Hollander has experimented with poems organized into specific patterns or shapes on the page. Several of these poems have been printed in *Types of Shapes.*[28] The first poem is arranged in the shape of a key on the page and words about unlocking the heart ''tight in a coffer of chest.'' Another poem is written in the shape of a light bulb and is about darkness and light. Another verse is shaped like a bell. A section on concrete poetry and related experimental poetry forms appears in *Writing Aids Through the Grades.*[29]

One term for much of this poetry is shaped whimsey. This is a story of a poem typed or printed in a certain shape and the shape is the subject of the poem. A cut-out shape of a raindrop formed from

[26] Solt, Mary Ellen, Edited with an Introduction by. *Concrete Poetry: A World View.* Bloomington: Indiana University Press, 1968.

[27] *Ibid.,* p. 7.

[28] Hollander, John. *Types of Shapes.* New York: Atheneum, 1969.

[29] Carlson, Ruth Kearney. *Writing Aids Through the Grades, op. cit.,* pages 109–119.

construction paper might be the shape for a poem on "Raindrops Coming Down." An umbrella painted wi colors might symbolize the visual form of a rain storm. grade child created a poem titled "All Alone" and p words in the shape of an Egyptian pyramid.

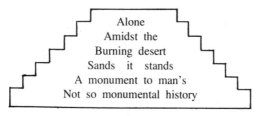

Alone
Amidst the
Burning desert
Sands it stands
A monument to man's
Not so monumental history

A younger child created a large blue and orange ball and placed it at the top of the stairs.

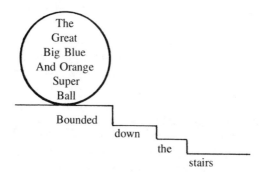

The
Great
Big Blue
And Orange
Super
Ball

Bounded

down

the

stairs

Another poem was shaped on a huge white cloud with the words:

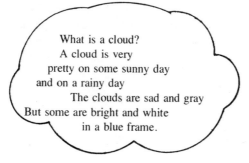

What is a cloud?
A cloud is very
pretty on some sunny day
and on a rainy day
The clouds are sad and gray
But some are bright and white
in a blue frame.

Many poems can be attractively arranged through experiments with calligraphy. For instance, a child can paint an outline of a huge dinosaur or unicorn. Then, he can create a poem about the dinosaur or unicorn and print his poems within the outline of the animal. An interesting book which correlates poetry and calligraphy is *Words and Calligraphy for Children* by John W. Cataldo.[30] An interesting chapter, "Poem and Image" discusses the painting-poetry experience which shows shadows. As another activity children are asked to choose a word from a list of several words and to paint a personal idea of the word in watercolors. After the painting is finished, the child is asked to write a paragraph about the word. For instance, one child selects the word "Fear" and expresses his ideas in a large green painting. The child then writes a paragraph about a huge monster which is rushing toward her causing such fear.[31]

The classroom teacher can motivate most children to create poems of many styles if models are provided. The poet uses words as an artist uses a palette of colors. A part of the act of creating a poem is a personal individual act of the child author. However, the teacher may help the child to investigate words and their nuances and the tunes which words and phrases sing. Words in the aural context of the poem and words in spatial relationships are used in different contexts. Some word growth occurs in repetitive auding experiences in which a child listens attentively and creatively to the reading of poetry by his teacher, his peers, his parents, or by professional actors and poets. The listener should become attuned to words and phrases which are fresh and original. He should avoid the use of clichés like a plague. Some poems by Eve Merriam appearing in the book *It Doesn't Always Have to Rhyme* offer a facility in word usage which is pleasant and amusing. Words are placed together in fresh relationships. For instance, the poem, "Mr. Zoo" describes a man through the characteristics of various animals such as being a "lionhearted man," "a roadhog in his car" and "a bear

---

[30] Cataldo, John W. *Words and Calligraphy for Children*. New York: Reinhold Book Corporation, 1969.
[31] *Ibid.,* unpaged.

for work." [32] Several poems such as "Nym and Graph" discuss homonyms and homographs cleverly.

Another author who helps pupils increase their word facility and imaginative power is Mary O'Neill. She has authored numerous books which facilitate the self-expression of pupils. An early volume, *Hailstones and Halibut Bones: Adventures in Color* [33] has motivated thousands of pupils and adults to create color poems. A second book *What Is That Sound!* makes pupils more cognizant of sound images such as the squeak of leather or the clang of a chain.[34] A volume *Fingers Are Always Bringing Me News* [35] causes authors to be more cognizant of tactile images. *Words Words Words* by the same author depicts words in many clever ways which differentiate between delight, joy, and happiness. Mary O'Neill states that many of the "loveliest things, have never yet been said." [36] A somewhat different book by the same author is *Winds*.[37] This book poetically depicts winds in many guises and includes "Sirocco," a hot wind from the Libyan desert which blows across the Mediterranean Sea. The poet discusses such clouds as cirrus, cumulus and stratus and helps pupils to visualize clouds in various shapes and forms.

Another poet, Natalia Belting introduces young prospective authors to words in a context which cleverly depicts an idea or image. She also presents the aural imagery of words arranged on lines in poetic tunes and phrases. *The Sun Is a Golden Earring,* presents poetic metaphors which reenact beliefs of persons ranging in habitat from Siberia to Malaya. The Milky Way is compared with a "long-stitched seam" by the people in Siberia and the "Sky is a tent

[32] Merriam, Eve. *It Doesn't Always Have to Rhyme.* Drawings by Malcolm Spooner. New York: Atheneum, 1964, p. 12–13.
[33] O'Neill, Mary. *Hailstones and Halibut Bones: Adventures in Color.* Illustrated by Leonard Weisgard. New York: Doubleday and Company, Inc., 1961.
[34] O'Neill, Mary. *What Is That Sound!* Drawings by Lois Ehlert. New York: Atheneum, 1966.
[35] O'Neill, Mary. *Fingers Are Always Bringing Me News.* Drawings by Don Bolognese. New York: Doubleday and Company, 1969.
[36] O'Neill, Mary. *Words, Words, Words.* With decorations by Judy Piussi-Campbell. New York: Doubleday and Company, 1966.
[37] O'Neill, Mary. *Winds.* Illustrated by James Barkley. Garden City, New York: Doubleday and Company, 1971.

roof.'' [38] A similar book by the same author is *The Stars Are Silver Reindeer* which presents numerous images and metaphors of the stars and constellations.[39] A third poetic volume by Belting is *Calendar Moon*.[40] All of these volumes include words used poetically and beautifully by the author.

In addition to books which use words with facility, child authors can enjoy reading modern poems in such a book as *Faces and Places. Poems for You* selected by Lee Bennett Hopkins and Misha Arenstein.[41] Pupils can read poetry in this book for pure enjoyment, but they can also re-read many poems to look for fresh unhackneyed ways of describing things and feelings. For instance, in "Shells," Lilian Moore depicts "shells caught in green weed hair." In "Night Train" Adrien Stoutenburg speaks of a train as "yellow lights running across the darkness with a sound of many black doors slamming in a long hall." [42]

In addition to poetry books offering sights and sounds of words, teachers can provide for developmental activities which assist young authors in finding ways to use words poetically. Robert A. Wolsch has included a chapter, "Using Language Poetically" in a book of practical teaching suggestions entitled *Poetic Composition through the Grades*.[43] It has previously been stated that poetic composition of a high quality requires both artistic techniques and a sense of humanity. During the past few years adults are becoming increasingly more aware of the words of childhood and youth. Perhaps there is a generation gap, but older persons are struggling to narrow the non-communicative space between old age and youth. Numerous poems written by urban pupils are being publicized in books with a nationwide circulation. Some of these vol-

[38] Belting, Natalia. *The Sun Is a Golden Earring.* Illustrated by Bernarda Bryson. New York: Holt, Rinehart and Winston, 1962.
[39] Belting, Natalia. *The Stars Are Silver Reindeer.* Illustrated by Esta Nesbitt. New York: Holt, Rinehart and Winston, 1966.
[40] Belting, Natalia. *Calendar Moon.* Illustrated by Bernarda Bryson. New York: Holt, Rinehart and Winston, 1964.
[41] Hopkins, Lee Bennett, and Misha Arenstein. *Faces and Places. Poems for You.* Illustrated by Lisl Weil. New York: Scholastic Book Services, 1971.
[42] *Ibid.*, p. 54.
[43] Wolsch, Robert A. *Poetic Composition through the Grades,* A Language Sensitivity Program. New York: Teachers College Press, Teachers College, Columbia University, 1970.

umes are therapeutic ones including poems about the hates and anxieties of youth in a topsy-turvey world. Many poems are vignettes of inhumane persons forcing suffering persons to endure their poverty. A few poems reflect a bitter antagonism between a Black adolescent poet and the white man who relegates his Black brother to menial positions such as those of a shoe shine boy or a scrub woman. Such poems appear in *I Heard a Scream in the Street: Poems by Young People in the City* selected by Nancy Larrick.[44] Another book edited by Nancy Larrick is *Somebody Turned on a Tap in These Kids.*[45] This volume includes chapters by such poets as Myra Cohn Livingston, Claudia Lewis, June Jordan, Richard Lewis, and Eve Merriam as well as ones by many others. It also includes a chapter "Straight Talk from Teenagers" by Warren Doty, Samuel Robinson and Students. Some of this "straight talk" will disturb persons unfamiliar with the open language of ghetto youth who wish to debunk the pretentious, hypocritical ways of schools and society.

Another book of this same type is *The Voice of the Children* collected by June Jordan and Terri Bush.[46] This volume includes both poetry and prose written by twenty-six Brooklyn authors from nine to seventeen years of age. The writings were created in a Saturday morning writer's workshop directed by June Jordan and Terri Bush. Some of the writing is beautiful, often the words are bitterly resentful, but these young poems express themselves in a clear, authentic style.

Another similar book is *Stuff: A Collection of Poems, Visions and Imaginative Happenings from Young Writers in Schools—Opened & Closed,* edited by Herbert Kohl and Victor Hernandez Cruz.[47]

---

[44] Larrick, Nancy, Selected by. *I Heard a Scream in the Street, Poems by Young People in the City.* Illustrated with Photographs by Students. New York: M. Evans and Company Incorporated, 1970.

[45] Larrick, Nancy, Edited by. *Somebody Turned on a Tap in These Kids: Poetry and Young People Today.* New York: Delacorte Press, 1971.

[46] Jordan, June, and Terri Bush, Collected by. *The Voice of the Children.* New York: Holt, Rinehart and Winston, Incorporated, 1970.

[47] Kohl, Herbert, and Victor Hernandez Cruz, Edited by. *Stuff: A Collection of Poems, Visions & Imaginative Happenings from Young Writers in Schools—Opened & Closed.* Illustrations by Sean Chappell and Phillip Crowder. New York: The World Publishing Company, 1970.

A volume which indicates a few motivational devices used to stimulate writing is *Wishes, Lies, and Dreams: Teaching Children to Write Poetry* by Kenneth Koch and the Students of P.S. 61 in New York City.[48] Koch says that he does not really teach children to write poetry but he helps them to find their own feelings, spontaneity, sensitivity, and inventiveness.[49] He helps remove the barriers of rhyme. Koch has many imaginative assignments which he describes in this book. Children are assisted in eliminating clichés by helping them to enter into an experience from another viewpoint such as how might you hurt people if you were the snow? Children collaborate on poetry creations as partners and in some instances all of the children in a class work cooperatively on one class poem. Koch has pupils create noise poems by two techniques. First they are asked to make comparisons of sound by thinking of things which are alike. Then they write whole lines which imitate a particular sound. As Koch continues to work with these poems, he teaches children to create sestinas which were invented by Arnaut Daniel. These are poems of 39 lines.[50]

Numerous suggestions have been made of ways to bring more artistry to the creation of better children's poems. Poetry experiences should be organized in a way to free young authors from too much supervision by adults; yet it is hoped that pupils can breathe new songs similar to those created by primitive Eskimo and Nahuatl poets who looked for a world of beauty rather than one of junkies, garbage, poverty, and hatred between races. Some day the urban child of the ghetto may leave his despair and dark bitterness behind.

Perhaps some inspiration can come from *Talkin' About Us: Writings by Students in the Upward Bound Program,* edited by Bill Wertheim with the assistance of Irma Gonzales.[51] In this volume appears a description of a lesson which grew out of an assignment,

---

[48] Koch, Kenneth, and The Students of P. S. 61 in New York City. *Wishes, Lies and Dreams: Teaching Children to Write Poetry.* New York: Chelsea House Publishers, 1970.

[49] *Ibid.,* p. 25.

[50] Koch, pages 222–223.

[51] Wertheim, Bill, Edited by, with the Assistance of Irma Gonzales. *Talkin' About Us: Writings by Students in the Upward Bound Program.* New York: New Century, Educational Division, Meredith Corporation, 1970.

"The Responsibility of Being Human." Marti V. J. J. Hilyard expressed herself in "A Letter to My Sister" which concludes with the words:

> I cannot give you my eyes that you might see the world that I see, nor can I give you the dreams that I dream. You cannot give me yours. I can but offer my hand and my heart and together we will find our own identities, our own worlds, and our own dreams. And though our hands may separate, our hearts will beat the same beat together in a warm south wind.
>
> Love
Marti [52]

As teachers work alongside the child to increase his potential creative powers, it is hoped that ways can be found to create artists who will accept the responsibility of being human.

QUESTIONS FOR DISCUSSION

1. Carlson sets forth an aesthetic theory for children's poetry— one that puts a good deal of emphasis on the aptness of form and technique to what is said. Do you accept this theory of children's poetry?

2. Do you share Carlson's opinion that experiments with poetic forms, including concrete poetry and shaped forms of other kinds, can help children to investigate words—their sounds, their nuances, their usefulness in recording experiences? In your own education, or in your work with students, what evidence have you seen of the value of such experimentation?

3. Carlson implies that reading and listening to poetry help children understand the values of different forms of *language*. How is this understanding helped, if at all, by the assigning of poems reflecting social bitterness and racial hatreds? Is there, as Carlson implies, value in asking students to read pieces by embittered and alienated members of society?

[52] *Ibid.*, page 101.

Selected Rhymed Forms
Robert Wolsch

This excerpt from Wolsch's study of ways to teach poetic composition to children at various ages mentions some additional verse forms and presents examples of children's accomplishments in these forms. Children need subjects for use within these or any other forms, and Wolsch suggests a few possible subjects.

SELECTED RHYMED FORMS

There are several varieties of rhymed patterns which are suitable for elementary school composers. They include the jingle, the limerick, the clerihew, and the ballad.

Jingles

Jingles are playful, easily remembered verse forms in which more emphasis is placed on sound than on sense. Some famous ones are:

Hickory, dickory, dock . . .
Eeny, meeny, miny, mo . . .
Rueben, Rueben, I've been thinking . . .

Other kinds of jingles include:

Nursery rhymes: Little Miss Muffet
Songs: war songs—(The King of France went up the hill)
       romantic lyrics—(Where are you going, my pretty maid?)
       popular songs—(Where, oh where has my little dog gone?)
       lullabies—(Rockabye baby)
Street cries: Peanuts, popcorn, cracker jacks. Hey, get your cold
  drinks.
Historical personages: Lucy Locket
Words accompanying games: Here we go round the mulberry bush
Counting-out-rhymes: One, two, buckle your shoe

Teachers show that jingles jingle and bounce as suggested by the word jingle. These verse forms consist usually of a succession of sounds or a repeated phrase. Children usually enjoy writing, listening to, or reading them. They have a place in the compositional diet of youngsters, like multi-colored "sprinkles" add to the delights of certain desserts. Jingles are not to be equated with the term poetic composition and served as a total poetic diet. They might, instead, be saved for special times and places like birthdays, holidays, when someone needs cheering up, to spoof, or to play with language.

Limericks

Limericks have been popular for more than two hundred years. They are as unbending as an English castle, the country in which they seem to have started. The limerick is a predesigned form well suited to humorous and nonsensical subjects. It has a highly metrical bounce, moves swiftly, and has the set rhyme scheme of *aabba*. The final line is often a variation of the first line. Some modern limericks include a witty final line, a "punch line," rather than merely a repetition of the first. The surprise ending is often intensified by the last line rhyming with the first two lines instead of the third and fourth. The ideas often move from possible in line 1 to improbable in line 5.

There was an old teacher of math
   In such need of a dunk in the bath
   That when she described
   A perpendicular side
We all held our noses and laughed.

Robert, grade 7

Some youngsters get caught up in the spirit of composing limericks. No sooner do they finish one than they are off working on another:

Little Zachary Zump
   Sat on his camel's hump
He slipped and fell
   Right down a well
Did little Zachary Zump.

Little Zachary Zump
   Sat on a tiny stump
He started to drink
   Some red and green ink
And fell over kerplunk.

Billy, grade 3

Limericks often begin with a subject, a name, or a locality, such as these:

There was a young fellow
   named Ben,

or

On the way to
   Washington

Teachers may wish to remind children that limericks may also be used as a literary form of poking fun, or as another way of playing with language. Limericks draw attention to real or imaginary situations and people.

Clerihews

A clerihew is a humorous verse form consisting of two couplets of unequal length. Often a ridiculous biography or satire, the humor is developed in a "deadpan" manner. The silly or trivial is usually treated with pomposity.

C. Columbus
Sailed by compass
He left his insignia
Somewhat East of India

Robert, grade 7

C. Ovington Bloomer
Started a football rumor
Joe Namath can't throw
And the Jet team is slow

Kenny, grade 5

Clerihews are fun, too. Teachers who have used jingle and limerick forms may want to experiment with this relatively new verse form. Some youngsters may want to design verse forms that bear their own name. Others might experiment with the names of famous historical personages, or popular movie, sports, or television personalities.

Notice what is often included in the clerihew: a recognizable name, something about an accomplishment, and a personal reaction to this accomplishment.

Ballads

Ballads are usually story poems. Using the plain language of the common people, they describe dramatic situations with repetitive meters and refrains. Put to music, sung, or danced to, they are akin to folk songs, work songs, sea chanties, cowboy songs, lullabies, play games, chants, spirituals, blues, and school songs. They may add great interest to the classroom.

Subjects for ballads are everywhere. They may focus on superstitions, ghosts, heroes, and villains. They can be sad, funny, realistic, or nonsensical. They may be spiritual and uplifting or mean and biting, but they are usually impersonal. The characteristics are repetition, dialogue, action verbs, plain language, little description, short stanzas. Some are made up of couplets, tercets, and a refrain imposed between the strong lines. When a quatrain is used, the second and fourth lines often rhyme *abcb*. Additional lines may round out the ballad.

Some ballads form from a solo line followed by a single response.

> Can I stay home from school today?
>   No, you can't my darling.
> Can I go out in the street to play?
>   No, you can't my darling.
> Can I skip my meat and eat my pie?
>   No, you can't my darling.
> Can I sock my brother in the eye?
>   No, you can't my darling.
> No, you can't. No you can't.
>   No, you can't my darling.

Allan, grade 5

Robert used firsthand experiences for his ballad. He used a single idea, a follow-up idea, and a nonsense refrain:

> Johnny got spanked and his brother went, "Nyaa, nyaa."
> Bing-bang boppity no no.
> Then he got spanked and he cried, "Waa, waa."
> Bing-bang boppity, no, no.
> Bing-bang boppity no no.
> Bing-bang boppity no.

Robert then decided to use the same theme with another meter:

Bing-bang the baby cried, "Waa waa"
Bing-bang the baby cried, "Waa."
Nyaa nyaa the brother teased, "Nyaa, nyaa"
Nyaa Nyaa, Waa Waa
They both cried Waa.

Robert, grade 6

Blues. Blues are a special kind of ballad. They may be about failures, lonesomeness, school, parents, boredom, fear, living conditions, world conditions, despair. Blues are personal. The first line is often repeated twice, followed by a second rhyming line to complete the thought. The following came from a fourth grader after the teacher had discussed the subject of blues.

I cried last night
  When mom closed my door
I cried last night
  When mom closed my door
Tonight I'll cry no more, no more.

Franklin, grade 4

Narrative ballads. The next selection exemplifies the use of the quatrain in a lengthy narrative ballad-like poem.

THE BATTLE FOR KING'S MOUNTAIN
In the Southern Carolina hills there stands a mountain bold,
On which the Tories and Rebels fought, is how the legend's told;
The mountain boys and patriots, 900 stalwart men
Advanced upon the Britishers, 1100 then.

Clad in buckskin, armed with a rifle, the men for Liberty
Defied King George and all his troops as their personal enemy.
Then the signal, a wild war whoop, rang out upon the hill,
And rebel riflemen charged in to get the finishing kill.

But then from the redcoat lines, there burst a withering fire
Which blazed down on the Patriots and forced them to retire,

Then with fixed bayonets, the British assaulted in vain,
But were shot down where they stood, so they bled, lest they be slain.

Regrouping with their leaders the Rebels invaded again,
And with their prize "sharpshooters," "picked off" the Englishmen
While under the barrage of a fire a solitary man
Stole past the Tory sentry to the powder wagons ran.

Then seizing a barrel of powder with his tomahawk he split,
And to the redcoat lifeline a glowing spark was lit.
The wagons with a deafening roar disappeared in smoke,
Whence the British troops surrendered and King George's morale broke.

In 1776 a Declaration signed,
Gave the citizens a nation, a nation in its prime
The Americans fought and struggled to make their country free,
And secured a land of promise from sea to shining sea.

Bill, grade 6

So lengthy a narrative poem is not common in the elementary school.

Work songs. Work songs are interesting topics for class discussion. Poetry has always accompanied work and play. Children have endless poems for rope skipping, ball bouncing, and rowing. Some compose poems and work songs for snow shoveling, grass cutting, garbage can lugging, bed making, carpet sweeping, dish washing, window washing, sweeping, and rope climbing. Some teachers read work songs of various occupations and times and allow children to compose their own related to their social studies units, their chores, their fears, their boredom, and their victories as they relate to work experiences.

Harry, a fourth grader, made the following observation on sweeping:

SWEEPING
Push on the broom
Push on the broom
Watch all the dirt
Fly away zoom.

Helen, John, and Sylvia also wrote songs for work and play.

DISH WASHING
Dishes, swishes
    Look what we just ate
Dishes, swishes
    Rinse away the plate
Now the plates
    are nice and clean
Cleanest plates
    I've ever seen

Helen, grade 4

ROPE CLIMBING
Hand over hand
Hold on with your feet
When you get the knack of it
You will say it's neat!

John, grade 7

ROPE JUMPING
Rink-a-dink-a
Choppa-choppa
Bing-bang Boo
I love me
Do you love you?

Sylvia, grade 3

QUESTIONS FOR DISCUSSION

1. What additional subjects or topics might be useful for children to write about in the forms Wolsch presents?

2. What kinds of classroom exercises would encourage children to work in these forms? Might you consider having children work in groups to compose pieces in these forms?

Exploring Poetry Patterns
Iris Tiedt

This article supplements Carlson's and Wolsch's discussions of various kinds of poetry by providing information about several other short forms, including free verse, haiku and cinquain. Tiedt teaches at the University of Santa Clara in California and is currently editor of *Language Arts* (formerly *Elementary English*).

Many teachers are finding that students of all levels of ability respond with enthusiasm and success to the writing of poetry. In order for students to enjoy writing poetry, however, it is important that first experiences be pleasantly rewarding. For this reason the forms introduced should be sufficiently simple so that emphasis can remain on the ideas to be expressed.

FREE VERSE

Beginning experiences with free verse will lead the child to compose verse that is simple and expressive. Without the need to pro-

From *Elementary English* Vol. 47, No. 8 (December 1970), 1082–84. Copyright © 1970 by the National Council of Teachers of English. Reprinted by permission of the publisher and the author.

duce rhyming lines, the child can concentrate on ideas and images. Poets whose work can be used to introduce children to free verse include: Carl Sandburg, Hilda Conkling, E. E. Cummings, and Walt Whitman. Here is one selection from the sensitive poetry of Hilda Conkling.

DANDELION
O little soldier with the golden helmet,
What are you guarding on my lawn?
You and your green gun
And your yellow beard,
Why do you stand so stiff?
There is only the grass to fight!

Children will enjoy developing their own ideas in poetry form in this manner.

ANIMALS
Animals can be big.
Animals can be little.
They can be red and yellow,
And blue, and all colors.
They bite and play.

Laura Janetsky
Teacher: Frances H. Emery

The child who produces this little poem in the primary grades is developing a positive attitude toward poetry. She will continue to enjoy poetry as her taste and ability mature. Included here, too, are these examples of delightful imagery as children wrote about the moon.

The moon is a white rabbit
Jumping up and down.
While we are asleep,
It jumps up;
And when we wake,
It jumps down.

Robert Rogers

The moon is a sun drowsing,
  but never going to sleep
The stars are faces in the sky.
Time is how long it takes you
  to do your homework.

Phyllis Dyer
Teacher: Mrs. Norville

Whitman's *Leaves of Grass* also provides many excellent passages for stimulating the writing of free verse. The following picture of a stallion is a good example to use with older students.

A gigantic beauty of a stallion, fresh and responsive to my caresses,
Head high in the forehead, wide between the ears,
Limbs glossy and supple, tail dusting the ground,
Eyes full of sparkling wickedness, ears finely cut, flexibly moving.
His nostrils dilate as my heels embrace him,
His well-built limbs tremble with pleasure as we race around and return.

After reading the description of this proud stallion, students can select an animal to describe in a similar manner. Examination of this example of free verse will show them that there is no rhyme and that there is no set pattern or rhythm. The free variation of the length of lines, form, and content permits emphasis to remain on the thoughts to be expressed. Students can also experiment with patterning their lines like those of Whitman.

HAIKU

Haiku, the ancient form of Japanese poetry that has been discovered by modern writers, offers another interesting possibility. Sans rhyme and artifice, the haiku form consists of three short lines totalling seventeen syllables. Originating in thirteenth century Japan, haiku generally follows these specifications:
  1. The poem consists of only three lines patterned as follows:
     a. Line 1–5 syllables
     b. Line 2–7 syllables
     c. Line 3–5 syllables

2. The season, location, and references to nature are usually included in the poem.
3. There is no rhyme.
4. Few articles or pronouns are used.

Translations from the ancient masters are available in different editions of haiku collections some of which are listed in the bibliography. This example by Kyoshi appears in *Cricket Songs.*

Lightly a new moon
Brushes a silver haiku
On the tips of waves.

Even young children are able to compose delightful haiku that compare favorably with those written by adults. Here is one by a fourth grade child.

The snowflakes fell hard.
The ground was covered with them;
Not one flake the same.

Martha
Teacher: Doris Schade

CINQUAIN

The cinquain, a simple five-line verse form, has been attributed to Adelaide Crapsey, a minor American poet who was the author of *Verse* published by the Manas Press in 1914. This verse consists, as the name suggests, of five lines which may be patterned in this manner.

Line 1: One word (which may be the title)
Line 2: Two words (describing the title)
Line 3: Three words (an action)
Line 4: Four words (a feeling)
Line 5: One word (referring to the title)

A third grade boy wrote this cinquain:

Bed—
Soft, warm,
Fun, bouncy, tumbling,
Fun on my bed;
Comfortable.

Mike McCord
Teacher: Frances H. Emery

MORE INVENTED PATTERNS

If you become enthusiastic about having students write poetry, as I have been, you will find yourself searching for additional patterns to challenge students who have become involved in the composition of poetry. It was this search that led to my creation of four new poetry patterns that have proved to be very successful frames for ideas. While lending some structure, a pleasant patterning, the framework is not dominant or confining.

The diamante (dee ah mahn' tay) is a seven-line diamond-shaped poem that follows this pattern:

It is suggested, furthermore, that the poem be developed according to the following specifications:

Line 1: subject noun (1 word)
Line 2: adjectives (2 words)
Line 3: participles (3 words)
Line 4: nouns (4 words)
Line 3: participles (3 words)
Line 2: adjectives (2 words)
Line 1: noun-opposite of subject (1 word)

Notice that this poem creates a contrast between two opposite concepts as in the following example:

Air

Balmy, soft,

Floating, wafting, soothing,

Typhoon, wind, gale, cyclone

Twisting, howling tearing,

Bitter, cold

Blast.

Vera Harryman

A second innovated form is the Septolet which consists of 7 lines (14 words) with a break in the pattern as indicated.

Kitten

Padding stealthily

Amongst green grasses

Most   intent.

Bird

Ascends   rapidly

Causing great disappointment.

Beverly Oldfield

The Quinzaine (kan zen′) consists of 15 syllables in 3 lines (7, 5, 3) which make a statement followed by a question, thus:

Boys screaming in the distance—
When will they drop to stillness
  On this dusk?

Irma Johnson

The Quintain (kwin ten′) is a syllable progression: 2, 4, 6, 8, 10, as illustrated here:

Poems
Read for pleasure
Before the bright firelight
Words meant for all those who enjoy
Delightful, soothing, lovable music.

L. Wille

Students, too, can experiment with the invention of new verse patterns. As they develop new patterns, others in your classes can be invited to try using these poetry forms. Students will find that poetry provides a stimulating means for expressing their ideas.

BIBLIOGRAPHY

Behn, Harry, *Cricket Songs*. Harcourt, 1964.

Conkling, Hilda, *Poems by a Little Girl*. Stokes, 1920.

Dunning, Stephen, et al., *Reflections on a Gift of Watermelon Pickle*. Scott, Foresman, 1966.

Henderson, Harold G., *An Introduction to Haiku*. Doubleday, 1958.

Lewis, Richard, comp., *In a Spring Garden*. Dial, 1965.

Lewis, Richard, comp., *Miracles*. Simon and Schuster, 1966.

Mizumura, Kazue, *I See the Winds*. Crowell, 1966.

Sandburg, Carl, *Early Moon*. Harcourt, 1930.

Sandburg, Carl, *Wind Song*. Harcourt, 1960.

Tiedt, Iris M. and Sidney W. Tiedt. *Contemporary English in the Elementary School*. Prentice-Hall, 1967.

Walter, Nina, *Let Them Write Poetry*. Holt, 1962.

QUESTIONS FOR DISCUSSION

1. Tiedt suggests that students often be encouraged to observe limiting formal patterns when learning to write poetry. Do you think that this method is helpful, or do you feel that children should find their own forms in poetry?

2. Does the effort to observe a formal pattern stifle a young writer's effort to find a way of communicating his ideas and feelings? If the writer has to attend to his form, does he take his eye off his subject or adjust what he wants to say to fit the form? What is your experience (as writer, or as teacher) with this problem?

Let the Children Write
Margaret Langdon

Teachers of all grades face the problem of how to evoke fresh and honest writing from their students rather than stale clichés and dishonest posturing. Margaret Langdon, teacher at an "all-age" (mainly 12 to 16 years) school in England, gives an account of her teaching technique and how she came to discover it in her book *Let the Children Write*. The selection that follows describes the goals Langdon was seeking when she began to experiment with her new technique.

Though Langdon does not discuss the applicability of the techniques she discusses to the teaching of younger children, her method is worth studying for its possible usefulness in the elementary schools.

. . . In their written work, I felt that the children were using a medium which was unnatural to them—a stultifying, deadening medium, which made all their expression come out as from a sausage machine, in a string of dull, stodgy sausages of things which they thought they *ought* to write, and say and think.

From *Let the Children Write* (London: Longman Group Limited, 1961), pp. 4–18. Reprinted by permission of the publisher.

It was harder for me to bear the dullness of expression, because I have always been aware of the value of words. They excite me. At the same time, the relationship between truth and expression is very real to me, and I am uncomfortable when people try to cloak a hypocritical thought with a platitudinous phrase. I feel very strongly that people should think for themselves, and say what they think.

How was I to get this over to the children? Obviously they were being embarrassed by the conventional methods of expression which is expected from them at school. I knew they had the thoughts, the ideas, the experiences: how could I help them to express these in an acceptable educational form, without brushing the dust from the butterflies' wings as I did so?

Wordsworth talks of "emotion recollected in tranquillity," and it was from the idea of feeling that I started my search for a new expressive medium. Poetry is the natural medium of emotion in writing, but I knew at once that this was a dead end as far as modern children are concerned. In these days, if anything is more soul destroying than marking essays, it is teaching poetry to teenagers. Do you recognize (and I'm sure you do if you have had anything to do with children of twelve to sixteen years of age) that blank, withdrawn, politely supercilious look which curtains their faces when they feel that you are being particularly "square"? Any normal poetry lesson produces that look; so, firmly, my medium must be non-poetic.

Emotional, non-poetic, I was getting on a bit. What else?

Brevity, I felt, was an essential. Much as children loved to babble on in their talk, when it came to writing, any inspiration which they had, took wings when confronted by the stern "Two pages at least" or "Not less than 250 words." Have you seen children stop and count and add a bit more, and count again? And they are supposed to be creating! For normal essays, when asked, "How much have we to write?" I firmly insisted, "Start at the beginning and go on until you have reached the end." I felt that length should be no criterion of value.

Because of brevity, simplicity became an essential. All the padding, the filling in, the stretching out, of one poor small idea, could be left out, and the idea, stated clearly and briefly, could stand on its own merits—could even grow in stature because it had to be thought out clearly, in order to be expressed simply. One idea, or experience told simply in two words or two lines is surely better than two pages filled with meaningless words, written in order to fill the space. I thought of the dignity and simplicity of Biblical language and decided that I was on the right track.

All that I had to do now, was to perform the Heculean task of encouraging the children to recollect an emotional experience and express it briefly, simply and with honesty. It was the emotion part which gave me most trouble. How was I to get an emotion over, naturally, easily and without causing them to be embarrassed?

As these children were due to take an external examination in English, I felt I must continue their conventional lessons as normally as possible, but that I could spare one half-hour period a week to attempt a new, drastic experiment.

April 1st gave me my first real break.

*   *   *

It happened that April 1st was a weekday. For several years we have either been on holiday with an early Easter or, luckily, it has fallen on a Saturday. This year it fell on a school day and I could tell from the glint in the teenagers' eyes that they had not overlooked the fact. But they are only children after all, and shoe-laces, mysterious packages, empty egg-shells and imaginary spiders brought back my own childhood efforts. I could still remember vividly the horror with which I had tried to brush off that—Spider! Imaginary Spider! Here was my opportunity to produce a strong emotion, yet a completely unembarrassing one.

The class was waiting with its usual tolerant lethargy.

"You'll only want your exercise books and pens today," I said. I watched their faces curtain still more. A test, they thought.

"Look. There's a spider on the wall, a huge one. Quick—write down the first thing which comes into your head about it. Now—as quickly as you can."

Startled eyes jumped to the wall, incredulous eyes looked back at me. What is she getting at? April fooling?

"Make it brief and snappy—don't stop to think just write what *you* feel," I urged.

Hesitantly, at first, pens scratched on books, but before they had had time to cross out, correct or alter—

"Start on the next line, and say something about its body. Describe it as *you* see it."

This time they started more easily, a bit strange, but still—

"Another new line and write three adjectives about its legs."

"Now write of its web. Do you see any contrast between the spider and the web? Now round it off with a final sentence."

As they were writing, I stood silently, feeling the revulsion against the spider, real and intense, and hoping that some miracle would happen to cause these children to have the same feeling and to be able to write it down without any words having been given to them.

This time I prayed before I opened the books. "Please, just one. If only it has got through to just *one* of them."

SPIDERS
Spiders are horrible and ugly, the very thought
  of them sends shivers down my spine.
This one has a bloated body, black and brown,
Its legs are long and spindly and fine,
The web is beautiful, dew-spangled, delicate,
But it is a trap.
The fly, though small, fights frantically, fiercely.

Janet Stainer

The first sentence showed me that the feeling had got through all right. The words, chosen quickly and emotionally were firm, descriptive and real.

I turned to the next one.

A nasty spider is clinging to the wall.
His body is bulgy, squashy, bloated.

His legs are hairy, horribly black.
The web is precise and elegant, tucked away in a corner,
To catch an ugly fly, it is a pity to use so beautiful a web.
When the fly is caught, it is wrapped and stored away
For ugly, hungry spider.

Jennifer Pragnell

Here again, was the same grasp of words, as if the emotion itself supplied the right word almost without thought.

But these were girls, careful, anxious to please and to do the right thing. What of the boys? Deliberately I searched through the pile and found the book of a slapdash, careless boy whose work was a constant battleground for him and for me.

The spider is on the wall.
Quickly I hit it with a newspaper.
Its legs are long
They look ghostly in the dark.
Its body is fat, floppy and filthy,
Its web looks like a net,
A safety net in a circus.
The web catches the flies
The spider bites them,
And wraps them,
And keeps them,
Until it is hungry.

Philip Shears

This was more forthright than the girls' efforts, but here again was the same directness of expression and individuality of treatment which made these writings real and valuable.

Naturally I had the realist in the class who started rather accusingly, "I can't see a spider on the wall," but he went on:

I hate the things anyway.
With bent skinny legs.

Why do they have to be so swollen and stout?
The beautiful web is a merciless trap for flies,
They are a menace, a scrawny menace.

David Beale

So we were all satisfied.

Correction of the exercise, I found very simple. There were few
spelling mistakes and, apart from an occasional grammatical slip,
there was little to alter. One or two children, clinging to the conventional style, had found it difficult to break their work into lines,
and needed to be shown how much more effective the writing
looked if it was written out in this way, though, of course, if it was
well read, the effect would be the same however it was written, so
long as it was correctly punctuated. With regard to the "breaking,"
I was most interested to find that so many children, right from the
start, used a natural break with which to begin a new line, and that
these breaks succeeded in giving the sentence its right, emotional
value and balance. . . .

Though it was obvious that the children wrote a form of modern
verse, I never gave a hint that they were producing poetry, but now
I started to encourage them to be aware of their use of words.

THE SPIDER'S WEDDING
I sat on the barn's steps and watched the black spider coming towards
    me.
I felt like screaming
But I moved aside a little, and the dark creature went up a beam.
It stopped
And turned back
And stared at me, and stared.
It said,
"Move on. My business has nothing to do with you.
I shall stand here until you go."
So I moved on, looking back over my shoulder to see what it would do.
As it went on, I ran back silently to see.
After a few minutes, back the spider came
Proud now, with an air of arrogance.

By his side, walked shyly, another spider.
A new bride.
When they came by me they stood
And stared and stared,
Then they went on.
"Ha. A spider's wedding," I thought.

June Robinson

We had lessons, for instance, on alliteration, which some children had used quite naturally and effectively in their first attempts. These lessons were quite apart from the creative writing periods, and, though I hoped that the result would be transferred, I didn't labour the point when the children were engaged in the written work.

Throughout the year, I had insisted that the children read as much and as widely as possible. I barred nothing except the out and out "comic" and the modern, paper-backed travesty of a picture book. This, with the ever-present help of the television, had given the children a wide and good vocabulary, and I tried to encourage this by lessons on word associations and thought transference, showing how one word gives the thought of another. The children found this link most interesting to follow, with the natural result that their thoughts moved more freely and they discovered, to their surprise, that far from having not an idea in their heads as they had so often protested, having been given a start, ideas flowed in a most stimulating way and their thoughts quickened and became alive.

THE SPIDER
The spider is an ugly thing.
Its legs are long and hairy and jointed.
Its body is fat and ferocious,
It is not elegant at all.
I wonder that flies are attracted.
I would like to free the fly, but the spider might eat me.

Christopher Waters

The poem by June Robinson was written some weeks later than the above, as a piece of free writing but it was obviously inspired by the early stimulus.

*   *   *

The next thing to do was to give this new expression a name. No word with a poetical or emotional bias would do, and it was while I was actually talking to the children about their work that the word *Intensive* came into my head. I hesitated to use it at first, for fear they should not fully understand the meaning, but no other word seemed to express what I wanted quite so well, and, as it happened, the children used it easily and correctly right from the start, so "Intensive Writing" it became.

QUESTIONS FOR DISCUSSION

1. What is your own assessment of Langdon's technique of giving direct instructions to the children concerning the kinds of things they should write, line by line?

2. What other emotions do you think that children might be called upon to express, in intensive writing sessions, without embarrassment or sentimentality?

3. What is the relation of students' reading to effective writing, according to Langdon?

4. How can you tell the difference in children's writing between honest and dishonest emotions? How can you cultivate the expression of honest emotion?

Wishes, Lies, and Dreams
Kenneth Koch and the Students of P. S. 61 in New York City

All writers, children or adults, need to believe that they have something worth saying before they will care enough to set down their feelings. In order to achieve belief, writers need a perspective on experiences, a way of organizing or viewing them, that furnishes insights which can promise pleasure in writing. One task for a teacher, therefore, is to help children find ways of looking at their experiences that will stimulate their desire for expression.

In this selection, Kenneth Koch, a poet, playwright, and teacher of creative writing to adults, describes some stimuli he used with a group of elementary school students in a New York public school. What Koch discusses is partly a technique for organizing the work of a group of children, but, even more important, it is a set of approaches to experience, ways of defining experience, that children find congenial and that will encourage them to write what they themselves will accept as poetry.

I wanted to find, if I could, a way for children to get as much from poetry as they did from painting.

From *Wishes, Lies, and Dreams: Teaching Children to Write Poetry* (New York: Random House, 1970). Copyright © 1970 by Kenneth Koch. Reprinted by permission by publisher, author, and International Creative Management.

IDEAS FOR POEMS

My adult writing courses had relied on what I somewhat humorously (for its grade-school sound) called "assignments." Every week I asked the writers in the workshop to imitate a particular poet, write on a certain theme, use certain forms and techniques: imitations of Pound's *Cantos,* poems based on dreams, prose poems, sestinas, translations. The object was to give them experiences which would teach them something new and indicate new possibilities for their writing. Usually I found these adult writers had too narrow a conception of poetry; these "assignments" could broaden it. This system also made for good class discussions of student work: everyone had faced the same problem (translating, for example) and was interested in the solutions.

I thought this would also work with children, though because of their age, lack of writing experience, and different motivation, I would have to find other assignments. I would also have to go easy on the word "assignment," which wasn't funny in grade school. In this book I refer to assignments, poetry ideas, and themes; in class what I said was "What shall we write about today?" Or "Let's do a Noise Poem." My first poetry idea, a Class Collaboration, was successful, but after that it was a few weeks before I began to find other good ones. Another new problem was how to get the grade-school students excited about poetry. My adult students already were; but these children didn't think of themselves as writers, and poetry to most of them seemed something difficult and remote. Finding the right ideas for poems would help, as would working out the best way to proceed in class. I also needed poems to read to them that would give them ideas, inspire them, make them want to write.

I know all this now, but I sensed it only vaguely the first time I found myself facing a class. It was a mixed group of fifth and sixth graders. I was afraid that nothing would happen. I felt the main thing I had to do was to get them started writing, writing anything, in a way that would be pleasant and exciting for them. Once that happened, I thought, other good things might follow.

I asked the class to write a poem together, everybody contributing one line. The way I conceived of the poem, it was easy to write, had rules like a game, and included the pleasures without the anxieties of competitiveness. No one had to worry about failing to write a good poem because everyone was only writing one line; and I specifically asked the children not to put their names on their line. Everyone was to write the line on a sheet of paper and turn it in; then I would read them all as a poem. I suggested we make some rules about what should be in every line; this would help give the final poem unity, and it would help the children find something to say. I gave an example, putting a color in every line, then asked them for others. We ended up with the regulations that every line should contain a color, a comic-strip character, and a city or country; also the line should begin with the words "I wish."

I collected the lines, shuffled them, and read them aloud as one poem. Some lines obeyed the rules and some didn't; but enough were funny and imaginative to make the whole experience a good one—

> I wish I was Dick Tracy in a black suit in England
> I wish that I were a Supergirl with a red cape; the city of
>   Mexico will be where I live.
> I wish that I were Veronica in South America. I wish that I
>   could see the blue sky . . .

The children were enormously excited by writing the lines and even more by hearing them read as a poem. They were talking, waving, blushing, laughing, and bouncing up and down. "Feelings at P.S. 61," the title they chose, was not a great poem, but it made them feel like poets and it made them want to write more.

I had trouble finding my next good assignment. I had found out how to get the children started but didn't yet know how to provide them with anything substantial in the way of themes or techniques. I didn't know what they needed. I tried a few ideas that worked well with adults, such as writing in the style of other poets, but they were too difficult and in other ways inappropriate. Fortunately for me, Mrs. Wiener, the fourth grade teacher, asked me to suggest some poetry ideas for her to give her class. (I wasn't seeing them regularly at that time—only the sixth graders.) Remembering the success of the Collaborations, I suggested she try a poem in which every line began with "I wish." It had worked well for class poems and maybe it would work too for individual poems, without the other requirements. I asked her to tell the children that their wishes could be real or crazy, and not to use rhyme.

A few days later she brought me their poems, and I was very happy. The poems were beautiful, imaginative, lyrical, funny, touching. They brought in feelings I hadn't seen in the children's poetry before. They reminded me of my own childhood and of how much I had forgotten about it. They were all innocence, elation, and intelligence. They were unified poems: it made sense where they started and where they stopped. And they had a lovely music—

I wish I had a pony with a tail like hair
I wish I had a boyfriend with blue eyes and black hair
    I would be so glad . . .

Milagros Diaz, 4 [1]

Sometimes I wish I had my own kitten
Sometimes I wish I owned a puppy
Sometimes I wish we had a color T.V.
Sometimes I wish for a room of my own.
And I wish all my sisters would disappear.
And I wish we didn't have to go to school.
And I wish my little sister would find her nightgown.
And I wish even if she didn't she wouldn't wear mine.

Erin Harold, 4

It seemed I had stumbled onto a marvelous idea for children's poems. I realized its qualities as I read over their work. I don't mean to say the idea wrote the poems: the children did. The idea helped them to find that they could do it, by giving them a form

[1] Here, as elsewhere . . . the number following the child's name indicates the grade he or she was in when the poem was written.

that would give their poem unity and that was easy and natural for them to use: beginning every line with "I wish." With such a form, they could relax after every line and always be starting up afresh. They could also play variations on it, as Erin Harold does in her change from "Sometimes" to "And." Just as important, it gave them something to write about which really interested them: the private world of their wishes. One of the main problems children have as writers is not knowing what to write about. Once they have a subject they like, but may have temporarily forgotten about, like wishing, they find a great deal to say. The subject was good, too, because it encouraged them to be imaginative and free. There are no limits to what one can wish: to fly, to be smothered in diamonds, to burn down the school. And wishes, moreover, are a part of what poetry is always about.

I mentioned that I had told Mrs. Wiener to ask the children not to use rhyme. I said that to all my classes as soon as I had them start writing. Rhyme is wonderful, but children generally aren't able to use it skillfully enough to make good poetry. It gets in their way. The effort of finding rhymes stops the free flow of their feelings and associations, and poetry gives way to sing-song. There are formal devices which are more natural to children, more inspiring, easier to use. The one I suggested most frequently was some kind of repetition: the same word or words ("I wish") or the same kind of thing (a comparison) in every line.

Once I understood why the Wish Poem worked so well, I had a much clearer idea of what to look for. A poetry idea should be easy to understand, it should be immediately interesting, and it should bring something new into the children's poems. This could be new subject matter, new sense awareness, new experience of language or poetic form. I looked for other techniques or themes that were, like wishes, a natural and customary part of poetry. I thought of comparisons and then of sounds, and I had the children write a poem about each. As in the Wish Poems, I suggested a repetitive form to help give their poems unity: putting a comparison or a sound in every line. Devoting whole poems to comparisons and sounds gave the children a chance to try out all kinds, and to be as free and as extravagant as they liked. There was no theme or argument with which the sounds or comparisons had to be in accord: they could be experimented with for the pleasures they gave in themselves. In teaching painting an equivalent might be having children paint pictures which were only contrasting stripes or gobs of color.

In presenting these poetry ideas to the children I encouraged them to take chances. I said people were aware of many resemblances which were beautiful and interesting but which they didn't talk about because they seemed too far-fetched and too silly. But I asked them specifically to look for strange comparisons—if the grass seemed to them like an Easter egg they should say so. I suggested they compare something big to something small, something in school to something out of school, something unreal to something real, something human to something not human. I wanted to rouse them out of the timidity I felt they had about being "crazy" or "silly" in front of an adult in school. There is no danger of children writing merely nonsensical poems if one does this; the truth they find in freely associating is a greater pleasure to them—

A breeze is like the sky is coming to you . . .

Iris Torres, 4

The sea is like a blue velvet coat . . .

Argentina Wilkinson, 4

The flag is as red, white, and blue as the sun's reflection . . .

Marion Mackles, 3

Children often need help in starting to feel free and imaginative about a particular theme. Examples can give them courage. I asked my fourth graders to look at the sky (it was overcast) and to tell me what thing in the schoolroom it most resembled. Someone's dress, the geography book—but best of all was the blackboard which, covered with erased chalksmear, did look very much like it. Such question games make for an excited atmosphere and start the children thinking like poets. For the Noise Poem I used another kind of classroom example. I made some noises and asked the children what they sounded like. I crumpled up a piece of paper. "It sounds like paper." "Rain on the roof." "Somebody typing." I hit the chair with a ruler and asked what word that was like. Someone said "hit." What else? "Tap." I said close your eyes and listen again and tell me which of those two words it sounds more like, hit or tap. "It sounds more like tap." I asked them to close their eyes again and listen for words it sounded like which had nothing to do with tap. "Hat, snap, trap, glad, badger." With the primary graders [2] I asked, How does a bee go? "Buzz." What sounds like a bee but doesn't mean anything like buzz? "Fuzz, does, buzzard, cousin." The children were quick to get these answers and quick to be swept up into associating words and sounds—

A clink is like a drink of pink water . . .

Alan Constant, 5

A yoyo sounds like a bearing rubbing in a machine . . .

Roberto Marcilla, 6

Before they had experimented with the medium of poetry in this way, what the children wrote tended to be a little narrow and limited in its means—but not afterwards. Their writing quickly became richer and more colorful.

After the Comparison Poem and the Noise Poem, I asked my students to write a Dream Poem. I wanted them to get the feeling of including the unconscious parts of their experience in their poetry. I emphasized that dreams didn't usually make sense, so their poems needn't either. Wishes and dreams are easy to doctor up so they conform to rational adult expectations, but then all their poetry is gone.

[2] At P.S. 61 some first and second grade classes are combined in one primary grade.

Their Dream Poems contained a surprising number of noises, and also comparisons and wishes—

> I had a dream of a speeding car going beep beep while a train
> went choo choo . . .

Ruben Luyando, 4

> I dream I'm standing on the floor and diamonds snow on me.
> I dream I know all the Bob Dylan songs my brother knows . . .

Annie Clayton, 4

My students, it was clear, weren't forgetting things from one poem to the next; they had been able to write more vivid poems about their dreams because of the other poems they had recently written. To encourage them in combining what they knew, I next asked them to write a poem deliberately using wishes, noises, comparisons and dreams all together.

The Metaphor Poem, which I had the fourth graders write next, was a variation of the Comparison Poem, and more difficult than it, probably because it isn't as natural to children to make metaphors as to make comparisons; metaphors require an extra act of thought. Some children wrote Metaphor Poems and many wrote new Comparison Poems. Something of this kind which the children found easier was the Swan of Bees Poem, which required in every line not a *like* or an *as,* as in the Comparison Poem, but an *of.* The idea was to put in every line a strangely composed object, like a swan of bees. "Swan of bees" was a spelling mistake a third grader made in his Comparison Poem: he meant to write "swarm" but wrote "swan" instead. Believing that his error had created something interesting and beautiful, I wanted to share it with the class; I was pleased to have a live example of the artistic benefits that can come from error and chance. The children seemed to find the swan of bees as beautiful as I did, and when I proposed they write a poem full of such things they responded enthusiastically. Being able to create things out of no matter what suggested marvelous possibilities—

I have a sailboat of sinking water
I was given a piece of paper made of roses . . .

Eliza Bailey, 3

I had a dream of my banana pillow
And of my pyjamas of oranges . . .

Madelyn Mattei, 3

This was only one of many poetry ideas I had which were directly inspired by the children's work. After my students had written a few basic poems like Comparisons, Wishes, and Noises, I began to be guided more by my sense of where they were in their development as poets and what they might be ready for next.

A poetry theme that all my classes were ready for at this point was the contrast between the present and the past. To give their poems form and to help them get ideas, I suggested that they begin every odd line with I Used To and every even line with But Now. Like Wishes and Dreams, this poem gave the children a new part of experience to write about. It gave them a chance too to bring in comparisons, dreams, and other things they had learned—

I saw a red doll and feel I am red
But that was a dream . . .

Thomas Kennedy, 3

I used to be a baby saying Coo Coo
But now I say "Hello" . . .

Lisa Smalley, 3

I used to have a teacher of meanness
But now I have a teacher of roses . . .

Maria Ippolito, 3

Some of the content brought into their poetry by this theme surprised me. Among the primary and third graders metempsychosis was almost as frequent a theme as the conventionally observed past:

I used to be a fish
But now I am a nurse . . .

Andrea Dockery, 1

I used to be a rose but now I'm a leaf
I used to be a boy but now I'm a woman
I used to have a baby but now he's a dog . . .

Mercedes Mesen, 3

I used to be a design but now I'm a tree . . .

Ilona Baburka, 3

I had forgotten that whole strange childhood experience of changing physically so much all the time. It came very naturally into the children's poems once I found a way of making it easy for them to write about change—that is, by suggesting the pattern I Used To/But Now.

I gave other assignments in my first two months at P.S. 61, but these were the ones that worked out best. Each gave the children something which they enjoyed writing about and which enabled them to be free and easy and creative. Each also presented them with something new, and thus helped them to have, while they were writing, that feeling of discovery which makes creating works of art so exhilarating. The success of these particular assignments, as well as of some I gave later, was due partly to their substance and partly, I think, to the accident of my finding an effective way to present them. A child's imagination can be reached in many ways. Some ideas that didn't turn out so well, such as a poem about mathematics, would doubtless have worked better if I had been able to find a way to make them suggestive and exciting. In these first poems, in any case, I thought the children had come to like poetry, and had become familiar with some of the basic themes and techniques that make it so enjoyable to write.

The repetition form, which I often suggested they use, turned out to have many advantages. Repetition is natural to children's speech, and it gave them an easy-to-understand way of dividing their poems into lines. By using it they were able to give strong and interesting forms to their poems without ever sounding strained or sing-song, as they probably would have using rhyme. And it left their poetry free for the kind of easy and spontaneous music so much appreciated by contemporary poets, which rhyme and meter would have made impossible—

> I wish planes had motors that went rum bang zingo and would be streaming green as the sea . . .
>
> *Argentina Wilkinson, 4*

> One of the saddest things are colors because colors are sad and roses are sad two lips are sad and having dates is sad too but the saddest color I know is orange because it is so bright that it makes you cry . . .
>
> *Mayra Morales, 3*

Children can be fine musicians when the barriers of meter and rhyme aren't put in their way.

Another strategy I'd used more or less instinctively, encouraging the children to be free and even "crazy" in what they wrote, also had especially good results. They wrote freely and crazily and they liked what they were doing because they were writing beautiful and vivid things. The trouble with a child's not being "crazy" is that he will instead by conventional; and it is a truth of poetry that a conventional image, for example, is not, as far as its effect is concerned, an image at all. When I read "red as a rose," I don't see either red or a rose; actually such a comparison should make me see both vividly and make me see something else as well, some magical conjunction of red and rose. It's another story when I read "orange as a rose" or even "yellow as a rose"—I see the flower and the color and something beyond. It is the same when one writes as when one reads: creating in himself the yellow and the rose and the yellow rose naturally gives a child more pleasure and experience than repeating a few words he has already heard used together. As I hope I've made clear, the best way to help children write freely is by encouragement, by examples, and by various other inspiring means. It can't be done by fiat, that is, by merely telling them to be "imaginative and free."

The best poetry assignments I found in my second stint at P.S. 61 (December 1968 to February 1969), like these first ones, added something new to what the children could write about and did it in a way that interested and excited them. My first December visit to the school was during a snowstorm, and I thought there would be considerable sentiment for a snow poem. To help the children avoid wintry Christmas-card clichés I proposed that instead of writing about the snow they write as if they were the snow, or rather the snowflakes, falling through the air. I said they could fall anyplace they liked and could hurt and freeze people as well as make them happy. This made them quite excited. Children are so active and so volatile that pretending to be something can be easier for them than describing it—

> If I were the snow I would fall on the ground so the children could pick me up and throw me into the air . . .
>
> *Ana Gomes, 6*

> We would cover the sun with clouds so it could not melt us . . .
>
> *Carmine Vinciforo, 6*

Later they wrote poems about animals and objects, and for these poems too I suggested that they be the animal or object rather than describe it—

> I'm the floor of a house. Everytime someone steps on me I laugh . . .
>
> *Billy Constant, 4*

A Lie Poem worked out very well. I asked the children to say something in every line which wasn't true, or to simply make the whole poem something not true. I know "lie" is a strong word; I used it partly for its shock value and partly because it's a word children use themselves. "Fantasy" is an adult word and "make-believe" has fairytale and gingerbread associations that I wanted to avoid. The Lie Poem, like the Wish and Dream Poems, is about how things might be but really aren't—though, as in Jeff Morley's "The Dawn of Me," it can lead to surprising truths.

Color Poems—using a different color in every line, or the same color in every line—were a great hit. The children had been using colors in their poems all along and they liked devoting whole poems to them—

> Yellow, yellow, yellow. The sky is yellow. The streets are yellow. It
> must be a yellow day . . .

Elizabeth Cabán, 5

I also had the children write poems while listening to music. The school had a phonograph on which I played for my different classes records by De Falla, Ravel, Mozart, and Stravinsky, while they wrote images and lines which the music suggested to them. The immediacy of the music, like that of the snowstorm earlier, was inspiring—

> This whole world appears before me.
> I wish to soar like a bird in the yellow-green sky . . .

Ruben Marcilla, 6

> I was looking at the sun and I saw a lady dancing and I saw myself
> and I kept looking at the sun then it was getting to be nighttime then
> the moon was coming up and I kept looking at it it was so beauti-
> ful . . .

Ileana Mesen, 4

My fifth grade class wrote two sestinas. The sestina is a seemingly difficult form, but acutally the only hard thing about it is remembering the order in which the six end-words are repeated. I did the sestina as a class collaboration: I wrote the end-words, in proper order, on the blackboard, and asked the students for lines to fit them. This way the children got the pleasure of solving the puzzle aspect of the poem—making their lines and ideas fit the form—without the troublesome remembering part. The sestina taught the children something new about the poetic possibilties of repeating individual words. Erin Harold's ''Gardentail,'' which was written a week later, I think shows its influence:

Gardenia's walking over Nellie
And Gardenia is a mouse
Her tail's still over Nellie
Who would rather step on tail
Gardenia's walking through the grass
But her tail is still on Nellie
Gardenia's going uphill
Gardenia's going downhill
She's wading through a stream . . .

Erin Harold, 5

There are other strict forms—the pantoum, for example—which could be made easy for children to write and would teach them something they would enjoy using in other poems.

A poetry idea which, like I Used To / But Now, brought a new part of their experience into the children's poetry, was one about the difference between how they seemed to other people and how they felt they really were. I suggested a two-line repeating form, as in the Used To Poem: I Seem To Be / But Really I Am. The sixth graders were particularly affected by this theme, being at an age when private consciousness and social image are sometimes seriously different. For one thing, there are hidden sexual and romantic feelings which one doesn't confess—

I seem to be shy when she passes by but inside of me I have a wonderful feeling . . .
As we went for a walk in the park I felt a wet kiss hit my dry skin.

Robert Siegel, 6

Other contrasting themes I thought of but haven't yet tried are I
Used To Think / But Now I See (or Know); I Wish / But Really; I
Would Like / But I Would Not Like.

I asked my students to write poems using Spanish words, which
delighted the Spanish-speaking children and gave the others an experience of the color and texture of words in another language. I
chose Spanish because so many children at P.S. 61 speak it, and I
wanted them to be able to enjoy their knowledge of it. There is
such emphasis in the schools on teaching Spanish-speaking children
correct English that the beauties and pleasures of the Spanish language are usually completely forgotten. I chose twenty Spanish
words in advance, wrote them on the board, and asked the children
to include most of them in their poems. This worked out best in the
fifth-grade class, where I asked the students to invent a new holiday
(it was near Christmas) and to use the Spanish words in describing
its main features—

On my planeta named Carambona La Paloma
We have a fiesta called Luna Estrella . . .
We do a baile named Mar of Nieve . . .

Marion Mackles, 5

   . . . the estrellas are many colors
And the grass is verde.

Esther Garcia, 5

The children were not limited to the words I wrote on the board; I
told them they could write their whole poem in Spanish, and some
did.

The best assignments to begin with, I think, are Class Collaborations, Wishes, Comparisons, Noises, Lies, and Colors. Children are excited by all of them, and each can show them some of the special pleasures of poetry. Many other assignments are possible, of course, aside from the ones I've described. Among those Ron Padgett used at the school were collaborative poems by two students and poems about what you could see with a third eye. At Muse, David Shapiro had the children write poems while he played the violin; another time he borrowed a white mouse from the Muse live animal collection and had each child hold it in his hand and then write a poem about what it would be like to be a mouse. The success of any assignment depends upon how one goes about presenting it and more generally how one approaches the whole subject of teaching children to write.

QUESTIONS FOR DISCUSSION

1. What are some other organizing ideas or verbal formulas that children might enjoy using in writing poems?

2. Are there any dangers or disadvantages in asking children to perform specific poetic "assignments"—i.e., to use particular forms and to repeat words or phrases within those forms? Does this sort of activity depress children's ability to find new ideas and perspectives for themselves? Why or why not?

3. Do you share Koch's reluctance to encourage children to seek rhyme in their poems?

4. At the end of this selection, Koch says, "The success of any assignment depends upon . . . how one approaches the whole subject of teaching children to write." How does Koch approach the subject? What characterizes his way of working with children? Does it differ from the approaches suggested by other authors in Part II? Is Koch indeed "teaching" children to write?

A Model for Writing Adventure Stories
Patrick Groff

Most of the articles in this section have dealt with the writing of poetry, but poetry is by no means the only form of imaginative expression from which a child in elementary school can profit. The writing of stories also allows children to explore and test different constructions of their world. But some children, as Patrick Groff, Professor of Education at California State University, San Diego, points out, will not find story writing easy and will need encouragement and help.

Groff proposes that teachers offer such students a model, such as a fairy tale, for writing a story. He assumes that having a plan to work with will help even the most uncertain writer since it will offer him or her a ready guide to the invention of material. Groff's proposal has the support of scholarship, for folklorists argue that "fairy tales" have had, across cultures, quite similar structures; these discoveries lead one to speculate on whether it might be possible to locate other "types" of fiction for which one might build models that might help the hesitant young writer to get started. The question a teacher faces in considering whether to use such a model is whether it will suppress the distinctive, individualistic, imaginative activity of students. On this issue it will be useful to consider Leslie Whipp's comments (p. 302ff) (and also the comments in a different context in his "Morning Haze," which follows on p. 241).

From *Elementary English* Vol. 46, No. 3, (March 1969), 364–67. Copyright © 1969 by the National Council of Teachers of English. Reprinted by permission of the publisher and the author.

During written composition we are confronted with some rather pit-eous appeals from desperate-sounding children:

"I don't know what to write."

"I don't know what to write about."

"I can't think of anything to write."

"I can't think of anything else to write." and so on.

All too often this seeming despair and obvious pleading com-mences almost as soon as the class has settled down to write. When "Jimmy," for example, raises his hand the teacher can invariably predict he is about to make such an entreaty. Experienced teachers realize, of course, such comments from some children can be in-terpreted in many ways. Jimmy's repeated calls for help can be a signal that he is truly frustrated in his attempts to string together on paper the thoughts that run so quickly through his head. When this is so, he obviously needs and should get some help.

What kind of help is useful in this situation? From the nature of such pleas we know it will have to be specific above all. And it surely must be immediately applicable by the reluctant writer. May I propose that help can be given such children in the form of a spe-cific writing model they can follow. This is a visible structure that will stand still long enough for them to supply details to its specific outline. This model will allow the child to deal with just one part of a story at a time. He will need to keep in mind only the details of it part-by-part. Thus he can delay his thinking of the bits and pieces of subsequent parts of his story until later.

Certain kinds of stories have been found to have such specific models. For example, it was discovered some time ago by a Rus-sian folklorist, Propp, that fairy tales contain certain stable and con-stantly reoccurring elements or parts.[1] Propp found, furthermore, that the sequence or the time of occurrence of these elements or "functions" in fairy stories was also constant. That is, the sequence of "happenings" from fairy tale to fairy tale was found to be the same, to be identical. The sequence was not accidental, as one might suppose; not in a different order in different stories.

This evidence allows us to construct a model for the faltering

[1] Propp, V., *Morphology of the Folktale*. Bloomington: Indiana University, Trans-lated in 1958. Written in 1928.

young writer to follow when he wants to write an imaginative or fanciful adventure story. If he can follow the model it may help him write longer, more intricate, and consequently more self-gratifying stories.

Good to know is that the usefulness of this guide or model is not restricted by the characters or scenes of action the child decides to use in any story he writes. He may use as many and any characters or scenes he wishes, although these are ''stock'' characters, obviously. Propp showed that all fairy stories do have a hero (a good guy) and a villain (a bad guy). There also will be here a provider, someone who gives the good guy what he needs. There may be some person of power, authority, or responsibility to tell the good guy he should or should not do something. There is often seen some victim of the bad guy (besides the good guy), and some helper of the good guy. In the fairy tale we also see the sought-for person or object, often a princess or half a kingdom, magical agent in some form—an animal, an object, a special power.

THE SEQUENCES OR FUNCTIONS

The pattern, or order of events, in which characters can perform in a story becomes one guide for the structural approach. The actions or functions in the model are these:

1. The good guy is introduced. Who he is, what he does, who he associates with, his group, his family, where he lives is told.

2. One of the members of the good guy's group, associates, or family is shown to be missing or absent or dead.

3. The good guy is ordered, urged, warned, or bidden not to do something, or to do something. This is usually done by a person of power or authority.

4. This request or order given to the good guy is disobeyed by him.

5. The bad guy makes a sudden appearance. He asks someone some questions, the answers to which he hopes will aid his evil purposes. He disappears.

6. The bad guy gains some information through persuasion, magic or deception about those he would harm. This usually includes the good guy.

7. The bad guy tries to trick the good guy in order to take something the good guy has. Here the bad guy can be dressed or disguised as someone else.

8. The good guy is tricked, hurt, and unknowingly helps the bad guy.

9. The bad guy "harms" a person in the group to which the good guy belongs or one the good guy likes. This harm can be stealing from, spoiling things, kidnapping, trickery, using a "spell," fighting, threatening, tormenting, causing an expulsion of someone, as well as hurting physically. (*All the previous actions prepare for this one, create the possibility of its occurrence, or facilitate its happening.*) and/or

9a. One member of the good guy's group lacks or needs something.

10. The good guy learns about what has happened or of the need. Being the good guy means he must help, of course. He may be torn between fear and honor, fear and honesty, ambition and loyalty, pride and love, etc.

11. The good guy decides what he will do. He must make a self-sacrifice and this must be made for the sake of someone else. This task may be given the good guy. In modern stories at this moment of decision the good guy must *not* be able to see or reason his way through. This is the "dark moment" of the story. Often a strong reversal or twist in the good guy's behavior is necessary for him to come to the decision as to what must be done. *At this point the direction of view of the story is not to what has happened, but to the future—what will happen.*

12. The good guy leaves the place he is in in order to carry out his plans.

13. On his way the good guy meets someone who can help him. To get this help he must either answer correctly questions this person asks, do a good deed, or pass a test of strength given him.

14. The good guy passes the test.

15. The good guy gains, receives, or takes a magical object or agent from the person who tested him. This can also be some special scientific know-how or machine in stories of modern times.

16. The gaining of this object or agent helps the good guy get to where he wants to go.

17. The good guy meets the bad guy. They fight or contend.

18. The good guy is hurt or mastered in the fight somewhat.

19. The bad guy is beaten or loses out. He can be killed, captured, may escape, or admits his faults.

20. The misfortune seen in item number 9 is straightened out.

21. The good guy returns to his home or to join his friends or group.

22. On the way the good guy is set upon by either the bad guy, the bad guy's friends, or by some mysterious being or force.

23. The good guy escapes, is hidden, or hides from his attackers. He sometimes has the magic to change into someone else to elude them.

(A great many fairy tales end at this point.)

24. The good guy arrives home but is not recognized.

25. As a test to prove who he is the good guy is asked to perform a difficult task involving physical danger, quickness of wit, a test of his strength or endurance, or his powers of magic.

26. The good guy accomplishes the task.

27. Now he is recognized as the good guy.

28. The bad guy, who is on the scene, does something that reveals he is the bad guy.

29. The good guy is given something for his work or efforts.

30. The bad guy is punished.

31. The good guy is given a new position or job of importance, or traditionally, the hand of the princess. This may be gaining full or social status.

The following is an example of a story outline deliberately set in very modern times but based on the fairy tale outline. The numbers in the story, (1) etc., refer to the numbers described above.

(1) A pilot on a space team is working on some special equipment. (2) His helper on the equipment gets sick and must go home. (3) The pilot's boss tells him not to get too close to the equipment. Doing this makes one see everyone as friendly for a short time. (4) In his work the pilot disobeys. (5) On the bus home the helper meets a strange man who questions him about his work. (6) The effects of the equipment cause the helper to tell some secrets. (7) This strange man calls the pilot on the phone and gets some more secrets since the pilot, too,

is affected. (8) The pilot gives the man some information. (9) The strange man visits the helper's house and after knocking him out steals more secrets. (10) The helper tells the pilot about this. (11) and (12) The pilot decides to go searching for the stolen information. (13) and (14) He convinces a scientist who he is. (15) The scientist gives him a powerful machine to help him find the thief. (16) This helps him find the thief. (17) They fight. (18) The pilot is hit a few times. (19) He overcomes the thief, and (20) gets back the secrets. (21) On the way home (22) a friend of the thief tries again to get the information. (23) But the pilot gets away from him safely.

This very brief example of how the model works suggests that stories generated from it will almost always have action, suspense, danger, and other exciting and entertaining features—at least at the level of quality seen in the typical television adventure series. We know these are the kinds of stories the reluctant writer likes to read, likes to listen to, and likes to see on television. Very likely they are the kinds he wishes he could write about.

The use of this guide obviously requires some understanding of its parts. It would be appropriate, first, for the teacher to read some folk tales or some stories he has written to demonstrate the parts of the model. It may be wise, too, to have a group of children dictate a few stories based on the model as the teacher records them before they begin to write. In this way they can be led to understand each part and to visualize how each of the parts of a story interrelates with the others.

Not all of the thirty-one actions need be used in the beginning by either the teacher or the children as they write stories, of course. Nor need much be written about each action. (The illustrative story ends on item twenty-three.) Neither should children feel they must refer to the outline at all times. If young writers will keep to the sequence of actions given in the guide, however, they will find they will be able to use more and more actions from story to story.

Some teachers may wonder about the use of a guide that requires so much conformity to a prearranged scene. Doubtless such an outline may not be necessary or appropriate for the able, productive, or creative child who apparently has realized the conventions or actions from literature from his reading or listening to stories. It should be remembered, however, that literature is full of conventions many children are not remotely aware of. These conventions can be seen in fables, myths, and epics, the older forms of literature, as well as in fairy tales. Modern professional writers have confessed their writings are governed by these conventions. Accordingly, the child in using the guide would be doing something all successful writers do, at least intuitively.

The guide should be seen, then, as one means of isolating the parts of stories for the reluctant writer so he can see how a certain kind of story is put together. One must admit from the example given that knowing this is no guarantee of a production of stories of great quality. For that matter, however, what is? If the use of the guide results in some building of the reluctant writer's self-confidence in his ability to write, it will do enough. It will have served its purpose nicely. Creativity is another matter.

QUESTIONS FOR DISCUSSION

1. Groff's essay implies that a writer finds it helpful, as he works toward discovering details and distinctive ideas, to have a basic, reusable plan with which to work. Would this thesis have any bearing on the teaching of other kinds of composition in the elementary classroom? Might models of other kinds of writing—not just adventure stories—be useful to the student?

2. Can you think of forms of fiction other than adventure stories or fairy tales that might, upon analysis, reveal recurring patterns? Would it help to enumerate the structure in such patterns for the student to follow?

3. Does the teacher endanger the imaginative life of students by encouraging them to work with well-defined structures such as that identified by Groff? Is the individual student likely to be discouraged from seeking patterns of his own discovery in his experiences if he is offered the crutch of a model for a standard sort of story?

Morning Haze
Leslie T. Whipp

Most of the previous essays in this section have taken for granted the idea that it is good to encourage "creativity" and "imagination" in children.

In the following essay, Whipp challenges this way of looking at the teaching of writing in elementary schools. He contends that facile talk of "creativity" and "imagination" diverts attention from the precise ways in which children use language. Whipp, using haiku to illustrate his comments, argues for analytically exact description of the language of children's poetry as a way to an understanding of the growth of children's ability to use language. He argues also for increased efforts to establish conditions in which children will want to use language for their personal satisfaction, instead of the customary exercises in "creativity" and "imaginative writing."

Leslie Whipp, of the University of Nebraska, has served on the staffs of the Tri-University Project in Elementary Education and of several federally funded institutes for the training of teachers.

From Geoffrey Summerfield, ed., *Essays and Addresses on Composition* (Lincoln, Nebraska: The University of Nebraska Tri-University Project, 1969), pp. 51–66. Reprinted by permission of the University of Nebraska Press and the author.

My title comes from a delightful old haiku:

Morning haze:
  as in a painting of a dream,
  men go their ways.

> *Buson* (*1715–83*),
> tr. H. G. Henderson [1]

Neither the subtitle nor the poem give much of a clue to the subject of these notes, though. As it happens, that subject is creative or imaginative writing in the schools.

That's not a very promising sort of subject, in fact. Not to sensible people, at least. "A field of corn and a bird in flight/These give sensible folk delight." [2] One certainly would not expect to find a field of corn and a bird in flight here. On second thought, perhaps one would. An essay on creative writing is very often "a field of corn," and an essayist on "creativity" often "a bird in flight." Essays on creative writing, in fact, are remarkably uncreative, essays on the nature and place of imaginative language singularly unimaginative, and the genre on the whole uninspired. If you read on, you must indeed have some serious interest in the teaching of creative writing. I'll try not to give you a field of corn and a bird in flight.

Instead I'll seek to argue a thesis. I want to argue that conventionally in talking about and thinking about and teaching creative writing, or "imaginative" language, we pursue the associations of "creative" or "imaginative" and ignore the associations of "writing" or "language." Further, I will argue, if one instead pursues the associations of "writing" and of "language," he will be led to some radically different teaching practices.

I propose to proceed initially by recalling what we know, that is, by examining the kinds of things we customarily say about "creative writing" or "imaginative language" in our classrooms, for by

[1] Harold G. Henderson, ed. and tr., *An Introduction to Haiku* (Garden City, New York: Doubleday & Company, Inc., 1958), p. 104.
[2] James Stephens, "Sensible People," *Collected Poems*. (New York: The Macmillan Company, 1954), p. 345.

looking at the kind of language which frequently patterns with this familiar subject, we may make discoveries about the well-known notions of "creative writing" or "imaginative language."

One of the burning questions, or set of questions, which often recurs, and one which I suspect you expect me to try (and fail) to answer is this: "How do we stimulate or motivate kids to do imaginative or creative writing? How do we get them to turn on their imaginations? How do we get them to use their imaginations?" Now what interests me about these questions is not their answers. It is instead the language of the questions themselves. Notice what these questions assume. Notice what part of the phrases "creative writing" and "imaginative language" they hook into. They might logically hook into either one of two sets of expressions. They might hook into the expressions "creative" and "imaginative" or they might instead hook into the expressions "language" or "writing." Now the expressions "creative" or "imaginative," or related expressions such as "imagine," or "imagination" or "creativity" very often come into talk about mental faculties or abilities—particularly the faculty of the imagination. And the expressions "language" or "writing" often involve the notions of public conventions, shared systems of communication, and in a profound and complex sense, rule-governed behavior. Now what part of the phrases "imaginative language" and "creative writing" is it which this first set of conventional questions pursues?

"How do we stimulate or motivate kids to do imaginative or creative writing? How do we get them to turn on their imaginations? How do we get them to use their imaginations?"

These questions assume, do they not, that eliciting creative writing in the classroom is a matter of "turning on" a mental faculty, like "turning on" a hidden motor by remote control. They are looking for the stimulus, the motive, the electrical impulse which will turn this motor on. They are concerned with the process, and with the process conceived in a certain way, in terms of faculty psychology: "How do you get kids to use their imagination?"

What strikes me as important about this first set of questions, then, is this: they are concerned with mental events. They inquire about psychology. Further, they assume for their psychology a faculty psychology, not a Freudian psychology, not the terms of clinical or physiological or contemporary child psychology, but the terms of nineteenth century theoretical psychology. And these questions do not inquire about writing or language. They are concerned with process, not with product. They pursue the associations of "creative" or "imaginative," not the associations of "language" or "writing."

Here is a second set of questions which are also frequent in talk about creative writing: "Will not the use of models in teaching creative writing stifle the imagination? Will it not prevent the child from using his own imagination? Will it not hamper and kill creativity and individuality and spontaneity? Will it not impede the development of the child's own *style?*" Here again one observes that the questions pursue the associations of "creative," not of "writing." And again one observes the questions are concerned with psychology, with the functioning of that mental faculty "the imagination." But we observe a second thing in these questions, an emphasis on individual difference, on the idiosyncratic, that which is distinctive to one single mind, the individual style.

Now look at the third set of conventional things to say about creative writing. Once our students have written, we might say of them individually, "He has a great imagination," or "He knows (or does not know) how to use his imagination," or "You haven't imagined this completely enough," or "You didn't feel that very strongly did you?" or "He has no imagination whatsoever." Or "He always copies what someone else does, he's not inventive or creative. There's nothing new, nothing individual, about what he writes." We might talk like that. Or we might say, "This is really awfully bad writing, and I have to resist the urge to correct it. But I know that one must resist that urge. Correcting creative writing is disciplining the undisciplined: how can it be disciplined and creative? How imaginative if restrained by rules?" Or it might go like this: "One must never correct a student's creative writing. To correct it is to reject it, and since it is the expression of the individuality of the child, to reject the writing is to reject the child." These, too, are conventional kinds of things to say about creative writing. Whether or not you or I agree with them is irrelevant now. What is relevant is the phrasing of the assertions themselves, the assumptions of this kind of talk.

And the notions which inform this talk again include the notions of the imagination as a psychological faculty, and of creative writing as the expression of the individuality, or difference, or distinctiveness of a particular mind, an emphasis on novelty and originality. We also have, though, the notions of sincerity and depth of feeling here, as well as the notions of the sensitivity and sacredness of the individual creative imagination.

In less casual and apparently more philosophical talk about creative writing, we might raise such questions as these: "What part does the intellect, the rational faculty, the reason, play in imaginative writing? What part does the emotion play? What part the imagination?" And we would expect that the answers would assert that creative writing was (or was not, probably was) the product of the imagination. The answer might go on to assert either an antithesis of imagination and reason or the need for a synthesis of the imagination and reason. Or in the words of Professor James E. Miller, Jr., a Whitman scholar, writing on imagination in the elementary schools: "I must also insist that it [the imagination] has a separate but equal status with the intellect. Indeed, it is possible that only the integration of both faculties develops each to the full. . . . Reason and imagination make up the whole man." [3] Even in the apparently more profound and less casual talk, we again find the emphasis on the psychological; we again find the pursuit of the implications of "creative," and "imaginative."

Now what sort of model or picture is it which would make these different notions cohere? Where do we find them coming together explicitly? In fact, the assumptions of much of the talk we have looked at so far are nicely gathered together in a little poem by James Stephens entitled "Demiurge," [4] and he goes beyond these assumptions to some we have not yet observed:

[3] James E. Miller, Jr., "Imagination and the Literature Curriculum," in Alexander Frazier, ed., *New Directions in Elementary English* (Champaign, Illinois: National Council of Teachers of English, 1967), p. 21.
[4] Stephens, pp. 248–249.

1

Wise Emotion, some have thought,
Is that whereby a poem's wrought:
More will have it, that the Hive
The Bee comes from, and all alive.

Is Thought: while others fret to tell,
Imagination, like a well,
Bubbles all that is to be
Into shape and certainty.

2

Imagination does but seem:
Thought is wisdom, in a dream:
And Emotion can, with strain,
Tell a pleasure from a pain

These, the Sleepy Ones and Dull,
That nothing sow, and nothing cull,
Nothing have that's fit to sing
The Wide-Awake, The Living Thing.

3

The living, ever-waking Will:
The ever-spacious, ever-still:
Wherefrom, as from a fountain, springs
All that praises, soars, sings:

All that is not dull and dense,
Bogged in thought, and clogged in sense,
Comes unbid, and surge on surge,
From the Will, the Demiurge.

In the first two stanzas, Stephens is clearly recalling what is conventionally said about the genesis of poems, the paradigm of creative writing. Imagination? intellect? emotions—some people, he says, argue for one or another of these faculties as the source of linguistic creativity, of "All that praises, soars, and sings." But they're wrong. Really, he says, it is the "Will." Notice that he, too, phrases his answer in terms of psychology, and in terms of fac-

ulty psychology. While he objects to the conventional answers, he
is giving an answer of the same kind as the conventional answers.
But he goes beyond that, to lead us to assumptions we have not yet
been aware of, assumptions which I suspect underlie and explain
how we come to talk the way we do about creative writing.

Notice the language with which he characterizes the creative experience:

Wherefrom, as from a fountain, springs . . .

Comes unbid, and surge on surge
From the Will, the Demiurge.

The creative product springs up, as from a fountain, comes invol-
untarily, unbid, comes surging, rhythmically pulsing up, comes
from the depths, from the mysterious "demiurge." Now that language reminds me of another poem about writing poems, about creative writing. That other poem is Samuel Taylor Coleridge's
"Kubla Khan."

James Stephens's surging fountain of creativity obviously echoes
Coleridge's fountain surging from a deep romantic chasm:

And from this chasm, with ceaseless turmoil seething,
As if this earth in fast thick pants were breathing,
A mighty fountain momently was forced:
Amid whose swift half-intermitted burst
Huge fragments vaulted like rebounding hail . . .

And Stephens:

The living, ever-waking Will:
The ever-spacious, ever still:
Wherefrom, as from a fountain, springs
All that praises, soars, and sings:

All that is not dull and dense,
Bogged in thought, and clogged in sense,
Comes unbid, and surge on surge,
From the Will, the Demiurge.

This echo suggests that in the background of this conventional kind of talk about creative writing, the pursuit of the psychological associations of the terms of "creative" or "imaginative," there may well be what goes along with Coleridge's surging fountain:

> A damsel with a dulcimer
> In a vision once I saw:
> It was an Abyssinian maid,
> And on her dulcimer she played,
> Singing of Mount Abora.
> Could I revive within me
> Her Symphony and song,
> To such a deep delight 'twould win me,
> That with music loud and long,
> I would build that dome in air,
> That sunny dome! those caves of ice!
> And all who heard should see them there,
> And all should cry, Beware! Beware!
> His flashing eyes, his floating hair!
> Weave a circle round him thrice,
> And close your eyes with holy dread,
> For he on honey-dew hath fed,
> And drunk the milk of Paradise.

Now several of the notions we have seen informing conventional talk about creative writing are found in this passage. The creative writer is there, the speaker, the I, and there too is an account of the creative process. There is the stimulus or motive, the revived song of the "Abyssinian maid." There is the great profundity of feeling which results from the stimulus or motive—"To such a deep delight 'twould win me." And there is the creativity which in turn results from the depth of feeling, the creative product:

> That with music loud and long,
> I would build that dome in air . . .

And there is the reverence of this creative act:

And all should cry, Beware! Beware!
His flashing eyes, his floating hair!

And there is even a description of what is currently taken to be the appropriate teacher response to a student's piece of creative writing:

And close your eyes with holy dread . . .

Or is that pushing the analogy too far?

In any event, the extent to which one can find in this Romantic poem about writing poems several of the notions we have seen informing conventional talk about creative writing raises an interesting question. Is it perhaps possible that there is implicit in the background of our conventional talk about imaginative or creative writing, a picture of an early nineteenth-century vision of creative writing?

I referred a bit ago to James E. Miller, Jr., writing an essay on imagination and elementary schools for the National Council of Teachers of English, an essay published in 1967. Professor Miller begins that essay by quoting the first couple of stanzas of Wordsworth's "Ode on Intimations of Immortality from Recollections of Early Childhood." [5] Professor Miller, from whom we have already found the conventional school talk about imagination, in order to find a poetic paraphrase of his position, goes to Wordsworth. And Stephens, who summarizes conventional school talk, echoes another Romantic, Coleridge. Wordsworth tells us that imaginative creativity is the spontaneous overflow of powerful feeling; Coleridge pictures for us what that is like: This is the Romantic vision, the Romantic dream. The subtitle of his picture, you will recall, is "A Vision in A Dream." Stephens, too, pictures for us what that is like. He gives us a picture of a dream, of the same dream.

And do not the conventional kinds of things we say about creative writing—the way we phrase our questions, indeed the questions themselves, and the way we phrase our judgments, indeed the

[5] Frazier, pp. 15–16.

judgments themselves—do these not reflect this same picture? Does not our conventional school talk about creative writing reflect a painting or picture of this early nineteenth-century dream of the creative imagination?

> Morning haze:
>> as in a painting of a dream,
>>> men go their ways.

One might say (and not at all facetiously) that in continuing to use the conventional talk about creative writing in the classroom, we are those men, going about in a morning haze.

To the extent that my samples of conventional language are both accurate and representative, it seems that we may indeed have been elaborating in our teaching talk and teaching behavior on an early nineteenth-century picture of creative writing, pursuing the associations of the expressions "creative" and "imaginative."

One might also, however, by his teaching talk and behavior, elaborate the expressions "writing" and "language." It seems to me that in thinking of, reading about, teaching, reading, and evaluating creative writing, one should in fact deliberately seek to pursue the associations of these expressions, perhaps to the exclusion of the associations of "creative" and "imaginative." This involves shifting our attention from the creative process to the created product, from concern about processes of generation of a poem or play or story to examination of the poems, plays, and stories themselves. Such a shift, of course, is consistent not only with fairly old developments in the study of language and literature, but also with more recent developments in research on creativity itself.[6]

One obvious consequence of this shift is the challenging responsibility to be knowledgeable. As long as we dealt with the imponderables of nineteenth-century theoretical psychology, we could, as teachers of creative writing, proceed by definition and dogma, by impulse and intuition, by guess and by gosh. When our staples

---

[6] See, for example, John Curtis Gowan, et. al., eds., *Creativity: Its Educational Implications* (New York: John Wiley & Sons, Inc., 1967), especially Chapter 8, "Research and Summary," pp. 285ff.

were postulated entities and hypostatized faculties, undiscoverable and hence irrefutable, we didn't need knowledge. Assuming there were no stars in all the shrouded heavens we were free to navigate by the seat of our definitions.

When we pursue the associations of writing and language, however, we step out of this pedagogue's paradise. Language is observable, systematic, and meaningful. It is subject to overt and explicit observation and generalization, whether one is thinking of oral or written language, of intonation (or pauses) in speech or of the equally complex and subtle system of punctuation in writing, of the developing syntactic, rhetorical, and conceptual capabilities of school children, or of the patterning of syntactic, rhetorical, and conceptual features of a given kind of writing. That is to say, by pursuing the associations of "writing" and "language," one is to assume responsibility for *knowing,* in a precise and detailed sense, something about the language development of students and about the qualities of the kinds of writing (narrowly defined) which one seeks to enable them to learn.[7]

Perhaps an illustration of what it is like to pursue the implications of "writing" and "language" will clarify. A group of teachers in Hawaii and I recently began to look carefully at haiku, seeking to make statements descriptive of some aspects of haiku language. Some of what we observed is concisely represented in the six haiku which follow. The first three are by mature writers:

After the bells hummed
    and were silent, flowers
chime a peal of fragrance.

> *Basho (1644–1694)*
> *tr. Harry Behn*

Women, rice-planting:
    all muddy, save for one thing—
that's their chanting.

[7] See, for example, F. Goldman Eisler, *Psycholinguistics: Experiments in Spontaneous Speech* (London: Academic Press, 1968), and Margaret E. Ashida, "Something for Everyone: A Standard Corpus of Contemporary American Expository Essays," *Research in the Teaching of English,* 2:1 (Spring, 1968), pp. 14–23.

Raizan (1653–1716)
tr. H. G. Henderson

Wake up, old sleepy
    butterfly! Come, come with me
on my pilgrimage!

Basho (1644–1694)
tr. Harry Behn

And the next three are immature haiku, all by children about age
11:

A bunny is cute.
It is fuzzy and furry,
Hop, little bunny.

Loyal to country
Faithful always to master
Is the loyal dog.

Apple blossoms
Like white butterflies
All about to fly away.

Of the three, we would all agree that the third is by far the most
imaginative and creative, although we might disagree if asked to
explain what we meant by saying that.

The three mature poems represent fairly well some of the prominent syntactic features of haiku. The first consists of a single main
clause plus dependent elements, the second of an incomplete clause
used as a main clause, the third of two main clauses. Now look at
the children's syntax. In the first immature haiku, each line is a
separate clause. A bit of trouble here with the English haiku convention of run-on lines. But notice that the writer has (though with
some inconsistency of perspective) used the imperative structure
("Hop, like Basho's "Wake up!") with the noun of indirect
address ("little bunny," like Basho's "old, sleepy butterfly").

She's having a bit of trouble, but she's coming along; unable to stretch her syntax over this three line frame, she finally draws upon one English haiku convention which avoids that problem.

In the second child's haiku, the student has by golly stretched his syntax over all three lines, but at considerable cost to his grace and dignity. He's coming along, though, making progress, in respect at least to this feature of haiku: he sees what is asked of him syntactically, though he has trouble delivering it. The third haiku delivers the goods: a single incomplete clause stretched over all three lines, and very nicely stretched at that.

Notice too the "is" verbs in the first two children's haiku—not the verbs of the mature haiku. Progress in coming to be creative and imaginative in writing haiku means in part deleting or replacing such verbs as these, as the third child perceived.

So much by way of illustrating some of what a teacher of haiku should be able to say about the syntax of mature haiku and of the progress kids are making in approximating that syntax. I mentioned other features as well, rhetorical and conceptual. One instance of a rhetorical feature, a traditional rhetorical feature, is that of figurative comparisons. In the first mature haiku, one finds the metaphors "flowers chimed" and "peals of fragrance," metaphors involving a mixture of sense perceptions, speaking of fragrance as if it were like sound. In the second we have the implication of the unmuddied chanting, again involving a mixture of senses, of the visually perceived mud and aurally perceived chanting. In the children's haiku, one finds only one comparison, that is the comparison of the apple blossoms to the butterfly in the third and best of the children's haiku. Significantly in this very impressive but still immature haiku, the comparison is both explicit (it is a simile) and simple (it does not involve a mixture of sense impressions).

I've exemplified syntactic and rhetorical considerations. What of the conceptual? The mature haiku use the nouns "butterfly," "bells," "flowers," "fragrance," "women," and "chanting." The immature use the nouns "bunny," "dog," "master," "country," "blossoms," and "butterfly." Citing the nouns in this way is one economical way of indicating what the haiku are written about, and that is one conceptual feature of haiku. The first two children's haiku are indeed about nature, but about animals, and domesticated animals at that, animals that recur in children's poetry generally, but not in mature haiku. Again, the third child's haiku is clearly superior: this child would appear to understand what mature haiku are written about.

Notice that the choice of subject for the first two children is probably not in any profound or simple sense a matter of what interests the child: butterflies and birds and bugs and blossoms—the frequent stuff of mature haiku—do interest kids. What is rather more operative, I take it, in the children's choice of what to write about, is their sense of what is appropriate to write about in haiku (or, in this case perhaps, more generally in academic kid poetry). And the third child has a rather more refined sense of this than do the first two, has acquired a better sense of the conceptual form of haiku.

In effect I have been illustrating some of the kind of talk which comes from pursuing the associations of "writing" and "language" instead of the associations of "imaginative" and "creative." I have been seeking to illustrate the detailed knowledge for which a teacher of creative writing becomes responsible when he does pursue these associations.

One might well ask what has happened to the creativity of creative writing. In the most imaginative and creative of the immature haiku, the haiku with the apple blossom-butterfly comparison, the writer most nearly approximates the mature usage. That, I take it, is in part what we mean by saying that this haiku is the most imaginative and creative of the three. I don't mean to redefine the expressions "creative" and "imaginative"; I only mean to clarify one way in which they conventionally do work for us.

Further, I wish to suggest that in acquiring the language of haiku to the extent that he has acquired it, in getting the hang of part of the haiku way of saying things, the third child has acquired as well part of the haiku way of seeing things. The insight, imagination, creativity (I wish to suggest) is consequent upon, the result of experience with, in a complex sense, the language forms of the haiku. It may be, that is to say, that our conventional emphasis on singularity, individuality, and idiosyncracy impedes the very end for which we use it. Individual insight, significant individual insight, cre-

ativity of the sort which contributes to the sum of human experience, as first-rate literature does, seems likely to be a consequence
of the mastery of existing forms of expression. Getting a way of
saying is a significant means of getting a way of seeing.[8]

This leads me to further recommendations, recommendations
concerning practice, not simply teacher talk or the way we generate
teacher talk. In speaking of progress in acquiring the syntactic, rhetorical, and conceptual forms of haiku, I was assuming the learning
writer's problem to be one of adding forms to his language learning
repertory. His problem is conceived then as a problem in language
learning, in language acquisition. In fact, all of our students have
considerable experience at language learning outside of the
classroom. If we were to seek to capitalize on this experience, if we
were to seek to reproduce in teaching creative writing some important features of the child's non-academic language learning experience, we would proceed quite differently than we conventionally do
in teaching creative writing. I have three pair of particular recommendations of this sort to make.

The first pair concerns preparation for the writing. In an ordinary, non-academic language learning situation, one observes as a
listener and some time later produces as a speaker, always observing a particular kind of language in use, and observing many different instances of particular kind of language, e.g., dinner table
conversation, or what slightly older kids say on the playground
when no adults are about, or what adults say when attending a
baseball game ("Ole John swings a mean stick!"), etc. What does
this imply for teaching creative writing? First, that students should
receive in a peculiar sense an opportunity for learning the relevant
kinds of writing, i.e., an opprortunity for the implicit and as it were
intuitive observation, generalization, and delayed reproduction of
the distinctive features of these kinds of language, that they be exposed as listeners and as readers to many instances of the particular
kinds of writing, narrowly defined, that they might later come to
produce. This in turn implies a prior identification of these kinds,

[8] Cf. Frances Christensen, "A Lesson From Hemingway," *Notes toward a New Rhetoric* (New York: Harper & Row, 1967), pp. 25–26.

and the selection of appropriate instances of them. The Nebraska Curriculum in English for Grades K through 12 can be seen as an ambitious and groping attempt to do this.[9]

The second of my first pair of particular recommendations is this: that these opportunities for this learning be so arranged as both to match the students' present linguistic and conceptual strategies and to anticipate and prepare for integration of the literature curriculum and the composition curriculum, as well as a careful articulation of creative writing curriculum through several grade levels. And it questions the effectiveness of the spur of the moment assignment in creative writing, as well as the effectiveness of even planned exercises in creativity when they are planned without detailed reference to kinds of imaginative language read or written at surrounding grade levels.

The next pair of recommendations concerns a closely related feature of ordinary, non-academic language learning situations—the role in those situations of children slightly older than the learner. The role seems to be an important one in providing a source of language for the learner to observe, internalize, and imitate. This implies that part of the experience of students with creative writing should involve hearing somewhat older children perform. Second graders should fairly routinely have competent third, fourth, and fifth graders telling them original stories and poems. Senior high students should routinely perform their own stuff for junior high students, as part of the study of literature in the junior high school. One might well recruit creative hippies or high school dropouts to recite their poetry or dialogues or skits to high school juniors and seniors.

Second, the reading of the kids, their literature study, should include a considerable segment of student writing read, talked about, and analyzed just as if it were by John Keats or William Faulkner or J. R. R. Tolkien. Good creative writing, carefully

[9] *A Curriculum for English,* Grades 1–12, Developed by the Nebraska Curriculum Development Center, Department of English, University of Nebraska, Lincoln, Nebraska, under funds from the U.S. Office of Education and under the direction of Paul A. Olson and Frank M. Rice, Co-Directors. The Curriculum is published by the University of Nebraska Press, Lincoln, Nebraska 68508.

selected, from third, fourth, and fifth grade students should be seriously treated as literature, as textbook material, in the third grade classroom.

The third pair of recommendations is related to the second: it concerns the status and functioning of the language forms the child learns in an ordinary, non-academic language learning situation. Consider as a paradigm what a child sees when observing the language of an older child complaining about the food he is served for supper. The language comes into a behavioral set that includes older people interacting, and the language is working incidentally to that interaction. Perhaps the parents respond sympathetically, perhaps angrily; perhaps they regard the complaint as adolescent rebellion, or as a transfer of hostility from a frustrating school situation. But whatever they do, they do *something* with it, and the older child is doing something with it. Indeed, on occasions the adults do the same thing with such language as the older child is doing. In short, in ordinary language learning situations kids observe language which *is* meaningful to, which works for, which is used by, which is taken seriously by—adults.

The implication of this, it seems to me, nearly undoes us all. I am not at all sure we can take creative writing seriously as adults in most school classrooms today. And in the experience of most of our students, no other adults do either. The fact is, I think, that most teachers and a good many professors (even some in English departments) can't abide poems. Philippe Aries speaks of "childhood . . . becoming the repository of customs abandoned by the adults," [10] and for a great many school students today, creative writing is one such custom. The same writer briefly sketches the history of hoops:

> From being the plaything of all ages, and an accessory used in dancing and acrobatics, the hoop would gradually be confined to smaller and smaller children until it was finally abandoned altogether, illustrating once again the truth that, in order to retain the favour of children, a toy must have some connection with the world of adults. [11]

[10] Philippe Aries, *Centuries of Childhood* (New York: Random House, 1962), p. 71.
[11] Aries, p. 95.

Toys and uses of language. As a teacher one has to demonstrate by his behavior that imaginative language does indeed "have some connection with the world of adults," that adults do indeed take this kind of language seriously. The teacher, the mature model in the classroom, must obviously use these kinds of language. He need not use them in a publishable way, but he does need to use them. He needs to use his own compositions as part of the literature to which he exposes his students. He needs to be seen reading and studying and analyzing these kinds of language. Not in order to be seen, and not in order to prepare for a lesson, but in order to do the kinds of things one writes or reads poems to do. That's one way of being serious about creative writing, of demonstrating that you do take this use of language seriously. And I recognize that it is a large order.

The second may be still more difficult. It is that you take seriously the imaginative language that kids do in fact use. Partially I have in mind respecting their use of the rhetoric of mass media art forms, but chiefly I have in mind something else. In order to illustrate this, and the immense difficulty of taking it seriously in the classroom, I include a poem written by my ten-year-old son. This boy at the time that he wrote this poem was a model student in a WASP middle-class neighborhood in Squaresville, the City of Churches, Lincoln, Nebraska, and still is for that matter. He is consistently the teacher's pet, he consistently gets top grades in all subjects, he religiously practices his piano for one hour each day, and he recently got a medal, of which he was justly proud, for perfect attendance at his church choir. His mother and I returned home one summer day to find that this ten-year-old boy had of his own volition composed a poem on my typewriter. The poem totaled 44 words in 29 lines, usually one word to a line. It was entitled "Description of Donald," and it read as follows:

Dumb,
Stupid,
Rotten,
Punky,
Damn,
Fuckin',

Shittan,
Bastird,
Son of a Bitch,
Dirty,
Ass Hole,
A Brat,
A Show Off,
A Hot Shot,
Bully,
Greedy,
Liar,
Non Sportsmen Like,
Butt,
Crummy,
Cruddy,
Queer,
Poopy,
Reformed,
Retarded,
Spoiled,
Nut.

P.S.
He can also go Hell.

I must say that I was surprised and a bit dismayed by this poem. And I must also admit that, from what I know of the boy my son was describing, there was in my son's description more truth than poetry. Granting all that, still, my son *is using* poetry. And it is obvious, I think that this poem could not have been written in school.[12] In school, I'm afraid my son might well have written "A bunny is cute" or "Faithful always to master/Is the loyal dog." When a child *cannot* come to write "the loyal dog" in school, then we can claim to take creative writing seriously in the classroom.

---

[12] It is true, however, that my son could readily identify the model from which he derived the form of his poem, and that it was a poem he had read in school some months before. Interestingly, it was a poem about a railroad and a train, so that the elongated form, with lines like cross-ties on a railroad, functioned quite differently than it did for my son; my son, I take it, applied the form creatively to represent visually the immense heap of garbage he was piling on the offending Donald.

When we are prepared to take creative writing seriously, when we are able to create language learning situations in the classroom, and when we can claim to be knowledgeable about the language of creative writing, and the progress our students make in acquiring that language, perhaps we will still go about in a morning haze, as men in a painting of a dream. That may be an occupational hazard of our profession. But perhaps we can also increase the effectiveness of our efforts to teach creative writing.

QUESTIONS FOR DISCUSSION

1. Do you find Whipp's analysis of the language in the children's haiku informative? If not, in what ways does it fall short? Do you accept Whipp's evaluation of the children's work, *particularly* of their development as writers of haiku?

2. Whipp implies that there are some features of language, and of the poet's attitude and choice of subject, that characterize mature haiku. Do you share this belief? Could similar statements be made about other distinctive forms of poetry? about forms of writing other than poetry?

3. Would the kinds of observations Whipp makes about the language of haiku be useful to children? Might a teacher attempt, through discussion, to bring children to explicit awareness of these features? Or should the features be known to the teacher without being discussed directly in the classroom?

4. What particular techniques for teaching, if any, are implied in the way Whipp talks about the language of haiku and the different accomplishments of the different children? Should a teacher try to lead students to write increasingly mature haiku? How?

5. Professor Whipp argues that mastering a form of expression is a way of discovering what can be said or expressed in that form. Have other authors in this anthology set forth similar views? How

does Whipp's argument compare with theirs—in what is said? in cogency?

6. Whipp has some suggestions about the curriculum (not merely in composition) for the elementary grades. What is your evaluation of his curricular proposals? How do they compare with the suggestions of other authors in this anthology about curriculum?

RESPONDING
TO
STUDENTS'
WRITING

On Value in Children's Writing
Wallace W. Douglas

A major responsibility of teachers of composition is to read and respond to their students' writing. Even if the teacher encourages students to respond to each other's work, he or she still must examine the students' works to note evidence of progress in the ability to discover ideas, to address a subject, and to control language. To do this successfully teachers of writing need to consider the details of each piece of student writing. Their judgments on that writing need to be appropriate to the student's age and rate of growth, and should recognize difficulties, if any, that the students are having.

In this essay, Wallace W. Douglas, of the Northwestern University Curriculum Center in English, offers guidance in seeking the distinctive features of children's writing that will reveal a student's progress, problems, and feelings. He uses several examples of writing by students at different ages as illustrations. His essay also introduces the reader to the reactions that one sensitive reader gives to elements in children's writing.

From Stephen Dunning, ed., *English for the Junior High Years* (Champaign, Illinois: National Council of Teachers of English, 1969), pp. 33–62. Copyright © 1969 by the National Council of Teachers of English. Reprinted by permission of the publisher and the author.

In my first paper I tried to raise some questions about the way teachers view that part of ''English'' that has to do with children's writing and with children writing—that is, ''composition.'' As things stand now, the purpose of composition is generally supposed to be that of giving children a command of various conventions of language and of forms of writing that are characteristic of adult public (and usually published) discourse, or that are said to be. It is said that the children are being prepared for the time when they will need to use such language and such forms of writing; though if the ceaseless correcting that their papers suffer means anything it must be that children are expected to use in their school writing just those forms that writing in school is supposed to teach them for future use.

This view of composition has meant that the writings of children are reduced to practice exercises in correct and efficient communication of an adult sort. As a consequence, the writings of children must be judged in relation to the nature and requirements of adult writing situations. Hence they must almost necessarily be either disvalued as faulty examples of the kind of writing the practice is supposed to prepare children to do, or valued precisely because they approach adult writing to some degree and are, therefore, by just that much unlike the writing of children.

I propose, as an exercise in proof of my proposition, that you consider the following papers written by two boys in second grade. You do not need to evaluate them, though given our habits you will probably find it hard not to. Instead of evaluation, just try to figure out what you can say about the two boys as writers. After that, perhaps you might try to predict their future in school—which is a form of evaluation, of course.

1A

CHRISTOPHER COLUMBUS

Columbus lived in Italy. He left from Spain. He bought 3 boats from the Queen. It took him 48 days to get to America. He thought the world was round. His boats were called the Nina, Pinta, and Santa Maria.

2A

Columbus went on a boat to sail to India. But a man said, "We're going to chase." So they jumped in and swam back to Spain. When they got back they were wet. So they took their clothes off and let them dry. When they were dried a fish ate them. So they were cold. So they were sad. So they sailed back to India to get killed.

1B

ABRAHAM LINCOLN

Abe lived in Kentucky with his sister, mother, and father. One day Abe's father came home from the fields and said, "We're moving to Indiana." So they moved to Indiana. About two months after they moved, a milk sickness spread. Abe's mother caught it. She died. A few weeks after she died, Abe's father said, "I am going back to Kentucky. I'll be back in about four weeks." Abe's father left. When Abe's father came back he had another person with him. Abe asked why he had her with him. He answered, "She is your new mother."

His new mother said, "You are so pale and your house so dirty, why let's clean up."

Some time has passed and Abe is now 22 and he leaves them. He became a lawyer. Then he become a senator. Soon he became President. He freed the slaves. But one day when he went to a play, he died.

2B

ABRAHAM LINCOLN GETS KILLED IN A WAR

One day in Feb. 20, 1960, Abe was hunting. Suddenly he heard a shot. Abe ran fast to his home. He made it. He called his mom. He looked all around but he found her. She was dead. The telephone rang. Abe answered the telephone. The man said, "There is a war." Abe said back, "My mom died." All of a sudden a shot came and hit Abe. The man came over. He saw Abe dead. He knew the war started. He heard a shot. He ducked. The man took a gun and shot the whole wide world. Only a couple people were left. Suddenly the man got shot. The name of the country Abe was fighting was France. The French people one. That's all I can tell you.

I shall leave these very remarkable pieces now, hoping, however, that you will keep them in mind, insofar as you can, while I try to make some suggestions about reading the writings of children, and also about how, considering the needs of children, we ought to plan (not necessarily organize) classroom occasions for writing.

My procedure here will be very simple. I am just going to take some children's writings that I have found interesting and discuss their formal and expressive qualities. I do not know whether my examples (or are they specimens?) are typical or even very significant. The only thing statistical about my procedure has been that I selected them in a random sort of way, random, perhaps, in the sense of whimsical. And my conclusions are based rather on speculation than on experiment. Even so, I hope that you will be able to feel some degree of validity in them.

I am going to try to consider these as the writings of children. I know this is nearly impossible. As Sybil Marshall has said,

> However good the children are, they will not produce adult work.[1] Their work will be essentially childlike, and to assess this work anyone is up against a very real difficulty. For though he was a child once himself, though he may have made a serious study of child psychology and development, though he may have spent years at work among children, the fact is inescapable that he is an adult now. His memories of childhood are remembered with an adult memory, his knowledge is an adult's knowledge, and his conception of what is childlike is adult, too. The absolutely impossible thing for most people is to see anything as a child sees it, unclouded by maturity, and not through a mirror of assimilated experience.[2]

So perhaps I shall not succeed in what I propose. But I should like to try.

I

The papers I shall try to discuss were written by two boys in a special class for talented fourth, fifth, and sixth grade children, who

---

[1] But notice. Even Mrs. Marshall cannot escape. Is the sign of "goodness"—i.e., excellence—in the writing products of children that they be like adult work?

[2] Sybil Marshall, *An Experiment in Education* (Cambridge: University Press, 1963), p. 107.

meet in a group for a half day twice a week. They work on language and social studies only, by their choice.

The first selections (figs. 1–4) are by a nine-year-old boy in fourth grade. They come from a journal in which the children are required—or at least expected—to make daily entries. (I suppose that's about as close as an American child ever gets to the freedom of writing "from the impulse of [his] own mind.")

I am afraid that what I noticed first in these selections was the third and fourth lines of the first poem:

Here I am
I want my bottle.

And I do think they are worth noticing, though perhaps not entirely for the reason you will be thinking, which indeed was my own first response.

For with a more responsible reading, I began to feel the lines in the poem as a whole. That is to say, putting it the proper way round, I began to feel the poem as a whole, and so, of course, the lines withdrew, as it were, into the structure of language that the boy had made.

As soon, then, as I began to read the poem as a reader I began to see some of the things that had been done in its making; or, if I must, that give the appearance of having been done. I do not myself think that it is appearance only, but I am willing at least to state that concession.

First of all, I noticed the title and especially the way it is set on the page. At the very least, this shows that the boy is feeling and, presumably, is pleased by the rhythm in the phrases.

Then I caught the reference to Alan Sherman's song of a few years ago, and that made me wonder whether the last three lines might contain a reference to the ad for Grant's Scotch: "While you're up, bring me a Grant's."

That may be questionable. I take it as obvious that the poem reflects—legitimately so, I should say—the lyrical form now being used for a good many popular songs. I don't mean lyrics such as those found in Broadway show-stoppers like "Hello, Dolly" but those rather of the sort that the Beatles have been doing lately. Of

> Hello, Mama   Feb. 26
> Hello Papa:
> Hello mama
> Hello papa
> Here I am
> I want my bottle
> And on the way there
> If you don't mind
> Would you please get me a big
> pastrami sandwich

Figure 1

> The Moose   Feb. 28
> The moose I'm talking about is not
> real. It's a plastic one that's about
> a foot long from the nose to the
> tail. His antlers are about four
> inches long from tip to tip. His
> tail is about an inch long. His
> nose is about a half of a inch
> wide. Moose are found mostly in
> Canada.

Figure 2

course the boy doesn't have their range of social reference. He is, after all, a child, in the first place, and not a performer, in the second place. But still I think that the details of the implied scene—which is, by the way, very nicely conceived and done—and also,

Welcome Song   Mar. 4

Give our men a hoot
Give our men a cheer
And after you do that:
You give the men a beer

Figure 3

Spring is Coming   Mar 6

Here comes the god called Mercury
With good news to proclaim
He has come to tell us
That spring has come again
He has come to tell
The things that we must do
To prepare Chicago
For March the twenty two

Figure 4

though less importantly, the structuring of the lines both suggest the style of that genre of popular song.[3] Note the plain, rather understated presentation of the details: no introduction, no scene-setting, no transitions, no emotive words. Just this is what happens, this is the way it is.

[3] It is not a question of imitating the style, but rather of using it, with greater or lesser awareness of conscious intent. Had it been a case of imitation, we would, no doubt, have to be asking questions about the poem's success as an imitation. As it is, I think we can quite properly ask questions of a better sort, about its quality as a poem of its own kind. Of course we must also ask questions about its quality as expression, because, in one way or another, being an expression is part of being a poem.

And that, of course, bring us back to the third and fourth lines—

Here I am
I want my bottle

—which is surely as pure a cry of want as ever you are likely to hear. But then immediately comes a denial of infancy and its needs—

And on the way there
If you don't mind
Would you please get me a big
    pastrami sandwich.

There is a double contrast here. First the pastrami is posed against the milk; adult food against infant. Second there are the contrasting sentence structures: the fairly childlike form of the first four lines against the complex structure of the last four, especially the very adult controlled politeness of the parenthetical "If you don't mind."

The effect is quite extraordinary. But what I have to emphasize is the value that the boy must have found in, received from, making this poem. I do not mean only whatever abstract, intellectual—conscious—satisfaction inheres in the recognition of having made something that is excellent in its own kind, though that is indeed a very important part of any successful writing experience. But in considering this paper, I think we must also be aware of the immediate, concrete—and very likely unconscious—feeling of control or at least order that would be expressed by, and, in the expressing, would be produced by, such a powerful formal organization as this poem.

The writer of the second group of papers (figs. 5–14) is a twelve-year-old in the sixth grade.

We have ten journal entries from him. With one exception (fig. 12, "The Moon") they divide quite easily into two equal groups. The impression left by the first group (figs. 5–9) is one of typicality, not to say ordinariness. Patriotism, baseball, doings with the family—these, it can be said with some confidence, are all subjects

The Flag

The flag rippling proudly in the
wind . . . .
It gives your heart a feeling of warmth
to see your country's flag.
Its bright red, white and blue colors
leave your eyes bewilderd.
a symbol of cloth
Showing everyone, and everyone it meaning.
A countries story written out on a
peice of cloth.
That is what <u>our</u> flag is.

Figure 5

My Plane Trip

My first plane trip was to Madison, Wisconsin, it was
bye a Northwest Orient Airlines Fan Jet. My family and I
went into the plane and sat a while before it took off.
Slowly but surely we moved to the runway and then
with a big burst of speed (200 M.P.H.) we wer off.
It was quiet and as smooth as can be.
We first flew to Milwaukee, Wisconsin and stopped there
a while and then took of again to Madison.
In three hours we were back at the Madison Airport.
We came back to Chicago on a Prop. Jet. It was so much
Fun my family plans to do it again!

Figure 6

Baseball

It is summer
I am at Wrigly feild (Home of the Cubs)
The sun is shining bright.
The ballgame is to begin right after the pledge.
Its the Cubs and the Giants yells
a fan in the crowd.
The First batter is up!
It is a realy important day for the Cubs.
I felt so good because I had never
been to a baseball game before.
It was real fun day for me and I
hope to do it many times more.
(As it turned out the CUBS won
5 to 4. RON SANTO hit his 28 home-
run in the seuenth inning, I yelled so
loud I had a sore throat after it.
Anyway the game was tied 4to 4 and they
had to start extra Innings they went All the
way to the 11th inning because a run
was scored by AL SPANGLER
and the CUBS won. 5 to 4.
Baseball is Great.)

Figure 7

Springfeild, Illinois Here I Come

About two months ago My family and I took a trip to Springfeild, Illinois on a Central Ill. Railroad. In the train there was a diner and many other cars. We were going very fast and it was fun looking out the back window of the train. When we got to Springfield we ate lunch in a park near the train station. After that we went to the Licoln home the air was very Fresh there and "Honest Abe's" house was in very good condition. It was very Fun in Springfield and I was sad to go but I had to do It sometime. We came home from Springfeild at 9:00 P.M.

Figure 8

My Vacation

Last summer My family and I went to Lake Deltan. It was very beautiful there. We were in cottage Number 3. Our cottage was on a cliff overlooking the beautiful blue lake. Every day we would wake up and hop in to our row boat, then we would row across the six mile lake to the other end. Then we would bring our boat up on to the land so it would'nt wash away. We would build a fire and warm our hands. We left in one week, I hope to go again

Figure 9

that any normal boy is expected to write about. And then there is
what he says about his subjects. The flag as a mere piece of cloth,
but yet a symbol of the country's story, bringing with its "proud"
ripple a feeling of warmth to the heart—certainly all that must
come from the boy's experience of official literature: sermons,
schoolbooks, assembly speeches, perhaps even some American
Legion speaker on the Fourth of July. The details in the piece on
baseball are of a similar order: easy, characterless, the kind that are
needed by reporters and other writers in a hurry. Even the three entries on family trips are pretty official too. They are themes, themes
only; there is no other word for them.

I should note in "The Flag" the statement that the red, white,
and blue "leave your eyes bewilderd," which is a little unexpected
at the least. In "Springfeild, Illinois Here I Come," there is the detail about the boy's surprise when he finds the air in the Lincoln
house fresh, not musty. That seems to be a recording of a personal
and felt experience, one that was strong enough to remain in the
boy's consciousness. Perhaps something might be made of the title
for that piece. It is rather nice and jaunty, but why did he think he
needed a title for a journal entry? Perhaps the rather elaborate ty-
pography (or unschoolroomish handwriting) of "Baseball" is also
worth noting.

But aside from those golden bits, the first group of entries in this
journal makes about as good an example of school writing as one is
likely to find. And the first thing one wants to do is to ask why a
talented child, one who by choice is working on language study in
a special class, should use space in "his" journal for such impersonal writing. Did he not feel the journal to be his? Did he not
know what a journal is for? Or is it merely that one of his abilities
as a talented child is to be able to deal with school and teachers,
and he cannot break the habit, even when given a chance? After all,
he is twelve years old and in the sixth grade, which means that he
has had six years of schooling, which is quite time enough to
become experienced, in the bad sense of the word.

I suppose I am responding to the weakness or suppression of affect in the pieces. But perhaps the case need not be considered a
serious one, for obviously something seems to have happened to

The Garbage Can

The garbage can is a neat little device.
You can throw everything in it.
The person that throws it in it gets all the credid but
really the poor tired, (little, or big garbage can should
get all the credit for holding the garbage (junk). There
are green garbage cans and red ones. The Garbage's
only friend is the Garbage Man. Pretty soon Garbage
Ladies will come into being. As Patrick Henry once
said GIVE ME LIBERTY or GIVE ME
DEATH.
                                    Yours Truly,
Figure 10   Your Favorite Garbage Can

Flowers
Flowers, their colors red, yellow, green

Figure 11

The Moon
The moon is a semi-heavenly body.
Without the moon there would be no moon
Man or moon lady. There would be no Apollo-
Shot or Moon Shot (which are really the same).
I am glad that the moon is there, arn't you?
(you better be glad;)

Figure 12

The Cinjumhi

The Cinjumhi is a funny little insect. It lives in your feet, . Where ever your feet go he goes with you. The Cinjuphi can Jump high high into the sky. It lives in your feet so your feet can Jump high. Old Cinjumhis loose their spring and they settle in old peoples feet (that is the reason that old people cannot Jump high.) The first person in America was Christopher Colombus Cinjumhi, he got so nervous and exited that he Jumped right out of Christopher Colombus's foot and across the Atlantic Ocean he jumped right on Amereia. The Cinjumhi of My foot has a good heritage he was George Washingmachin's Cinjumhi. Also his Uncle was the Cinjumhi president

The Cinjumhi →

the super-
← Springs

Figure 13

Time

Time is a tricky little varmit. People get mixed up like this they say: Now is Now and then is then so now then, then is now and now is then so ther and now are the same. Do you follow me? We say the Wright brothers were the first people to Fly, but really Time was. You can not feel time, or see it. Its Favorite game is hide-and-seek which he plays at night, in the day he is there and in the night he isn't. Now then, if now is then and then is now now and then are then and now and then and now are now and then, so now and then are then and now so now and then are ... . NOW AND Then!

Figure 14

the boy after the writing of "My Vacation," and in the second five entries (figs. 10–14) there is feeling enough. Clearly they are written from a different impulse of the boy's mind. The "persona" is less public and official; so are the forms and style. The quirkishness, whimsy, and wit that surfaced a few times in the first group are now apparent throughout. And instead of a neutral, typical, impersonal voice doing a job it knows how to, we hear the voice of an individual in something like its full complexity.

What seems to be apparent in the expression is the need to be in a dominant position, or the need to experience the feelings that go with being so. This is very conspicuous in the fantasies on the garbage can and on the Cinjumhi; it seems to appear in the final parenthesis of "The Moon." But I think it would be too easy to say that these pieces simply express the drives of a boy nearing adolescence. It is something of a problem, to be sure, what this boy does begin to do when he sheds the mask of the official school writer; but clearly he is finding himself able (or needing) to use writing as an expressive outlet.

"The garbage can is a neat little device," he says patronizingly, using a boyish idiom and making a pretty good topic sentence. Then he begins his "paragraph development" with a fairly reasonable specific fact: "You can throw everything in it." The effect is, perhaps, a little harsh, but still it cannot be denied that garbage cans are for throwing things in; and of course "you" is a general pronoun, which perhaps somewhat removes the writer from direct involvement. It is not that others do the throwing, but merely that whatever is implicated in the notions of throwing and garbage cans is something that is part of everyone's life and experience.

In his next sentence, the boy is all sympathy for the "poor tired, little, or big garbage can," not only for what it suffers—having things thrown into it—but also for being deprived of "all the credit," presumably for the job it does. Then—did that last sentence strike at some sensitive area?—the boy withdraws from his fantasy, goes back to his official and learned voice that knows all about "developing paragraphs," and gives us another "specific detail": garbage cans are green and red, which is a rather odd statement.

At this point, however, the boy almost gives up what has been—fairly obviously—a typical "paragraph development," right out of the books. First he shifts from the container to the contained: "The Garbage's only friend is the Garbage Man." He holds the form of the sentence to the mode of plain statement about the world; but for its content he turns again to a pre-rational world where life is everywhere: garbage cans are poor, tired, and unrewarded; garbage has a friend. Again the device is used to carry an expression of sympathy. And again the expression (or the identification implicated in it) seems to send him back to the language of exercises in paragraph development. Garbage ladies are going to "come into being" (a curiously adult phrase) to supplant garbage men because the books say that women are taking over jobs formerly done by men, especially, no doubt, in Russia.

The effect of the sentence is close to a burlesque of social studies information. And perhaps it was this that led the boy to the mocking allusion to Patrick Henry that he finishes with. One or two other things need to be said, however. First, here the boy once again shows his familiarity with the conventions of adult writing. "As Patrick Henry once said" is a typical introduction for an allusion. And using an allusion to summarize or pull together a set of loosely connected statements is a device that is found fairly often in adult writing, especially of an oratorical sort. Second, though this allusion may seem logically unpredictable, its meaning is really quite open, given the implications that seem to be carried in the somewhat surrealistic structure and texture of the whole "paragraph." For in this entry, the first of the ten that seems to be something like a personal expression, the boy does seem to base his writing on some sort of interplay between constraint or convention and freedom or revolt, to which this allusion comes as a wholly proper climax.

The boy and his uncertain feelings are pretty clear in his lovely fantasy on the Cinjumhi. On the one hand, there are the self-denying distortions in the figure of the Cinjumhi at the bottom of the page; on the other hand, there are the assertions of very great power; jumping the Atlantic Ocean, the super-springs, the association with quasi-legendary figures. There is also some evidence of an effort—really rather a considerable one—to strengthen the masking function of the symbol. The Cinjumhi is "a funny little insect" (cf. the garbage can—"a neat little device"). It is located in the feet, where it naturally, obviously, and neutrally "ought" to be, considering the connection with jumping. The boy's own Cinjumhi has very respectable antecedents, though not through a father, it would appear. Since the Cinjumhi "can jump high into the sky," the symbol may contain some expression of escape, though of course the possibility of separating the Cinjumhi from its human host would also be a neutralizing device of some complexity.

Perhaps there is still another protective device in the way the boy follows the schoolbook formula for "the paragraph." Note the repeated pattern in the opening sentences of four of the last five selections:

> The garbage can is a neat little device.
> The moon is a semi-heavenly body.
> The Cinjumhi is a funny little insect.
> Time is a tricky little varmit.

The one sentence that does not follow the pattern is the one that he fails to finish:

> Flowers, their colors red, yellow, green.

II

I am not sure how much may be made of the writings of these two boys. Very likely it will be said that two gifted boys in a special class where, presumably, expression is being encouraged are slim grounds for generalizing. To which objection will be added the fact that the writings in hand are themselves special cases, having been free work, done to the children's own demands and interests, with a minimum of teacherly direction or interference. If neither writers nor writings are typical, to say nothing of the inadequacy of the sample, what use discussion? None, I suppose, unless we are willing to make two stipulations: first, that the difference between gifted and ordinary is one of degree, not of kind; and, second, that there is some value (at least a heuristic one) in the questions that develop when individual or special cases are examined in relation to perceived or imagined probabilities. And I have to say that for me at least the writings of these two boys do raise questions that seem generally applicable, or at least that seem to be worth examining for general significance.

Let me begin with the case that is most difficult for my argument, that of the nine-year-old in the fourth grade. I am sure you will long since have begun to wonder what relevance he and his works may have for you, since his writing is at a very far remove from what is generally done in schoolrooms. I concede the fact. Obviously the boy's poems have a kind of independent life. You don't need to know him or be his teacher to get some pleasure from them. They can exist and give pleasure in their own terms, because they are pretty clearly "works" as well as expressive sounds. This may be especially true of the poem about Mercury. It seems to have no personal meaning at all and to be interesting for its formal qualities alone—the achievement of a jauntiness in rhythm and tone that is peculiarly satisfying or pleasing.

To a degree the same thing can be said of the writings of the second boy, the twelve-year-old in sixth grade. Of course he doesn't produce anything like the "works" of the first boy. Yet it would be hard not to find at least some independent pleasure in the "persona" suggested by his style. For one thing, he writes like a person who has a strong feeling for words as such. "George Washingmachin" in "The Cinjumhi" is a fine touch, and the word-play in "Time" is very engaging, unless the apparent disorganization is taken to be symptomatic. Even the clichés in "The Flag" and "Baseball" show the boy's responsiveness to sounds and patterns of words. And as I have already suggested, he seems to have some feeling for form, even though he may not have the means to realize it completely.

Yet when one looks at all the entries of the two boys, what stands out immediately is the number of them that share neither the expressive nor the artistic values that I have been discussing. In his middle three entries—all of them reports of personal doings—the second boy falls into a mode of expression that is, to say the least, impoverished and constrained. In "Flowers" and "The Moon," which sound like the beginning of reports, he seems plaintive and uncertain as well as inarticulate. In none of these does he show even a suggestion of the fluency he had in "Baseball" and "Time." The effect is as if we were dealing with the writings of two quite different boys.

The same is so of the first boy's curious entry on the moose. This looks very much like any ordinary piece of school writing, one of those practice exercises, the staples of classroom times for writing, that are intended to increase the accuracy or clarity (or some other, similar, abstractions) of the writing that children will be doing some day. As school writing goes, his effort is certainly "better" than those of his older classmate. But it still has its roughnesses: the omission of the apostrophes in two out of three contractions, the use of "a" (the indefinite article) before a word beginning with a vowel sound, comparatively monotonous and unfluent sentences.

Perhaps the boys simply weren't very much interested when they were doing these pieces. Presumably all of us, not just children, experience periods of relative unsuccess, if not actual failure, in the goings-on of living, including writing and other productive actions. And lack of interest is as good an explanation for them as any that is now likely to be brought forward. *Et bonus dormitat Homerus,* and even Shakespeare wrote *Love's Labour's Lost.*

But of course, as teachers, and concerned with the regularities on which planning is dependent, we want to know what it is that leaves the boys without interest. It may have been what they were writing about. That is, for the one boy, moose, or at least that moose, may have had so little value or such strong negative value as to prevent marshalling of the energy necessary for expression and productive work. And so for the other boy, with his flowers, moon, and trips. This conclusion hardly provides the kind of regularity on which increment, sequence, and development can be built, especially if we consider the possibility that the affect content of the subjects may have been, in some sense, temporary or depending on circumstances of the moment.

It is also something to consider, that the boys did choose these subjects; they were not assigned. Such a fact may lead us away from the niceties of learning theory into the "inviolate retirement" of basic motivations, or it may simply suggest that children are very powerfully affected by our teaching, so that even when free, they choose to do what they have learned they will be rewarded for, even though what is chosen may be in some sense antipathetic to them and hence productive, if of anything, of either withdrawal or at least restriction of reward. At any rate, it seems clear that when we discuss children's lack of interest in subjects as a cause of failure in either communication or artistic production, we are touching very complicated problems indeed. And perhaps the best conclusion is that we must be prepared for failures which have nothing to do with achieved competence or innate talents. It seems to me that we must, therefore, go very carefully when we think about planning programs for writing in the schools. Must we, perhaps, even give up the very notion of "program"?

But unfortunately there is another, and perhaps equally plausible, explanation for these unsuccessful or unsatisfying writings. Maybe it will be a more useful one, since it brings us close to matters which at least seem to be subject to correction or improvement by instruction. Perhaps the boys were put off less by their subjects than by the kind of writing they had chosen to do. I know, as you do, that we have very little that is either precise or even useful in the way of a theory of writing kinds; so I am not sure what sense there is in that last notion of mine. But still I suppose we can at least distinguish, broadly, between writing that appears to be directed toward an audience and writing that, in some way, seems to be done for reasons of self-satisfaction. If those are not generally useful classes, at least they seem to work here. Whatever success these boys had came to them in the entries for which the audience seems to have been themselves, and the end, consequently, the creation in themselves of a pleasure or satisfaction that, whatever its ultimate psychic cause, had its immediate cause in what they were doing.

No doubt "what they were doing" is somewhat question-begging. I am willing to settle for saying that it means something like "expressing themselves for their own purposes" and "making or attempting to make self-sufficient structures in words." And I guess I had better say at the same time that I am not disturbed if those definitions connect children's writing with the old romantic senses of the word "poetry." "Poetry, in a general sense," Shelley said, "may be defined to be 'the expression of imagination'; and poetry is connate with the origin of man." Then, after a short and vivid passage of epistemological speculation, he goes on:

> A child at play by itself will express its delight [in the internal and external impressions that are "driven" over man's brain] by its voice and motions; and every inflexion of tone and every gesture will bear exact relation to a corresponding antitype in the pleasurable impressions which awakened it. . . . In relation to the objects which delight a child, these expressions are what poetry is to higher objects.[4]

The passage has its fame, though perhaps more as an example of lavish prose than as a statement of reasoned principles according to which action can be planned. Yet I think that in it, as in many other pieces of romantic criticism, there is a conception of man and language and the functional relationship between them, which, if we attended to it, would offer us quite firm basis for planning.

But that is a matter for another time. Right now I want to indulge myself in some speculation concerning what seems to me to be the central fact about these writings. I mean that the unsuccessful ones are all attempts at communications (in fact, reports) directed toward general audiences. The relatively successful pieces are expressions which seem to be directed toward no audience but the children themselves. (In the latter case, it should be understood, I include internalized objects as constituents of the personality.) It occurs to me that this fact—if you will allow me to use that word in connection with what I have just said—may be an important one for those who are interested in putting sequence, increment, and development into the "composition component" of the English curriculum. Perhaps there is a question here: Does writing for a general audience somehow create conditions that weaken a child's command of whatever practical knowledge is necessary for the creation of satisfying pieces of writing?

Here the operative word is "general." I do not for a moment suppose that children cannot sense and respond to the demands of a real audience. We hear them doing it all the time, for example as they adjust the register (sometimes perhaps even the dialectical forms) of their speech to the various occasions of school life and business, or as they make accommodations of tone, gesture, or posture. But such adaptations are made in response to the exigencies of

---

[4] From the second paragraph of the "Defence of Poetry."

an immediate, concrete situation. The audience is physically present; in most cases, it is also known. In some sense, it is part of the child or at least of his experience. Note the child's (anyone's, for that matter) difficulties fixing his register and tone when he has to talk to someone unknown, especially if the person carries signs in his speech, dress, or manners that suggest his membership in a class different from that of the child.

But the first fact about a general audience is that it is not real, not present, and not known. Even to conceive such an abstraction, let alone then write to it, would, I should think, require conceptualizing and imaginative powers of a very high order. My own suspicion is that even adult professional writers are not really up to the job, and perhaps indeed not very much interested in it. Children, then, so much the less.

But the boys whose papers I have been discussing are young and perhaps not yet much touched by the procedures of the school, and certainly they are in a very special situation, where, no doubt, the play of the fancy is highly rewarded. So before drawing any general implications from their work, I should, I suppose, see whether I can make similar observations of other examples.

III

The papers I shall discuss next were written by tenth grade children in more or less formal circumstances which they may well have regarded as like those of a test, even though they were told that their work would not be graded. The assignment was designed so that the children would have to work in two different kinds of writing situations. They wrote one paper without any preparation; the other they did after some reflection and gathering of material at home, in the interval between two school days. It may be odd that the impromptu theme was to be "a thoughtful opinion, perhaps a paragraph or two, about summer school." For the prepared theme, though, the children were told "to be ready to describe some room—or a part of a room—in the place where you live. What room or part of a room you decide to write about is important." Both papers were to be done in fifteen minutes.

I know that the terms of the assignment are very difficult. Write "a thoughtful opinion" and "be ready to describe a room" gave the children no indication of what formal requirements were being set them; and their uncertainty would hardly have been eased by hearing that, in the first case, they could write "perhaps a paragraph or two." And one can well imagine that many of the children must have wondered why their choice of room was so important. Finally, how many even very skillful writers could plan and execute a piece of writing, even a short one of "perhaps a paragraph or two" in just fifteen minutes?

In response to that last question, it may be said that letter writers do so all the time. And as a matter of fact, any realistic appraisal of the writing done in American schools would lead, I suspect, to the conclusion that most of it is on the order of letters. One reason for this may be just the problem of writing for a general audience that I have mentioned. Writing has to be written to someone, real or otherwise. Even though a child cannot cope with the concepts involved in "general audience," he still always has an audience of some sort. The trouble is that it is generally an unacknowledged one, a friend, a relative, a teacher that is present to the child's feelings but not to his consciousness. But of course individuals of that sort are very seldom the recipients of arguments, analyses, reports that are cast in any of the forms of public discourse.

The situation would not be so bad if we were willing to accept its consequences. But in fact we are always complaining about lack of form, structure, organization, or what not. Such complaints can only mean, it seems to me, that we are unsatisfied by the forms appropriate to personal sorts of writing. Yet if we make formal stipulations in our assignments, they are perhaps less than helpful for the problem. One teacher says, "I find that it is necessary to set a definite length (number of sentences or page portion) when dealing with seventh graders. This seems to give them a framework for planning." No doubt. But what is a child to do with such rather linear directions, except produce pieces that are like letters or—at best but hardly as a result of planning—the informal essay, as it used to be called? The fact is that we give children all too little chance to experience in their reading examples of the forms of public discourse that, with greater or lesser awareness, we set as models for their writing.

The first papers in this group (set I) were done by a girl in a high ability section; the second (set II) by a boy in one for children of low ability. I shall make some general comments on both sets, before trying to see what, if anything, they may tell us about children and the problem of audience.

Set I

I

My bed distinguishes my room from any other room in my home or in any other house. Many people have single beds such as I have. Several people even have canopies over their beds, but I have a semi-canopy with long flowing white curtains which surround the head of the bed. The curtains are ruffled and at certains times of the year, artificial flowers are hung on the ruffles.

My animal friends, a thirty-seven year old teddy, a black musical lamb with pink ears, and a light-gray elephant with red feet and a curled nose, peer out from behind the curtains. They sit and play on a white eyelet bedspread. The lamb likes the flowered eyelet with the pink blanket showing through the holes. He also likes the maple with a fruitwood finish of which my bed is made.

My bed is the center of activity in my bedroom. On it, I may do my homework or watch television with my animal friends.

II

Summer school is a good idea, because it provides extra learning opportunities as well as extra help. ———— High School has a plan whereby a student may take summer courses for the enjoyment of gaining knowledge or in order to make up credits for graduation. This plan seems best, because some students need extra help, while others yearn for advancement. Summer school gives one a chance to broaden his learning experiences before he enters the business-world.

Some drawbacks are presented by summer school, however. One could be working to save money for college, while broadening his experience with the business world. A job would help earn money for the future. It would also help give one an idea of life after schooling, thereby preparing one for life. It could help one decide on ones future occupation.

Both going to summer school and getting a job would help one.

Set II
I

As I open one of the sliding doors in my room, the first unforgettable sight I see is the brown stained cherry wood on the walls. Across from the entrance there is three sun windows on the the other wall is two more. My dresser and desk lay along the east wall. There is also a cozy little rug (circular shape) that covers the entire middle portion of the room. The room looks so clean homy I just like to sit in there and think of the days doings.

II

I think that summer school shouldent be forced to take if a person flunks a subject. I think when he or She gets in hi-school, they should realize the importance of a high school education and not to fool around and flunk. Because summer school is just another discouragement after another (flunking). If he or she still insists on flunking courses they should have their hi school education lengthened an extra year or so whichever it takes to complete it.

Ignoring for the moment the attitudes and values expressed by the girl, and thinking only of the qualities of the language, what one notices at once, and with some uneasiness, is its excessive correctness: for example, the careful shift of the terminal preposition in "of which my bed is made," the equally careful comma after the artificially placed "On it" in the last sentence of the first paper, the two all too precise "one . . . his" constructions, and the rather heavy "both . . . and" correlative.

A second disturbing quality in the language is its prevailing formality and fussiness. A bed is said to "distinguish" a room. The writer has a "home"; other people only have "houses." Some kind of parallelism is sought in "Many people . . . several people," evidently without any thought for meaning. Toys move and have their little feelings. Students in a suburban high school have "learning opportunities" and "learning experiences," and knowledge is said to be gained, experience to be broadened. Young people enter the business world, earn money for the future; they get ideas about life after schooling and thus are prepared for life. It is all very genteel, very schoolroomish; and quite, quite dispiriting.

Obviously the girl has pretty clear ties to modern literary culture, if only in its schoolroom forms. Not so the boy in the low ability section. For him, writing—the written dialect—means little more than a transcript of speech. In his first piece, for example, he must surely use the run-on sentence, so called, and fail to hold "homy" to the rest of its sentence by punctuation chiefly because he has been unable to find graphic equivalents for the pauses, hesitations, and rhythms of his speech. Or perhaps he simply made too literal a copy of the paratactic structure of speech.

In the erratically constructed sentences of his second piece there is an example of what happens with a child who is unfamiliar with the conventions according to which written discourse is organized. We say he doesn't think ahead, and we put him into low ability sections. But really his trouble is that, for various reasons, he is mainly used to ordinary conversation, with all the discontinuities and meanderings by which human beings constantly and easily adjust the patterns of their talk, in a kind of flowing response to the totality of the experience.

Obviously these two children are at or near the extremes of the ability in school children to deal with the comparatively rigid patterns of written English. For the girl, secure in the culture of the school, at ease with the graphics of writing, the papers must have been easy and satisfying to write. No doubt she thought she was "putting across" her subjects; and no doubt she was. For that "light-gray elephant with red feet and a curled nose," the product of years of faithful teaching and quick learning, must have mightily pleased both her and her teacher. But there is more to her than that, and I would be quite unfair if I left the impression that her papers get their entire value from being successful examples of the rather specialized genre that school writing is. The world itself, the rich, intractable world of fact and feeling, is not entirely concealed, not entirely shut away by the heavy shroud of the girl's words and her complacent, vulgar value system. The two little misspellings throw their own kind of light into the naughty schoolroom world. And the lamb who likes "the flowered eyelet with the pink blanket showing through the holes'' may be a means of expressing and controlling some feelings that were quite the girl's own.

Taking everything into account, perhaps the girl does deserve to be placed in a high ability section. Yet the fact remains that the only worthwhile matter in her papers is that little section, in the first one, on the toys, where for a moment she seems to free herself from the schoolroom's restrictive conventions of language and form. Her second paper is a collection of platitudes, of which the best that can be said is that it probably represents a reasonably competent assessment of an audience; the worst, that it does represent the child's own value system. In general the papers suggest a deplorable lack of contact with the real world, a dangerous refusal to look beyond words to facts. It is perhaps also to be noted that even in the passage on the toys the total effect is somewhat regressive and rigid.

For the boy, it is clear, words-in-writing come hard. If he gets any satisfaction from his papers, it seems unlikely that he would find any corroboration, approval, or support shown by his teacher. Would he have known, after writing it, how fine a last sentence he gave the paper on his room? ''The room looks so clean homy I just like to sit in there and think of the days doings.'' Would he have been complimented on that rhythm, that cadence (complete with alliteration), that easy, clear, and full expression of real feeling? Would any notice have been taken of the thought and feeling in the sentence fragment in the second paper? ''Because summer school is just another discouragement after another (flunking).'' Who would there be to get beyond his curious spellings, his odd punctuation, his trouble with verb form and number—and to listen to him? And considering his probable reputation, and his placement, who would there be to suppose that he should be listened to at all?

For that matter, how many of us now have noticed the very considerable freedom of expression in the boy's first paper? He begins, of course, with a perfunctory catalog that is straight out of the directions in some book. (''A description of a room may be begun by imagining yourself opening the door for a visitor. What is the first thing he would see? The next? Or perhaps you can organize your description by following around the walls of the room.'') But he sustains virtue for only a moment, and then, forgetting the books (though perhaps not the audience he was feeling), he gets to expressing himself pretty directly about items of value to him. At that point, incidentally, his paper rather stops being a piece of writing, and somehow it takes on a kind of general interest. For the moment the boy has triumphed over the rules and all his learnings.

But the triumph is in fact an intensely personal one, and perhaps for that reason somewhat unconnected with the purposes (whatever they may be) of a "description," such as the assignment required. In the first part of the paper, where he seems to try to meet the requirements of a description as he understands them, the boy was considerably less successful in making contact. I think the reason for this is simply that he chose there to take a more or less impersonal approach to his subject without knowing enough of the various stylistic conventions of the impersonal registers so as to be able to use his own language. Like many of his seniors, he had available only the very special variety of impersonal English that is taught and cultivated in schoolrooms. Only when he gave this up and let himself just write down something he might have said did he get close to anything like an interesting piece of writing, let alone a full and expressive communication.

Curiously, what success the boy had in his second paper seems to have come precisely because he refused to use the kind of language which the assignment presumably called for. As in the first paper, he simply took down what he said to himself (or to whomever he conceived to be his audience). The result seems to be a struggling jumble of sentences, straggling back and forth from one level of generalization to another, without any apparent signs of direction or confidence, though not without a topic sentence. Probably the result would universally be judged a bad theme; yet withal it seems to me a rather successful communication. For the boy did manage to get out a simple, practical, workaday comment and solution. In fact he showed himself to be a good deal more in touch with the world of things and facts than was the girl, for whom, it would seem from her paper, words were everything.

In sum, taking "writing" in the broadest and most creative sense, it is not at all clear which of these students is superior. Indeed, the boy may come off slightly the better. But that, it will be said, is a more or less romantic judgment based on an analysis that is quite remote from what *must* go on in the classroom, because of what society or parents or employers or somebody wants. There, in the classroom, it is said, the only problem is how to bring writing like the boy's up to the cleanness of the girl's. And of course spelling, punctuation, grammar, and paragraphing are important, and it would be very nice indeed if the boy—and all those like him—could turn out papers that would be mechanically inoffensive. But would it not also be nice if the girl—and all others like her—could say as much as the boy? Is it not also a great problem to bring the girl up to being as expressive as the boy? Perhaps the true problem of the classroom is a double one: how to clean up the boy's writing, how to emancipate the girl's thoughts and feelings from the constraint of schoolroom conventions. But the girl's tight, inhibited, rather impersonal style points the same way as the boy's mechanical errors. They are both, as it were, indexes of discomfort. And so the double problem is, perhaps, a single one after all: how can the composition class, the teaching of writing, and indeed writing itself be made to seem natural and pleasurable, the occasion and means of a satisfying (even a self-consummatory) experience instead of, as they too often still are, a chance for teaching (though not necessarily for learning) that mysterious entity known as "good English"?

IV

No doubt the conditions for successful and pleasurable writing are many and various among individuals; probably no one of them can be considered sufficient to the desired end; and only a few are under control of the school. Yet, recognizing all those and other qualifications, it does seem possible to say that among the conditions that children need if they are to achieve success in written works is some sense that the writing they are doing is real and of value to them. To have this sense they must either have or be able to feel that they have a fairly distinct audience.

Very young children and also, perhaps, the very talented seem to be able to find an audience within themselves. It may be said of them that they retain a contact with "the visionary gleam"; "the shaping spirit of the imagination" remains with them. They are open to experience, willing to express themselves, able to find sympathy with others. They can see *and* feel an experience in its moment, in all its existential particularity; they are able to take into their awareness "all the varied sensings and perceivings" that are going on within themselves; and retaining that which "dissolves, diffuses, dissipates" the rigid givens of conventional perceptions, the standard responses to experience, they can give effect to the human organism's tendency "to expand, extend, develop, mature" in a constant process of recreating the self in an environment that is, to some degree, made by the self.[5]

> O Lady! we receive but what we give,
> And in our life alone does Nature live:
> Ours is her wedding garment, ours her shroud!
>   And would we aught behold, of higher worth,
> Than that inanimate cold world allowed
> To the poor loveless ever-anxious crowd,
>   Ah! from the soul itself must issue forth
> A light, a glory, a fair luminous cloud
>   Enveloping the Earth—
> And from the soul itself must there be sent
>   A sweet and potent voice, of its own birth,
> Of all sweet sounds the life and element! [6]

Children who are free in that way can, it seems, demonstrate considerable powers of expression in language. They can arrange words into shapes that at least give every appearance of being self-consistent and internally determined. It looks as if they can find in working with words the same kinds of satisfactions that acknowledged literary artists are said to do. Or at least, reading what such children write, we seem to be able to make the same kind of infer-

---

[5] The material in this paragraph is drawn from the Intimations Ode, the Dejection Ode, *Biographia Literaria* (Chapter XII), and from Carl Rogers, "Toward a Theory of Creativity," in Harold H. Anderson (ed.), *Creativity and Its Cultivation* (New York: Harper & Row, Publishers, 1959), pp. 69–82, esp. p. 72.
[6] The Dejection Ode, lines 47–58.

ence about causes that we do in the case of literary artists. Even children who cannot make works that have the qualities of wholes can be supposed to receive from parts of their writing some quantity of the pleasure that derives from creation.

I should think that teachers ought to try to develop, in every way possible, and all through the school years, situations in which as many children as can will be able to exercise their creative powers. Yet evidently this is not, cannot be enough. For the shades of the prison house do begin to close:

> —But there's a Tree, of many, one,
> A single Field which I have looked upon,
> Both of them speak of something that is gone:
> >   The Pansy at my feet
> >   Doth the same tale repeat:
> Whither is fled the visionary gleam?
> Where is it now, the glory and the dream? [7]

To put it directly, children—or some children—do begin to have thoughts to develop; opinions to express, reports to make, analyses to detail, arguments to expound. Some children will perhaps want to put their interests and concerns into writing. To help at this stage of growth and schooling, teachers probably ought to be constantly trying to restore or preserve, to whatever extent possible, the freedom in awareness that seems to be characteristic of young or talented children. In particular they should be trying to assure that children remain autonomous as to the actions and feelings involved in writing, insofar as autonomy is a feasible condition in classrooms. This means that they must be willing to accept the children's own perceptions of need, purpose, and value in writing. Or to put it another way, they must be willing to let children find their own audiences, fulfill their own intentions in whatever writing they choose to do.

There seems to be no necessary reason why teachers cannot serve as appropriate audiences for children. Of course, as Sybil Marshall is quoted in the beginning of this paper, age and interests do make

---

[7] The Intimations Ode, lines 51–57.

for difficulty in the relationship, on both sides. But no doubt compromises can be worked out, especially if the teacher can remain a reader and not become a judge, and if the child does in fact find himself needing to write something for such an adult. On the whole, though, it seems likely that children will receive satisfaction from their writing more often if they are doing it for their fellows.

Insofar as a child may be representative of those to whom he writes, he should be able to feel what they will discover themselves to have wanted to read after it has been produced for them. Responses to any product will, no doubt, vary among individuals, in the world out there, those with whom the writer is trying to make contact. But again, to the extent that a child's responses are representative, he will know what it is necessary for him to do to succeed. Thus he will have what may be the most important condition for success in any creative or productive activity; that is, an internal locus of evaluation. If he does succeed, it will be for reasons that he can at least feel, if not understand; if he should fail, then too the causes will be open to him, his to change, if he wishes to.[8]

Obviously classrooms favorable to the conditions of creativity and expression, such as those I have been sketching, would be very different indeed from those we know today. Yet it seems to me that some change in that direction is a most serious need in our time. We must free ourselves, so that our students may be free. The situation is as Carl Rogers describes it:

—if we can add to the sensory and visceral experiencing, which is characteristic of the whole animal kingdom, the gift of a free and undistorted awareness, of which only the human animal seems capable, we have an organism which is aware of the demands of the culture as it is of its own physiological demands for food or sex; which is just as aware of its desire for friendly relationships as it is of its desire to aggrandize itself; which is just as aware of its delicate and sensitive tenderness towards others as it is of its hostilities towards others. When man's unique capacity of awareness is thus functioning freely and fully, we find that we have, not an animal whom we must fear,

---

[8] Some of the ideas in this paragraph are drawn from a comment on editor and audience in Norman Podhoretz, *Making It* (New York: Random House, Inc., 1968), p. 223.

not a beast who must be controlled, but an organism able to achieve, through the remarkable integrative capacity of its central nervous system, a balanced, realistic, self-enhancing, other-enhancing behavior as a resultant of all these elements of awareness. To put it another way, when man is less than fully man—when he denies to awareness various aspects of his experience—then indeed we have all too often reason to fear him and his behavior, as the present world situation testifies. But when he is most fully man, when he is his complete organism, when awareness of experience, that peculiarly human attribute, is most fully operating, then he is to be trusted, then his behavior is constructive. It is not always conventional. It will not always be conforming. It will be individualized. But it will also be socialized.[9]

And it is such growth in awareness that English and especially composition are all about.[10]

QUESTIONS FOR DISCUSSION

1. Douglas argues that children's writing should be judged and valued according to standards developed specifically for and appropriate to such writing (as distinguished from standards applicable to adult writing). Do you agree? If not, why not?

2. What standards has Douglas developed to judge children's writing? Would Whipp accept Douglas' standards? Do *you* accept them? If not, why not?

3. What is your evaluation of the pieces of student writing that appear (in type) on pages 289–290?

4. Douglas implies disappointment at seeing "school writing" in some of the examples he gives. Do you think disappointment with this sort of writing is an appropriate response? Why?

[9] Carl R. Rogers—"Some Directions and End Points in Therapy," in *Psychotherapy: Theory and Research,* edited by O. Hobart Mowrer—Copyright 1953—The Ronald Press Company, New York.
[10] The author here expresses his gratitude for permissions to use students' work in this paper.

5. Douglas occasionally guesses at the feelings and attitudes communicated (perhaps unconsciously) by the student writers. Is this a fair approach to student writing? Can it be done reliably? If a teacher does it, how might he or she use the guesses arrived at? Ought they to guide the teacher's way of working with the student? How?

6. Are you willing to make Douglas' stipulation that "the difference between gifted and ordinary is one of degree, not of kind"? Why or why not?

7. Do you find Douglas' distinction between writing done for an audience and writing done for the students' own selves a useful distinction? Does it parallel James Britton's distinctions? Is it useful in evaluating children's writing? in planning a curriculum for writing?

8. What might be your answers to the question with which Douglas concludes part III? Do you agree that the goal implicitly suggested by Douglas is worth seeking? Has Douglas answered his own question later in the essay?

9. What sorts of audiences is Douglas advocating for young writers in part IV? Can a teacher, by his or her behavior, make it easier or more pleasurable for the student to seek out those audiences? How?

Conflicting Claims: Parental Expectations and Professional Expertise

Leslie T. Whipp

One can respond to students' writing by noting the freshness and honesty with which the students express what they see and feel or by judging the development of the features of the student's language and perception, or both. In the following essay, Leslie Whipp presents still another way to respond to student writing, that is, to describe as fully and as precisely as possible the language, the structure, and the substantive content of successive pieces produced by a student and then to look at the results for signs of progress in the student's handling of language. In the present selection, Whipp applies his analytical techniques to a child's myth written in prose, but he would argue that the same techniques will work on any form of children's writing. Though his title implies that he would use his techniques to gather information for discussions with parents, Whipp would probably assert also that whatever decisions the teacher makes about the emphases and procedures to be used in teaching, and about advice to students, ought to come from analyses such as he proposes here.

   Leslie T. Whipp developed the techniques presented here while on the faculty at the University of Nebraska, where he worked with the Nebraska Curriculum Center in English.

From *Elementary English* Vol. 49, No. 2 (1972), pp. 171–78. Copyright © 1972 by the National Council of Teachers of English. Reprinted by permission of the publisher and the author.

Mechanics and correction are largely irrelevant to composition instruction and composition language learning, as I have previously argued.[1] What a student must learn is immensely more subtle, complex, and useful than are mechanics, and most of it is still indescribable. Further, such intervention as "correction" plays little part, in fact, in a child's learning of language.

One might be prepared to grant all that and still be intimidated at the prospect of acting on it in the classroom. The kids expect mechanics-correction teaching, one's colleagues expect mechanics-correction teaching, supervisors and administrators expect mechanics-correction teaching, parents expect mechanics-correction teaching. That's intimidating. So far as the kids are concerned, though, they'll prefer alternatives, any alternatives, once they've experienced them. Colleagues, supervisors, and administrators will be neutralized so long as kids do not perform significantly worse on standard achievement tests, and there is no reason to expect that under any other system the kids would do significantly worse on these tests than they do under mechanics-correction teaching. But parents? Parents are a horse of a different color. Most, I'd guess, couldn't care less. Some will care positively, some negatively, and the vocal minority are likely to be those who care negatively.

I'd guess they *do care,* they are serious, and want their kids to learn. Their problem, though, is simply ignorance of "composition concepts," i.e. ignorance of what there is to learn in learning to write well. If that is indeed the problem, then one solution would seem to be some attempt to educate them. Two forms which this might take are (1) a brief explanatory paper, prepared by you and sent home early in the year, or two or three times during the year, making a fairly extensive analysis of a single student paper (or of a pair of student papers), illustrating the "composition concepts," which implicitly the kids are acquiring. And (2) a brief list of composition concepts relevant to a student's file of papers, a list which enables you to speak in parent-teacher conferences of items which the student does command.

[1] In "The Child as Language Teacher," *EE,* April 1969.

I want to try to illustrate the first sort of parent education device here. I'll record the steps I go through to derive it as well as the final product. There are in effect four steps: the first is a detailed analysis of each sentence in the story; the second is a topical summary of items discovered in the sentence-by-sentence analysis; the third is a sample prose elaboration for parents of the most significant features summarized in the second step. And the fourth step is the readiness to apply the first three steps to another instance of a child's composition.

STEP 1: SELECTION OF MATERIAL FOR ANALYSIS

In this case, I have a set of papers from a third grade classroom in Hastings, Nebraska, taught by Georgia Bishel. In the set, there is one which was a preliminary joint effort by the whole class, as well as many others which were efforts of individual members of the class. The story produced jointly by the whole class makes a convenient starting place, a source of a norm or stable point in terms of which to perceive individual motion in the other stories in the set, though obviously not a norm in the sense of a criterion in terms of which to evaluate the individual efforts of the class. To derive the description of the norm or stable point, I analyzed the story produced by the class as a whole, one sentence at a time, as follows:

(a) Long, long ago lived a greedy man named Judas, in the deep dark woods. 1 sentence; 1 T-unit [2]; 14 words

      (1) initial time reference
      (2) time reference varied from story formula, "Once upon a time"
      (3) name with conventional moral implications

---

[2] The term is from Kellogg Hunt, *Differences in Grammatical Structures Written at Three Grade Levels,* USOE Cooperative Research Project 1998 (Tallahassee, Fla.: Florida State University, 1964). In effect, I use it to designate an independent clause plus all subordinate elements, or an incomplete sentence punctuated as a separate sentence.

    (4) overt reference to literary tradition (Biblical: "Judas")

    (5) description by adjective in determiner + ——— + subject noun slot

    (6) early injection of moral problem

    (7) natural description

    (8) association of natural description with moral description

    (9) myth as having to do with moral problem

    (10) sentence inversion

    (11) human figure as character in myths

    (12) initial place reference

(b) He was a tax collector and he kept all the money. (11 words in 2 T-units, 5 in the first T-unit, 6 in the second)

    (1) compound sentence, "and" compounding of T-units

    (2) description by vocational class

    (3) descriptions by habitual action

    (4) description 2, 3 thematically related to moral description in sentence *a*

    (5) repetition of grammatical subject in pro-form

(c) He also hunted rabbits. (4)

    (1) description by habitual action

    (2) parallel syntax

    (3) animal figure as character in myths

    (4) action thematically related to moral description in sentences *a* and *b*

    (5) animal figure conventionally appropriate to the role it has in the story

(d) He caught all the rabbits he could see. (8)

    (1) terminal adjective clause

    (2) all + clause (intensity)

    (3) repetition of description by habitual action

        (4) description thematically related to description in first three sentences

        (5) parallel syntax

        (6) repetition of subject form

(e) He threw away the fur and left the meat out to rot. (12)

        (1) compound verb

        (2) repetition of description by habitual action

        (3) description thematically related to sentences *a*, *b*, *c*, and *d*

        (4) association of negative moral quality with negative physical process ("rot")

        (5) miming syntax: dividing verb to speak of dividing a thing ("rabbit")

(f) Many people were starving because he had taken all the rabbits. (11)

        (1) terminal "because" clause

        (2) shift of grammatical subject terminating a section of the narrative

        (3) occurrence of phrasal repetition "all the rabbits"

        (4) description by effect of habitual action

        (5) effect of habitual action explains moral judgment implicit in sentences *a*, *b*, *c*, *d* and *e*

        (6) tense contrast between verbs of main and subordinate clause

        (7) characterization by relating character to others

(g) The god of the rabbits saw this and disipproved of his greed, and wanted to put a stop to it. (20)

        (1) divine being as character in myth

        (2) divine being as moral judge in myth

        (3) divine being judging by conventional moral principle

        (4) double compounding of the verb

      (5) shift of grammatical subject at initiation of new segment of the narrative

      (6) long sentence to introduce impressive good guy

(h) But first he warned him, but it did no good. (10: 5, 5)

      (1) contiguity of longest and shortest T-units

      (2) brevity to speak of confrontation

      (3) brevity to speak of futility

      (4) occurrence of negative + brevity

      (5) anticipation of subsequent action

      (6) "but" compounding of T-units

      (7) characterization of good guy by action

(i) He still did it. (4)

      (1) brevity to speak of futility

      (2) repetition (paraphrase) to speak of futility

      (3) negative: shift of notional subject without corresponding shift of form of grammatical subject

      (4) intensifier "still"

      (5) characterization of bad guy by action in response to admonition

(j) So he called his noble birds, and they carried the god down to earth. (14: 6, 8)

      (1) characterization by adjective in determiner + ——— + object noun slot

      (2) characterization of good guy by relation to others (noble birds as servant entourage)

      (3) action implicity relating divine and human realms, the central point of nature myths

      (4) "And" compounding of T-units

      (5) "So" relation of bad guy, good guy actions

(k)   When the god touched the ground, he changed into a rabbit.
      (11)

         (1) metamorphosis action appropriate to myth
         (2) initial "when" clause
         (3) identification of victim with divine being
         (4) phrasal repetition ("the god") patterning with variation
             of filler in subject slots

(l)   That same day, Judas went out to hunt rabbits. (9)

         (1) initial time reference with new section of narrative
         (2) shift in subject slot with new section of narrative

(m) He saw the large, unusual rabbit, which he wanted to catch
     and kill. (13)

         (1) terminal adjective "which" clause
         (2) "which" clause with compound infinitive
         (3) length with preparation for confrontation
         (4) compound adjective in determiner + ———— + object
             noun slot
         (5) description by size (visual) in determiner + ———— +
             object noun slot
         (6) description by abstraction of viewer response ("un-
             usual") in determiner + ———— + object noun slot

(n)   Judas threw his net over the large and unusual rabbit. (10)

         (1) variation of pronoun to noun in subject slot with climac-
             tic bad guy action
         (2) repetition of phrase "the large and unusual rabbit" with
             climactic bad guy action
         (3) compound adjectives in determiner + ———— + object
             noun slot
         (4) implicit limitation to bad guy point of view
         (5) irony of "unusual"

(6) adjective ("large") related to bad guy's fault ("greedy")

(o) Just as the net came down on the rabbit god, he changed himself back to the god he was. (19)

(1) initial time reference with new narrative section
(2) grammatical subject shift with new narrative section
(3) prepositional phrase ("on the rabbit god") used to shift notional subject
(4) initial time reference very precise at good guy response
(5) terminal adjective clause ("he was") shifting to author perspective (contrast n-4 above)
(6) transformation involving appearance-reality deception related to the nature of the bad guy's moral confusion (he mistakes wealth for the Good instead of charity, as he mistakes the rabbit for an animal instead of a god)
(7) initial adverb clause ("just as")
(8) co-occurrence of initial adverb clause and terminal adjective clause
(9) maximum T-unit length for ante-climactic good guy response

(p) "So!" If you want to hunt and kill rabbits, I'll change you into a fox, so you can do it all your life. (23)

(1) shift to direct discourse at climax
(2) maximum T-unit length for climactic good guy response
(3) metamorphosis as moral punishment
(4) moral justice as climax
(5) climax as end
(6) compound infinitive in initial "if" clause
(7) initial "if" clause
(8) terminal "so" clause
(9) co-occurrence of initial "if" and terminal "so" clause
(10) repetition of verbal form from first sentence ("lived," "life") in terminal sentence
(11) use of quotation marks to mark direct discourse

(q) The-End.

    (1) transition from actions of fictional characters to action of story teller

    (2) transition explicit

STEP 2: SUMMARY OF NORM CHARACTERISTICS

1. Lengths
   a. 17 sentences total
   b. 20 T-units total
   c. 192 words
   d. 9.5 words/T-unit average
   e. 2 words/T-unit minimum
   f. 22 words/T-unit maximum
   g. 6 consecutive sentences on a single subject (character description)
   h. maximum sentence length progressive
   i. sentence brevity expressive (futility)
   j. sentence length expressive (impressive, climactic)
   k. paragraph length doesn't come in, since the scribe started each sentence flush with the left margin.

2. Syntax
   a. subject-verb inversion does occur in one declarative sentence, the initial sentence (1/16)
   b. subordinate clauses appear in 5/16 sentences
      (i) initial and terminal adverb clause ("if," "when," "just as," "so"), but no such clauses occur medially
      (ii) only terminal adjective clauses appear (either with no conjunction or with "which")
      (iii) co-occurrence of initial and terminal subordinate clauses
      (iv) length of long sentences tends to come from subordinate clauses
      (v) no nominal clauses
   c. compounded T-units ("and," "but") in 3/16 sentences

    d. compounded verb phrases, infinitive phrases, and adjectives

    e. adjectives only in determiner + —————— + noun slot in either subject or object positions, usually object positions

    f. syntactic parallelism in functionally parallel sentences (sentences *b, c, d, e*)

    g. miming syntax (sentence *e*)

    h. co-occurrence of initial adverbials of time and shifts in the narrative

3. Character
    a. Characterization by
        (i) stereotype name (literary tradition)
        (ii) association with physical description
        (iii) habitual action
        (iv) association with negative physical process
        (v) relationships with other people
        (vi) moral adjective
        (vii) ironic adjective
        (viii) visual adjective
        (ix) animal-moral stereotypes (rabbit, fox)
        (x) vocational classification
    b. Characters include divine, human, animal
    c. divine character associated with sustained moral order
    d. human character associated with transgression of moral order
    e. animal characters are transformations of human and divine characters

4. Plot or narrative
    a. five stages
        (i) introduction of human character
        (ii) introduction of divine character
        (iii) preliminary confrontation of human and divine character
        (iv) climactic confrontation (metamorphosis)
        (v) judgment (metamorphosis)

    b. progressive confrontations
    c. role of metamorphosis
       (i) as feature of myth
      (ii) as metaphor of moral theme

5. Rhetoric
    a. variation of initial time references
    b. progressive specificity of initial time references
    c. verbal phrasal repetition
    d. variation and repetition of grammatical subjects with stages of narrative action
    e. posing of moral problem implicitly in the first sentence
    f. myth as concerning maintenance of moral order
    g. moral justice as climax
    h. shift to direct discourse as climax
    i. terminal sentence ("The-End") as bridge from fictional to real world

6. Interpretation
      (i) little (defenseless victim) big (adult aggressor) opposition
     (ii) little (good, associated with divine)-big (bad) opposition
    (iii) good-little triumphs
    (iv) a moral order, a higher law, avenges innocent little ones by punishing bad big ones (*avenges,* not *protects*)
     (v) moral law, the higher law, is defined in human consequences (selfishness-charity; self and society, I and We opposition)

STEP 3: FORMULATION OF THE INSTRUCTIONAL MATERIAL FOR PARENTS

"You are doubtlessly concerned about just how much your child has developed in his abilities to use writing as a way of expressing himself, and of exploring and explaining and understanding his experience. In order to help him develop these abilities, our class has been reading and writing myths this term. After reading several, we began to compose our own, first by composing a myth jointly, all members of the class contributing something to the composition. Since this myth serves well to illustrate some of the composition concepts your child is acquiring or extending in writing his own myths. I thought you might like to see it, and when your child brings some of his myths home, you might appreciate them more by comparing the features he includes with those of the class myth.

"The class myth (recorded by one of the children, and reproduced here just as he recorded it) reads as follows:

THE FIRST FOX

Long, long ago lived a greedy man named Judas, in the deep dark woods. He was a tax collector, and he kept all the money. He also hunted rabbits. He caught all the rabbits he could see. He threw away the fur and left the meat out to rot. Many people were starving because he had taken all the rabbits. The god of the rabbits saw this and disipproved of his greed, and wanted to put a stop to it. But first he warned him, but it did no good. He still did it. So he called his noble birds, and they carried the God down to earth. When the god touched the ground he changed into a rabbit. That same day Judas went out to hunt rabbits. He saw the large unusual rabbit which he wanted to catch and kill. Judas threw his net over the large and unusual rabbit. Just as the net came down on the rabbit god, he changed himself back to the god he was. "So!" If you want to hunt and kill rabbits, I'll change you into a fox, so you can do it all your life. The-End.

"There are several interesting features. A good deal of progress from the second grade is evident in the spelling and punctuation. And lengths are surprisingly significant; as children extend their language ability they learn to lengthen their structures. The average sentence length here is 9.5 words, which is pretty good for third graders. They have good variety in sentence length, too, with a minimum of 4 words, a maximum of 22 words per sentence. The most surprising feature of sentence length is the great expressiveness the kids have achieved with it; notice how the shortest sentence (4 words) expresses futility, while (still more surprisingly) the longest sentences progressively express more and more impressiveness (introduction of the god, transformation of rabbit into god, and judgment of Judas). The kids also sustained the initial character description of Judas through six sentences, which is a considerable elaboration for the third grade.

"The way they are putting their sentences together is equally interesting. Although they do use compound sentences (as in the second sentence), they are expanding their sentences primarily through adding adverbial or adjectival clauses at the beginning or end (or both, as in the next to the last sentence). When they compound phrases, they compound only verb or infinitive phrases (as in the fifth and thirteenth sentences).

"One of the nicest features of the syntax, though, occurs in sentences in which we have a divided grammatical construction (the compound verb) to speak of dividing, or "miming syntax," grammar which acts out, as it were, what it speaks of, grammar which is itself a sort of metaphor.

"The way the kids work with the characters in the myth is particularly instructive. They see that the characters in myths are divine and animal as well as human. And they have drawn upon an astonishing number of devices in order to sketch these characters. They characterize chiefly by the nature of the habitual action they attribute to the character, as in sentences 4 and 5, or by individual action, as in sentences 8 and 9. But they also characterize by name ("Judas"), by vocational classification ("tax collector"), oral adjective ("greedy"), association with natural description ("in the deep dark woods"), association with unpleasant natural process ("rot"), animal-moral stereotypes ("rabbit," "fox"), and by relationships with other characters (sentences 6 and 10). The nicest touch, however, comes in sentences 13 and 14, with the adjective "unusual," for the adjective has a double function; the rabbit appears to be unusual to Judas only in its size, appealing to his predatory acquisitive instinct, but the writers and the readers know that the rabbit is far more unusual than Judas can know, as the writers indicate in the next sentence by the phrase "back to the god he was." This ironic change of perspective from sentences 13 and 14 to sentence 15 reproduces the main theme of the story, of course, the short-sightedness and limited awareness of the greedy man. That's a very nice bit of characterizing indeed.

"The narrative structure of the story works very smoothly, with the stages in the narrative signalled by changes in the grammatical forms of sentence subjects, as well as by initial time references. And the way the initial time references narrow in increasing specificity accentuates the progress of the narrative still further. The preliminary confrontation, when the god warns Judas, serves nicely both to build suspense for the final confrontation and to make it clear that Judas deserves whatever he gets, pig-headed sinner that he is!

"Several remarkable touches make the story coherent and pointed—the shift to direct discourse in the last sentence, the verbal repetition between the first and last sentence (''lived,'' ''life''), the semantic relationships between key words (''greedy,'' ''tax collector,'' ''kept,'' ''money,'' ''hunted,'' ''caught,'' ''large''), the use of repetition of words, phrases, and ideas, etc.

"The class myth is representative of many, many myths in several respects—in explaining how a natural phenomena came to be, in couching the explanation in terms of moral justice, in involving punishment and transformation, and in relating divine and human orders of experience. These are some of the features you recognize as conventional to myths.

"The most significant thing, of course, is the way the kids *use* the conventions of the myths to order and express their view of the world. They have essentially an opposition of the little, innocent, and defenseless with the big, evil, and adult, but there is a moral law transcending the arbitrary power of the adult in their universe, and that law avenges wrongs done to the innocent, defenseless, and small. It is particularly noteworthy, I think, that the law avenges, and does not directly intervene to protect: there is a kind of tough-mindedness in their view of the universe, as expressed in this myth.

"This story, of course, represents the work, perhaps the best work, of the class as a whole. What I've spoken of as ''norms'' are only very loosely ''norms'' at all. Many myths don't have all of the features found in this one, and many of the features found in others are not found in this one. So the features one does find in this one are perhaps less "norms" than "suggestions," or "composition concepts." Individual children vary considerably in their acquisition of these many kinds of composition concepts, and in the consistency with which they employ them after they have acquired them. Your child may well exceed the norm in some dimensions (his handling of lengths, perhaps) and not meet the norm in others (modes of characterization, for example), in the particular story he shows you, and might on another day produce myths which show progress in quite other dimensions still. But wherever he is in his progress, and whatever dimensions he is currently expanding and exploiting, if you'll take the time to compare his work with this story along the several dimensions I've summarized above, I suspect you'll share my admiration for the immensity of the learning task he is currently managing."

STEP 4: APPLICATION TO OTHER STORIES

Be prepared to make such a comparison yourself. Below I reproduce two more myths from the same set from which I took the myth already analyzed; one of the two is from a group of slow third graders, one from an above average group. Try analyzing them.

THE FIRST BLUEJAY

Once a God came down from the sky. "I'm hungry," he said. So many people brought him food, all but a man that was lazy and slept all the time. "Why don't you bring me food young man," the God said loudly. Then the man woke up and said, "Go away I'm sleep." So the God did and turned the old man into a bule jay. And the is the way the bule jay came to be.

The End

HOW THE FIRST SHARK CAME TO LIFE

Once there was a man who was the meanest man in the country. People called him Mac Mulligen. He was in love with meanness. He would catch fish, and then burn, bary or rip up the fish and throw on the ground to rot. No one had fish to eat most of the poor people lived on fish but now some of them died because they had no fish to eat. The fish god seen this he got so mad that he made the man into a fish he named him the shark and Mac Mulligen went on killing and eating fish.

The End

At this point, you might well object, "Good God! Who'd expect a parent to read that!" "What's he sending this stuff to me for? I can't understand it!" Perhaps it might go that way, although I would not want to sell parents quite that short. Nor would I wish to base my policies toward parents generally on the putative responses of only indifferent or ignorant parents. Or on the murkiness of my own prose; when you write such an analysis it will at least be understandable.

But perhaps it is not essential that such parents understand or even read such an analysis. What is essential is that you *have* the knowledge, and analytical competence which you claim in teaching language arts at all, that you have the competence to perceive and foster the acquisition of the expressive resources of the language, and that parents know you have this competence and are willing to share it.

QUESTIONS FOR DISCUSSION

1. If you were to use Whipp's analytical techniques, what indications could you discover that would show development of the students' writing? (Here we are talking about signs of development, not the criterion by which development is judged.)

2. What criteria for talking about acceptable progress or improvement in writing does Whipp use? Do you think them suitable or satisfactory criteria? Why?

3. Do you find any parts of Whipp's analyses helpful enough so that you would want to develop the skill needed to make these analyses? If so, which parts, and why do they seem valuable to you?

TEACHING SOME STRUCTURES AND CONVENTIONS IN LANGUAGE

Nobody Writes a "Paragraph"

O. S. Trosky and C. C. Wood

Among the doctrines of rhetoric traditionally offered to students at almost every age and in any grade are those that govern the construction of paragraphs—the paragraph usually seen as an isolated structure to be composed by and for itself. The propositions that paragraphs have "topic sentences" and that they are characterized by "unity," "coherence," and "emphasis" are set forth at the beginning of many courses in composition.

One alternative doctrine holds that paragraphing is a way of organizing material so that related ideas are visibly grouped together and the reader knows (from seeing the end of a paragraph) that he has reached the end of a group of related ideas. (See the National Council of Teachers of English publication, *The Sentence and the Paragraph,* for a discussion of the two doctrines, and some others.) O. S. Trosky and C. C. Wood, both of the University of Manitoba, describe how they teach students to organize ideas by employing some procedures for classifying data and how they lead students to view paragraphs as groups of sentences containing related information.

From *Elementary English* Vol. 49, No. 3 (March 1972), pp. 372–75. Copyright © 1972 by the National Council of Teachers of English. Reprinted by permission of the publisher and the author.

Schools try to teach pupils to write. From the beginning to the end of public school part of the emphasis in English courses is on getting the student to express himself, simply, directly and in an organized manner. In addition to "creative" writing, students are expected to produce reports, written contracts, and essays in many subjects and on many topics. It seems sensible to assume that the teaching of writing should make some contribution to the skill required to produce written work in all school subjects.

At higher levels particularly, the schools consciously attempt to contribute to skills in written communication through the use of models of good form and through emphasis on organization and planning as necessary preliminaries to writing. Yet, when students write, teachers often say, "These students can't organize their thoughts"; and students often complain, "I knew it, but I couldn't write it down."

When we began to think about this problem we knew that the approach to the writing of longer themes or essays in any subject was commonly through the early study and practice of paragraph writing, and, later in school, through emphasis on organizing paragraphs into larger communications. We began to wonder if we could find a way to show pupils, early in their school careers, that a paragraph in a writing of any length, is not a separate entity, but that it is merely a part of a longer discourse marked off in some way because the information therein is more or less complete in itself. We wondered if, at the same time, we might be able to show pupils how to sort out information so that they could see which items would be sufficiently alike to merit their being placed together and marked off as a paragraph in a larger piece of written work.

We were interested in working with younger students because it seemed that, if we could get them used to sorting and classifying ideas, they would have a useful tool for the rest of their school work, not to mention possible uses and adaptations for later life. Having observed how young children can sort and classify physical materials we thought that, if we used ideas and words with which they were familiar, they could sort and classify these as well, once they were given some practice in simple procedures. Our reading and our experience in schools led us to believe that we could try out some of these procedures with a group of nine- to twelve-year-olds.

The question, then, was, would the children be able to sort and group ideas, and would this sorting and grouping make their written communication more effective?

Since the work had to begin with ideas or topics about which students would have some information, we decided to find out which topics would best produce ideas for sorting at three different levels, grades four, five, and six. To do this we enlisted the aid of certain teachers in a suburban school beginning in the fall. Through the cooperation of the staff, we were able to demonstrate at each level a technique of "brainstorming" or class production of ideas. The teachers then continued to work with this technique, at their convenience, for the remainder of the school year. They found that certain topics would produce from the class a sufficient number of ideas for sorting and classification. No attempt at rigid classification was made. The teachers merely reported those topics which the classes had suggested, and which had been the most productive of ideas.

At this stage we were not too concerned with the production of written work. We were more interested in making pupils aware of the fact that they were able to produce ideas, and that these ideas could then be sorted into categories based on similarities which the pupils themselves could observe. The work was done as a class exercise. The class invariably could tell why they had grouped ideas in certain ways, and the answer to this question provided the name, or label, for the group of sports, flowers, clothes, etc., so classified.

Due to other commitments this preliminary work was not followed up immediately. As opportunity permitted, the intervening time was spent in noting pertinent background material in this area. This reading indicated that the idea was worthy of further study, and that some idea of the real nature of the whole process as it applied to the classroom situation should be sought. The problem was to get a teaching sequence providing for interest and variety, and simultaneously providing for experiences to strengthen the procedure for organizing ideas into simple and effective communication.

We approached a school in Winnipeg, and, through the cooperation of the principal and the classroom teacher we were given the opportunity to work with a heterogeneous class of Grade V students for one half hour each Thursday for several months.

Our previous experience had indicated that there was sufficient class interest in the approach to allow us to use a problem-solving technique. As certain problems arose, the students were asked to offer solutions. The consensus of the class determined the choice of solution. (There was a conscious effort on our part to accept the students' choice regardless of our own bias.)

We first told the class that we knew that they had many ideas about different topics, and that we thought it was difficult in most instances for them to organize their ideas so that someone else would appreciate the extent of this knowledge.

Class discussion of several ways of recording this knowledge led to the conclusion that one of the best ways, under the circumstances, would be to write the knowledge down so that everyone could see it.

The class then presented orally every idea each student had related to a particular topic. We offered the first topic, "sports" and each idea, as it was given, was recorded on the chalkboard. No exceptions were made. When the contributions were exhausted (we had several sections of chalkboard covered with ideas by this time), the students were asked to identify the activity in which they had just engaged. One student's response, "List your ideas," was acceptable to the class, and this became STEP I. The first procedure was repeated several times on succeeding days. Topics such as "Seasons," "Christmas," "Plans For Point Douglas" (a recent field trip) were used.

To obtain the second step in the sequence, the students were asked, "What would we want to do with all these ideas we have listed here?" The class suggested putting the ideas into some kind of order. They liked one member's statement, "Group them," and this became STEP II. As several ideas were grouped by the class, the groups of ideas were recorded elsewhere on the chalkboard, and the ideas so grouped were marked off the original list. *Each idea suggested for grouping in a particular way was accepted as long as there was some reason for it.* In some instances, when the placement of the idea in a particular group was not clear to us, we simply asked, "Why?" This procedure was practised until the students became used to it.

The following problem was then posed: "Why have we been putting these ideas together?" Class response indicated that in each case they had a reason based on some similarity they had observed. We then asked, "How shall we show that they belong together?" Once again the students were asked to judge. The response most acceptable: "Name each group," then became STEP III, and was added to the sequence of procedures.

When it appeared that the class was ready for the next step, students were confronted with the problem of what could be done with any particular group of ideas. The class decided that they could, "Talk about them." As they talked about a particular group of ideas, their contributions were recorded on the board. At this point a difficulty arose concerning the order of the talking and recording. The tendency was to talk about the ideas in the order in which they appeared in the original group list. Upon a class suggestion, the ideas were first numbered into some logical sequence, and then the writing, or paragraph, began to have some logical form. Thus, "Number the ideas within the group" became STEP IV. STEP V was then named: "Write about these ideas." These five steps were practised several times with the class, using such topics as: "The Sugar Beet Industry," "Winter," "Our School."

The class itself edited the sentences as they were being written on the board, including further suggestions for improvement after the paragraph had been written.

Following these class practice sessions it was possible to ask individuals to write about one of the groups of ideas, allowing each student to choose the group he would prefer. Usually the name of the group was included in the topic sentence. (The words, "Topic Sentence," were not used.) This key sentence appeared in the paragraph generally at the beginning, sometimes at the end, and on some occasions it was implied rather than stated.

When each student had completed his writing, paragraphs on each different group of ideas were selected arbitrarily and these were written randomly on the board. The students were led to realize the need for ordering or numbering each group of ideas so that the whole would appear in a sensible order. Thus, "Order the paragraphs," became STEP VI. Students became aware that writing about groups before ordering them was too time-consuming. They suggested that the groups of ideas might be ordered before the writing. This suggestion was accepted.

Up to this point the class was involved in the following steps:

STEP I—List Ideas

STEP II—Group the Ideas

STEP III—Name Each Group of Ideas

STEP IV—Number the Ideas in Each Group

STEP V—Order the Groups

STEP VI—Write About the Ideas in Each Group (Paragraph)

This sequence of procedures is merely a beginning. The conscious application of such routines, over a period of years, should give students an awareness of a system of organization which they may apply to any area of written communication at any level. It allows the student gradually to see that a paragraph is seldom an entity, being rather a part of something larger. If the student wishes to take a small part of a succession of developed ideas, he may, because of this selection, move into many areas of creativity as well, depending on his unique selection and treatment of an idea that appeals to him. Thus, in time, some students may come to realize that art, or creativity, depends on selection and individual emphasis, and that any communication in writing, whether structured for reporting or for entertainment, is his own particular creation.

QUESTIONS FOR DISCUSSION

1. What might be the value of a "problem-solving approach" to the handling of classroom activities such as those described in the article? What sorts of problems can the children try to solve in the classroom?

2. Are there any procedures for classifying ideas or objects that might be taught to students in elementary grades? Do you think it would be useful to teach such procedures, directly, to children in these grades, instead of allowing them to find their own ways of organizing and classifying?

3. The authors imply that what they are teaching supports students' creative impulses. Do you think they are right, or would their procedure inhibit students' interest in creative thinking and writing?

Three Notes on the Teaching of Writing
A. F. Watts

A. F. Watts, author of *The Language and Mental Development of Children,* devotes most of his book to an examination of changes in children's ways of using language as they grow up and enlarge their understanding of their world, but he also explicitly suggests a few techniques for teaching. Three of his notes containing such suggestions are included here. In addition to being of interest in their own right, they should be compared with suggestions by Kellogg Hunt (pp. 64ff) and Frank O'Hare (pp. 346ff), since each of these writers agrees that giving children practice in the deliberate use of specific forms of language is a way to help increase their sophistication in using language.

HOW FAR CAN WRITING BE TAUGHT?

The virtues of good prose writing have been variously stated. The most important are: (1) clearness, (2) interest, (3) orderliness, (4) simplicity, (5) appropriateness, and (6) euphony. How shall we secure them?

From A. F. Watts, *The Language and Mental Development of Children* (London: George G. Harrap & Co., Ltd., 1944), pp. 138–44. Reprinted by permission of the publisher.

We have already suggested that the progress of children in the art of writing English is marked by a control over an ever-widening range of words correctly used, a growing sensitivity to the kind of diction best suited to the subject written about, an increasing skill in the construction of sentences designed to match the increasing complexity of their thought processes, and a steadily developing power of planning a piece of writing as a whole, with due attention to order and proportion in the ideas expressed.

It has been suggested that the best writing by children comes largely from wide reading in interesting books. By comparison, manuals which promise aid in teaching the child to write well are rarely worth the time and trouble spent on them. The argument against the manual is that children who have not felt the need of using a particular device or construction in their writing do not develop the need as the result of a set lesson on its value. It is not found, for example, that children who have had lessons on metaphors and similes, or on the construction of complex sentences with material supplied for them, produce compositions which contain more metaphors and similes or more dependent clauses than children who have received no such lessons. Neither can children be taught to write well who have no ear for a good cadence, or who take no pleasure in words for their own sake.

We have indicated, however, some of the lines along which useful instruction can be given. We have said that a feeling for order and arrangement in compositions can be gradually instilled but only in connexion with subjects of suitable difficulty. We have also suggested that the teacher can do much to convince the child that good writing is not necessarily fine or fulsome writing. Clearness and precision may be taught negatively; that is, by the unremitting eradication of faults of woolliness and verbosity. In other words, it is the art of presenting such ideas as one has that can be cultivated by teaching. But interest and euphony are natural virtues not easily come by. Generally, one must say that the best instruction has its roots in a close criticism of the pupils' own efforts at writing well. Formal and prescriptive teaching is by no means sure of securing good results; indeed, it may be that the wisest plan is that of Coleridge's teacher who set exercises and in correcting them "showed no mercy to phrase, metaphor, or image unsupported by sound sense or where the sense could be conveyed with equal force and dignity in plainer words."

In fine, it may be that on the whole the teacher had best confine himself to discreet praise, popularizing the kind of writing he values when he finds it in the work of his pupils, and to practising the arts of criticism and correction which, properly understood, will not be destructive or negative in their effects and restricted to blue-pencilling (or red-inking) errors in spelling, punctuation, capitalization, and grammatical concord, but will manifest themselves in stimulating encouragement and guidance, informed by sympathy and directed with insight and skill.

THE THREE-SENTENCE COMPOSITION

It is an excellent practice to require children from time to time to write all that is of interest or importance to them about a topic in no more and no fewer than three sentences. They are thereby compelled to exercise whatever judgment and skill they can command for a perfectly definite purpose. They must understand what a sentence is; they must get their ideas clear before they put pen or pencil to paper, they must learn to concentrate on what is essential to their purpose and ignore what is not; and they must order their effort so that what they have to say is properly introduced, suitably developed, and brought to a satisfactory conclusion.

The method thus gives the teacher a sound criterion for judging the work of his pupils, and it is one which they can be readily taught to appreciate. Well-taught children, for instance, will usually be able to detect such faults as failure to get quickly off the mark, inability to distribute ideas evenly among the sentences, weakness in sentence-construction, lack of due emphasis on important points, and so on. They can also be depended on to make sensible suggestions for the improvement of poor efforts. If an occasional assembly can be arranged at which some of the best three-sentence compositions from several classes are read aloud by their authors, then the measure of applause that may well be allowed to follow will serve to indicate the degree of success achieved in presenting a subject with interest and conciseness. Time and thought will not have been wasted if, in preparation for such assemblies, a three-sentence composition has been subjected to repeated revision.

Careful attention will need to be given, of course, to the choosing of topics so that children of limited capacity do not attempt flights of thought and language that are beyond their range. Simple narrative work, for instance, is better suited to such children than explanations of semi-scientific processes or the recapitulation of arguments. Wisely managed, children who are trained in the way suggested will learn what type and length of sentence suit them and what sort of linguistic techniques are not so far beyond their reach as to be impossible of acquirement.

As a guide to the kind of thing which may be expected, from the abler children at least, after a little instruction and exercise, the following samples of finished work are tentatively offered as criteria for use in the evaluation of the efforts of other children. It should be understood that these samples represent not always the first versions but often the second (and sometimes third) revisions by their authors. In comparing one age with another development will be seen to take place in sentence-length, sentence-complexity, phraseology and vocabulary, in the skilful subordination of the less important to the more important ideas, and, above all, in the imaginative grasp of the chosen subject.

A Three-Sentence Written Composition Scale

AGE 8

Once a woman kept a hen that laid an egg every day. She thought to herself that if she gave her hen twice as much food it would lay twice as many eggs. But the hen got fat and lazy and wouldn't lay any eggs at all.

AGE 9

Joan of Arc was a brave French girl who was told by the angels that God wanted her to drive the English out of her country. She went to the King and told him her story and he gave her permission to lead his soldiers into battle. But after she had won many great battles somebody betrayed her to the English who had her burnt as a witch.

AGE 10

One day a dog stole a piece of meat from a butcher's shop and ran off home to enjoy it. On his way he had to cross a stream and looking down he caught sight of his reflection in the water. He thought it was another dog with another piece of meat and in snatching at it he dropped his own piece of meat which disappeared down the stream.

AGE 11

The Pied Piper of Hamelin is a poem about a plague of rats which invaded the town of Hamelin a long time ago. The people were in despair until the Pied Piper said he would rid them of their vermin on condition that they paid him a thousand guilders. After charming the rats into the Weser he was refused the reward and so in revenge he charmed away the children of Hamelin into a cavern in the hills and they have never been heard of since.

AGE 12

The Children's Hour covers a large variety of subjects to suit the different tastes of listeners, and although it previously occupied a whole hour, in this way getting its name, it is now cut down to forty minutes. It is broadcast every evening at 5.20 and is arranged by Uncle Mac, whose task it is to provide for the entertainment of the children. Generally, the entertainment takes the form of stories or interesting talks by well-known people, while programmes of music are often included.

AGE 13

Swimming is an excellent form of exercise for people of all ages as it keeps the arms and shoulders, the legs and back in a healthy condition, and compels the swimmer to devote his attention to deep and regular breathing. Swimming is also a good sport which gives pleasure to all who practise it, whether old or young, especially when the weather is sunny and warm. In addition, it is very refreshing to take a plunge in the hot days of summer into a cool stream or outdoor swimming bath.

AGE 14

The Ancient Mariner is a fairly long poem and is said to have been written by Samuel Taylor Coleridge in order to get money for a holiday. It tells the story of an old mariner who sailed away down towards the South Pole, shot an albatross, thus causing by his unlucky act the death of all his shipmates, and was then driven back into the Tropics where he suffered terribly from exposure and thirst before his ship found its way home again. It is a thrilling story which calls up in a vivid fashion to the mind of the reader everything that happened to this unfortunate man.

THE WELL-CONSTRUCTED LONG SENTENCE

An alternative method of helping children to plan what they have to say in advance of saying it and also to "write clearly, neatly, and succinctly," to use Dr. Johnson's words, is to set them to describe objects or pictures in single sentences. We have already referred to our picture-scale in the chapter dealing with continuous speech. Of the series of pictures already referred to the least understood by little children were those that showed actions in progress linked in the relation of cause and effect. Through lack of experience as well as through lack of insight a good many of the children under seven years of age were uanble to think themelves imaginatively into certain of the situations depicted, though to do this was essential for the successful description of what was seen.

The complexity of the sentences which children brought up in the same linguistic environment employ will depend, then, partly upon the number of things which they are able to grasp together in a single act of attention and partly upon the range and subtlety of their powers of interpretation (*i.e.,* on their ability to see the relations in which these things stand to one another).

We have indicated in our picture-scale what we think is the upper limit of the ability of infants in describing what they see. But at the mental age at which the scale abruptly ends we find the factor of interpretation beginning to assume more and more importance. The following sentence, for example, descriptive of a picture in a child's reading-book, could only spring from a mind of exceptional capacity, even though the boy who framed it was but ten and a half years old: *This is a picture* (he wrote) *of a young man seated on a chair looking sad and lonely, with his arm in a sling and his dog resting his nose against his master's knee and looking up at him as much as to say, "I am sorry."* But even in the simpler descriptions we have found something more than mere description of externals. At the upper limit it is doubtful whether many of us could express without undue effort much more than is conveyed in the following description of the familiar school picture, "When did You Last see Your Father?" *It shows us a boy standing in front of a table where some soldiers, evidently Roundheads, are questioning him as to the whereabouts of his cavalier father, while his mother and his sisters are anxiously watching him from behind.*

The close study of carefully chosen pictures followed by attempts to describe their subjects in single comprehensive statements should be well worth the attention of those teachers who still have some regard for what has been called "the architecture of the long sentence," which, well-contrived, is "the fine flower of prose writing." The skilful management of the long sentence is not a simple matter. It involves a mastery of balance and rhythm; it calls for the proper emphasis of the more important elements and for the due subordination of what is less important; it entails the most economical packing of ideas, and this in turn necessitates learning how and when to substitute phrase for clause and phrase for word. All this calls for assiduous application and constant scrutiny and revision of what one has written. But in the end we shall be able to appreciate what Bacon called "the choiceness of the phrase and the round and clean composition of the sentence, and the sweet falling of the clauses." What thought, and feeling too, must have gone to the construction of the well-wrought sentences that follow, the first representing the sixth revision by a girl of thirteen, and the second the fifth revision of a boy of fourteen:

(a) *The Return of Persephone.* This picture shows us Demeter welcoming with outstretched arms her long-lost daughter, Persephone, who is being borne up in the arms of Hermes from the underworld where King Pluto had for so many months kept her a prisoner.

(b) *The Angelus.* Here we see a potato field where two poorly dressed peasants, a man and a woman, have ceased work for a time and are standing with bowed heads in an attitude of prayer, listening to the Angelus which is ringing in the distant church.

QUESTIONS FOR DISCUSSION

1. What is your evaluation of the steps proposed by Watts in the first note for securing "the virtues of good prose"? What comments would Douglas, Moffett, and other teachers represented in this collection have on Watts' suggestions, given the views presented in their own pieces?

2. What values do you see in Watts' proposed "three-sentence compositions"? What might be undesirable results, if any, of practicing this rather strict form? Will the student have the chance to learn about kinds of connections among statements—to learn in a way that he could not if he were writing longer pieces? ("Connections among statements" might include the relation between a statement and supporting data, between an item of description and another similar item, or between a statement of result and a statement of causation.)

3. Is the philosophy of teaching that Watts implies here at odds with an effort to encourage students to express feelings and to seek creativity? How or how not?

A Generative Rhetoric of the Sentence

Francis Christensen

Whether the student's writing be transactional, objective, expressive, or creative, the teacher will probably always face the question of whether it is possible, through direct instructional activities, to affect the kinds of sentences the student writes. Is it appropriate to offer drills or pattern practice in the hope of getting students to vary sentences and to write richer, more detailed, more complex sentences than they would write without the drill? Francis Christensen's answer is yes.

Christensen's essay was written initially for college teachers, but the teaching techniques he advocates have been employed with good results in elementary school, in the judgment of teachers. Christensen uses the terminology and concepts of traditional grammar to describe composing activities that can be undertaken deliberately by students in order to give what Christensen says will be more varied texture to their writing.

Francis Christensen taught for many years at the University of Southern California, and was a member of the faculty of Northern Illinois University.

From *Notes Toward a New Rhetoric* (New York, Harper & Row, Publishers, Inc.) Copyright © 1967 by Francis Christensen. Reprinted by permission of the publisher. This material also appeared in *College Composition and Communication* (October 1973).

If the new grammar is to be brought to bear on composition, it must be brought to bear on the rhetoric of the sentence. We have a workable and teachable, if not a definitive, modern grammar; but we do not have, despite several titles, a modern rhetoric.

In composition courses we do not really teach our captive charges to write better—we merely *expect* them to. And we do not teach them how to write better because we do not know how to teach them to write better. And so we merely go through the motions. Our courses with their tear-out work books and four-pound anthologies are elaborate evasions of the real problem. They permit us to put in our time and do almost anything else we'd rather be doing instead of buckling down to the hard work of making a difference in the student's understanding and manipulation of language.

With hundreds of handbooks and rhetorics to draw from, I have never been able to work out a program for teaching the sentence as I find it in the work of contemporary writers. The chapters on the sentence all adduce the traditional rhetorical classification of sentences as loose, balanced, and periodic. But the term *loose* seems to be taken as a pejorative (it sounds immoral); our students, no Bacons or Johnsons, have little occasion for balanced sentences; and some of our worst perversions of style come from the attempt to teach them to write periodic sentences. The traditional grammatical classification of sentences is equally barren. Its use in teaching composition rests on a semantic confusion, equating complexity of structure with complexity of thought and vice versa. But very simple thoughts may call for very complex grammatical constructions. Any moron can say "I don't know who done it." And some of us might be puzzled to work out the grammar of "All I want is all there is," although any chit can think it and say it and act on it.

The chapters on the sentence all appear to assume that we think naturally in primer sentences, progress naturally to compound sentences, and must be taught to combine the primer sentences into complex sentences—and that complex sentences are the mark of maturity. We need a rhetoric of the sentence that will do more than combine the ideas of primer sentences. We need one that will *generate* ideas.

For the foundation of such a generative or productive rhetoric I take the statement from John Erskine, the originator of the Great Books courses, himself a novelist. In an essay "The Craft of Writing" (*Twentieth Century English,* Philosophical Library, 1946) he discusses a principle of the writer's craft, which though known he says to all practitioners, he has never seen discussed in print. The principle is this: "When you write, you make a point, not by subtracting as though you sharpened a pencil, but by adding." We have all been told that the formula for good writing is the concrete noun and the active verb. Yet Erskine says, "What you say is found not in the noun but in what you add to qualify the noun . . . The noun, the verb, and the main clause serve merely as the base on which meaning will rise . . . The modifier is the essential part of any sentence." The foundation, then, for a generative or productive rhetoric of the sentence is that composition is essentially a process of *addition.*

But speech is linear, moving in time, and writing moves in linear space, which is analogous to time. When you add a modifier, whether to the noun, the verb, or the main clause, you must add it either before the head or after it. If you add it before the head, the direction of modification can be indicated by an arrow pointing forward; if you add it after, by an arrow pointing backward. Thus we have the second principle of a generative rhetoric—the principle of *direction of modification* or *direction of movement.*

Within the clause there is not much scope for operating with this principle. The positions of the various sorts of close, or restrictive, modifiers are generally fixed and the modifiers are often obligatory—"The man who came to dinner remained till midnight." Often the only choice is whether to add modifiers. What I have seen of attempts to bring structural grammar to bear on composition usually boils down to the injunction to "load the patterns." Thus "pattern practice" sets students to accreting sentences like this: "The small boy on the red bicycle who lives with his happy parents on our shady street often coasts down the steep street until he comes to the city park." This will never do. It has no rhythm and hence no life; it is tone-deaf. It is the seed that will burgeon into gobbledygook. One of the hardest things in writing is to keep the noun clusters and verb clusters short.

It is with modifiers added to the clause—that is, with sentence modifiers—that the principle comes into full play. The typical sentence of modern English, the kind we can best spend our efforts trying to teach, is what we may call the *cumulative sentence*. The main clause, which may or may not have a sentence modifier before it, advances the discussion; but the additions move backward, as in this clause, to modify the statement of the main clause or more often to explicate or exemplify it, so that the sentence has a flowing and ebbing movement, advancing to a new position and then pausing to consolidate it, leaping and lingering as the popular ballad does. The first part of the preceding compound sentence has one addition, placed within it; the second part has 4 words in the main clause and 49 in the five additions placed after it.

The cumulative sentence is the opposite of the periodic sentence. It does not represent the idea as conceived, pondered over, reshaped, packaged, and delivered cold. It is dynamic rather than static, representing the mind thinking. The main clause ("the additions move backward" above) exhausts the mere fact of the idea; logically, there is nothing more to say. The additions stay with the same idea, probing its bearings and implications, exemplifying it or seeking an analogy or metaphor for it, or reducing it to details. Thus the mere form of the sentence generates ideas. It serves the needs of both the writer and the reader, the writer by compelling him to examine his thought, the reader by letting him into the writer's thought.

Addition and direction of movement are structural principles. They involve the grammatical character of the sentence. Before going on to other principles, I must say a word about the best grammar as the foundation for rhetoric. I cannot conceive any useful transactions between teacher and students unless they have in common a language for talking about sentences. The best grammar is the grammar that best displays the layers of structure of the English sentence. The best I have found in a textbook is the combination of immediate constituent and transformation grammar in Paul Roberts's *English Sentences*. Traditional grammar, whether over-simple as in the school tradition or over-complex as in the scholarly tradition, does not reveal the language as it operates; it leaves everything, to borrow a phrase from Wordsworth, "in disconnection dead and spiritless." *English Sentences* is oversimplified and it has gaps, but it displays admirably the structures that rhetoric must work with—primarily sentence modifiers, including relative and subordinate clauses, but, far more important, the array of noun, verb, and adjective clusters. It is paradoxical that Professor Roberts, who has done so much to make the teaching of composition possible, should himself be one of those who think that it cannot be taught. Unlike Ulysses, he doesn't see any work for Telemachus to work.

Layers of structure, as I have said, is a grammatical concept. To bring in the dimension of meaning, we need a third principle—that of *levels of generality* or *levels of abstraction*. The main clause is likely to be stated in general or abstract or plural terms. With the main clause stated, the forward movement of the sentence stops, the writer shifts down to a lower level of generality or abstraction or to singular terms, and goes back over the same ground at this lower level.[1] "He has just bought a new car, a 1963½ Ford, a Galaxie, a fastback hardtop with four-on-the-floor shift." There is no theoretical limit to the number of structural layers or levels, each at a lower level of generality, any or all of them compounded, that a speaker or writer may use. For a speaker, listen to Lowell Thomas; for a writer, study William Faulkner. To a single independent clause he may append a page of additions, but usually all clear, all grammatical, once we have learned how to read him. Or, if you prefer, study Hemingway, the master of the simple sentence: "George was coming down in the telemark position, kneeling, one leg forward and bent, the other trailing, his sticks hanging like some insect's thin legs, kicking up puffs of snow, and finally the whole kneeling, trailing figure coming around in a beautiful right curve, crouching, the legs shot forward and back, the body leaning out against the swing, the sticks accenting the curve like points of light, all in a wild cloud of snow."

---

[1] Cf. Leo Rockas, "Abstract and Concrete Sentences," CCC, May 1963. Rockas describes sentences as abstract or concrete, the abstract implying the concrete and vice versa. Readers and writers, he says, must have the knack of apprehending the concrete in the abstract and the abstract in the concrete. This is true and valuable. I am saying that within a single sentence the writer may present more than one level of generality, translating the abstract into the more concrete in added levels.

This brings me to the fourth, and last, principle, that of texture. *Texture* provides a descriptive or evaluative term. If a writer adds to few of his nouns or verbs or main clauses and adds little, the texture may be said to be thin. The style will be plain or bare. The writing of most of our students is thin—even threadbare. But if he adds frequently or much or both, then the texture may be said to be dense or rich. One of the marks of an effective style, especially in narrative, is variety in the texture, the texture varying with the change in pace, the variation in texture producing the change in pace. It is not true, as I have seen it asserted, that fast action calls for short sentences; the action is fast in the sentence by Hemingway above. In our classes, we have to work for greater density and variety in texture and greater concreteness and particularity in what is added.

I have been operating at a fairly high level of generality. Now I must downshift and go over the same points with examples. The most graphic way to exhibit the layers of structure is to indent the word groups of a sentence and to number the levels. Since in the narrow columns of this journal indentation is possible only with short sentences whose additions are short, I have used it with only the first three sentences; the reader is urged to copy out the others for himself. I have added symbols to mark the grammatical character of the additions: SC, subordinate clause; RC, relative clause; NC, noun cluster; VC, verb cluster; AC, adjective cluster; Abs, absolute (i.e., a VC with a subject of its own); PP, prepositional phrase. With only a few exceptions (in some the punctuation may be questioned) the elements set off as on a lower level are marked by junctures or punctuation. The examples have been chosen to illustrate the range of constructions used in the lower levels; after the first few they are arranged by the number of levels. The examples could have been drawn from poetry as well as from prose. Those not attributed are by students.

1

1 He shook his hands,
    2 a quick shake, (NC)
        3 fingers down, (Abs)
            4 like a pianist. (PP)—Sinclair Lewis

2

2 Calico-coated, (AC)

2 small bodied, (AC)

2 with delicate legs and pink faces (PP)

    3 in which their mismatched eyes rolled wild and subdued, (RC)

1 they huddled,

2 gaudy motionless and alert, (AC)

2 wild as deer, (AC)

2 deadly as rattlesnakes, (AC)

2 quiet as doves. (AC)—William Faulkner

3

1 The bird's eye, / , remained fixed upon him;

    2 bright and silly as a sequin (AC)

1 its little bones, / , seemed swooning in his hand.—Stella Benson

    2 wrapped . . . in a warm padding of feathers (VC)

4

(1) The jockeys sat bowed and relaxed, moving a little at the waist with the movement of their horses^{2-VC}.—Katherine Anne Porter

5

(1) The flame sidled up the match, driving a film of moisture and a thin strip of darker grey before it^{2-VC}.

6

(1) She came among them behind the man, gaunt in the gray shapeless garment and the sunbonnet^{2-AC}, wearing stained canvas gymnasium shoes^{2-VC}.—Faulkner

7

(1) The Texan turned to the nearest gatepost and climbed to the top of it, his alternate thighs thick and bulging in the tight jeans^{2-Abs}, the butt of his pistol catching and losing the sun in pearly gleams^{2-Abs}.—Faulkner

8

(1) He could sail for hours, searching the blanched grasses below him with his telescopic eyes^{2-VC}, gaining height against the wind^{2-VC}, descending in mile-long, gently declining swoops when he curved and rode back^{2-VC}, never beating a wing^{2-VC}.—Walter Van Tilburg Clark

9

(1) The gay-sweatered skaters are quick-silvering around the frosty rink, the girls gliding and spinning[2-Abs], the boys swooping and darting[2-Abs], their arms flailing like wings[3-Abs].

10

(1) He stood at the top of the stairs and watched me, I waiting for him to call me up[2-Abs], he hesitating to come down[2-Abs], his lips nervous with the suggestion of a smile[3-Abs], mine asking whether the smile meant come, or go away[3-Abs].

11

(1) Joad's lips stretched tight over his long teeth for a moment, and (1) he licked his lips, like a dog[2-PP], two licks[3-NC], one in each direction from the middle[4-NC].—Steinbeck

12

(1) We all live in two realities: one of seeming fixity[2-NC], with institutions, dogmas, rules of punctuation, and routines[3-PP], the calendared and clockwise world of all but futile round on round[4-NC]; and one of whirling and flying electrons, dreams, and possibilities[2-NC], behind the clock[3-PP].—Sidney Cox

13

(1) It was as though someone, somewhere, had touched a lever and shifted gears, and (1) the hospital was set for night running, smooth and silent[2-AC], its normal clatter and hum muffled[2-Abs], the only sounds heard in the whitewalled room distant and unreal[2-Abs]: a low hum of voices from the nurse's desk[3-NC], quickly stifled[4-VC], the soft squish of rubber-soled shoes on the tiled corridor[3-NC], starched white cloth rustling against itself[3-NC], and outside, the lonesome whine of wind in the country night[3-NC], and the Kansas dust beating against the windows[3-NC].

14

(1) The beach sounds are jazzy, percussion fixing the mode [2-Abs]—the surf cracking and booming in the distance[3-Abs], a little nearer dropped bar-bells clanking[3-Abs], steel gym rings, flung together[4-VC], ringing[3-Abs], palm fronds rustling above me[3-Abs], like steel brushes washing over a snare drum[4-PP], troupes of sandals splatting and shuffling

on the sandy cement^{3-Abs}, their beat varying^{4-Abs}, syncopation emerging and disappearing with changing paces^{5-Abs}.

15

(1) A small negro girl develops from the sheet of glare-frosted walk, walking barefooted^{2-VC}, her bare legs striking and coiling from the hot cement^{3-Abs}, her feet curling in^{4-Abs}, only the outer edges touching^{5-Abs}.

16

(1) The swells moved rhythmically toward us irregularly faceted^{2-VC}, sparkling^{2-VC}, growing taller and more powerful^{2-VC}, until the shining crest bursts^{3-SC}, a transparent sheet of pale green water spilling over the top^{4-Abs}, breaking into blue-white foam as it cascades down the front of the wave^{5-VC}, piling up in a frothy mound that the diminishing wave pushes up against the pilings^{5-VC}, with a swishmash^{6-PP}, the foam drifting back^{5-Abs}, like a lace fan opened over the shimmering water as the spent wave returns whispering to the sea^{6-PP}.

The best starting point for a composition unit based on these four principles is with two-level narrative sentences, first with one second-level addition (sentences 4, 5), then with two or more parallel ones (6, 7, 8). Anyone sitting in his room with his eyes closed could write the main clause of most of the examples; the discipline comes with the additions, provided they are based at first on immediate observation, requiring the student to phrase an exact observation in exact language. This can hardly fail to be exciting to a class: it is life, with the variety and complexity of life; the workbook exercise is death. The situation is ideal also for teaching diction—abstract-concrete, general-specific, literal-metaphorical, denotative-connotative. When the sentences begin to come out right, it is time to examine the additions for their grammatical character. From then on the grammar comes to the aid of the writing and the writing reinforces the grammar. One can soon go on to multi-level narrative sentences (1, 3, 9–11, 15, 16) and then to brief narratives of three to six or seven sentences on actions that can be observed over and over again—beating eggs, making a cut with a power saw, or following a record changer's cycle or a wave's flow and ebb. Bring the record changer to class. Description, by contrast, is static, picturing appearance rather than behavior. The constructions to master are the noun and adjective clusters and the absolute (13, 14). Then the descriptive noun cluster must be taught to ride piggy-back on the narrative sentence, so that description and narration are interleaved: "In the morning we went out into a new world, a glistening crystal and white world, each skeleton tree, each leafless bush, even the heavy, drooping power lines sheathed in icy crystal." The next step is to develop the sense for variety in texture and change in pace that all good narrative demands.

In the next unit, the same four principles can be applied to the expository paragraph. But this is a subject for another paper.

I want to anticipate two possible objections. One is that the sentences are long. By freshman English standards they are long, but I could have produced far longer ones from works freshmen are expected to read. Of the sentences by students, most were written as finger exercises in the first few weeks of the course. I try in narrative sentences to push to level after level, not just two or three, but four, five, or six, even more, as far as the students' powers of observation will take them. I want them to become sentence acrobats, to dazzle by their syntactic dexterity. I'd rather have to deal with hyperemia than anemia. I want to add my voice to that of James Coleman (*CCC,* December 1962) deploring our concentration on the plain style.

The other objection is that my examples are mainly descriptive and narrative—and today in freshman English we teach only exposition. I deplore this limitation as much as I deplore our limitation to the plain style. Both are a sign that we have sold our proper heritage for a pot of message. In permitting them, the English department undercuts its own discipline. Even if our goal is only utilitarian prose, we can teach diction and sentence structure far more effectively through a few controlled exercises in description and narration than we can by starting right off with exposition (Theme One, 500 words, precipitates *all* the problems of writing). The student has something to communicate—his immediate sense impressions, which can stand a bit of exercising. The material is not already verbalized—he has to match language to sense impressions. His acuteness in observation and in choice of words can be judged by fairly objective standards—is the sound of a bottle of milk being set down on a concrete step suggested better by *clink* or *clank?* In the examples, study the diction for its accuracy, rising at times to the truly imaginative. Study the use of metaphor, of comparison. This verbal virtuosity and syntactical ingenuity can be made to carry over into expository writing.

But this is still utilitarian. What I am proposing carries over of itself into the study of literature. It makes the student a better reader of literature. It helps him thread the syntactical mazes of much mature writing, and it gives him insight into that elusive thing we call style. Last year a student told of re-reading a book by her favorite author, Willa Cather, and of realizing for the first time *why* she liked reading her: she could understand and appreciate the style. For some students, moreover, such writing makes life more interesting as well as giving them a way to share their interest with others. When they learn how to put concrete details into a sentence, they begin to look at life with more alertness. If it is liberal education we are concerned with, it is just possible that these things are more important than anything we can achieve when we set our sights on the plain style in expository prose.

QUESTIONS FOR DISCUSSION

1. What is your evaluation of the kinds of sentences produced by Christensen's methods, particularly examples 13 through 16? Are these the kind of sentences one might encourage children to write?

2. Would Christensen's techniques, if taught to children, support or work against the emphases we have observed in the essays earlier in this book, particularly the emphases on children's use of direct experience in writing and on "creative" writing?

3. It has been suggested that Christensen's major contribution to the rhetoric of the sentence is his identification of different "levels of generality" (or "levels of abstraction"). Do you find this con-

cept useful to you personally? Is it a concept that you think can usefully be taught to young children?

4. It may be that Christensen is assuming a connection between techniques of writing about experience and ways of learning about (making discoveries about) that experience: that the techniques foster the discoveries. Do you believe that this connection is sound? Does your experience support it? contradict it?

5. After reading this essay, do you think that direct instruction in ways of producing specific kinds of sentences is desirable? Or do you think it unwise to give the kind of emphasis Christensen advocates to sentences in isolation from the total piece of which the sentences are part?

Sentence-Combining
Frank O'Hare

The work of Francis Christensen on "generative rhetoric" and the work of transformational grammarians have kept alive the question of whether direct instruction in the management of language can improve the quality of students' composition. Further, studies of the ways in which children's language develops in maturity and fluency have raised questions about whether that growth can be accelerated by direct instruction. In 1966–67, John Mellon of Harvard University worked with a group of seventh graders to find out whether teaching students to use some of the essential steps in composing sentences that had been suggested by transformational grammarians (particularly addition, deletion, and embedding of parts of sentences) could help students grow more rapidly in syntactic maturity than, according to Kellogg Hunt, students typically grow. Mellon found that he could accelerate the students' progress toward producing more complex and "mature" sentences, but his students apparently did not improve their ability to produce essays that pleased adult readers.

In 1969–1970 Frank O'Hare, of Florida State University, also working with seventh graders, employed the same concepts from transformational grammar that Mellon used, but changed some of Mellon's procedures and

From *Sentence-Combining: Improving Student Writing without Formal Grammar Instruction* (Urbana, Illinois: National Council of Teachers of English, 1973), pp. 67–76. Copyright © 1973 by the National Council of Teachers of English. Reprinted by permission of the publisher and the author.

terminology. In the following selection, the final chapter of O'Hare's report of his research, he describes the success of his efforts and advances a cogent argument for the efficacy of direct instruction in the handling of syntax as a way of helping children to improve the complexity of their sentences and the overall effectiveness of their writing. (Note that O'Hare is not advocating instruction in grammatical theory, or in grammar itself, as a way of improving students' writing. He is talking about the use of exercises in the management of sentences—exercises based on the findings of grammarians.)

While O'Hare and Mellon each worked with seventh graders, O'Hare contends that the techniques he used would be applicable with younger children, too. Teachers interested in learning in detail about his techniques and exercises should consult the complete report of his study, which is available from the National Council of Teachers of English, 1111 Kenyon Road, Urbana, Illinois 61801.

The present study was designed to measure the effect of written and oral sentence-combining exercises on the free writing of a seventh grade experimental group. The experimental group was given intensive practice in combining groups of kernel statements, by addition and deletion, into single sentences which were structurally more complex than those students would normally be expected to write. In order to facilitate the sentence-combining operations a series of signals capitalizing on the students' inherent sense of grammaticality was developed. An important, perhaps crucial, dimension of these signals was that they were in no way dependent on the students' formal knowledge of a grammar, traditional or transformational. Also important was an acceptant classroom atmosphere designed to allay possible syntactic fears and to produce a student confident in his ability to manipulate sentence structure. Specifically, the present study was designed to answer two questions. In comparison with the control group who were not exposed to the sentence-combining exercises, would the experimental group in their free writing (1) write compositions that could be described as syntactically more elaborated or mature? and (2) write compositions that would be judged by eight experienced English teachers as better in overall quality?

CONCLUSIONS

As a result of the analyses of data presented in Chapter Four, it was concluded that the experimental group wrote compositions which were syntactically different from the compositions written by the control group. The experimental group wrote significantly more clauses and these clauses proved to be significantly longer. As a consequence the experimental group wrote T-units which were significantly longer than those of the control group. When compared with the normative data presented by Hunt (*Grammatical Structures Written at Three Grade Levels,* 1965), the experimental group's compositions showed evidence of a level of syntactic maturity well beyond that typical of eighth graders and in many respects quite similar to that of twelfth graders.

When eight experienced English teachers were asked to judge the overall writing quality of thirty pairs of experimental and control compositions, sixty compositions in all, that had been matched by sex and IQ, they chose a significantly greater number of the experimental compositions. Therefore, it was concluded that the experimental group wrote compositions that were significantly better in overall quality than the control group's compositions.

Given the design features of the present study, it seems reasonable to attribute the superior performance of the experimental group to the experimental treatment. For these reasons it has been judged that sentence-combining practice that is in no way dependent on formal knowledge of a grammar has a favorable effect on the writing of seventh graders.

IMPLICATIONS

The present study has demonstrated that the writing behavior of seventh graders can be changed by certain written and oral language experiences and that it can be changed fairly rapidly and with relative ease. In a sense this assertion questions the belief that growth in writing ability is *necessarily* a slow and difficult process. In showing that significant qualitative and syntactic gains can be achieved in approximately eight months, the present study suggests that, at least for seventh graders, a part of the composing process is directly amenable to alteration.

In the Epilogue to his NCTE report written two years after his original study, Mellon repeatedly asserted that "the sentence-combining practice had nothing to do with the teaching of writing" (*Transformational Sentence-Combining: A Method for Enhancing the Development of Syntactic Fluency in English Composition,* 1969, p. 79). The present researcher rejects such an assertion. Both Mellon's and the present study's experimental groups practiced writing sentences. The sentence-building process involved semantic as well as syntactic considerations: How does it sound? Does it make sense? Does it include all the input information (the kernels)? All of these questions, which surely include rhetorical considerations too, were an integral part of both treatments. At least by implication, both treatments favored sentences that were syntactically more mature than those the students were accustomed to producing. Football coaches have their players practice play after play in an "a-game" setting, often with no opposition, so that they will be able to execute efficiently in an actual game. Surely the coach at practice is teaching football. Similarly, students exposed to sentence-building exercises, even in an "a-rhetorical" setting, are in a very real sense being taught writing. Both treatment groups ended up writing sentences that were syntactically more mature. The present study's experimental group wrote compositions that were judged better in overall quality. The acceptance or rejection of Mellon's overall hypothesis depended entirely on whether his students wrote syntactically more maturely. Mellon reported that the students were generally able to complete the sentence-combining exercises. But the crucial question was whether they had developed syntactic manipulating skills that would show in their writing. Mellon's study was clearly concerned with the teaching of writing skills. It is, therefore, difficult to understand how sentence-building exercises can be defined out of the teaching of writing.

Indeed, sentence combining has both theoretical and practical attractiveness when considered as part of a composition program. Rhetoric and sentence-combining practice should be viewed not as mutually exclusive or even discrete but rather as complementary.

Gleason ("What Is English," in *CCC*, 1962), in an article discussing the place of language study in the curriculum, argued that the choppy style and the run-on style

> are basically the same. Each chooses one device to the exclusion of all others. The style is bad, not because of any individual choice, but because of the monotonous patterning. . . . to produce a good style it would be necessary to select out of a wider stock of available devices, and to work them all into an appropriate, pleasing over-all pattern. (p. 5)

Gleason went on to ask what a student must be made aware of if he is to understand and control style.

> He must know the options. The wider his repertoire and the deeper his understanding of the peculiarities of each, the better equipped he is to write. . . . As in teaching a foreign language, the accurate, casual control of patterns comes out of specific patterned drill and conscious manipulations. (pp. 5–6)

This is precisely what sentence combining provides. It expands the practical choices, the options truly available to the inexperienced young writer *when he needs them*. Christensen (*The Christensen Rhetoric Program*, 1968) claimed that "Grammar maps out the possible, rhetoric narrows down the possible to the desirable or effective" (p. 572). Sentence combining helps the writer enlarge the "practical-possible" so that it can be utilized during the composing process. The young writer, who has been exposed to sentence-building practice and who is developing into what was earlier called "the student as syntactic authority" as a result of intensive experiences with the manipulation of sentence structure, should be in a better position to deal with run-on or choppy styles. Armed with an expanded practical repertoire of syntactic choices, he would be better able to avoid "monotous patterning" and to work his "wider stock of available devices" into "an appropriate, pleasing overall pattern" as advocated by Gleason. Clearly a desirable curricular outcome for the teacher of writing.

Although the findings of the present study relate specifically to seventh graders, there is no obvious reason for assuming that sentence-combining practice should not be used in elementary and senior high school, as well as in junior high school.

The English department at Florida High School spent a good deal of time planning the seventh grade language arts program for the control group. (Remember that the experimental group was exposed to shortened versions of each of the control group's units.) And yet, despite the sophistication of the control group's program, with its small classes, well-qualified, experienced teachers, an abundance of free reading, carefully planned instruction in composition, and a relaxed atmosphere in which student talk and classroom interaction were encouraged, the control group showed only "normal" growth—.27 words per T-unit—in syntactic maturity, very similar to Mellon's control group which increased by .26 words per T-unit. If the control group's program had such a negligible effect on their syntactic maturity and overall writing quality when compared to the experiences of the experimental group, it seems reasonable to advocate the use of sentence-combining practice with, at the very least, seventh graders. The case for the efficacy of sentence-combining practice becomes even more attractive when the results of research in composition are reviewed. Neither Braddock (*Research in Written Composition,* 1963) nor Meckel ("Research on Teaching Composition and Literature" in *Handbook of Research on Teaching,* ed. N. L. Gage, 1963) uncovered a single study reporting a statistically significant composition treatment effect. Since the present study did discover a significant composition treatment effect, its sentence-combining system, which enables students to build sentences and manipulate syntax with greater facility, should surely be utilized in our schools.

In elementary school, simple adjective and relative clause insertions and repeated subject and verb deletions could be practiced orally in, perhaps, second grade. Written exercises could start in third or fourth grade. The present study's sentence-combining signal system can easily be expanded to incorporate a wider range of syntactic structures which could be practiced in junior and senior high school.

Students exposed to sentence-building techniques could use these syntactic manipulative skills at the prewriting or rewriting stage in their work in composition. They would be better able to ''unchop'' the choppy sentence and eliminate the run-on sentence. One can readily envisage individual or classwide work on improving sentences or even paragraphs in a rhetorically oriented setting. Students could practice rewriting whole paragraphs, given either in kernel form or in a choppy or overly elaborate style. Experienced in sentence manipulation and trained to think in rhetorical terms, they would be in a better position to make meaningful rhetorical choices because they would have a wider repertoire of syntactic alternatives from which to choose.

The present researcher certainly agrees with Mellon's statement that sentence-combining exercises could be regarded as ''a valuable addition to the arsenal of language-developing activities Moffett (*A Student-Centered Language Arts Program,* 1968) includes in his language arts program'' (*Transformational Sentence-Combining,* 1969, p. 80). Whether these activities are ''naturalistic'' or ''non-naturalistic'' is, perhaps, irrelevant. The crucial questions are (1) Would they work? and (2) Would students enjoy them? A skillful teacher should be able to ensure that both questions are answered in the affirmative.

Practice with intensive sentence-manipulation exercises need not be restricted to the lower grades. Hunt's data, shown in Table 1 (p. 22), indicate a wide gap between the syntactic maturity level of twelfth graders and that of superior adults. Indeed, *The Christensen Rhetoric Program* (1968), although heavily dependent on the students' prior knowledge of grammatical terminology, does teach sentence-building operations in order to improve college freshmen's writing ability.

Although Christensen agreed with Mellon that a mature style can be taught, he strenuously disagreed with what he called Mellon's conception of good style. He criticized Mellon for concentrating on relativization and, especially, nominalization, and also suggested that ''we shouldn't teach subordination as it is hard to read'' (''The Problem of Defining a Mature Style,'' in *English Journal,* 1968, p. 576). Christensen based this argument on an examination he made of modern professional and semiprofessional writers. These writers,

Christensen claimed, wrote what he called "cumulative sentences," which feature a high proportion of final free modifiers and are indicative of a mature style. However, another researcher, Johnson ("Some Tentative Strictures on Generative Rhetoric," in *College English,* 1969), after analyzing the prose of a different group of professional writers—a very prestigious collection indeed—and comparing them with Christensen's "best" writer, Halberstam, concluded that

> If we are to measure the degree of skill in a writer by the percentage of words he has in free modification, we should rate Cather, Fitzgerald, Forster, Isherwood, Baldwin, Auden and Orwell as less skillful than Halberstam. (p. 163)

Johnson also suggested that "students had best devote far more time to mastering subordination than Christensen would have them do" (p. 161). She noted that Edmund Wilson's style is one that is not cumulative but periodic and that Wilson

> depends for modifications, not on verbal clauses, appositives and absolutes so much as on relative and subordinate clauses. . . . (p. 162)

It is obvious from the evidence advanced, both by Christensen and Johnson, that we are a long way from defining satisfactorily a mature style or styles. Relativization and nominalization, final, medial, and initial free modifiers, short base clauses, all would appear to have their place in any definition of what constitutes a mature style.

What is bad about any style is its obviousness. Repeated cumulative sentences draw attention to themselves; their lack of variety only has unfortunate stylistic consequences. Therefore it would surely be a mistake to favor any one particular syntactic pattern to the exclusion of other possible patterns. Syntactic manipulative exercises should exploit the entire range of syntactic alternatives allowed by the grammar of English. What the young writer needs is as much practice as possible on every conceivable combination of syntactic operations.

In *Notes Toward a New Rhetoric* (1967) Christensen raised an interesting point that may help to explain something that the present researcher noticed in an entirely subjective examination of the post-treatment compositions. Christensen claimed that "solving the problem of *how to say* helps solve the problem of *what to say* . . ." (p. 5). Does this mean that form can, in some sense, generate content? It was evident to this researcher that the post-treatment compositions written by the experimental group had much more detail, more "meat" to them. The treatment group seemed to "see" more clearly. They had more to say. Perhaps the syntactic manipulative skill the students had developed, because it entailed a wider practical set of syntactic alternatives, *invited* or *attracted* detail. Perhaps knowing *how* does help to create *what*.

An alternative explanation seems plausible. Since the experimental group had become more skillful manipulators of syntax, perhaps their fear of syntax had dissipated. Confidence is very likely a self-generating process, feeding on itself. Released from syntactic roadblocks, confident, seeing a wider range of choices, the student's mind could grapple, at ease, with additional syntactic-semantic considerations. It is of interest to note that although the sentence-combining exercises did not include practice with adverb clauses, the experimental group produced a significantly greater number of adverb clauses in their free writing. The "confidence" factor has a theoretical attractiveness that invites further study. An important dimension of the present study was the systematic attempt to build student confidence by accentuating the positive. Perhaps grammar study and too much concern with error build barriers between the beginning writer and the composing process. Sentence combining concentrates on student success. It not only has students write, it shows them *how*.

Since this researcher is advocating work with cumulative sentences as well as with sentences similar to those in the present study, it might be of interest to illustrate how readily adaptable the present study's sentence-combining signals are to Christensen's system or similar programs. In an article describing and evaluating the latest developments in rhetorical theory, McCrimmon ("Will the New Rhetorics Produce New Emphases in the Composition Class?" in *CCC*, 1968, p. 128) cited his favorite example of a cumulative sentence, written by one of Christensen's students. Reduced close to basic kernel form, with sentence-combining signals added, it would look like this:

A girl develops from the sheet of walk.
The girl is *small*.
The girl is a *Negro*.
The walk is *glare-frosted*.
The girl is *walking barefooted*.(,)
Her bare legs are striking the cement.(,)
Her legs are *recoiling from the cement*. (AND)
The cement is *hot*.
Her feet are *curling in*.(,)
Only the outer edges of her feet are
    touching the hot cement.(,)

Note that the only additional signals that had to be developed are (AND) and (,). The (AND) simply means insert an *and* where appropriate on that line. Perhaps the comma signal (,) is not really necessary. Remember that underlined (italicized) words are retained and the remainder of the sentence deleted. The final sentence is rather easy to produce:

A small Negro girl develops from the sheet of glare-frosted walk, walking barefooted, her bare legs striking and recoiling from the hot cement, her feet curling in, only the outer edges touching.

Similarly, the following example from Sinclair Lewis can be readily handled by the development of two additional signals, (⧓) and (A). HE with the cross through it means delete *he*. And (A) means supply *a*. The present researcher is indebted to Brown ("Concepts, Kernels, and Composition," in *South Atlantic Bulletin*, 1970, p. 44) for the reduction of Lewis's sentence to near kernel form. The signals, of course, have been supplied:

He dipped his hands in the bichloride solution.
He shook them. (AND ⧓)
The *shake* was *quick*. (, A)

His *fingers* were *down*. (,)
His fingers were *like the fingers*
of a pianist above the keys. (,)

Insertion of each sentence into the top sentence according to the present study's signal system would result in the following sentence:

He dipped his hands in the bichloride solution and shook them, a quick shake, fingers down, like the fingers of a pianist above the keys. (Brown, p. 42)

Style has been conceived of in many ways; at times it is all-embracing, at others very narrow. Christensen ("The Problem of Defining a Mature Style") called it "syntax as style" (p. 572). Milic ("Against the Typology of Styles," in *CCC*, 1967) defined it as

[the individual's] habitual and consistent selection from the expressive resources available in his language. . . . his style is the collection of his stylistic options. . . . Options or choices are not always exercised consciously. (p. 72)

McCrimmon cited the following all-encompassing definition of style given by Young and Becker ("Toward a Modern Theory of Rhetoric: A Tagmemic Contribution," in *Harvard Educational Review*, 1965):

A writer's style, we believe, is the characteristic route he takes through all the choices presented in both the writing and prewriting stages. It is the manifestation of his conception of the topic, modified by his audience, situation, and intention—what we call his "universe of discourse,"

and made the following comment:

Since all the choices cited here include those made in all three of the major classical stages, this definition subsumes invention and arrangement under style. (p. 125)

The present researcher is interested in the implications for the *teaching* of composition of considering the part of style defined above by Milic and Christensen as at least as important as invention or arrangement—style, that is, in the sense of the final syntactic choices made in the process of writing. Although lexical choices are not uncommon, the final choice made by every writer is more frequently a syntactic one. The last thing a writer usually does is to put words down on paper in a particular order. Perhaps English teachers have not sufficiently realized the desirability, indeed the necessity, of helping their students acquire the ability to put words down on paper, to manipulate syntax.

The present study's findings strongly suggest that style, rather narrowly defined as the final syntactic choices habitually made from the writer's practical repertoire of syntactic alternatives, is an important dimension of what constitutes writing ability. Whether Young and Becker were correct in asserting that style subsumes invention and arrangement obviously cannot be answered from the findings of the present study. But it is nevertheless an interesting and an important question for rhetorical theory and practice.

Most teachers of writing either ignore or neglect the importance of syntactic manipulative ability. They certainly do not give it its proper due. And they fail to do so, perhaps, because they are concentrating on another important dimension of the writing process— that of observation and experience. Composition teachers should realize that it is not enough for a young writer to have something to say. Finally, he must be able to express it, to manipulate sentence structures in order to recapture the experience for his reader. An examination of the sentence about the small Negro girl, a sentence with all the hallmarks of a professional writer, and also of how that sentence *might* have been written should make this point clearer. Here is the "professional" example again:

> A small Negro girl develops from the sheet of glare-frosted walk, walking barefooted, her bare legs striking and recoiling from the hot cement, her feet curling in, only the outer edges touching.

After due consideration has been given to the importance of the writer's observation and experience, to the concreteness of the meticulously sequenced images, to the viewer's eye movement, all of these can be reflected in a series of sentences which are, perhaps, typical of the writing of a rather observant high school student, not that of a professional writer:

> A small Negro girl develops from the sheet of walk which is glare-frosted. She is walking barefooted. Her bare legs strike the hot cement and then they recoil from it. Her feet curl in so that only the outer edges are touching the hot cement.

In terms of observation and experience the "professional" example is no different from that of the hypothetical high school student. Both examples recreate the writer's visual experience. They carry the same experiential and observational load. The only difference between them is in the writers' handling of the syntax. It is true, of course, that the "professional" writer was able to recreate the rhythmic quality of the scene by blending syntax and image. Although there is no necessary connection between the observational experience, the ordered sequence of concrete images, and the manipulative syntactic skill of the writer, their brilliant fusion, their complementary confluence, made the difference. In the last analysis, however, the "professional" writer was able to accomplish this only through his ability to manipulate sentence structure. Teachers of writing surely ought to spend more time teaching students to be better manipulators of syntax. Intensive experience with sentence combining should help to enlarge a young writer's repertoire of syntactic alternatives and to supply him with practical options during the writing process.

The attractiveness of the sentence-combining signals in the present study lies in their simplicity, their consistency, their flexibility, and their practicality. The previous examples illustrate how simple it is both to learn to use the signals and to expand and adapt them. The elimination of the study of transformational grammar and of transformational nomenclature makes all of this possible. With the threat of grammatical failure removed, the developing writer can get on with solving sentence-structure problems and confidently face the real issue—that of blending form and idea in any given rhetorical situation.

One final comment: Although this researcher has rather strenuously urged that more attention be paid to the syntactic manipulative skill and for a more important place for "style as syntax" in the curriculum, he is merely suggesting a possible new emphasis in rhetorical instruction and is in no sense denying or even questioning the importance of the other members of the classical rhetorician's tripod, invention and arrangement. In the last analysis the question as to which of these comes first, which is more important, becomes totally irrelevant. In their essential inseparability, they are more than a tripod. Invention, arrangement and style are a trinity, one and indivisible.

QUESTIONS FOR DISCUSSION

1. Not much is known about "the composing process"—the succession of mental and physical activities through which children or adults go as they move from the conception of an idea to a completed written sentence. Does O'Hare's work shed any light on the process? Does it promise to help teachers understand the process better? In what ways?

2. From what you know of students in grades 2–6 and from what you can see of O'Hare's procedures, do you concur that his techniques might usefully be employed in the elementary grades? Where might they be used? How much time might be devoted to them? How might they be related to other elements in the teaching of writing?

3. Do you agree with O'Hare's comments on what constitutes good style and bad style? Reconsider Christensen's essay, and determine whether you think O'Hare's response to it is fair.

4. O'Hare implies that his technique of teaching writing differs appreciably in spirit and philosophy, as well as in technique, from methods commonly used in the schools. Do you agree? In what ways do the methods differ?

5. Does O'Hare's technique make it possible, or desirable, for the teacher to abandon his or her concern for what is grammatically "right," in favor of a concern for syntactic options and how they might work in a piece of writing?

Developing a Vocabulary of the Senses
Alexander Frazier

Elementary teachers frequently face the question of whether they should try, through their comments and observations in class discussions, to introduce students directly to new words they can use in talking about their experiences, or whether teachers should rely upon the students' reading and, perhaps, on lists of new words in the readings as the primary stimulus to vocabulary building.

Alexander Frazier, of the School of Education at Ohio State University, presents an organized vocabulary for talking about sensory experiences —experiences that appeal directly to one or more of the five senses— and implies that teachers should draw on it deliberately in their talk with students.

Frazier assumes the desirability of giving students many experiences that will engage their senses, and he suggests that the building of students' vocabulary be part of teachers' efforts to help students develop skill in presenting their sensory experiences through language. Since Frazier does not specifically detail the kinds of classroom applications this vocabulary may have, teachers should consider how they might use this vocabulary with their students.

From *Elementary English* Vol. 47, No. 2 (February 1970), pp. 176–84. Copyright © 1970 by the National Council of Teachers of English. Reprinted by permission of the publisher and the author.

The multi-sensory base of learning, long understood by teachers of young children, has recently received renewed attention in programs designed for the disadvantaged. Classrooms have been equipped more richly with objects to be manipulated, pictures and filmstrips to be looked at, and models or artifacts of one kind or another to be both observed and handled. Study trips to the zoo or the fruit and vegetable department of a supermarket have provided a fund of sensory images and impressions to be extended back in the classroom. Sometimes deliberately planned experiences have been added to the curriculum to sensitize children to differences in texture, color and shape, volume and pitch, odor, and taste.

Such multi-sensory enrichment has usually been seen as compensating for environmental deficits. The belief has been that by multiplying the objects, occasions, or events from which valued kinds of learning can be derived, children from poor backgrounds will be helped to catch up with other children. Thus the added experiences have often been considered to be in themselves sufficient to produce learning.

But in view of more rigorous evaluation of programs like Head Start, doubt is now being widely expressed as to whether experience alone is enough. Viewing a filmstrip of farm animals, getting a chance to feel and smell a pineapple and finally to taste a bit of it, or trying to identify with eyes closed a series of noises made by a set of household articles—what does all this really add up to?

Something more would seem to be needed than just new experience. While the range of things more to be done with experience is being freshly explored by workers in early childhood education, we may wish to remind ourselves that we already know a good deal about what it takes to develop one of the products to be expected from new experience—additional or more precise meanings for words already in the vocabulary and also brand new words.

The young learner develops vocabulary as he does other aspects of language from the language he hears around him as well as through the occasions he has for using language purposefully. He learns the meanings valued in the discourse of those to whom he listens and with whom he communicates. Experience may be said to have been fully experienced only when it has been worked through in terms of language. The meaning of experience has to be extracted, clarified, and codified, so to speak. Perhaps, then, one of our chief challenges in working more productively with disadvantaged and indeed with all children is to attend more carefully to the development of vocabulary from whatever experiences they are having.

What is offered here is a vocabulary of the senses that teachers may find useful to refer to as they do try to make the most of talking things through with younger children. The list presents the words first in alphabetized order under each sense and then by certain categories of common interest in sensory education. The list has been developed out of a number of different situations, including workshops or other inservice sessions with teachers in the schools of Collier County, Florida; Rome, Georgia; and Columbus, Ohio.

THE SENSE OF SOUND

A List of Words

babble	cackle	coo	eavesdrop
bang	caw	crackle	echo
bark	chant	crash	
bawl	chat	creak	fizz
bay	chatter	croak	
beat	cheep	croon	gab
bell	cheer	crow	gabble
bellow	chime	crunch	giggle
blab	chirp	cry	gobble
blabbermouth	chuckle		gong
blare	clack	deaf	gossip
blast	clamor	deafening	groan
bleat	clang	din	growl
blubber	clank	drawl	gruff
boom	clink	drone	grumble
bray	cluck	drum	grunt
buzz	converse	dumb	gurgle

harmony
hear
hiss
hoarse
honk
hoot
howl
hubbub
hullabaloo
hum
hush

jabber
jangle
jaw
jeer
jingle

knock

laugh
laughter
lecture
lisp
listen
loud
low

melody
melodious
mew (meow)
moan
monotone
monotonous
moo
mum

mumble
murmur
mute
mutter

neigh
noise
noisy

overhear

pad
patter
peal
peep
pitch
plunk
pop
prattle
preach
purr

quack
quiet

racket
rant
rap
rasp
rattle
rave
recite
rhythm
ring
ripple
roar

roll
rumble
rustle

say
scream
screech
shriek
shrill
shout
silent
silence
sing
singsong
siren
sizzle
slam
smack
snarl
snort
snuffle
song
sonic boom
sound
soundless
speak
speech
speechless
splash
splutter
squall
squawk
squeak
squeal
stammer
stereophonic

still
strum
stutter
supersonic
swish

tap
tattle
thud
thump
thunder
tick
tinkle
toll
tom-tom
tone
tongue-tied
toot
tread
trill
trumpet
tune
twang
twitter

undertone
uproar

vocal
voice
volume

wail
warble
weep
whimper

whine	whisper	yap	yip
whiney	whistle	yell	yodel
whinny	whoop	yelp	yowl

SOME USEFUL CLASSIFICATIONS

to hear—eavesdrop, hear, listen, overhear

to talk—blab, chat, chatter, converse, drawl, gossip, jabber, lecture, lisp, mumble, murmur, mutter, prattle, preach, rant, rave, recite, say, shout, speak, stammer, stutter, tattle, whisper

to express grief or sadness—bawl, blubber, cry, groan, moan, wail, weep, whimper

to express happiness—cackle, chuckle, giggle, laugh, roar, squeal, whoop

a loud or penetrating noise—bang, bellow, blare, blast, boom, bray, cheer, clamor, clang, crash, din, howl, racket, roar, scream, screech, shriek, shout, slam, squeal, thunder, uproar, wail, whistle, whoop, yap, yell, yelp

a soft or low noise—buzz, chirp, chuckle, creak, croon, drawl, fizz, giggle, groan, growl, gurgle, hiss, hoarse, hum, jingle, mew (meow), moan, mumble, murmur, purr, rumble, rustle, sizzle, snarl, squeak, swish, thud, tick, tinkle, undertone, warble, whimper, whisper

animal noises—bark, bay, bleat, bray, cackle, caw, cheep, chirp, cluck, coo, croak, crow, gobble, growl, grunt, hiss, honk, hoot, howl, mew (meow), moo, neigh, peep, purr, quack, screech, snarl, squeak, squeal, twitter, whimper, whinny, yap, yelp, yip, yowl

a confused noise—babble, buzz, cackle, shatter, din, hubbub, hullabaloo, hum, racket, twitter, uproar

an angry noise—bellow, growl, grumble, grunt, jaw, jeer, mutter, roar, shout, snarl, snort, splutter, yell

a musical sound—chant, chime, harmony, hum, jingle, melody, peal, plunk, rhythm, song, trill, tune, volume, yodel

musical instruments—bell, chime, drum, gong, tom-tom, trumpet, whistle bell sounds—boom, chime, clang, peal, ring, tinkle, toll

percussion sounds—bang, beat, boom, clang, rattle, rumble, thump, thunder

wind instrument sounds—blare, bleat, toot, trumpet

stringed instrument sounds—plunk, strum, twang

inexpressive sounds—drone, monotone, sing-song

pleasant sounding—harmonious, melodious

unpleasant sounding—deafening, monotonous, singsong, whiney

not hearing—deaf

noiseless—dumb, mute, quiet, silent, soundless, speechless, still, tongue-tied

THE SENSE OF SIGHT

A List of Words

admire	blink	colorless	fade
appear	blond	crystal	faded
appearance	blot		faint
array	blue	dappled	fair
attractive	blur	dark	farsighted
auburn	blurred	darken	flash
	bright	dazzle	flashy
beautiful	brighten	dazzling	flicker
beauty	brightness	dim	foggy
becoming	brilliance	dingy	freckled
binoculars	brilliant	dirty	
black	brindle	discolor	gaudy
blank	brown	discolored	gawk
blare	brunet	distinct	gaze
blaze		drab	glance
blazing	clean	dusky	glare
bleached	clear	dye	glasses
bleary	color		gleam
blind	colorful	eye	gleaming
blindness	colored	eyewitness	glimmer

glimpse
glint
glitter
glittering
glisten
glistening
gloom
gloomy
gloss
glossy
glow
glowing
goggle
good-looking
gorgeous
gray
green
grimy

hallucination
handsome
hazy
homely
hue

illusion
image
indistinct
invisible

light
look
looking glass

magnify
microscope

mirage
mirror
misty
mottled
murky

nearsighted
notice

observe
observant
observer
observation
ogle
orange

pale
pastel
peek
peep
peer
periscope
perceive
perception
picture
pigment
pink
polished
pretty
purple

radiance
radiant
recognize
red
reflect
reflection

reflector
reveal
review

scan
scene
scrutiny
see
shade
shadowy
sharp sighted
sheen
sheer
shimmer
shimmering
shine
shining
shiny
show
showy
sight
smeared
smudged
soiled
sooty
sparkle
sparkling
speckled
spectacle
spectator
spectrum
splotched
spotted
spy
squint
stain

stained
stare
streak
streaked
stripe
striped
sunny
survey

tarnish
tarnished
telescope
tinge
tint
transparent
twinkle
twinkling

ugly
ugliness
unattractive

view
viewpoint
visible
vision
vista
visual
visualize

watch
watchful
well-groomed
white
witness

yellow

Some Useful Classifications

to see or look at—admire, eye, gawk, gaze, glance, glare, glimpse, goggle, look, notice, observe, ogle, peek, peep, peer, perceive, recognize, review, scan, see, sight, spy, squint, stare, survey, view, watch, witness

to show or reflect light—glaze, brighten, dazzle, flash, flicker, glare, gleam, glimmer, glint, glitter, glisten, glow, reflect, shimmer, shine, sparkle, twinkle

to alter or change color or clarity—blot, blur, brighten, darken, dim, fade, flicker, magnify

something to see or look at—appearance, hallucination, illusion, image, mirage, picture, reflection, scene, sight, spectacle, view, vision, vista

a look at something—glance, glimpse, look, observation, peek, peep, survey

color or an aspect of color—auburn, black, blond, blue, brown, brunet, dye, gray, green, hue, orange, pastel, pigment, pink, purple, red, spectrum, tinge, tint, white, yellow

one who sees or looks—eyewitness, observer, spectator, spy, witness

brightness—blare, blaze, brightness, brilliance, dazzle, flash, flicker, glare, glint, gloss, glow, light, radiance, sheen, shimmer, shine, sparkle, twinkle

darkness—blindness, gloom, shade, tarnish

instruments of seeing—binoculars, glasses, looking glass, microscope, mirror, periscope, reflector, telescope

attractive looking—attractive, beautiful, becoming, good-looking, gorgeous, handsome, pretty, well-groomed

unattractive looking—homely, ugly, unattractive

easy to see—clear, distinct, transparent, visible

hard to see—bleary, blurred, dark, dim, indistinct, invisible, murky

unable to see well—blind, nearsighted, farsighted

able to see well—observant, sharp sighted, watchful

bright—blazing, bright, brilliant, dazzling, flashy, gaudy, gleaming, glittering, glistening, glossy, polished, radiant, shimmering, shining, shiny, showy, sparkling, twinkling

dark—black, dark, dim, dusky, gloomy, murky, shadowy, sooty

colorless—blank, bleached, drab, faded, pale

mottled—bleary, blurred, brindle, dappled, freckled, mottled, speckled, spotted, streaked, striped

discolored—dingy, dirty, discolored, grimy, smeared, smudged, soiled, sooty, splotched, spotted, stained, tarnished

THE SENSE OF TOUCH

A List of Words

alive	feathery	hit	powdery
	feel	hot	prickly
blush	feeling	humid	pull
blushing	feverish		push
bristly	firm	itch	
brush	flabby		rough
bumpy	flat	juicy	rub
	fluffy	jumpy	
caress	flush		sandy
chill	flushed	lifeless	scratch
chilly	fondle	light	scratchy
coarse	fumble	limp	sharp
cold	furry	lukewarm	shiver
coldness	fuzzy	lumpy	shivering
contact			shivery
cool	gooey	massage	shudder
crawly	grab	maul	shuddering
creepy	grasp	moist	shuddery
crisp	grainy		shove
cuddly	greasy	numb	silky
	gritty		slap
dab	gummy	oily	slick
damp			slimy
deadened	hairy	pat	slippery
downy	handle	peck	smooth
dull	hard	pet	soft
dry	heavy	pinch	solid
dusty			

spongy	strike	thorny	velvety
springy	stroke	tickle	vibrate
squashy	sweaty	ticklish	vibrating
squeeze		tingle	
stiff	tag	touch	
sticky	tap	tough	warm
sting	temperature	toughened	warmth
stinging	tepid		wet
stretchy	texture	uneven	woolly

Some Useful Classifications

to touch something—brush, caress, dab, feel, grab, grasp, handle, hit, pat, pinch, rub, scratch, smooth, squeeze, strike, tag, tap, tickle

to respond to a stimulus—blush, chill, cool, flush, itch, shiver, shudder, tingle, warm

a touch—brush, caress, contact, dab, hit, pat, pinch, rub, scratch, squeeze, sting, strike, stroke, tag, tap, tickle

a feeling (as a result of being touched or affected by something)—blush, chill, coldness, feeling, flush, itch, shiver, shudder, tingle, warmth

warm or hot feeling—blushing, feverish, flushed, hot, humid, lukewarm, sweaty, warm

cool or cold feeling—chilly, cold, cool, crisp, shivering, shuddering

dry feeling—dry, dusty, hot, powdery

wet feeling—damp, humid, juicy, moist, squashy

sticky feeling—gooey, gummy, sticky, sweaty

oily feeling—greasy, oily, slimy, slippery

smooth feeling—flat, greasy, oily, sharp, silky, slick, slippery, smooth, velvety

rough feeling—bristly, coarse, dull, grainy, gritty, hairy, lumpy, rough, sandy, scratchy, uneven

soft feeling—downy, feathery, flabby, fluffy, furry, fuzzy, limp, powdery, silky, soft, spongy, squashy, velvety, woolly

hard feeling—crisp, firm, hard, solid, stiff, tough

springy feeling—alive, flabby, jumpy, shuddering, spongy, springy, squashy, stretchy, vibrating

solid feeling—firm, hard, solid, tough
light feeling—downy, feathery, fluffy, light, powdery
heavy feeling—heavy, solid
feeling full of movement—alive, jumpy, shivering, shuddering, vibrating
feeling without movement—chilly, cold, dead, lifeless
unclean feeling—greasy, gritty, gummy, slimy, sticky, sweaty
uneasy or uncomfortable feeling—chilly, cold, crawly, creepy, feverish, flushed, jumpy, shivery, shuddery
unable to feel—cold, deadened, numb, toughened
responsive to touch—jumpy, ticklish

THE SENSE OF TASTE

A List of Words

acid	gingery	ripe	tainted
appetizing	green	rotten	tang
			tangy
biting	high-seasoned	salty	tart
bitter	honeyed	savor	taste
bland	hot	season	tasteless
		seasoned	tasty
	insipid	seasoning	
curdled		sharp	unappetizing
	luscious	sip	unflavored
delicious		sour	unpalatable
distasteful		spice	unripe
	mellow	spiced	unseasoned
		spicy	untainted
flavor	nauseating	spoiled	
flavored		stale	vinegary
flavorless	palatable	sugary	
flavorsome	peppery	sweet	yummy

Some Useful Classifications
to taste something—savor, sip, taste
to give taste to something—flavor, season, spice

a taste—flavor, savor, taste

an agent to alter taste—flavor, seasoning, spice

sweet tasting—honeyed, sugary, sweet

sour tasting—acid, curdled

sharp tasting—bitter, salty, sharp, tangy, tart, vinegary

hot or spicy tasting—biting, gingery, hot, peppery, spiced, spicy

bland tasting or tasteless—bland, flavorless, insipid, tasteless, unflavored, unpalatable, unseasoned

ripe tasting—mellow, ripe

unripe tasting—green, unripe

spoiled tasting—curdled, rotten, spoiled, tainted

good tasting—appetizing, delicious, flavorsome, luscious, tasty, yummy

bad tasting—biting, bitter, distasteful, nauseating, rotten, sour, spoiled, stale, tainted, tasteless, unappetizing, unpalatable, unripe, unseasoned, vinegary

having a taste—flavored, high-seasoned, seasoned, spiced

THE SENSE OF SMELL

A List of Words

aroma	incense	pungent	sniff
aromatic		putrid	spice
			spicy
bouquet	moldy		stench
	musty	rancid	stink
deodorant		rank	stinky
deodorize		reek	strong-scented
deodorized	odor		strong-smelling
deodorizer	odorless		sweet-scented
		scent	sweet-smelling
fragrance		scented	
fragrant	perfume	smell	
fumes	perfumed	smelly	whiff

Some Useful Classifications

to smell something—scent, smell, sniff, snuff, whiff

to give out a smell—perfume, reek, smell, stink

to add to or disguise a smell—to deodorize, perfume, scent, spice
a smell—aroma, bouquet, fragrance, fumes, odor, perfume, scent,
  smell, stench, stink, whiff
an agent to add to or disguise a smell—deodorant, deodorizer,
  incense, perfume, scent
sweet smelling—aromatic, fragrant, perfumed, scented, strong-
  scented, sweet-scented, sweet-smelling
sharp or spicy smelling—aromatic, pungent, spicy, strong-scented,
  strong-smelling
spoiled smelling—moldy, musty, putrid, rancid
bad smelling—rank, smelly, stinky, strong-scented, strong smelling
lacking in smell—deodorized, odorless

Warnings about the limitations of such a vocabulary list would
hardly seem necessary. This list touches on only one aspect of experience. Words can be mistaught as ends in themselves rather than
made the product of experience. Specificity of the sort that single
words represent soon exhausts itself when elaboration of meaning is
the goal, as it often is in teaching; the learner then has to resort to
restatement, modification, or metaphor to say what he wants to say.

Still, vocabulary lists can have value. Perhaps their chief use is
to remind us as adults of what there is to be learned. Perhaps we
need to spell out more clearly our ends in vocabulary development
as we have in other aspects of language learning. Certainly we are
agreed that we need to be more conscious of all our goals, especially as we try to improve our effectiveness in teaching language
to the disadvantaged.

As always, our problem is to keep our concern for ends from in-
terfering with our respect for means. Experience must come first.

QUESTIONS FOR DISCUSSION

1. To select a word is to interpret, perhaps to evaluate, the experience being discussed. Is it appropriate to discuss with children the
kinds of interpretations they are offering of their experiences and
how their words suggest these interpretations? How might the
teacher help students to see the differing interpretations communicated by words nearly synonymous?

2. Frazier suggests that there is a danger in excessive specificity in using words to represent experience. Do you share his concern? Is this a concern that might be discussed with students as they look at professional writing and at each others' papers?

3. As you read the articles by Watts, Christensen, and O'Hare, consider whether Frazier's "vocabulary of the senses" could be combined with the teaching techniques they discuss so as to give students some understanding of how to compose words into sentences to produce varied effects. Is it useful to talk with children about the effects gained (or lost) by the language choices they make? The purpose of expanding one's vocabulary, of course, is to widen one's range of choices for the expression of ideas and feelings. To what extent should the making of these choices in language be discussed as a deliberate process in the elementary classroom?

Spelling, etc.
Nancy Martin and
Jeremy Mulford

As has been emphasized in the preceding selections, many teachers believe that the primary goal of instruction in writing is to help students discover their worlds, order them, respond to them, and perhaps to exercise their imaginations upon them. Concern with syntactic correctness, proper spelling, and neat handwriting should be secondary, in the opinion of these teachers, since such concern may distract students' attention from writing and may even quench any interest in writing that the students may be developing. Teachers who are concerned about syntactic and other ''basic'' matters need to put such matters into perspective in relation to other elements of writing.

The following article by Nancy Martin and Jeremy Mulford argues that teachers should focus attention on syntax, spelling, and handwriting only when such attention is necessary to help children communicate what they want to say to their intended audiences and will not distract children from deciding what they want to say and how to say it.

Nancy Martin is on the faculty of the University of London Institute of Education; Jeremy Mulford is an experienced teacher in primary schools who, at the time this essay was published, was director of the National Association for the Teaching of English—Schools Council project on ''Children as Readers.''

From Anthony Jones and Jeremy Mulford, eds., *Children Using Language,* pp. 153–73. © 1971 by Oxford University Press. Reprinted by permission of the Clarendon Press, Oxford.

Teachers commonly talk about the "basic skills," especially in connection with reading, writing and arithmetic. The phrase itself provides the explanation for this. First, any concern with what is of lasting value seems to imply a need for solid foundation, a basis. Secondly, "skill" has the attraction for a teacher of seeming to be something which can not only be objectively defined but also exist in its own right and *therefore* be passed on as a sort of entity. Because of this, it is not surprising that the notion of "skill" is often translated into the image of a "tool." Now a tool in the literal sense is useless without the competence to use it. But "tool" in the figurative sense incorporates that competence; and so it reassuringly obscures the fact that, in the case of writing for example, skill cannot be adequately defined merely as something the teacher imparts and which the pupil comes to possess in so far as he is ready to do so. We say "reassuringly" because this conception puts a considerable onus on the teacher—he is then *in charge* of *what is to be learned;* and usually, the more one is in control of a situation, the more reassured one feels. We would go on to suggest that the teacher who does not question what he means by "skills"—whose notion of them expresses, or has lurking behind it, a feeling that skills are in some sense entities—will be all the readier to see the conventions (of spelling, punctuation, etc.) as "basic" to writing. For the conventions are by definition held in common, impersonal, and can be considered in isolation. By an easy extension, competence in using them can also be considered in isolation, and hence as something which the teacher who possesses it can impart to pupils who don't. This, to repeat, is reassuring. But we would maintain that a child who observed all the conventions with perfect competence, yet whose writing was uniformly unengaged, should not be called a skilled writer—not even in a "basic" sense. Indeed, it would be precisely what is basic that was lacking in his writing behaviour. We use, here, the phrase "writing behaviour" in order to stress the *activity* of writing, the process, as against the *product*.

Christian Schiller writes in *Talking and Writing* [1]:

---

[1] Edited by James Britton (Metheun).

It can be argued that logically reading comes before writing; but there must have been a first writer before there was a reader. Young children like to be such a first writer, putting down, regardless of others, what they want to say. It is not writing in the sense that it is written to be read; often it cannot be read except by the writer. Even if it can be read by others it is not the written word that is read, but a record of speech. John wants to talk about some experience he has enjoyed, and he records what he would say. If his pencil is very slow it helps occasionally to record it for him. Here is such a recording of a boy just seven, who lived in the country.

> "One day in autumn I went for a walk in a wood, and in a tree I saw a nest. I thought it was rather strange to see a nest in autumn, especially when a bird flew off it. I wondered what bird's nest it was. I thought it was a hooded crow's nest, but I knew it couldn't be in the part of England where I lived. I wanted to try and climb the tree, but the tree was too thin. The colours of the bird that flew from the nest were black and white. I thought it was very strange to see a bird's nest in autumn. I wished I could see inside the nest, but I knew I couldn't because the tree would break. So I came away, and I am still wondering what bird it was in the nest."

These words were spoken by a human voice; and black marks lying still and silent on a page cannot convey the melody and rhythm of the spoken sounds. But if one is familiar with the way an eager boy of seven will relate an adventure, slow at first with quickening pace as he lives again the event, something of this melody and rhythm can be felt; and it is this melody and rhythm which give to the words a quality beyond that of sense, a quality of being alive. But there is more than melody and rhythm; these simple words arranged simply have a shape, a beginning, a middle, and an end; and the simple shape is the more eloquent because the end is almost but not quite a repetition of the beginning. Hearing these words in our inner ear we can vicariously share his adventure, what he saw, what he did, what he felt in the wood one day in autumn.

There is no evidence to lead us to think that he spoke, or would write, deliberately in the way he did, or that he strove consciously to give his words a living quality. Doubtless he used language, as for example he would use paint, to say what was in him to say without concern for giving a considered impression. But in fact, however unconsciously his words were chosen and arranged, they give us something living of himself. He is using language, as he uses paint, not merely to say something but to express something of himself. Already he has begun to grasp the discipline of the material he uses.

Set out in printed words, punctuated and spelt in our contemporary convention, the composition looks exemplary. But it was not consciously spoken in sentences; and punctuation and spelling had no part in the creative act. It is not in these conventions that the discipline has been felt, but in *the choice of what to say and how to say it.* . . .

We have quoted at length because we feel the passage is a classic statement and deserves the widest currency. "The choice of what to say and how to say it" seems to us the basic skill of writing, though perhaps the word "choice"—implying as it does, out of context, conscious choice—is not a very apt word to apply to the process, particularly in the case of young children. Yet, since all experience is the raw material of writing, there must be, in fact, selection and shaping in words. The process of writing seems to be primarily a matter of keeping the inward eye focussed on whatever bit of experience the writer wants to record or articulate, and letting the flow of words largely look after itself. When the flow stops from time to time, as it inevitably does, the focus of attention may shift to the words, and conscious choice begin to operate. But whatever the exact nature of this process and its possible varieties may be, we believe—as do Professor Britton and Mr. Schiller— that a function of writing prior to communication is self-discovery, the representation of experience to oneself, for one's own satisfaction. With this in mind, it may be helpful to consider briefly the nature and function of various conventions.

One fundamental distinction that must be made is that between the concept expressed in a particular grammatical form and the conventional means of expressing it. For example, an eleven-year-old might have a good practical understanding of conditionality, yet still write, "If my dad go to the football match on Saturday, he said he take me with him." Now there might be general agreement that the conceptual knowledge involved in writing this is much more important than the inaccurate rendering of the conventional inflexions; yet teachers commonly act as though this were not so.[2] Much concern with correct conventional usage is merely a concern with tidiness for its own sake (to which we are not necessarily hostile— it's a question of priorities); and quite often particular notions of tidiness, of acceptable usage, have a class base. "They ain't got no" is not a middle class usage, and therefore attracts teachers' red pencils. Yet in many working class environments it is the normal, accepted usage; and moreover, nobody for whom it isn't the accepted usage is likely to be in any doubt as to what it means. There is no Natural Law which states that a second negative cancels the first (Chaucer, a court poet, was not being unconventional for *his* time and social group when he used a double negative, for emphasis). For a teacher to unquestioningly impose [3] *his* accepted usages of this kind on a child may be at once pointless and harmful. Pointless, because it is often far from clear that it is advantageous to an adolescent about to leave school—let alone a primary school child—that he should have acquired arbitrary middle class linguistic habits. Harmful, because such impositions suggest a failure by the teacher to recognize the prior function of writing that we mentioned in the last paragraph, and because they act cumulatively as a threat to a child's sense of identity which he expresses when he employs the linguistic usages of his home environment.

It is, in fact, difficult if not impossible to judge where to draw the line between usages that are conventional only for tidiness's sake and those that have a greater significance. It is probably more helpful to distinguish between those that have chiefly to do with what we shall call "presentation," and those that are intrinsic to the communication of meaning. Thus, except in the trivial (because so extraordinary) case of a mis-spelling that is actually the spelling of another word which could reasonably fit the given context, incorrect spelling hardly ever affects significantly the communication of meaning. The margin of error has to be very great before decipherment becomes impossible. Even the famous example of

---

[2] On promoting the use of "the complex internal organization that language itself provides for representing relation of sequence and hierarchy and consequence" (James Britton), see Nancy Martin's article, "What are they up to?"

[3] The reader who objects to this split infinitive might, relevantly, ask himself why.

"egog" becomes comprehensible in such a sentence as "The egog rolled himself into a ball when the dog sniffed his prickles"—and might well remain so even if the rest of the spelling were grossly inaccurate. It is true that a writer (adult as well as child) may choose to write down a word that he thinks he can spell, but which doesn't precisely capture his meaning, just because he cannot spell the right word. But this would have to do with his awareness, or assumption, of what is socially acceptable.[4] It would be likely that, given only a rudimentary phonic sense, had he made an incompetent stab at the spelling of the right word, he would still have succeeded in communicating his meaning.

Much punctuation also belongs, essentially, to the category of "presentation." The following is taken from John Clare's "Journey from Essex" (in which he describes his journey back to his home in Helpstone, Northamptonshire, after escaping from a lunatic asylum in Essex):

> . . . I have but a slight reccolection of my journey between here & Stilton for I was knocked up & noticed little or nothing—one night I lay in a dyke bottom from the wind & went to sleep half an hour when I suddenly awoke & found my side wet through from the sock in the dyke bottom so I got out & went on—I remember going down a very dark road hung over with trees on both sides very thick which seemed to extend a mile or two I then entered a town & some of the chamber windows had candle lights shining in them—I felt so weary that I forced [sic] to sit down on the ground to rest myself a while & while I sat there a coach that seemed to be heavy laden came rattling up and stopt in the hollow below me & I cannot reccolect its ever passing by me I then got up & pushed onward seeing little to notice for the road very often looked as stupid as myself & I was very often half asleep as I went on the third day I satisfied my hunger by eating the grass by the road side which seemed to taste something like bread I was hungry and eat heartily till I was satisfied & in fact the meal seemed to do me good the next & last day I reccolected that I had some tobacco & my

---

[4] The importance of spelling is often assumed to belong to the Natural Order of Things. A symptom of this is the fact that the incorrect spelling of a person's name is commonly regarded as a particular embarrassment. Yet, Sir Walter Rawleigh (sic), for example, was not very eccentric for his time in varying the spelling of his signature according to whim.

box of lucifers being exhausted I could not light my pipe so I took to chewing tobacco all day & eat the quids when I had done & I was never hungry afterwards—I remember passing through Buckden . . .[5]

In reading this for the first time, one stumbles occasionally; but to understand precisely what is meant is not at all difficult.[6] This example indicates an important distinction: there is a fundamental difference between a passage that is grammatically, syntactically, incoherent, and one that is coherent but lacking the usual signs of this which we call "punctuation *marks*." A child's ability to construct sentences may be well in advance of his ability (or inclination) to use full-stops, capital letters, etc. Or, to look at the matter in another way: if all the punctuation marks were removed from, say, *Little Dorrit,* the result would not be a bookful of bad prose.

However, the *Little Dorrit* example raises another issue. Although much of the meaning of the book would not be lost if all punctuation marks were excluded from it, there would be a great many places where an ambiguity was thereby left unresolved (and unresolvable [7]), or an emphasis (and hence a bit of meaning) lost: such omissions could not be subsumed under the category of "presentation." There can be no doubt that, when punctuation marks are intrinsic to the communication of meaning in this way, they are

[5] J. W. and Anne Tibble, *The Prose of John Clare,* pages 248/9 (Routledge).

[6] It might be said that the lack of punctuation in this passage contributes to the directness of its impact; or alternatively, that the poignancy of it is all the greater because of the biographical implications of the lack of punctuation. These possibilities are a reminder that one cannot treat "presentation" as either a simple or a completely separate category. We cannot investigate the matter properly here; but its complexity can perhaps be suggested by imagining a text reproduced in a number of different ways: very inaccurately spelt in immaculate hand-writing, perfectly spelt in almost illegible hand-writing, perfectly spelt in decent hand-writing, typewritten on red paper, printed in huge capitals on newsprint, engraved on cloth paper surrounded by printer's flowers, the same only mis-spelt, and so on—the list could be endless, and it is safe to say that the total meanings communicated would be different— sometimes significantly, sometimes not—in each case.

[7] I.e., unlike three occasions in the Clare passage. There, technically, we cannot be sure whether a stop would properly come before or after "as I went on the third day," and before or after "the next & last day"; nor can we be sure whether it was the box of lucifers that was exhausted, or Clare himself. In practice, we are in no doubt.

performing their most important function. Yet although it is correct to distinguish between the two main functions of punctuation marks—between occasions when the reader can get by without marks and occasions when, strictly speaking, he cannot—it is important to recognize that, from another point of view, the two functions belong together: both become significant only if one considers the reader *in addition to the writer*. Thus, someone might write, "Thunder crashed immediately after the horse bolted the stable collapsed," and *he* would know whether he meant that the thunder crashed after the horse bolted, or that the horse bolted after the thunder crashed. This example returns us to the principle that we stated earlier, concerning "self-discovery" as against "communication."

In speech, children learn very early to say things in different ways on different occasions: that is, their speech is increasingly differentiated, and at a time when their writing is relatively undifferentiated. Despite this fact of development, children are often asked to write in ways they are not capable of—impersonal reports, for instance: they are asked to accept someone else's purpose and mode of writing before they have a sufficiently defined sense of themselves to be capable of seeing purposes separate from their own impulses of the moment. Indeed, it is not simply a matter of purposes. A seven-year-old is not much concerned with his reader beyond the fact that the writing is often seen as an "offering" to someone who is assumed to understand it just because *he* has written it. The child will not usually make any modification in what he writes, as an adult would, in order to communicate what he is saying. In short, he is writing above all for himself. An adult, too, writes primarily for himself on many occasions: the difference is that an adult's satisfaction in his writing typically includes a sense of his reader reading it—a sense of what is required if satisfactory communication is to take place and of the reader's likely responses, both local and total. The pedagogical implication of this is that great tact is necessary in the face of much writing by young children. If a child has still to reach the stage when the notion of a reader reading what he writes is meaningful to him, an explicit concern chiefly with "communication" (whether in terms of "purposes'' or of "presentation" or of *failure* to communicate) on the part of the teacher will be essentially incomprehensible to him. It will tend to stem the impulse towards self-discovery through writing; and if this happens, the teacher's concern will commonly be counter-productive even in its own cause. For a young child to put on record what he *wants* to say, to write so that his language closely fits himself, his experience, to his own satisfaction, seems to us to be skilled writing at this stage of his development; and there will be many occasions when it is better to let him *fail to communicate,* or communicate only inefficiently. We are not suggesting, though, that the teacher should merely wait and see.

The business of helping children directly with their writing is a difficult one. They readily interpret instruction as the learning of rules, and we suggest that the basic matter of writing about what concerns you is not readily susceptible to rules: this is the reason that we make a distinction between skilled writing behaviour and the learning of surface competences. When we try to formulate rules for writing such as "Have a beginning, a middle, and an end" or "Make a plan before you write" or "Here is a list of good words and here is a list of bad ones," we are formulating much simpler and cruder versions than are already being operated.[8] So we suggest that teachers should beware of rules of this sort, and go for indirect aids such as a rich language experience and opportunities to write from a wide variety of situations—opportunities that the children may take up in any way that fits their concerns. Moreover, it is perhaps relevant that sportsmen are reluctant to talk about the procedures that they operate since they think that being conscious of what they are doing prevents them from operating most efficiently. Poetry may be a better teacher of writing to primary school children than analysis. Poetry works indirectly, analysis is direct ("Why is this word a better one to use than that one?"). The following piece of writing came from a class of eight year olds who had been handling and talking and writing about a green iguana in their classroom:

[8] It is worth remembering that children's use of language at all depends on their operating very complex rules which they don't know exist—which are not for them at any analysable level of knowledge.

The iguana has a long tail to curl with
a long tongue to have fun with
a striped tail to sail with.

Janey

We suggest that the boldness and brevity of this (an example of Professor Britton's "poetic mode") might well be related to the fact that the children had a lot of poetry read to them, so that this *kind* of language was in their experience continually. The point here is that no one indicated its qualities or asked the children to write according to models. They were simply writing out of a rich language experience, of talking and reading.

But what about the conventions: can the learning of *them* be left to the influence of a "rich language experience"? The short answer is No; though we believe that such experience should be the main teacher, and that, without it, any direct teaching will be a null activity.

Several points need to be made about the timing of this teaching. First, despite the relative unimportance of the conventions, we are in no doubt that it is desirable that children should have a working knowledge of them by the time they leave school. This does not mean, however, that it is—by definition—better if a child is (say) a competent speller at the age of 10 instead of 15. Such forwardness *may* suggest qualities of intelligence and interest which it is pleasing to find in a child, but the achievement itself is of little consequence. A full recognition of this ought to release much pressure on the primary school teacher. And it should enable him more readily to take the second, related point: if a child is not ready for a particular piece of direct teaching, it will do more harm than good to subject him to it. Thirdly, a child is not "ready" at the same time to learn all the conventions: we need to work out an order of priorities (which may well not be related to their relative intrinsic importances), and the appropriate order of learning may vary from child to child. Which leads to the fourth point—one whose obviousness seems to make it all the easier to ignore: children reach readiness at different times. Fifthly, any concern with readiness is incomplete without a consideration of the possible formation of bad habits that have subsequently to be unlearned. We shall return to those points after discussing *preparatory* teaching.

Earlier, we reached the conclusion that the stronger a child's sense of an audience for whom he is writing, the more ready he will be to receive instruction in the conventions of presentation. Helping to create this sense of an audience in a child is, therefore, a prior task to teaching him what the reader's particular needs are. In this light, the frequency with which a teacher reads a child's work with the child beside him, or has it read to him by the child, and the frequency with which a child's writing is read out to other children or is pinned up on the wall, take on an added significance. Not only are these procedures generally encouraging, they also constitute specific preparation. And they will be further complemented if the teacher occasionally writes when his children write, and then reads out or lets them read out what he has written.[9] For the sense of an audience involves a sense of reciprocity: it will be reinforced if teacher and children occasionally exchange roles in this way. On the other hand, if a teacher merely collects up a class's writing at the end of a lesson, and hands it back the next day or the day after that, this will tend to arrest any developing sense of an audience. And with children whose sense of an audience is minimal, it is particularly crass to not only do this but also cover their work with corrections; for this must tend to condition them into *not wanting* an audience. It is safe to say that, especially in the early terms of the junior school but also afterwards, it is generally better for a child to receive a very brief face-to-face response to what he has written as soon as possible after he has written it (and that this response be usually an encouraging one) than for the teacher, even with the seemingly enlightened intention of wanting to sort out what corrections the child is ready for, to postpone the encounter for a few hours—or days, as sometimes happens. We are not seek-

[9] What we are advocating has nothing to do with the provision by the teacher of models. Nevertheless, we realize that the practice could amount to this in effect, and that therefore it could be dangerous—especially if the teacher's writing approaches the "formal" or "poetic" in Professor Britton's sense; or if he saw good writing as, for example, a matter of vividness gained by inserting "good" adjectives.

ing to abrogate the teacher's traditional function of correcting mistakes; rather, we want to emphasize the need to prepare for such correction, by increasing children's receptivity. The means which we have mentioned so far are indirect, but they can become gradually more direct to some purpose. Here it is convenient to refer to Margaret Spencer's article where she says, on page 138, of one piece of writing:

> The total immersion of the teller results in a version which has great sweep and power. It drives on, if somewhat confusedly for the over-sophisticated reader.

She invites a comparison with an "older child's attempts to retell a story about Romulus so that the characters and actions are clearly differentiated for the reader," and then comments:

> As the child's egocentrism declines, so he begins to put the reader in full possession of the facts of the tale, and the narrative flood decreases.

This suggests to us that early direct approaches with a child to the needs of a reader are best made chiefly in terms of *information* that he has omitted, rather than of ways, for example, that punctuation helps the reader along. If the teacher questions a child tactfully, almost by the way, about any informational gaps, the child will see this as a function of the teacher's interest, not as an indication that he has Done Something Wrong; and the practice will almost certainly have a useful cumulative effect.

Our stress, then, is on a developmental approach. For only in this way can a teacher coherently take account both of the need to promote the self-discovery that writing can be, and of the fact that skilled writing finally involves successful communication. But having said this, we do not want the reader to infer that we are advocating a rigidly linear developmental approach. For instance, we can see no harm and some point in a teacher telling a child, soon after he has started to write a few words at a time connectedly, that it is usual to start a piece of writing with a capital letter and to end it with a full stop. Similarly, he might tell the child that the names of people begin with a capital letter, and, a little later, say the same about towns or countries. A little later still, once the child was able to form all lower case letters satisfactorily, the teacher could go on to explain that capital letters don't come in the middle of words (that is, unless the child's name were McIntyre . . .). But it would be quite inappropriate to attempt to teach a child at the same stage that all sentences begin with a capital letter and end with a full-stop; or that all proper nouns begin with a capital letter. The first would involve the teacher in an explanation of what constitutes a sentence; the second, in a definition of the difference between proper nouns and other nouns. These far from simple matters would almost certainly be far beyond the child's understanding; and any partial understanding that the child did achieve would, at this stage, amount to clutter.

With regard to learning "readiness," we agree with recent thinking which holds that, generally speaking, it can be a dangerous concept. By the time a child *shows* that he is ready to learn something, he may be more than ready. However, we see teaching the conventions as a special case. There is a sharp distinction to be made between teaching *them* and teaching, for example, the operation of mathematical concepts. In addition to the relative unimportance of the conventions, we would point to the fact that, if children write engagedly about what concerns them, there will be no redundancy of the kind that occurs when children go on practising a mathematical operation after it has become a firm part of their knowledge. In other words, if children go on writing about things that concern them in ignorance of a certain convention, even after they have reached the stage when teaching of that convention would be meaningful to them, this will not (given a qualification we mention below) do any harm: the basic activity will be taking place. We believe that, if in doubt about a child's readiness to be taught a convention, a teacher should postpone teaching it—or, at least, that the teacher should be very ready to give up immediately he senses a child failing to grasp what he is attempting to teach. To continue would be likely to induce an anxiety in the child which would issue in a false sense of priorities when writing, and would probably be counter-productive in its own cause, too.

We know how easy it is to act as though a child's incompetence at the age of eight will stay with him for life unless something is done more or less immediately about it—especially when that is the dominant attitude of his parents, and Open Day is in the offing. But we want to emphasize that there is no pedagogical justification for the primary school teacher to be in a hurry over the conventions. We believe that many children go on committing an array of habitual errors—such as forming plurals by adding an apostrophe s, or putting inverted commas round indirect speech—until they leave school, precisely because their primary school teachers felt they just had to teach them these things—otherwise they wouldn't know them when they left school . . . Of course, a child can pick up bad habits unnecessarily *by default* of the teacher; but here again a distinction has to be made—in particular, between spelling and punctuation.

In order to write, whether just for himself or to communicate to somebody else, a child has to attempt the spelling of every word he uses: he is bound to spell or misspell each word, he cannot notspell it. On the other hand, as the Clare passage showed, it is quite possible to not-punctuate. The acquisition of competence in spelling will, therefore, characteristically involve a much greater element of *un*learning—unlearning of habitual misusages—than the acquisition of competence in punctuation. "But what," a teacher might ask, "does this mean in practice?" This question cannot be answered satisfactorily by us: a teacher simply has to learn to judge how much concern for the conventions he can evince without it beginning to get in the way, without it inducing in a child a false sense of priorities, or confusion. This will vary, perhaps considerably, from child to child—according to his age, his ability, his interest, his flexibility, his aspirations; the effects of his past experience, of his parents' expectations, of his friends' attitudes; his attitudes to reading, to writing, to learning generally, to the teacher, to the school. . . . The list could be much extended. Here is an obvious area for joint, comparative study by all the teachers in a school (or perhaps two groups of them, if the school has more than, say, eight classes). Time spent for an hour each week on such matters would be incomparably more interesting, and incomparably more useful from every point of view, than the same time spent by each teacher in isolation on what is commonly regarded as the drudgery of marking.

Reference to the ways in which children vary leads us to stress that the teaching of the conventions should largely consist of discussion with individual children or—less often—with pairs or groups. "Readiness" is an individual matter; and the occasion when it is especially appropriate to discuss a given point must also, usually, be an individual matter. Moreover, we have no doubt that strident markings on a child's work, in addition to being offensive as defacement, often have as their chief effect the reassurance of the teacher that he is not failing to do his job (cf. "Take out your reading books"); and that if corrections are not actually discussed with a child, they are likely to have *no* effect other than the latter and the alienation of the child.[10] It must be very dispiriting to come to expect more or less the same old number of red marks to the page, the same old brief comment (give or take a "quite" or a "very") and list of "corrections" at the bottom: it must surely be remarkable if the child's response *isn't* mechanical. Of course, a teacher cannot properly discuss a child's work with him anything like as frequently as he would wish, but this is not a reason for allowing his staple response to that work to be little or no more than a dull registering of trivial errors after the event. Let the extent (in terms of time spent) of the teacher's response, the extent of his engagement with a child and his writing, vary considerably. If necessary, let the majority of his responses amount to no more than quickly reading through a given piece of writing with the author beside him soon after he has written it, offering a brief comment (as encouraging as possible) which takes up something the child has written so as to show him that he has engaged with his reader, and initialling the piece—commonly without mentioning any errors. This will at least leave the teacher time for a full discussion with

---

[10] See M. L. Peters, *Spelling: Taught or Caught?*, (Routledge and Kegan Paul) on the need to draw children's attention specifically to their errors. This book contains much useful information and advice on the teaching of spelling. Although it is not altogether free of the attitude, "the earlier the better," on balance its priorities are similar to ours.

each child *sometimes*. And if writing is not a "special" activity, accordingly timetabled, but something that is going on most of the time somewhere in the classroom, then "sometimes" may well be several times a week.

We are not meaning to imply that when a teacher takes an opportunity to respond fully to a piece of writing, this necessarily involves him in questioning the child directly and closely about its substance. Sometimes, when the child has committed a confidence to paper or when the main burden of a piece is not its surface meaning,[11] tact will demand that the teacher approaches the substance indirectly, or moves away from it tangentially, associatively.

There can be a point in a child, most commonly after he has spent several terms in the junior school, writing out corrected spellings in a personal spelling book; but this should generally be restricted to occasions when the teacher is able to discuss more important matters as well. Otherwise, the child will be justified in feeling that the only or main consequence of his effort—and hence, the purpose of his effort—is a further task, one that is mechanical and boring. The teacher should select carefully from among the child's errors when he has made more than one or two, and should then regard his selections as one, relatively unimportant element in the matter to be discussed. What is fundamental is involvement by the teacher in the *substance* of the child's writing. Such involvement guarantees to the child that corrections are worth taking seriously: it will tend to maintain or renew his interest, often to the point where he *wants* to produce a fair copy. With older juniors, this is the moment when some teaching in punctuation is likely to be most effective. With younger children, and less able older children, it will usually be more appropriate to discuss mainly or exclusively other aspects of presentation (in particular, how the fair copy might be decorated or illustrated), with a view to fostering the sense of an audience that we referred to earlier. We should perhaps emphasize that we are not advocating this sort of approach as a *strategy* for getting a child to learn the conventions, but as a *justification* for considering them at all.

[11] On this subject, see, for instance, Ruth Griffiths, *Imagination in Early Childhood* (Routledge and Kegan Paul).

In the last paragraph, we mentioned the decoration of fair copies; and, of course, there is no reason why first drafts should not be decorated and illustrated as well (as we have already said, the majority of them will be only drafts). Indeed, the practice is to be welcomed. Because writing is made up of non-iconic symbols (i.e. it is not picture-writing), it can be a relief or sustaining to a child to deal, part of the time, in the direct representation or embroidery of things he is writing or has written about.[12] The less experienced he is as a writer, the more likely this is to be so; but it remains true of many children long after they have become minimally proficient writers; and it would probably remain so much longer still if most children were not conditioned into believing that they "can't draw" by the time they arrive at the secondary school or soon afterwards. (Everyone can draw. The notion that being able to draw means being able to produce life-like, "realistic," representations of an object is an unfortunate, culturally determined prejudice.) Which brings us to the problem of hand-writing.

We feel that the less emphasis hand-writing—in small, using a pencil—receives in the infant school, the better. This is not because we regard hand-writing as unimportant: from the point of view of successful communication, there is a case for saying it is more important than spelling and punctuation.[13] It seems clear to us that the business of trying to manipulate a pencil satisfactorily can be a considerable hindrance to a child's initial engagement with written code; and, in addition, it seems a reasonable hypothesis that a year or two after a child has started school, when his co-ordination has much improved, is a better time for intensive teaching of hand-writing. We cannot deal here with techniques for teaching the formation of letters; nor, in fact, are we competent to deal properly with the larger practical questions that our view raises. All we can say here is that, in particular, the infant teacher and the teacher of backward juniors should enable his children to use as many ways to

[12] This is not contradicted by the fact that it *can* be inept of a teacher to say unthinkingly: "That's nice, dear; now do a drawing of it." Sometimes all the creative effort a child can give to a subject for the time being may have been expended in the writing.

[13] Thus, it matters much less if a teacher is unable to remember unerringly that e comes before i after c, than if his hand-writing is difficult to read.

record written code as possible, in order to remove some of the pressure that ordinary hand-writing can produce. Materials produced by the Initial Literacy Project are very useful in this respect. In addition, transcription (not necessarily by the teacher) of taped dictation by a child, chalk on blackboards (or slates for that matter), and especially—if at all possible—typewriters [14] should be regarded as means of composing for daily use. A variety of this sort—and our list isn't meant to be exhaustive—will be enlivening, as well as a relief from pencil-pushing.

Throughout this article, we have discussed the teaching of the conventions in relation to the main business of composition. It might be inferred that all such teaching should be tied to what a child has written. Generally speaking this is so; but we want to make it clear that we are not necessarily against exercises, etc. In some measure, our attitude depends on the extent to which the understanding of a convention can be seen as a function, or an extension, of choosing "what to say and how to say it" in Mr. Schiller's sense. Thus, we believe that punctuation will, essentially, be best learnt gradually from discussion with the teacher about particular pieces that a child has written. But occasional exercises can help even with punctuation. We are not thinking of the conventional sort, in which children are asked to insert capital letters, commas, inverted commas, question marks, full-stops, etc., in the right order, into inert sentences that a textbook writer or eleven-plus examiner has thought up specially. Many older juniors *can* be drilled into completing these efficiently. But it is our experience that there is often very little, if any, transfer of such expertize to their own writing. (To occasionally type out a piece by a child just as he has written it, and then to ask him to correct it in collaboration with a friend, is a different matter.) On the other hand, if a group of children were asked to punctuate a number of sentences similar to the one about a horse bolting * . . . they should certainly gain something from the discussion that ensued when it was discov-

* See p. 301 of *Children Using Language*.

[14] For a very relevant description of research, by Dr. O. K. Moore of Yale University, into the beneficial effects of using typewriters, instead of pencil or pen, for the early teaching of reading and writing, see John Downing (ed.), *The First International Reading Symposium*, pp. 12–15 (Cassell).

ered that there was no right answer. Two or three exercises of this kind in the course of a term could help them to a proper respect for punctuation, *confirm* knowledge that they had already partially got, and hence perhaps influence them to use punctuation marks less haphazardly (for most children, the best time to do such exercises is in the last year or so of the junior school).

We are sure it is undesirable for there to be a continuous traffic of children coming up to the teacher for spellings while they write. It can happen that a child comes and asks for every other word: this cannot but get in the way of what he is about. Once or twice perhaps—but no more, unless the piece is especially long or technical. And in classes where all the children write at the same time, even moderate toing and froing can generate a usurping momentum. (Of course, we are not suggesting that a teacher should tell a child to sit down immediately if he has already been to him twice. What we have in mind is a largely tacit attitude prevailing in the class, which keeps *spelling* in its place.) Similarly, although we approve in principle of the use of dictionaries, we think they should be regarded, primarily, as a reading tool, rather than a writing tool.

In order to enable a child to use a dictionary effectively, it can be helpful for him to do a series of exercises on alphabetical order when he is ready (and all the children in a class, whether unstreamed or streamed, certainly will not be ready at the same time). Dictionary exercises in which a child finds out and writes down the "meaning" of words that a dictionary gives are more questionable, for two reasons. First, they treat meanings in a void. Secondly, so-called "junior" dictionaries are inevitably very arbitrary in their selection not only of words but of meanings. Which is why we said "in principle" just now. A "junior" dictionary can be as much a hindrance as a help to a child (more so than to an adult, who understands and can make allowances for the arbitrariness). Most if not all fourth year classrooms, and every junior school library, should have a set of the two-volume *Shorter Oxford Dictionary,* which briefly gives the life histories of words and meanings. Once a child is not daunted by the sight of large pages packed with words, it can actually be easier to use, as well as be incomparably more exciting. (One of us once found himself discussing original passages from

Chaucer and *Sir Gawayne and the Grene Knight*—and comparing them with the Penguin translations—with a group of ten-year-olds in response to interest that ensued when the *Shorter Oxford Dictionary* was introduced into the classroom.)

Basically, our attitude is that the conventions, and spelling in particular, should not become tin-cans that a child drags around with him whenever he is concerned with writing. Because of this, and because of the arbitrariness of written code, it seems to us desirable that the learning of spelling should be separated to some extent from composition. We see no harm and likely gain in a teacher looking with each child, intensively and systematically for a few minutes twice a week, at words and families of words that the child has had difficulty with; and sometimes this will be best done with a pair or group of children. We see no harm and likely gain in a child learning by rote spellings from a personal spelling book, and then testing himself with the help of a friend, for five minutes each day. There is a place, too, for occasional word games that have the aim of establishing spelling regularities and irregularities. The important thing is that the procedures adopted should become neither a burden nor a distraction. In other words, let the traditional priorities be turned on their head.

QUESTIONS FOR DISCUSSION

1. Do you think that teachers should require children in the elementary grades to set forth their ideas in language that conforms to the conventions of the teacher's social dialect? Do you share Martin's and Mulford's discomfort with teaching "arbitrary middle class linguistic habits"? Why, or why not?

2. Martin and Mulford urge caution in asking children to become aware, when they write, of a "communicative" purpose—a purpose other than satisfying themselves. Do you think that such caution is wisely urged? Do you think that it is possible to recognize when children might be ready to consider the needs and interests of readers as they write? How might the needs of readers be brought

to the attention of children without the suggestion that there are "rules" to be followed?

3. Does it seem to you likely that a teacher's asking a young writer to add more information in what he has written will help prepare him for later suggestions that he meet still other needs of a reader? Does asking for added information give the child an adequate awareness of the needs of a reader, or must the teacher be concerned, at the same time, for other elements in the child's writing that affect communication?

4. Does your experience, as student, as teacher, confirm Martin's and Mulford's suggestion that teaching children about spelling, punctuation, and syntax at the wrong time—before they are ready—can work *against* their learning what the teacher is trying to teach? How can the teacher tell when students are "ready" to learn the conventions?

5. What sorts of responses and comments do Martin and Mulford advocate that teachers make about students' writing? Does their position resemble or differ from that of Douglas? Whipp?

THE
TEACHING
OF
RHETORIC

"Rhetorical Writing" in Elementary School
Richard L. Larson

When children begin writing, they do so for their own satisfaction and pleasure rather than to communicate with an audience outside themselves. They may offer their writing for the pleasure and responses of their friends, but they think of their work primarily as their own. Teachers of composition, therefore, must decide how to alert children to the needs and interests of audiences—particularly adult audiences—and how to help children satisfy these needs without feeling that their personal goals and wishes in writing are being compromised. The problem is compounded by the recognized fact that as children grow up, their willingness to write, for their own pleasure or for anyone else's satisfaction, often diminishes, and that even when they write, the imaginative freshness and the frankness with which feeling is communicated often slacken. In considering how to help children become sensitive to the needs of their audiences, teachers need at the same time to try to avoid reducing the imaginative and expressive elements in their writing.

In the following essay Larson argues the need for teaching "addressed" writing in the elementary school and offers a few suggestions for doing so. Richard Larson has served as director and teacher in federally-funded summer institutes for teachers at all levels.

From *Elementary English* Vol. 48, No. 8 (December 1971), pp. 926–31. Reprinted by permission of the National Council of Teachers of English.

The distinctive characteristic of "rhetorical" discourse, according to one of the leading students of rhetoric in the twentieth century, Kenneth Burke (in *A Rhetoric of Motives*), is that such discourse is "addressed." By this Burke means that he applies the term "rhetorical" only to discourse in which a speaker or writer is talking or writing to one or more persons other than himself, for a particular purpose. Usually the talking or writing responds to the demands of a particular occasion which for specifiable reasons has prompted the speaker or writer to "speak out." A modern scholar of rhetoric, Professor Lloyd Bitzer of the University of Wisconsin (writing in the winter, 1968, issue of a new journal, *Philosophy and Rhetoric*), goes a step further and says that the term "rhetorical" is best applied, or perhaps should only be applied, to discourse prompted by the observation of some urgent weakness or difficulty in the world (air pollution, the death of a national leader, uncertainties about the nation's foreign policy—to name a few examples) and the conviction that by speaking out, by moving his hearers toward a particular action or feeling, the speaker can help to resolve the difficulty or eliminate the observed inadequacy in the world around him. "Rhetorical discourse," then, is a transaction between a speaker or writer and a listener or reader, deliberately entered into by the speaker or writer for a purpose, and is frequently initiated regardless of whether or not the listener or reader wishes to be a party to the transaction.

Since this definition embraces a great deal of the writing that appears in print, it is natural that "rhetoric" is becoming an increasingly important field of inquiry among students of English. The rhetorician, the professional student of the art of rhetoric, examines the connections between the content, form, and manner of expression in a piece of addressed discourse, and the responses of those who hear or read it; he tries to make generalizations about those connections or to evaluate the discourse itself or the impact it had upon its hearers or readers.

We need to be quite clear about the rhetorician's field of inquiry, not merely in order to make clear the focus of this article, but also because definition helps explain why the rhetorician has to date had relatively little impact on the teaching of composition in elementary school. Much, perhaps most, of the writing done by students in elementary school—even in the upper elementary grades—is not produced in response to an outside "occasion" for writing (other than an assignment by the teacher) and has no purpose of inducing belief or action in any audience. This is not to say, of course, that the writing of students in elementary school is not intended to be read; but this writing does not presuppose a particular reader or readers reading at a particular time or under particular circumstances. The writing is often shared with the writer's classmates, of course, unless the writer prefers to keep his work to himself. But to influence his classmates' beliefs or actions at a particular time is not often the goal of the writer. And others who read the student's work are not committed, not involved, not personally affected by what they are reading unless some particularly moving story or perception evokes special sympathy or tolerance. The teacher, the parents, the principal, other teachers, officers of the PTA—any or all of these may read what the student has written and may record reactions of general or selective praise, but with none of these readers either is there much likelihood that belief may be shaped or an attitude formed (except toward the skills and talents of the writer) or action inspired. Much of the writing done in elementary school, then, is audience-less and time-less: it can be read by any of a number of possible audiences under a large number of circumstances and still make approximately the same effect upon its readers: pleasure perhaps, admiration of the writer's facility with language, perhaps the discovery of new ways of "seeing" an experience. These are important and valuable effects—no doubt of it. But they are mostly not "rhetorical effects."

The absence of "rhetorical writing" from elementary classrooms results from some widely held assumptions about the goals of writing programs in elementary school and about the kinds of writing that one may most appropriately encourage children to attempt. These goals, as I understand them, are to help students develop fluency and confidence in the use of language, to encourage students to develop powers of exact observation, and to stimulate students to exercise their imaginations. Teachers hope children will come to enjoy writing and want to write; they want children to understand their worlds and their lives and to write about them honestly; and they want children to make new objects, new worlds, by applying their as yet uninhibited imaginative powers to data from the reality they already know—laudable goals all, of course. Though the students may be asked to read examples of forms of writing which are controlled by fairly precise rules or conventions—for example, the haiku, the limerick, the short descriptive sketch—they are often asked to compose in those forms for the sake of the verbal exercise and the discipline of working within a form, almost as if these were ends in themselves. The students themselves, of course, are rarely conscious of the rationale behind the writing exercises their teachers encourage. They write because they find the acts of perceiving and imagining to be fun, and they take pleasure in what they produce. They take particular pleasure in what they have done if their classmates and teacher comment approvingly on it; in short, their goal in writing is often to give themselves pleasure by making an attractive object and by giving pleasure to others around them. Because of his position of authority, words of praise from the teacher are especially welcome, but the praise is usually awarded to the student's display of verbal competence or to the freshness of his perceptions, not to observations or statements whose substance affects the teacher or other students or is important to them. It is the talent displayed, and not the topics or the substantive content vivified by that talent, or the effect of the writing on a reader, that draws the praise.

Thus encouragement of the student's writing gives pleasure; pleasure stimulates the willingness to write; the willingness to write helps develop fluency in writing; fluency is expected to assure that the student will be able and willing to practice precise observations, fresh verbal representations, and revealing comparisons—all of these considered to be the important abilities for a student to develop while he is in elementary school.

As far as they go, these goals and procedures—probably familiar to most elementary teachers—in the teaching of composition in the elementary school are worthy and important. But at some point during his school career the student is presumably expected to develop what, given the definitions in my first paragraph, can fairly be called "rhetorical" skills. The expectation is often exhibited first when a teacher suddenly advises a student by his comments that it no longer matters much whether the student or his classmates or his teacher or his parents take pleasure in what he has done; what he writes must conform to (frequently unspecified) standards of competence operating within the mind of the teacher, or it is unacceptable. The unacceptability of this work is signified by the awarding of a low grade, and by expressions of concern on the part of the teacher over the inadequacy or inaccuracy of the ideas contained in what the writer has written, or of his language.

One obvious trouble with this change of emphasis is that the student is rarely prepared for it. A second obvious trouble is that whereas the compositions written in elementary school were acknowledged by teachers and parents and administrators alike to be "non-rhetorical," the compositions written by the student at this unspecified time later in his school career are expected to display the technical proficiency of utterances designed to affect the thinking of the most fastidious readers, while these compositions are in fact difficult for the student to take seriously because he knows perfectly well that he is not addressing a reader or readers whose thinking he can affect or whose thinking he cares to affect. If we lament, as many teachers do, the disappearance from young students' writing of the freshness, fluency, and enthusiasm which we found in the work they did when they were in elementary school, the reasons for that disappearance may not be far to seek. They may lie, very simply, in the sudden shift of attitude toward what the student writes—the shift from the unstated but widespread admission that the student was engaged in non-rhetorical writing to the equally unstated but equally widespread expectation that he should "now" be producing rhetorically sophisticated pieces, to be judged as if they were something that (given the student's lack of previous training in rhetorical writing and the abstractness of the classroom situation) they cannot possibly be: pieces written in response to a specific external occasion and for a specific purpose, cogently reasoned, and addressed to a reader or readers capable of being moved by what they read.

It is, of course, entirely appropriate for teachers at some point in the student's career to want him to learn to address real audiences with conviction in a style that suggests mastery of the English language and of the conventions of standard usage. But as one surveys the years between, let us say, age nine and age fourteen, one finds it difficult to locate the time at which teachers and curricula expect students to begin to produce what one might call, again using the definitions in my first paragraph, "rhetorical" writing. Possibly the preferable time for this additional emphasis is when the student becomes capable of conceiving abstractions rather than simply perceiving or imagining concrete objects in the world; at about this same time he may become capable of grasping the notion of purpose and the possibility of shaping the real world around him by means of discourse that he himself produces. But the time at which these changes occur is hardly fixed with any precision, at least in the views of elementary teachers and curriculum supervisors with whom I am acquainted, and the time probably varies considerably from student to student. It is therefore difficult, or perhaps impossible, to say that "rhetorical" writing should appear in the curriculum in one particular year, but not in the immediately preceding year. I would like to suggest here, therefore, only that some work in "rhetorical writing" be included in the elementary school composition program of the student when, in the judgment of his teacher, he seems likely to be capable of understanding the concept of addressing a living audience in order to induce belief or move action in that audience, and that when such rhetorical writing activities are incorporated into the curriculum some of the fundamental concerns of the scholar (i.e., professional student) of rhetoric become part of class discussion on this writing.

I do not wish here to imply that the "non-rhetorical" writing exercises performed by students in the elementary grades have no value whatever in helping to develop in these students the abilities they will need for rhetorical writing. The fluency and the willingness to write that are quite explicit goals of such non-rhetorical exercises are obviously indispensable to the student who is going to attempt to address and move a specific audience. The capacity for exact observation of events and objects in the real world and the capacity to invent arresting analogies and illuminating comparisons are both essential to precise and vivid writing, whether it be rhetorical or not. The sheer practice in generating English sentences which one's fellow students will be able to read and want to take pleasure in is also, obviously, indispensable to effective rhetorical writing. Furthermore, the connection that the student may perceive between his ability to observe essential details and his selection of apt comparisons, on the one hand, and the kinds of response or feelings demonstrated by his readers, on the other hand, is an important early demonstration to the student that the way he writes may have something to do with the behavior of his readers.

I should also recognize that elementary teachers sometimes do encourage forms of writing that might be classed as rhetorical, even while giving the major portion of their time for instruction in writing to the kinds of non-rhetorical pieces I have been discussing. Notes on meetings, letters to parents inviting them to PTA meetings, instructions to delivery men—all of which I have heard listed as examples of "practical" writing activities carried on in elementary grades—might well in a broad interpretation of the term be classed as "rhetorical writing." I do infer, however, that when teachers assign these more nearly rhetorical activities, they rarely discuss them from the perspectives that the study of rhetoric might furnish.

What I am suggesting, then, is that teachers include among their lessons, for students capable of understanding the concept of purposeful communication, a more systematic examination of how rhetorical discourse "works." I propose that teachers invent, or better still allow their students to invent, circumstances in which they can write in order to modify the thinking or actions of the persons who they think might read what they write. These exercises need be by no means trivial or contrived. They might include written statements recommending books that they liked for reading by their classmates—brief statements, perhaps, possibly designed to be put on a small file card for reference by students using the classroom library. They might include written explanations and suggestions to the teacher concerning classroom activities that the writer thinks the class might enjoy or subjects the writer thinks the class might like to study. They might even include statements written to the principal of the school or to curriculum specialists concerning special events which the class might like to participate in or special kinds of study that the class might like to undertake. At the end of the course (or of the year), activities might include statements to parents either explaining what the class has been studying or why the class has been studying a particular subject, or evaluating each writer's own progress in school—a statement that might easily accompany (or replace) the student's report card. All of these writing activities have in common the genuine possibility that the reader's opinion or action might in some way be affected by an effective piece of writing produced by the students. Teachers and students as well can no doubt conceive other circumstances in which successful writing can result in action.

These pieces are, naturally, public, as are all rhetorical utterances. Class discussion can deal with the problems faced in writing these pieces, and the success with which each writer completed his task. Some of the emphases that might be established in class discussions are:

the kinds of data, or explanations for events, or reasons for requests, that might be more likely, and those that might be less likely, to achieve the writer's purpose in a given piece;

desirable ways to introduce the piece, and reasons why these ways are desirable;

the kind of person that the writer of each piece might wish to be, and the ways in which his language might help him or hinder him in his efforts to be that kind of person, in his reader's eyes;

the kind of attitude that the writer might wish to reveal or suggest toward his listener and toward his subject, as well as the ways in which his language helps him to establish this attitude;

the relative advantages of general and abstract language, specific and concrete language, and comparisons or analogies, in urging what the writer wishes to have his reader believe.

These topics, of course, are by no means the sum total of a rhetorician's concerns, but they are important elements in the study of rhetoric, and a teacher can introduce them as far as his students are capable of dealing with them, confident that he is giving his students a sound introduction to some of the fundamental emphases of the rhetoric of written English.

For teachers to whom the phrase "rhetorical writing" has a forbiddingly abstruse or academic ring, it is important to make clear what the teaching of this kind of discourse would *not* include. It would not include enumeration of rhetorical or syntactic techniques, such as the "topics" of invention or argument, and "schemes" (formal patterns) for the construction of sentences. It would not label pieces of children's writing according to some system of rhetorical categories. It would have nothing whatever to do with textbook presentations of the "methods of development" that are so disastrously offered in many of our texts on writing as the core of rhetorical study. The discussion would, instead, be pragmatic and empirical; it would confront students with situations—problems of writing in hopes of inducing action or belief in the reader—and discuss students' performances in these situations. From such trying out of rhetorical writing, students would, indeed, construct their own rhetoric—not by forming conscious or conceptual generalizations, but by seeing how language can (and why it sometimes cannot) make things happen.

As a part of this practice in discovering how writing can make things happen, teachers may find it useful to encourage students to take roles in an imagined dramatic encounter in which their written pieces may play a part. That is, students working in groups might assign to one or more members of the group the role of the intended reader (or listener) who is being addressed by the student, and might encourage that reader or listener to react to the discourse as if he were the person who is being addressed. The roles of reader or listener could be rotated among members of the group, so that each student would get the experience of feedback on his rhetorical performances. If the teacher was the person addressed in the pieces written by some of the students, the teacher might respond candidly in his own person to the statements made and the language employed by the writers of these pieces. Perhaps even a parent or an administrator could be brought into the classroom to receive and

respond to the pieces written by the students in one of these kinds
of rhetorical writing. Such reliance on dramatic interplay among
students or among students and adults within the classroom has the
support of experiences of British teachers, who have found that
improvised dramatic encounters help to build language fluency and
self-understanding among their students. At the very least, such experiences would give the student a feeling of what it means to compose discourse with the hope of evoking action or inducing belief in
someone from the real world on a subject that matters to the writer.
If this kind of honesty in making and responding to rhetorical performances were continued into the later years of a student's schooling, the kinds of frustrations experienced by the student who is
asked to offer an accomplished rhetorical performance (a "theme")
in an abstract world—without any possibility of its making an effect in the real world—might be considerably reduced.

The student in elementary school unquestionably needs the encouragement to experiment with language and to develop fluency
with language that opportunities for non-rhetorical writing—writing
for fun and for pleasure—give him. At the same time, the student's
progress toward developing the abilities he will need to carry on the
activities of his adult and professional life can be made smoother
and easier if he becomes aware of the distinction between writing
that has no specific audience or can appeal to any audience—writing undertaken to *explore* the world or to achieve the satisfaction of
making a new and pleasing object—and writing that is directed
toward a particular reader or readers for a specific purpose. Early
practice in rhetorical writing, with the teacher guided by some of
the insights and emphases that characterize the professional study
of rhetoric, can be a valuable part of the elementary curriculum in
writing, and may even be an essential part that has been substan-
tially neglected.

QUESTIONS FOR DISCUSSION

1. Do you find the distinction between "rhetorical" writing—writing that is "addressed" to a reader—and writing that is not "rhe-

torical" in that sense a useful distinction? How does one recognize each of the two kinds of writing? What signs does the language give that the writing is of one kind or the other?

2. Do you share the author's conviction that some work in "addressed" writing should be included among the composition activities of the elementary curriculum? If not, why?

3. What features of a piece of addressed writing, besides those mentioned by the author, might be worth calling attention to in class discussions? Or should the teacher not call attention directly to the insights afforded by the study of rhetoric? If he should not, what should be his emphases in class discussion?

4. Can you imagine any situations in which students' writing could elicit feedback from live audiences—situations that could be introduced into the classroom (or into students' work outside the classroom)—and thus show something of how writing is received in the world of human activities outside the school?

Teaching
Rhetorical Concepts
Robert Fichteneau

In this article, Fichteneau, Director of English in the Oakland Schools, Pontiac, Michigan, offers a group of lessons in rhetoric—on concepts of audience, purpose, invention and style—that have been developed for fourth graders. In examining the lessons, note the structure within the lessons. What has the author assumed about ways to introduce his subjects and how does he present the structure of his field (rhetoric)?

"What do you teach them anyhow?" is a familiar cry of the fourth-grade teacher to her third-grade counterpart after having just marked a pile of compositions for misspellings and mispunctuation. Typically, teachers equate composition with writing though the two are quite different processes. Writing is transcription; it is learning to take dictation from oneself. Composition involves the discovery of ideas, patterns for ordering those ideas, and such stylistic considerations as word choice and sentence structure as they relate to helping the writer communicate his intent and purpose to his audi-

From *Elementary English* Vol. 49, No. 3 (March 1972), pp. 376–81. Copyright © 1972 by the National Council of Teachers of English. Reprinted by permission of the publisher and the author.

ence. The two processes are understandably confused since both go on simultaneously. Yet if teachers and children are to understand that composition is not spelling, punctuation or handwriting but is a sincere attempt on the part of the writer to say something to someone, then aspects of the writing process will have to become a part of elementary school language arts programs.

Three years ago this writer asked a number of elementary teachers if there were any reasons why one had to wait until students were in secondary schools before helping them to understand some of the concepts basic to rhetoric. These teachers knew of none.

With the support of the teachers a series of basic lessons were developed for fourth-grade youngsters. The basic lessons present concepts of invention, arrangement and style, those concepts basic to rhetoric, basic to communication. The lessons treat the concepts one at a time. Once three lessons were taught, a fourth lesson asked the youngsters to use what they had learned by writing one or two stories.

BASIC LESSON 1

In the first basic lesson the youngsters were introduced to the idea that compositions are directed toward an audience. The lesson was structured in this way.

    I. What is an audience?
        A. Teachers asked a series of questions designed to evoke such terms as *reader* and *viewer* from the students.
           1. Are all movies alike? How are they different?
           2. Are some movies more interesting to you than others?
           3. What do we call people who watch movies—the people who decide whether a movie is interesting or not?
           4. (Repeat the same pattern illustrated in 1-3 using books instead of movies.)
        B. Once the term audience is discovered (or introduced by the teacher if necessary) ask questions to help students

begin to understand that a professional writer composes for an audience.

II. One of the first questions a writer asks is: Who is going to read my story, paragraph or poem?

    A. To help youngsters begin to realize why the question is important, ask questions to elicit the differences between books written for second-graders and those written for fourth-graders.

    B. To help the students generalize about differences between audiences, have them read a short excerpt from an encyclopedia written for older students and an excerpt on the same subject written for their age group. We used "Dinosauria" from *The Encyclopedia Americana* and "Stegosaurus" from *Dinosaurs and More Dinosaurs* by Jean Craig. In both instances the teacher read the excerpts aloud as the students followed the text on their own dittoed copy. A few questions helped the students note the obvious differences.

        1. Which example has the longer paragraph?

        2. Which tends to have shorter sentences?

        3. Which definition is easier to understand?

        4. Do you know the meanings of these words in the first example: *aberrant, quadruped, dentition, diminutive?*

    C. Most youngsters were able to generalize as follows: The second example is easier to read because of both structure and vocabulary. The second excerpt is written for younger readers.

    D. A further study of two other excerpts ("The Life of a Moth," *Basic Goals in Reading* 3[2] and a teacher-written definition) and the youngsters began to grasp some of what a writer must consider as he thinks about his audience.

III. Next the students were asked to retell a folk tale to a group of first-grade children. A time limit of two minutes was agreed upon.

    A. They were asked to write out what they would say to the first-graders for these reasons:

      1. So that they wouldn't have to depend upon their memory.

      2. So that they would finish telling their version of the tale before the younger children became restless.

      3. So that they could plan carefully just what they wanted to tell their audience.

  B. Before actually writing the folktale, youngsters discussed the first grade as an audience:

      1. For how long will they be able to attend?

      2. What will be of most interest to them?

      3. Would a picture or two help hold the attention of the children?

  C. Each fourth-grade student was then given a copy of "The Husband Who Was to Mind the House" and asked to follow as the teacher read it aloud.

  D. Once the teacher had read it the students were told to think about first-graders as an audience and then to write their two-minute version.

IV. When the writing was completed the students met in small groups to read what each group member had written.

  A. The groups were asked to read in terms of these questions:

      1. Are the sentences clear enough for first-graders to follow?

      2. Will this version of the tale hold the interest of the intended young audience?

      3. Will the picture or pictures help the audience follow the story?

  B. When the answer to any question was "no," the group was asked to help the writer find a way to change the answer to "yes."

V. With the cooperation of several first-grade teachers the fourth-grade students met with small groups of first-graders and read their folk tales.

While this first lesson ignores many aspects of the audience concept, it does introduce the concept. Later lessons explore some of the other aspects. One of the most favorable outcomes of this lesson is that the writers receive immediate feedback on what they have written. The feedback comes first from their peers who have struggled with the same task and then from a meeting with the actual audience. Feedback of this nature is much more important than any grade a teacher might place on the composition.

BASIC LESSON 2

The second lesson was one treating aspects of *invention*. Here, the students begin to discover that often a writer is asked to draw upon his own experience. One requirement for learning to write well is learning *how to use experience*. This particular lesson helped students learn how to discover what they knew about a topic—how to discover story material.

    I. Ways in which a writer might begin a story were brought out through questions once again.
        A. These questions helped students discover ideas:
            1. If you were asked to use this sentence as the opening of an imaginary story—*When I woke up, all of the lawns had turned bright purple!* how could you begin?
            2. What questions might you ask to help you get started?
            3. Would thinking of questions your reader might want answered help?
            4. Some readers might want to know *everything,* but *everything* would take too long to write.
            5. Since you can't tell *everything* about purple grass, concentrate on telling one thing.
            6. To decide what *one thing* to write on, ask questions about the opening sentence.
        B. Questions about "what caused the lawns to turn purple?" lead to imaginative answers.
            1. The red of the evening sun mixed with the blue of the sky and fell on the lawns in the form of purple rain.
            2. This led to "why did the red of the sun mix with the blue of the sky?"

C. Other questions center on effect.
    1. Were the lawns prettier now that they were purple?
    2. Does purple grass have a different taste?
    3. What does it taste like?
    4. What happened as soon as you (the writer) saw the purple lawns?
    5. Were you the only one who saw the purple color— maybe a fairy or gremlin did something to your eyes as you slept.

II. To demonstrate how questions are helpful in other ways the youngsters were asked to read this story:

THE LOCKET
My friend owned a locket. It was old but it was kind of pretty. Some queer looking scratches were on the back. Another friend wanted it

A. The fourth-grade youngsters were asked to determine what a reader might want to know that the story didn't tell him. Such questions as "Where did your friend get the locket?" and "What kind of scratches?" were suggested.

B. Each student was asked to write two questions that would aid his reader.

III. Next, the youngsters were given a picture which contained a gaily wrapped present, a pair of wooden shoes and an envelope addressed to Edward Paul, New Bond Street, London, England. They were asked how the three different objects might serve as an *idea* for a story that would interest other students in the room:

A. For a first step, the teacher suggested that they ask a few questions about each item.
    1. Shoes: "Where were they made?" "Who owns them?"
    2. Present: "Who wrapped it?" "Who is it for?"
    3. Letter: "From where was the letter mailed?" "Is Edward Paul a man?"

B. Next, they asked questions which included two items; finally questions which included all three.
1. "Are there more shoes in the present?" "Did the same person receive both the shoes and the present?"
2. "Does Edward Paul now have all three items?" "If so, does he know who sent the three to him?"
C. From the questions asked, each student selected those which he thought would make an interesting story for his classmates.
IV. When the writing was completed, the students met in small groups to read one another's stories. Each group was asked to determine whether or not the stories would be of interest to the audience. If any one story was not interesting, the group helped the writer determine how to make it interesting.

BASIC LESSON 3

The third lesson focused on arrangement. A writer arranges his material so that it will make sense to his audience.
I. What happens when a comic strip is not in a logical order? What happens when sentences are mixed up in a story? The students were first given a comic strip in which the frames had been disarranged.
A. They were asked whether they would read the mixed up version or rearrange first so that it made sense.
B. Each student rearranged it so that it made sense to him and then compared his arrangement with his neighbor.
II. The concept of time order, chronological order, was introduced through practice of arranging a series of events (1775—The famous ride of Paul Revere, 1968—The death of Martin Luther King and Robert Kennedy, etc.) in time order.
A. Students then practiced arranging a mixed up story. The story was a straight chronological narrative in which half of the sentences were not in sequence.

B. The final step before writing included studying a well written paragraph on preserving the shape and color of flowers from *Science in Your Own Back Yard* (Harcourt, Brace and World).

> To preserve both the shape and the color of flowers, you will need some fine white sand and a number of cardboard boxes. Pansies, dogwood, daffodils, and other sturdy flowers are good for this method of preservation. First, pour a thin layer of sand on the bottom of a box. A one-pound candy box is just the right size. Next, place several fresh flowers on top of the sand. Then, carefully and slowly, cover the flowers with more sand. Place the box in the sun. Keep it from being shaken and do not let it get wet. In two or three weeks your flowers will be ready.

Questions such as the following helped students discuss the paragraph:

1. What would be a good title for the paragraph, a title that would aid the reader?
2. This paragraph tells the reader "how to do something." It is important that the reader follow a certain order. How does the writer help the reader know what to do first? second? Are there particular words that aid the reader?
3. Read the first sentence again. What is the purpose of this sentence?
4. Why do you think the writer added the second sentence?
5. Question 2 asks you to find particular words that gave order to the paragraph. The words were *first, next,* and *then.* Think of a few more words which might be helpful in keeping order straight.

III. The students were then asked "to explain to their classmates *how to do something.*"

A. Emphasis was placed on (1) keeping the sequence of steps in chronological order and (2) giving the reader enough information so that he would be able to do the task himself.

B. To help the youngsters think about topics this list was presented:

> how to: shine shoes
>
> make popcorn
>
> set a party table for four
>
> toast marshmallows
>
> brush a dog
>
> exercise a horse
>
> make a kite
>
> build a backyard fort

Each student was asked to use a topic from the list only if he could not discover one of his own.

C. Students were reminded how asking themselves questions helped them on the previous assignment. Here it was suggested that they ask ''what will my reader need to know to be able to do the task I am writing about?''

IV. When the students finished writing they met in small groups. The groups asked these questions of each paper:

A. Has the writer included everything the reader needs to know?

B. Has he kept the directions in order? Will the reader know what to do *first, next,* and so on?

C. Will the writing hold the interest of the reader?

D. Has the writer paid attention to spelling and punctuation?

The group was also asked to help the writer make any of the improvements that the questions suggested.

This lesson is only a beginning step in helping students grasp the concept of arrangement. The main thrust of the lesson was to help youngsters realize that a writer must be concerned with whether or not his audience will be able to follow what he has written.

These three lessons complete the first cycle. The materials developed for the fourth grade included two other cycles in which the concepts of invention, arrangement and style were further developed. In later lessons the notion of writing for an audience was used to help youngsters discover why spelling, punctuation and other mechanical aspects were important. Mechanical aspects often keep a writer from communicating with his audience. Audiences, as a rule, are bothered by misspelled words and haphazard punctuation.

WRITING STORIES

Following each cycle of these basic lessons, the students were asked to put to use that which they had learned in writing stories. Three story topics were used after the first cycle.

 I. After reading and discussing excerpts from "Little Georgie, the Rabbit" (from *Rabbit Hill*) students were asked to select an animal for the main character of a story. The character was to be developed by adding one detail (a cane, a pair of sunglasses, rubbers on the feet, etc.). Once the detail was selected, the students were asked "to tell how the animal happened to get the detail" and "to tell what he does with it."

 II. Another story topic asked the youngsters to write about a particular incident from their own life. A suggested topic was "a story which tells how you did or did not get something you wished for."

 III. A third story was suggested after the students read "Pig Wisps" (from Sandburg's *Rootabaga Stories*). Here they were asked to write a story "about a letter of the alphabet."

Such a writing program has helped fourth-grade students come to understand some of the aspects of the writing process. The youngsters are discussing writing in terms of communication instead of in the conventional terms of red ink and teacher grades. Those students who have participated in the program have become involved with the processes of communication.

QUESTIONS FOR DISCUSSION

1. What similarities in structure, if any, do you see in the three basic lessons? Where does the teaching begin, and how does it proceed? Are the lessons useful examples of "inductive" teaching? Is the author in fact leading his students to "discoveries"?

2. The second lesson concerns ''invention'' and relates the activity of invention to the needs of a reader. Do you think that this is the best approach to teaching invention? What are other approaches to invention that might work as well or better with children?

3. Are there other forms of organization, besides chronology and process, that might be taught to elementary school children? Which? Devise lessons that would help teach them.

4. Does a writer of stories need to be concerned with the rhetorical concepts taught in the three basic lessons? How far is he concerned with those concepts? Can mastery of the activities taught in the basic lessons help in the writing of stories?